Applied Qualitative Research in Psychology

Edited by

Joanna Brooks and Nigel King

Published 2017 by
PALGRAVE

Palgrave in the UK is an imprint of Macmillan Publishers Limited,
registered in England, company number 785998, of 4 Crinan Street,
London, N1 9XW.

Palgrave® and Macmillan® are registered trademarks in the United States,
the United Kingdom, Europe and other countries.

ISBN 978–1–137–35915–5 hardback
ISBN 978–1–137–35912–4 paperback

This book is printed on paper suitable for recycling and made from fully managed
and sustained forest sources. Logging, pulping and manufacturing processes are
expected to conform to the environmental regulations of the country of origin.

A catalogue record for this book is available from the British Library.

A catalog record for this book is available from the Library of Congress.

Printed and bound by CPI Group (UK) Ltd, Croydon, CR0 4YY

Contents

Notes on the contributors

Vicky Alfrey completed her PhD at the University of Lincoln, UK, working with Harriet Gross. The topic of her thesis was the construction of identity in later life with reference to gardens and gardening, and the research involved a series of interviews with residents of sheltered housing schemes as well as an analysis of promotional materials for housing schemes. She has a BSc in Human Psychology from De Montfort University, Leicester and following a period of teaching in China after her PhD, she is at Exeter University teaching on the International Year One in Psychology programme.

Peter Branney is a Chartered Psychologist who has undertaken a programme of award winning, internationally leading work exploring how men engage with healthcare, how they experience threats to their health, and how to improve their experience of healthcare. To date, Peter has had almost twenty research grants, which combined are over half a million pounds and have attracted a Research Leadership Award from the Centre for Applied Social Sciences and nominations for the Researcher of the Year Award, Leeds Beckett University, UK and a Medipex & NHS Innovation award. Alongside methodological innovations, Peter's research has gone beyond the state of the art highlighting a clear policy gap in the needs of men using mental health services and providing key insights into the experiences of men living with penile cancer.

Alison Bravington is a Research Associate at Hull York Medical School, University of Hull, UK. Alison originally qualified in English Literature and worked for many years as a book editor and writer. She requalified with a Psychology degree and an MSc in Social Research and Evaluation before moving on to her PhD – a photo-elicitation study investigating the role of social context in recovery from cancer treatment. Alison has worked in applied health research since 2009 across multiple projects in end-of-life care evaluation, cancer care, and experiential learning in undergraduate practice placements, and has a special interest in the use of visual elicitation methods in qualitative research.

Joanna Brooks is a Chartered Psychologist and Senior Research Fellow at the University of Huddersfield, UK. She is the author of numerous publications using and describing qualitative methods, including (with Nigel King) *Template Analysis for Business and Management Students* (Sage, 2017). The focus of her work is on applied and health-related research topics, and Jo has a particular interest in the management and experience of chronic illness conditions and end of life care. Jo's research explores networks of care and support in health and social care, and her work includes the development and use of novel and inclusive qualitative research approaches in applied settings – including recently the visual interview technique, Pictor, with Nigel King and colleagues.

Kirsty Budds is a lecturer in psychology at Keele University. She is a critical social psychologist with research interests in women's reproductive health, reproductive timing, and experiences of the transition to parenthood and how these are shaped by cultural prescriptions of 'good' motherhood.

Viv Burr is Professor of Critical Psychology at the University of Huddersfield, UK. Her publications include *Invitation to Personal Construct Psychology* (2nd edition 2004, with Trevor Butt) and *Social Constructionism* (3rd edition 2015). Her research is predominantly qualitative and she has a particular interest in innovative qualitative research methods arising from Personal Construct Psychology (PCP), which is better known for its clinical applications. She is currently using PCP methods in two research projects. The first of these explores how older and younger generations perceive their own and the other generation, and the second (with Nigel King) examines the meanings that various outdoor spaces hold for people. Viv is co-editor of the e-journal *Personal Construct Theory and Practice.*

Flora Cornish is Associate Professor in the Department of Methodology at the London School of Economics & Political Science, where she teaches qualitative research methods to social science students. Her research investigates the role of community mobilisation in public health, particularly HIV/AIDS, with recent work focusing on the relations between local grassroots realities and globalising development policies and management practices, in the context of the evidence-based policy movement. She has particular interests in the critical and public significance of qualitative methods as means of understanding and advancing progressive social change.

Malcolm Cowburn is an Emeritus Professor Applied Social Science at Sheffield Hallam University, UK. His research has focussed on three areas; sex crime and responding to sex offenders; the management of diversity in prisons; and applied research ethics in social science. He has published widely in these areas. He was principal investigator of a (1999) Economic and Social Research Council (ESRC) funded pilot study exploring the response to diversity. He is co-author (with Steve Myers) of *Social Work with Sex Offenders: Making a Difference* (2016). He is current Alternate Vice-Chair of the National Research Ethics Service (NRES) South-West Committee, and has also served on the Social Care Research Ethics Committee and University Faculty ethics committees.

Helen Cowie is Emeritus Professor at the University of Surrey, UK, in the Faculty of Health and Medical Sciences and a Fellow of the British

Psychological Society. She has numerous publications in refereed journals on the subject of mental health and youth, emotional development, bullying, cyberbullying and peer support. She has authored and co-authored a number of influential books, including *Managing School Violence* (with Dawn Jennifer, Sage Publications), *New Perspectives on Bullying* (with Dawn Jennifer, Open University Press), *From Birth to Sixteen* (Routledge) and *Bullying Among University Students* (with Carrie-Anne Myers, Routledge). *Understanding Children's Development* (John Wiley), co-authored with Peter K Smith and Mark Blades and now into its sixth edition, remains one of the most popular undergraduate texts in the field. Her latest book, co-edited with Carrie-Anne Myers, *Bullying in Schools: Intervention and Prevention*, will be published by Routledge in 2017.

Frances Darby began her nursing career at the age of sixteen. Having qualified as a Registered General Nurse and worked in a busy district general hospital, Frances returned to the world of education in her thirties to study Sociology. After obtaining a BA (Hons) from the University of York, UK, she went on to complete her PGCE, a Masters degree and PhD in Health Studies and Sociology. She currently works as a research assistant and project officer in health and social sciences at Leeds Beckett University, UK.

Charles Elliott is an Associate of the Prison Research Centre at the Institute of Criminology, Cambridge, UK. He is the author of the seminal book *Appreciative Inquiry: Locating the Energy for Change* (International Institute for Sustainable Development, 1999), and a co-investigator on a three year Economic and Social Research Council (ESRC) funded, multi-prison study focusing on the challenges of ensuring equality and diversity in prisons. He has conducted Appreciative Inquiry (AI) related performance improvement exercises in over 60 prisons in the UK and has worked with a range of NGOs in Africa and Asia.

Harriet Gross is Professor of Psychology at the University of Lincoln, UK. Having undertaken her PhD at the University of Nottingham on childhood hearing impairment, she started academic life as a developmental psychologist. She is now particularly interested in people's experiences of their everyday experience and activities, and has been involved in a range of projects using qualitative methods to explore this experience. She has worked on topics as diverse as parenting, chronic illness, ageing, joyriding and fear of crime, and she has longstanding interest in the psychology of home and allotment gardening. In 2013 she was a member of team from the University of Lincoln, and garden designers Harfleet and Harfleet, that developed 'Digital Capabilities', a social media garden which won a Gold Medal at the RHS Chelsea Flower Show.

Beth Hardy is a Lecturer in Nursing at the University of York. She is a registered general nurse and in 2015 was awarded the Queen's Nurse title for her commitment to leading and developing Community Nursing. Beth originally used the Pictor Technique in her PhD research at the University of Huddersfield exploring the experiences of people receiving palliative care in the community. She has subsequently developed a particular interest in visual and participatory approaches in research. In addition to teaching across pre and post registration nursing programmes Beth is an active researcher with recent projects focusing on palliative care and the experiences of carers and older people.

Sarah Honeywell works for the UK Government Social Research service conducting qualitative and quantitative research on a range of issues related to health, education and employment. She has a Masters in Social Research Methods from the London School of Economics & Political Science, where she used qualitative methods to investigate the creation of collective identities and attitudes towards individuals' contributions to conflict resolution. At the time of writing, Sarah was Research Team Leader at The Key Support Ltd, leading a team which provided research for school leaders and governors. Her interests include how to make research accessible, including using qualitative methods to understand individual experience and tell an engaging story, applied research and evidence-based policy making.

David Hiles is Honorary Research Fellow at both De Montfort University, Leicester, UK, and the Centre for Counselling & Psychotherapy Education (CCPE), London. He has been a psychologist for some fifty years, and trained as a transpersonal psychotherapist in the 1980s. He has pioneered teaching qualitative methods at undergraduate, master, doctoral and post-doctoral levels, and has delivered masterclasses in qualitative inquiry in Brno, Czech Republic, and Jenna, Germany. His research interests lie in an expanded vision of cognitive psychology that is inclusive of human experience, empowerment, cultural practices, and a special focus upon narrative in everyday human cognition. He is critical of the naivety in some of the thinking underlying psychological research methods, especially with respect to paradigm assumptions, mixed methods, and the inference processes used in qualitative data coding.

Sunjay Jain is lead clinician for audit and clinical governance within the urology department at St James' Hospital, Leeds, UK. Sunjay was appointed to St James' in 2007 as a sub-specialist in uro-oncology. He qualified from Guy's Hospital, London in 1993 achieving MBBS with distinction and has held previous positions in Nottingham, Derby and Leicester. His research portfolio includes over 30 scientific papers. As well as cancer treatment, Sunjay has an interest in the diagnosis of urinary symptoms and in particular the management of all diseases of the prostate.

Dawn Jennifer has a research career spanning nearly twenty years. Her research has focused on emotional and psychological health and well-being, with a particular focus on understanding and addressing school bullying. Prior to emigrating to Australia, Dawn was the Regional Adviser for London with the Anti-Bullying Alliance, providing targeted support to schools, colleges and local authorities for their anti-bullying strategies and policies. For the past five years, Dawn has worked with the South Australian Government, first as the Senior Ethics Adviser with the Families and Communities Research Ethics Committee at the Department for Communities and Social Inclusion, and then as the Research Governance Officer with the Southern Adelaide Local Health Network.

Nigel King is Professor in Applied Psychology and Dean of the Graduate School at the University of Huddersfield, UK. He has a long-standing interest in the use of qualitative methods in real-world research. With a background in both organisational and health psychology, his research interests include professional identities and inter-professional relations in health and social care. He has published extensively in these areas, including *Interviews in Qualitative Research* (with Christine Horrocks, Sage, 2010), *Template Analysis for Business and Management Students* (with Joanna Brooks, Sage, 2017) and *Managing Innovation and Change: A Critical Guide for Organizations* (with Neil Anderson, Thomson Learning, 2002). Nigel is well known for his work on Template Analysis and, more recently, the development of a visual interview technique known as 'Pictor'.

Victoria Lavis is a Chartered Psychologist and Senior Lecturer in the Division of Psychology at the University of Bradford, UK. Since 2000, her field of research has focused on adapting and developing appreciative methodologies to help transform prisons in England and Wales. Her work aims to facilitate the development of cohesive prisons which are safe, respectful and decent for both staff and prisoners and which can promote and sustain the transformation and rehabilitation of offenders. She is Principal Investigator of a collaborative research project, funded by Economic and Social Research Council (ESRC). The three year, multi-prison study focusses on the challenges of ensuring equality and diversity in prisons.

Abigail Locke is a critical social psychologist whose research work specialises in issues around gender, parenting, identity and health. She has a particular interest in what society constructs as 'good' mothering and 'good' fathering and has applied this to a variety of topics including infant feeding, early parenting and fathers in primary caregiving roles. Abigail is currently Professor of Psychology at the University of Bradford, and Visiting Professor in Social and Health Psychology at the University of Derby, both in the UK. Abigail has previously held academic positions at the Universities of Loughborough, Huddersfield, Derby and Coventry.

Jane Melvin has had an extensive NHS career working within both hospital and community services for over twenty years. During this time, she has held varying roles in the field of cancer, palliative and end of life care and latterly has taken up the post as Macmillan Head of Services for North West England moving from a strategic lead position at a Clinical Commissioning Group in Manchester. As a result of her work as Macmillan Lead Nurse for the roll

out of the Gold Standards Framework programme in palliative care, Jane
became a founding member of the Macmillan Palliative Care Collaborative
(MacPaCC), a group of leading researchers from six universities across
England and Scotland. She then took up the role as Senior Research Fellow
at the University of Huddersfield, working on several Macmillan Cancer
Support funded studies including 'Unpicking the Threads'.

Delia Muir leads on public involvement and engagement at the Leeds Institute
for Clinical Trials Research (LICTR), UK. Her work focuses on how to
include patients and carers as partners throughout health research. She has
been recognised nationally for leading innovative public involvement activities as part of the NIHR Pressure Ulcer Programme of Research (PURPOSE).
Delia has a background in performance and is particularly interested in how
the arts can be used to stimulate conversations about health. In addition to her
academic career, she has worked extensively as a freelance theatre practitioner
and facilitator. This has involved working in a variety of contexts including
prisons, schools, music festivals and community spaces. Delia currently holds
a Wellcome Trust Engagement Fellowship.

Michael Murray is Professor of Social and Health Psychology and Head of
the School of Psychology at Keele University, UK. He has published journal
articles and chapters and (co-)authored and edited several books and collec-
tions on critical and qualitative approaches to health psychology including
Qualitative Health Psychology: Theories and Methods (with Chamberlain,
Sage 1999), *Critical Health Psychology* (Palgrave, 2014) and *Health
Psychology: Theory, Research & Practice* (with Marks, Sage 2015). He is
the Associate Editor of *Psychology & Health* and sits on the editorial boards
of several other journals including *Health, Psychology & Medicine, Health
Psychology Review*, and *Arts & Health*. His current research interests include
the use of participatory and arts-based methods to engage older people and
the development of narrative research methods.

Anthony Papathomas is a Lecturer in Sport and Exercise Psychology within
Loughborough University's School of Sport, Exercise and Health Sciences in
the UK. His research interests concern the role of sport and exercise across
clinical contexts. Drawing predominately upon qualitative methodologies, he
has published studies that address disability, chronic illness and mental health.
Anthony is an editorial board member for the journals *Qualitative Research
in Sport and Exercise*, and *Psychology of Sport and Exercise*. He also leads
the mental health strand for the Psychology Division of the British Association
of Sport and Exercise Sciences.

Brett Smith is a Professor at the University of Birmingham, UK. His research
focuses on disability, sport and physical activity. It has been published widely
in leading journals, such as *Social Science and Medicine, Health Psychology*,
and *Qualitative Research*. In addition to over 100 publications, Brett has
given over 150 invited talks to audiences in numerous countries around the

world, including to The Royal Society of Medicine and in the UK Houses of Parliament. He is founder and former editor of *Qualitative Research in Sport, Exercise and Health*. Currently he is Associate Editor of *Psychology of Sport and Exercise* and serves on 7 editorial boards, including *Qualitative Research in Psychology*. Brett is co-editor of the *Routledge Handbook of Qualitative Research in Sport and Exercise*.

Clare Strickland is an Assistant Clinical Psychologist for Bimingham and Solihull Mental Health NHS Foundation Trust. In this role, she works across two establishments: a medium secure unit and a community Dialectical Behaviour Therapy (DBT) service. Previous to this, Claire worked for a specialized service working with people with personality disorders within the prison service.

Andrew Thompson is a Reader in Clinical Psychology at The University of Sheffield, UK, and a visiting Professor of Clinical Psychology at the University of Hull. He is registered as a Clinical Psychologist and as a Health Psychologist. He has worked in the NHS for nearly twenty years and currently sees people in connection with providing psychological therapy to assist with adjustment to long-term health conditions. His research interests focus upon adjustment to conditions that affect appearance. He is an author on a recent handbook on the psychological management of appearance concern and also a handbook on the use of qualitative methods (both published by Wiley). He is an advisor to The All Party UK Parliamentary Group on Skin and an Associate Editor of the *British Journal of Dermatology*.

Leah Tomkins is a Senior Lecturer in Organisation Studies at the Open University UK. Her research focuses on the experiences of work and organisation, including the ways in which these are both enabled and constrained by discourse, especially the discourses of perfection, reliability and self-management which underpin our taken-for-granted understandings of organisation. She draws on the philosophies of hermeneutics and phenomenology to try to make sense of the identity work of people in organisations, critiquing popular notions of 'authentic leadership' and 'the caring organization' for downplaying the lived experiences of work in its day-to-day, un-heroic moments. Her work has appeared in a range of leading journals, including *Organization Studies, Organization, Academy of Management Learning and Education, Management Learning*, and *Business Ethics Quarterly*.

David Wilde is a Senior Lecturer at Nottingham Trent University, UK. He graduated from the University of Sunderland with a degree in Psychology with Human Physiology in 1996 and the following year obtained an MSc in Environmental Psychology from the University of Surrey. After working as an Environmental Psychologist for three years, he began working in the field of Cancer and Palliative Care at the University of Sheffield. In 2005, he attained a Diploma in Consciousness and Transpersonal Psychology from Liverpool John Moore's University. In the same year he joined the University of Manchester where he obtained his PhD in 2011. He then returned to the Cancer/Palliative Care field whilst working at the University of Huddersfield for 2 years. David's research interests cover Out-of-Body and Near-Death Experiences, anomalous experiences and mental health, cancer, palliative care and long-term-conditions, and patient & public involvement in research.

Lisa White is an Oncology Specialist Nurse, and works for Leeds Teaching Hospitals NHS Trust, UK. She has worked in various roles within Urology for 19 years and as a specialist nurse for 13 years. She specializes in the care and treatment of prostate cancer, supporting men along their prostate cancer journey.

Katie Wright-Bevans is a lecturer in social and community psychology at Keele University UK. Her research is informed by critical social psychology and action research, with a focus on marginalised groups, health promotion and community-led change. In her PhD research (supervised by Michael Murray) Katie examined intergenerational practice and social change through mixed qualitative methods including a document analysis, interviews and participant drawings. Much of this work involved communities as collaborators to investigate disadvantage and health promotion among older and younger people in one British city. Katie has an interest in traditional and more innovative qualitative research methods and in particular, how these can be used as tools in working with communities to collaboratively explore issues related to health, wellbeing and equality.

SECTION I

Introducing Applied Qualitative Research in Psychology

Applying Qualitative Research in Psychology

Joanna Brooks and Nigel King

The use of qualitative research methods in psychology has proliferated rapidly over recent years. In the United Kingdom, undergraduate psychology courses are expected, according to benchmarks stipulated by the discipline's professional body (the British Psychological Society [BPS]), to cover qualitative methods, and the great majority of psychology courses include at least one module covering qualitative research methods as a matter of course. The BPS's Qualitative Methods section (QMiP: Qualitative Methods in Psychology) is now over ten years old and one of the largest sections in the Society. In the United States, the American Psychological Association (APA) set up a new 'Society for Qualitative Inquiry in Psychology' (SQiP) as part of their methodology section in 2013. There is increasing international interest in the use of qualitative methods amongst students, academics and clinicians in many sub-disciplines of psychology.

This trend is reflected in the recent and continuing publication of a number of popular and excellent textbooks on qualitative psychology methods (see the recommended reading list at the end of this chapter). So why do we see the need for yet another qualitative psychology textbook? What this book has to offer is its focus on situating qualitative psychological research in real-world settings. We see ourselves as *applied* psychologists – our focus is on using psychology theory and methods in a wide range of 'real-world' settings, undertaking research that addresses practical issues and has a meaningful impact on the society in which we live.

In this book, we situate qualitative psychological research in applied settings, and demonstrate the genuine utility of qualitative research methods. By showing some of the many different ways in which sub-disciplines and areas of psychology have usefully applied qualitative research methods, we very much hope that this book will appeal to those potentially disengaged from the abstract notion of research methods by demonstrating how and why qualitative research matters. In this chapter, we will introduce you to qualitative psychology and discuss how qualitative research differs from other ways of undertaking research in psychology. We will explain why we think

3

qualitative research has an important role to play in applied settings for psychologists, and describe the purpose and structure of this book.

What is qualitative psychology?

Qualitative psychology is often introduced as an alternative to quantitative psychology and it is highly unlikely that you are reading a book such as this without some awareness of the differences between the two approaches. Often, 'qualitative' and 'quantitative' research are presented to those new to research and to research methods as two very distinct and opposing ways of undertaking research. This is not necessarily the case: sometimes using both qualitative and quantitative methods and taking what is known as a mixed-methods approach can be the most effective way to answer your research question (see Rachel Shaw and David Hiles in Chapter 15 for more on this). And this, of course, is the crux of the matter: your approach to research should be determined by what you are investigating, what you want to know and how you can best find this out. It is not that one type of approach is better than another, but that different research questions require different research methods to provide the best and fullest answer. In this book, we will show you how, in applied psychology research (and we will go on to define what we mean by 'applied' research shortly), qualitative work can usefully explore and elucidate real-world issues in a distinctive, informative and valuable way.

However, it is true that there are some key ways in which qualitative and quantitative approaches differ. Biggerstaff (2012, p. 177) suggests that 'a practical definition [of qualitative research] points to methods that use language rather than numbers'. Quantitative research is primarily concerned with accurate measurement of a phenomenon and with describing things like the frequency of an occurrence, or statistical associations between particular phenomena. Fundamentally, qualitative research in psychology is about the study of meaning. The focus in qualitative psychology is on people as meaning-makers, and on describing and understanding the ways in which we experience and interpret our world. As two distinct research paradigms, then, qualitative and quantitative research offer us rather different ways of thinking about the world (King and Horrocks, 2010).

Historically, the focus in contemporary psychology has been on quantitative research, and the relatively recent increase in qualitative work being undertaken in the discipline does mark a shift in approach. Psychology itself is a relatively new academic discipline, developing in the second half of the nineteenth century, and the early psychologists (such as William James) were certainly interested in thinking about notions familiar to qualitative psychologists such as subjective perception and personal accounts. However, from the beginning of the twentieth century onwards, mainstream psychology became increasingly concerned with establishing itself as a traditional 'science', measuring external and observable variables (Ashworth, 2003). Whilst other important fields of psychology such as psychoanalysis are based on qualitative psychology methods (such as the narrative case study), and key figures in psychology (for example, Jean Piaget) certainly made use of qualitative observational methods and interviews, it was not really until the 1980s that there was increased focus on the development of qualitative psychology research as a legitimate and defensible method (Madill, 2015).

As the contents of this book clearly demonstrate, qualitative psychology research is an umbrella term and not a single 'homogenous entity' (Smith, 2003, p. 2). There are a number of different qualitative research approaches with different perspectives and procedures (we will go on to look at this in more detail in Chapters 2 and 3). What you want to research and your research question will determine what is a suitable method for you (be that a qualitative or a quantitative method, and if a qualitative method which one) – as we discuss in Chapter 2, it is important that your research question is consistent with the approach you are using and vice versa. In this book, we will show how a number of research questions that one may wish to address in applied settings can be usefully and valuably answered using qualitative methods. Next, we will explain what we mean by 'applied' psychology and then we will move on to explain the relevance of qualitative psychology in applied settings.

What is 'applied' psychology?

So what is 'applied' research and how does it differ from other types of research? Notions of an 'applied science' originally derive from distinctions made in the natural sciences between 'pure' and 'applied' research. Traditionally, the notion of 'applied' research refers to taking knowledge derived from 'pure' or 'basic' research and applying it in the wider world beyond the four walls of the scientific laboratory. In this context, it is fairly easy to distinguish between the 'pure' and the 'applied' in terms of their focus on either the theoretical (refuting or supporting scientific theory) or the experimental (applying and utilising this knowledge).

'Applied' psychology is the application of psychological knowledge to solve practical issues and problems in real-world settings. As psychology covers a wide range of different areas, there are many different possible 'real-world' settings including health, clinical, educational, occupational, social and community settings. For qualitative psychologists, whose central focus is often on human experience, notions of 'pure' and 'applied' research can be difficult to reconcile with an essential concern with human beings as meaning-makers. Traditional notions of moving from basic to applied research are often based on reductionism, the idea that we can understand larger systems by reducing them to their constituent parts. For example, understanding an illness in terms of biochemical activity or in terms of genetics may be very helpful indeed in enabling researchers to identify a cure for that illness. However, reductionism can be more problematic when considered in terms of human behaviour and experience. Take the example of religious or mystical experience. Professor Michael

Persinger has suggested that stimulation of the temporal lobes (achieved by wearing a piece of apparatus known as 'the God helmet') is associated with subjects reporting 'mystical experience and altered states' (Persinger et al., 2010). But even if it is possible to identify which particular part of the brain it is that is 'activated' in 'mystical experience', this doesn't mean that such experiences are now explained and understood. Others researching mystical experience might suggest that is how one interprets or frames the experience which is the crucial determinant of the perceived nature of the experience. What qualitative research can do is capture what people make of such experiences – how, for example, such an experience might contribute towards or be impacted on by religious identity, as well as consider what other factors might contribute to this. In the United Kingdom, for example, Professor Adrian Coyle has shown how qualitative research can develop useful insights into the psychology of religion (e.g. Coyle, 2008). An important point here is that, especially for those undertaking research in applied settings, there is no such thing as 'decontextualised' experience: experience, mystical or otherwise, does not occur in a vacuum. Trying to create a traditionally scientific 'objective' setting for our research may well result in us creating a situation so artificial that it has little to tell us about what happens in the 'real world' outside of our controlled environment.

For qualitative psychologists, rather than defining 'applied' research as a dichotomous alternative to 'pure' or 'basic' research, we think that a more meaningful distinction can be made in terms of the main *focus* of a piece of research. This may vary from those studies aimed primarily at addressing academic debates to those with a very pragmatic and practical research focus. Thus, for qualitative research in psychology, one can consider at what point on this 'academic to practical' spectrum a particular piece of work is situated, and consider this in dimensional rather than dichotomous terms. This means that we can think about applied qualitative psychology in terms of applying qualitative psychological approaches to practical issues in the world beyond academia. This does not mean that very practically-focused research cannot contribute to academic knowledge: it means thinking about who the research is *principally* addressing. We believe that for qualitative psychologists whose work involves them taking a 'hands-on' approach to pragmatic research questions in real-world settings, it is essential that the methods they use should be able to genuinely incorporate the concerns of those whom the research is intending to help, as well as being accessible and intelligible to its intended audience. We also think that qualitative research has particular utility in applied settings, and we will now move on to explain why.

Why use qualitative methods in applied psychology?

We have briefly introduced what is meant by 'qualitative psychology' (more on this in Chapter 2) and 'applied psychology'. So why might qualitative methods be an appropriate choice in applied settings?

The first point to make is that qualitative methods will not always be the most appropriate choice. As we have already said, different research methods are appropriate for different research questions. As Willig (2013) points out, research questions are best conceptualised in creative terms rather than in any mechanistic sense – your question should be 'How can I find out about something?' rather than 'How can I apply appropriate techniques to this topic?' What Kinmond (2012) refers to as the 'So what?' test ('Why is this research relevant and what useful knowledge will this research provide?') is also likely to be especially pertinent in research undertaken in applied settings.

There may be both practical and philosophical reasons for choosing to use qualitative methods in applied psychological research. We have already suggested that qualitative methods can offer a rather different way of thinking about the world compared to quantitative methods, and we will address this in more detail in Chapter 2. Qualitative methods are often appropriate when a researcher is interested in examining a psychology-related topic in an applied setting in depth rather than in breadth. Qualitative methods can help psychologists and others understand particular cases in rich detail, which may very useful in illuminating what is happening in a particular applied setting, and why – they may well be able to help explain what is going on behind the headline numbers and statistics, or why people are behaving in particular ways. For example, we undertook a qualitative study in which we interviewed people who had back pain and their spouses (Brooks et al., 2013). We were interested in finding out why some of our sample had managed to keep working with their condition, whilst others (with a clinically comparable condition) had not. Our findings highlighted ways in which generally under-researched wider social circumstances, including stigmatising socio-cultural beliefs about 'benefit cheats' and 'malingering', can contribute to different occupational outcomes. We found that people out of work were so anxious about others being sceptical of their back pain condition that they seemed to have become entrenched in a position whereby it was crucial that they were perceived as completely disabled. This presents an obvious tension with accepted clinical recommendations for the management of back pain which emphasise remaining active – in adopting this stance and limiting activity, the chances of any return to work and economic activity become increasingly remote. Qualitative work may be able to usefully highlight potential limitations of mainstream theory and taken for granted assumptions – for example, discursive approaches (such as those used by Kirsty Budds and colleagues in Chapter 9 of this book in their work on 'older' mothers) can effectively challenge taken for granted assumptions and discourses, as well as informing and promoting action and change (Willig, 1999). Qualitative methods are also often very useful in applied settings when a research topic is relatively new and unresearched – for example, in exploratory work which is primarily looking to explore phenomena rather than seeking to confirm hypotheses. Qualitative work can generate new, relevant questions for future research (be that qualitative and/or quantitative). In Chapter 4 in this volume, you can find an example of this type of work: Peter Branney and colleagues describe how the one-day workshop events they ran with men with prostate cancer gave the research team the opportunity to learn more about the topic prior to designing a research programme.

As qualitative methods have become more accepted not just in the field of psychology but also more widely, their utility is increasingly recognised in applied settings. In health settings, for example, incorporating patient views is seen as increasingly important by those developing policies and initiatives (and see Delia Muir's discussion in Chapter 16 for more on this). There is an acknowledged need for more community-centred ways of working in health and social care, and an increasing focus on empowering individuals and communities to engage in participatory development of, and decision making about, health and social care services (National Institute for Health and Care Excellence, 2014). This shift has been mirrored by a change in the way that the public interacts with and contributes to health and social care research. Patient and public involvement in health care research has become increasingly common both in the UK and internationally (Gillard et al., 2012) and is often now a requirement for publicly funded research (there is additionally an important moral argument that society has a right to both shape and participate in publicly funded research). At the core of public involvement is recognition of the valuable understanding and knowledge gained through lived experience. Qualitative research can be very useful in exploring patients' perspectives (as well as allowing these stories to be heard), and qualitative work is now often a routine component of much applied health research (McParland and Flowers, 2012).

In applied settings, qualitative research can be accessible and powerful, and can incorporate rather novel ways of working to achieve research aims whilst including participant groups typically deemed 'hard to reach'. With the drive to see members of the public as active members of research teams rather than passive subjects of research, for example, there has been a burgeoning interest in participatory approaches to research, which often utilise qualitative methods. *Participatory research methods* seek to actively involve as 'co-researchers' those who would conventionally be regarded as 'participants', and places strong emphasis on learning from the process of research co-production as much as from research outcomes. Where conventional forms of knowledge production distinguish between knowledge producers and consumers, co-production offers an alternative to find ways of generating, disseminating and using knowledge that blur these boundaries (Borg et al., 2012). There are striking similarities between criticisms which have been levelled at participatory approaches and those levelled at qualitative methods, suggesting that both are 'soft' (critiques often founded on crucial misunderstandings around the appropriate criteria on which such research should be judged) (Hammersley, 1992; Cornwall and Jewkes, 1995). There are interesting parallels with debates around how to ensure and demonstrate the quality of participatory research, and the development over the last 30 years of an increasingly secure foothold in psychology for qualitative methods, driven by 'the development of qualitative research as *method*, with a concern for rigour and an interest in epistemology' (Madill and Todd, 2002, p. 5). Qualitative psychologists have the opportunity to usefully contribute to such applied research (e.g. drawing on their expertise to show how rich qualitative findings from individual participants might be meaningfully summarised and shared), and several of the authors in this book – see Peter Branney and colleagues, Chapter 4; Helen Cowie and Dawn Jennifer, Chapter 6; Michael Murray and Katie Wright-Bevans, Chapter 8; Victoria Lavis and colleagues, Chapter 12 – explicitly identify their work as taking a participatory approach.

Qualitative research can also offer alternative strategies to empower and engage participants by developing innovative methods which are accessible to and engaging for participants. For example, arts-based research, using a creative format (which may include visual arts, music, dance, performance, poetry or some form of narrative inquiry method be it autobiography or fiction) to develop, explore, collect, analyse and/or present data (Leavy, 2008) can facilitate engagement and inclusivity, disrupting habitual ways of looking at a substantive research topic and expediting knowledge translation and transferability (Leavy, 2008; Lapum et al., 2011). Such methods are also potentially far more accessible to diverse stakeholders and multiple audiences in applied settings (Gergen and Gergen, 2010). In Chapter 8, Michael Murray and Katie Wright-Bevans describe a community arts project undertaken with older residents of a disadvantaged neighbourhood, and explain how, as well as facilitating understanding, their approach promoted participants' social interaction and community empowerment. Participants in this project expressed particular satisfaction in being able to challenge negative representations of their community through public exhibition of the artwork they produced, which attracted attention from elected officials and the media as well as from other local residents.

Another example of the ways in which qualitative psychologists in applied settings have developed useful and innovative ways to facilitate reflection and talk is through the use of visual methods and materials (we will talk about this in more detail in Chapter 3). Pre-existing visual materials can be used to elicit verbal data – see Helen Cowie and Dawn Jennifer's chapter on the use of pictorial vignettes to actively engage children and young people in research. Alternatively, participants may themselves produce some form of visual material that can be treated as data in its own right, or used to facilitate talk. In Chapter 14, we and some of our colleagues present a study in which we used a visual tool called 'the Pictor technique' (King et al., 2013) – using this method, participants create visual 'Pictor' charts which are used both as a basis for a research interview and as part of the research data in analysis. The Pictor technique was developed in response to some challenges we encountered when asking health care professionals to reflect on how they worked with others to provide patient care. Often, in an interview situation, it can be hard for a participant to bring to mind all of those who were involved in a particular case, and equally difficult for the researcher to remember these details. When asked about their own involvement in and understanding of collaborative working, health care staff can sometimes present an 'official' version of care procedures, rather than an account of their own direct lived experience (Ross et al., 2005). Finally, especially when it comes to experienced professionals, the way they work can become so habitual and taken for granted that it is quite difficult for them to reflect on this in any depth in a research interview. The Pictor technique, which involves participants creating simple visual charts to represent a case of collaborative working, was developed in direct response to these challenges, and we describe how we used this method in a large qualitative study with different health and social care professionals in Chapter 14. This and other techniques used by qualitative psychologists to help facilitate self-reflection (see Chapter 13 of this book, in which Nigel and our colleague Viv Burr present their work using personal construct psychology methods to facilitate reflexive practice amongst social work students) have obvious applications in applied settings where the ability to demonstrate one's proficiencies as a 'reflexive practitioner' are often important elements of practice-based professional development.

Overview of the book

In this book, we take a highly pragmatic approach which first and foremost situates qualitative psychological research in applied real-world settings. There are very many excellent resources available for psychology students wanting to know how to undertake qualitative research (see the recommended reading list at the end of this chapter for examples of some very good textbooks on this subject). The differentiating focus in this book is on showing you how qualitative psychological research is actually undertaken by qualitative psychology researchers in applied settings. We have examples from a wide range of psychology sub-disciplines including (amongst others) health, organisational, educational, clinical, community, social, forensic and environmental psychology. Following an introduction to the different approaches taken by qualitative researchers (Chapter 2) and guidance on the main steps undertaken when doing a qualitative study in psychology (Chapter 3), we will then present examples of qualitative research undertaken in different areas of psychology. Expert psychology researchers working in these different areas will explain how they have used qualitative methods in their work to show you how qualitative research can be used in applied settings. Each chapter provides an overview of the particular area of psychology in which the work was undertaken, a description of the qualitative approach used, a summary of the applied setting in which the work was undertaken and a specific example of the author's research showing how qualitative methods contributed to understandings in this area of work. The final section of the book covers some of the specific issues that arise in applied qualitative research including public involvement in research and the use of mixed (qualitative and quantitative) methods. Finally, Flora Cornish and Sarah Honeywell offer some thoughts on how findings from qualitative research can be used in applied fields so that research findings can be translated into actionable findings with real-world impact. We hope that reading about these varied worked examples of qualitative research will give you an idea of some of the interesting qualitative research undertaken by applied psychologists – and inspire you in your own qualitative research work.

Recommended reading

There are a number of excellent textbooks available which provide a detailed introduction for psychologists looking for guidance on how to go about undertaking a qualitative research project. Some of the ones we use and recommend to our students are:

Braun, V. and Clarke, V. (2013). *Successful Qualitative Research: A Practical Guide for Beginners*. London: SAGE.
Forrester, M. (ed.) (2010). *Doing Qualitative Research in Psychology: A Practical Guide*. London: SAGE.
Frost, N. (2011). *Qualitative Research Methods in Psychology: Combining Core Approaches*. Maidenhead: Open University Press.
Langdridge, D. and Hagger-Johnson, G. (2011). *Introduction to Research Methods and Data Analysis in Psychology* (3rd edn). Harlow: Pearson Education Limited.
Smith, J. (ed.) (2007). *Qualitative Psychology: A Practical Guide to Research Methods* (2nd edn). London: SAGE.
Sullivan, C., Gibson, S. and Riley S. (eds) (2012). *Doing Your Qualitative Psychology Project*. London: SAGE.
Willig, C. (2013). *Introducing Qualitative Research in Psychology* (3rd edn). Maidenhead: Open University Press.
Willig, C. and Stainton-Rogers, W. (2013). *The SAGE Handbook of Qualitative Research in Psychology*. London: SAGE.

References

Ashworth, P. (2003). The origins of qualitative psychology. In J. Smith (Ed.), *Qualitative Psychology: A Practical Guide to Research Methods*. London: SAGE, 4–24.
Biggerstaff, D. (2012). Qualitative research methods in psychology. In G. Rossi (Ed.), *Psychology: Selected Papers*. Rijeka, Croatia: InTech, pp. 175–206.
Borg, M., Karlsson, B., Hesook, S.K. and McCormack, B. (2012). Opening up for many voices in knowledge construction. *Forum: Qualitative Social Research*, 13(1), Art. 1.

Brooks, J., McCluskey, S., King, N. and Burton, A. K. (2013). Illness perceptions in the context of differing work participation outcomes: exploring the influence of significant others in persistent back pain. *BMC Musculoskeletal Disorders*, 14, 48, doi:10.1186/147124741448.

Cornwall, A. and Jewkes, R. (1995). The use of qualitative methods: What is participatory research? *Social Science and Medicine*, 41(12), 1667–1676.

Coyle, A. (2008). Qualitative methods and 'the (partly) ineffable' in psychological research on religion and spirituality. *Qualitative Research in Psychology*, 5(1), 56–67.

Gergen, K. and Gergen, M. (2010). Performative social science and psychology. *Forum: Qualitative Social Research*, 12(1), Art. 11.

Gillard, S., Simons, L., Turner, K., Lucock, M. and Edwards, C. (2012). Patient and public involvement in the coproduction of knowledge: Reflection on the analysis of qualitative data in a mental health study. *Qualitative Health Research*, 22(8), 1126–1137.

Hammersley, M. (1992). What's Wrong with Ethnography? Routledge: London.

King, N., Bravington, A., Brooks, J., Hardy, B., Melvin, J. and Wilde, D. (2013). The Pictor technique: A method for exploring the experience of collaborative working. *Qualitative Health Research*, 23(8), 1138–1152.

King, N. and Horrocks, C. (2010). *Interview in Qualitative Research*. London: SAGE.

Kinmond, K. (2012). Coming up with a research question. In C. Sullivan, S. Gibson and S. Riley (Eds.), *Doing Your Qualitative Psychology Project*. London: SAGE, pp. 23–36.

Lapum, J., Ruttonsha, P., Church, K., Yau, T. and Matthews-David, A. (2011). Employing the arts in research as an analytical tool and dissemination method: Interpreting experience through the aesthetic. *Qualitative Inquiry*, 18(1), 100–115.

Leavy, P. (2008). *Method Meets Art: Arts-Based Research Practice*. New York: The Guilford Press.

Madill A. (2015). Let a thousand flowers bloom. *The Psychologist*, 28, 656–658.

Madill, A. and Todd, K.Z. (2002). Proposal to the Council of the British Psychological Society for the Formation of a New Section of the Society on 'Qualitative Methods in Psychology'. Retrieved 11 June 2015 from: www.academia.edu/1635472/ Madill_A._Todd_K._Z._2002_._Proposal_to_the_Council_of_the_British_ Psychological_Society_for_the_formation_of_a_new_Section_of_the_Society_on_ Qualitative_Methods_in_Psychology.

McParland, J. and Flowers, P. (2012). Nine lessons and recommendations from the conduct of focus group research in chronic pain samples. *British Journal of Health Psychology*, 17(3), 492–504.

National Institute for Health and Care Excellence (2014). Community engagement to improve health. NICE local government briefings 2014. Available from www. publications.nice.org.uk/lgb16.

Persinger, M.A., Saroka, K., Koren, S.A. and St-Pierre, L.S. (2010). The electromagnetic induction of mystical and altered states within the laboratory. *Journal of Consciousness Exploration & Research*, 1(7), 808–830.

Ross, A., King, N. and Firth, J. (2005). Interprofessional relationships and collaborative working: Encouraging reflective practice. *Online Journal of Issues in Nursing*, 10(1). Retrieved 30 January 2017 from: www.nursingworld.org/ MainMenuCategories/ANAMarketplace/ANAPeriodicals/OJIN/TableofContents/ Volume102005/No1Jan05/tpc26_316010.html.

Smith, J. (2003). Introduction. In J. Smith (Ed.), *Qualitative Psychology: A Practical Guide to Research Methods*. London: SAGE, pp. 1–3.

Willig, C. (Ed.) (1999). *Applied Discourse Analysis: Social and Psychological Interventions*. Buckingham: Open University Press.

Willig, C. (2013). *Introducing Qualitative Research in Psychology (Third Edition)*. Maidenhead: Open University Press.

Approaches to Qualitative Psychology

Joanna Brooks and Nigel King

2

In Chapter 1 we noted that qualitative research in psychology is not a homogenous entity, and in this chapter we will explain some of the different approaches to research taken by applied qualitative researchers. We will explain why these may be appropriate for different projects – and throughout, in keeping with the applied focus of this book, we will conceptualise qualitative research as a way of *addressing questions* rather than simply applying techniques.

Different ways of thinking about the world = different approaches to research

There are many ways to do qualitative research: that is to say there exist different qualitative research *methods*. *Method* refers to particular techniques used to collect and analyse research data. In Chapter 3 we will discuss the various data collection methods (e.g. different kinds of research interview) that can be used by applied qualitative researchers. It is important to note at this point that a researcher's choice of method is informed and underpinned by their choice of *methodology*. *Methodology* refers to the general approach taken to carrying out a piece of research. Methodologies are shaped by ways of thinking about the world and by different perspectives on both what we can find out about the world and how we can find this out. Different methodologies are, that is to say, shaped by different underlying *philosophical assumptions*.

As we saw in Chapter 1, generally speaking mainstream quantitative research in psychology takes a traditional 'scientific' approach to answering research questions, with the underlying assumption that the research phenomena being investigated exist independently and can be objectively observed and accurately measured. Central to this approach is *empiricism* – the view that knowledge of the world comes from direct experience of it. It follows from this that the way for researchers to gain knowledge of the world is to collect data through observation and measurement. From this perspective, the role of a researcher is to take a detached and objective approach to their research topic and to collect repeated data with a view to developing general laws or rules to explain research phenomena.

In qualitative research, however, the phenomena under investigation tend to be related to human experience – something that it is often quite 'messy' and complicated and certainly rather difficult to think of in terms of accurate measurement and objective observation. Qualitative researchers, examining how social worlds are experienced by their participants, are therefore likely to prioritise what the sociologist Max Weber (1864–1920) called *verstehen* (understanding) over *erklaren* (explanation). They are also likely to ask rather different research questions and to have rather different research goals compared to their mainstream quantitative psychology research colleagues. Applied qualitative psychologists are likely to want to understand human experience and behaviour in their social context rather than in a neutral controlled laboratory environment. Qualitative psychology researchers are likely to recognise and even welcome their own involvement and hence their 'subjectivity' in the research process.

The varied approaches to qualitative research derive from different ways of thinking about the world with differing implications for the kind of research we should undertake. This leads us to a couple of terms and concepts that many people can find rather difficult to grasp – it might even be that you are surprised to find these concepts being discussed in a book that focuses on applied real-world research. However, as you will see, in qualitative research in psychology, these concepts have very real and practical consequences for choices you make in terms of your research area, your research question, the data you collect, the analysis you undertake and the way in which you report your findings.

The two philosophical terms you need to have a grasp of are *epistemology* and *ontology*. The 'ology' bit of both words comes from the Greek word *logos* (study). *Epistemology* comes from the Greek *episteme* (knowledge) and therefore refers to the study of knowledge. Epistemology, then, is the philosophical theory of knowledge – the assumptions we make about *what* it is possible for us to know and *how* we can obtain this knowledge. *Ontology* comes from the Greek *ontos* (being) and refers to philosophical assumptions about the nature of being, which determine our understanding of what is real. So ontology is concerned with 'What is reality?', and epistemology is concerned with 'How can we know this reality?'

Understanding these concepts can be difficult, and it might be tempting to dismiss them as having no real-life or applied relevance for your own research. However, all research involves epistemological and ontological assumptions. It is true that, for those psychologists concerned solely with quantitative research, such assumptions are seldom explicitly addressed – but it does not mean that such research is not underpinned by particular epistemological and ontological beliefs. As we have already discussed, quantitative research in psychology (and in other social sciences) is often concerned with demonstrating the discipline's credentials in line with those prioritised by 'traditional "science"', measuring external and observable variables (Ashworth, 2003). This type of research can be said to take a *realist* position in both epistemological and ontological terms. Researchers adopting this position hold the view that there is a real-world or objective reality 'out there' that exists independently, and that they can have some kind of access to further knowledge about this world using appropriate methods and techniques.

However, as we have already pointed out, qualitative research in psychology is usually concerned with subjective human experience and human beings as meaning makers. Qualitative psychology researchers therefore have rather different assumptions from those of their quantitative psychologist colleagues about the 'reality' of human experience (ontology) and about what it is possible for us as researchers to 'know' or find out about this experience (epistemology). Importantly, though, there is no one particular philosophical position taken by qualitative psychology researchers. This means that the onus is on qualitative psychology researchers themselves to reflect on and be clear about the approach they are adopting. It is worth emphasising that the requirement to do this does not stem from a need to defend qualitative methods as such. Rather, it is needed because if, as researchers, we acknowledge that there are multiple philosophical positions we can take, then it follows that we need to be clear about our own approach so that others are able to understand, scrutinise and appropriately assess our work.

A common distinction made in discussions of the philosophical basis for research is between *realist* and *relativist* positions. Researchers taking a straightforwardly realist approach would assume that (in terms of ontology) there is a real world or objective reality 'out there' that exists independently of the researcher. Further, they would assume that (in terms of epistemology) it is possible through the correct use of appropriate methods to come to confident conclusions about this objective reality. The opposing relativist position would not accept that there is a single objective reality, or that we can come to any certain knowledge of reality through our research processes. However, when it comes to positioning yourself in qualitative research, the options available to you as a researcher are actually far more nuanced than a simple either/or choice between realism and relativism. In the remainder of this chapter we will introduce a way of thinking about and distinguishing between the different philosophical positions taken by qualitative psychologists. We will then present three well-known approaches used by qualitative researchers – grounded theory, interpretative phenomenological analysis (IPA) and discourse analysis – to show how specific methodologies are associated with particular epistemological and ontological positions.

Identifying a philosophical position as a qualitative psychologist

Writers on qualitative methods in psychology have distinguished between the different philosophical positions taken within the field in a number of useful and thoughtful ways (e.g. Reicher, 2000; Madill et al., 2000). Often, though, the emphasis is on the claims different qualitative methods make as to what they can enable us to know about the world – that is, the focus tends to be on epistemological considerations. Sometimes, methodological approaches that seem to have rather similar epistemological positions can differ importantly in terms of their ontology. To allow us to think about and describe both the epistemological and ontological positions underpinning different methodological approaches, we have found it useful to distinguish between four different philosophical positions in qualitative psychology research: (1) qualitative neo-positivism; (2) limited realism; (3) contextualism; and (4) radical constructionism (see Table 2.1). However, it is worth emphasising that divisions between these positions are not precise and inflexible – these are not four discrete positions. Nor are they positions that we are suggesting you need to choose and then identify yourselves with absolutely, irrevocably and unalterably – an assumption we quite often hear from novice qualitative psychologists. As researchers ourselves, we have undertaken work on projects from each of these stances, because the research question that needed answering was congruent with – and could be answered by taking – a particular approach. We are not presenting these as positions to adopt once and for all and to live your life by! Of course, you may find that some positions fit more comfortably with your personal perspective than others, and you will naturally be drawn to the types of project that enable you to use your preferred approach. We would, though, argue that willingness to be flexible about approach, at least to some extent, is important for an applied qualitative researcher.

Table 2.1 Different philosophical positions for qualitative research

Philosophical position	Ontology	Epistemology
Neo-positivism	Realist	Realist
Limited realism	Realist	Constructivist/relativist
Contextualism	Relativist (or indeterminate)	Constructivist/relativist
Radical constructionism	Relativist	Strongly relativist

King and Brooks (2017); reprinted with kind permission.

Qualitative neo-positivism

Research undertaken from a qualitative neo-positivist stance is strongly realist in terms of both ontology and epistemology, and assumes that individuals are part of a real world 'out there' that is both observable and knowable. It assumes that the accounts of research participants directly represent this reality, and that there is a relatively straightforward and unproblematic relationship between individuals' views and accounts of the world and the material world itself. A further important aspect of this stance is the assumption that researchers can (and should) take steps to remove any subjective bias from their research.

We have appropriated the term 'qualitative neo-positivism' from Duberley et al. (2012) who use it in the context of organisational and management research to refer to qualitative research that seeks to 'neutrally apprehend the facts "out there"' (p. 19). The term refers to and incorporates some notions from the positivist epistemological position associated with 'traditional' science: positivism suggests that the purpose of research should be to provide objective knowledge through unbiased observation of a real and perceivable outside world. Nowadays, as Willig (2001) notes, it is 'generally accepted that observation and description are necessarily selective, and that our perception and understanding of the world is therefore partial at best' (p. 3). Few researchers in contemporary times would unreservedly identify themselves as operating from a positivist stance, but it is not uncommon for qualitative research undertaken in some disciplines (business and management being one example – see King and Brooks (2017) to adopt what we refer to here as a qualitative neo-positivist stance. 'Naive realism' and 'crude realism' are other terms that have (often rather dismissively) been applied to research undertaken from this type of philosophical stance. Our use of the term 'qualitative neo-positivism' reflects our contention that, rather than simply exhibiting naivety, researchers adopting this stance may well have a clear and coherent rationale for so doing. Nonetheless, there is rather little qualitative psychology research that explicitly positions itself as neo-positivist, although there are times when such an approach is clearly appropriate in applied research. An example might be a piece of research that is strongly tied to existing psychological theory – perhaps in a mixed methods study with a strong quantitative lead. In this sort of work, a qualitative neo-positivist stance would allow for philosophical congruity between the quantitative and qualitative arms of a research project.

Limited realism

'Limited realism' as we use the term here refers to quite a range of varied but related philosophical positions also referred to in the literature as, for example, 'critical realism' (Archer et al., 1998) or 'subtle realism' (Hammersley, 1992) (and see Madill, 2008, for more discussion of the use of realism in qualitative psychology). As with researchers adopting the neo-positivist stance described above, researchers operating from a limited realist position conceptualise the world as having a concrete reality outside of human constructions of it – that is, they are committed to a realist ontology. However, this realist ontology is, for those taking a limited realist stance, integrated with a relativist epistemology. Simply put, a relativist epistemology sees our understanding of the world as always limited by our own perspectives and our standpoint within it; there are no technical, procedural solutions to remove the researcher from the outcomes of the research process, as neo-positivists would claim.

Limited realist research frequently draws on and seeks to develop existing theory: it is often concerned with producing causal explanations of social phenomena, and as such tends to seek at least some degree of (cautious and nuanced) generalisability. So whilst limited realist qualitative research does not claim objectivity, it also rejects the position of more strongly relativist stances (such as those we'll cover in the next two sections) which maintain that no interpretation of data is 'better' than any other. In research taking a limited realist stance, the aim is to develop an interpretation that is as credible as possible, and researcher reflexivity is an important part of the research process. An applied example of when such an approach might be appropriate would be a realist evaluation of a complex intervention being tried out in a health care setting (a realist evaluation focuses on examining what conditions might be necessary for a programme to succeed or fail, rather than simply asking 'Does the programme work?').

Contextualism

Researchers working from a contextualist stance are committed to both a relativist epistemology and a relativist ontology. From a contextualist stance, there is no single reality 'out there' that can be measured and investigated. Knowledge obtained through research is always context specific; thus, understanding context (in social, cultural and historical terms) is essential. Both the researcher and the research participant are seen as conscious beings who are always interpreting their worlds and acting on and in the world. All research undertaken from a contextualist stance is therefore openly acknowledged as subjective. Notions of knowledge as being universal and value-free are impossible from this perspective and, as such, it is neither meaningful nor appropriate to try to impose or measure objectivity or reliability – all accounts are subjective.

Researcher reflexivity is again important in both a personal and a methodological sense – in this sort of research, which recognises it as inevitable that the researcher's own perspective is brought to the project, researcher subjectivity is not merely accepted but welcomed. Common cultural understandings and the empathy engendered through recognition of a shared humanity are argued to be valuable and important in terms of both the research process and the research findings (King and Brooks, 2017). Contextualist research acknowledges that there are multiple possible interpretations that can be made of any research phenomena and that findings will depend upon the specific research context as well as the researcher's position. Findings from a piece of research undertaken from a contextualist stance may therefore be very context specific. In applied settings, such research might be undertaken to explore the experiences of particular people – perhaps those with a particular illness condition, or those with experience of a particular event. However, qualitative psychology researchers taking a contextual approach do understand their research and their data as being part of a broader existence. Contextualist research therefore seeks to firmly ground its results in participants' experiences and their social context. So, though it does not seek objectivity or any absolute sense of 'truth', it does concern itself with what is experienced as 'the truth' for particular people in particular contexts. It thus adopts a less thorough-going relativism than we see in the final position, introduced in the following section.

Radical constructionism

Radical constructionist approaches share a number of similarities with the contextualist approach to research described above. Radical constructionists similarly conceptualise knowledge as being historically and culturally located, and research knowledge as being co-produced by the researcher and the research participant. However, whereas contextualist approaches seek to 'ground' findings in participants' experience, radical constructionism challenges the notion that there are any absolute foundations for knowledge whatsoever. From a radical constructionist stance, 'reality' is only constructed through language – that is, reality is socially and culturally produced. It is pretty clear, then, that the epistemological position taken by radical constructionists is strongly relativist. Classifying radical constructionism in terms of ontology, though, is more problematic. Maxwell (2012) argues that constructionists do not really distinguish between epistemology and ontology (if we accept that language creates reality then it follows that there is no reality 'out there' because reality does not exist outside of our constructions of it). To the extent that radical constructionists equate their acknowledgement of diverse perspectives and constructions of meaning with ontological relativism, it may largely be to clearly distinguish their approach from both realist and contextualist approaches.

If radical constructionism is not concerned with any attempt to understand experience, even in a very contextually-bounded way, we may wonder how it can be of any relevance in an applied psychology context? We would suggest that it can be. Whilst the field might face legitimate criticism for being often primarily academic in focus, the applied value of such an approach can stem from its emphasis on raising awareness of and challenging limiting but socially dominant discourses, as well as on bringing about change through political and social action and informing recommendations for social and psychological practice (Willig, 1999).

Examples of specific approaches used in qualitative psychology

Having looked at the different philosophical positions that might be taken by qualitative psychologists, we will now consider three approaches used in qualitative psychology research. We have spent some time in this chapter looking at the range of philosophical positions available to qualitative psychologists because different philosophical positions have differing implications for how research should be carried out, including how data should be analysed. You will remember that we have already distinguished between method (the particular techniques used to collect and analyse data) and methodology (the general approach taken to carrying out a piece of research). In terms of how these concepts relate to each other, we can think of this as a hierarchy whereby philosophical assumptions shape methodological approaches, which in turn inform the choice of method. Some qualitative data analysis methods are directly linked to particular methodologies (that is, if you claim to be using that methodology, you are then obliged to use the particular method of analysis it specifies, and to follow its philosophical assumptions). We refer to these as *specific* approaches, and it is three of these that we will discuss now. Other methods of qualitative data analysis can be used within a variety of methodologies, although precisely *how* they are used will differ – for example, different styles of thematic analysis (e.g. Braun and Clarke, 2006; Brooks et al., 2015). These *generic* approaches are not distinct methodologies but rather particular styles of analysis that, as such, can be used in qualitative research from a range of philosophical positions. When using a generic approach, the onus is on the researcher to reflect on (and be explicit about) the position they are taking in their work (see King and Brooks, 2017). Specific methods such as the ones we are going to discuss now are, in contrast, embedded within distinct methodologies and clearly linked to particular ontological and epistemological assumptions.

Grounded theory

What is it?
Grounded theory is a qualitative research approach that was developed in the 1960s by two sociologists, Anselm Strauss and Barney Glaser (Glaser and Strauss, 1967). Glaser and Strauss developed grounded theory in response to concerns they had about the use of existing theory in sociological research. Glaser and Strauss argued that there was a tendency amongst researchers to look only to dominant existing theories to answer their research questions rather than progressing the field and advancing knowledge through the development of new theories. Glaser and Strauss suggested that not only was this leading to an increasingly large gap between theory and empirical

research, but it also meant that researchers were ignoring research questions they perceived themselves as being unable to address with the theories and methods available to them. Glaser and Strauss introduced grounded theory as an approach in which theory is developed from the data collected, rather than applying a theory to the data.

Over the years, a number of different versions of grounded theory have developed, and Glaser and Strauss themselves disagreed significantly and publicly on both the nature and the practice of the approach. In 1990, Strauss (with Juliet Corbin) published a detailed procedural guide for those wishing to use grounded theory, including a specific coding paradigm delineating three clear stages of analysis: open coding, axial coding and selective coding (Strauss and Corbin, 1990, 2008). Glaser (e.g. 1992) heavily criticised the method outlined by Strauss and Corbin as too prescriptive, going so far as to opine that what Strauss and Corbin described was not grounded theory at all, but another method entirely. In addition to Glaser's 'classical' grounded theory and the approach associated with the detailed guidelines provided by Strauss and Corbin, amongst other variants of grounded theory, is a social constructionist version introduced by Kathy Charmaz (e.g. 2014). Charmaz's constructivist grounded theory explicitly acknowledges the role of the researcher in theory construction – theories are therefore seen as being constructed by the researcher through their interaction with the data, rather than as emerging from within the data set itself.

Philosophical positioning

When grounded theory was being developed by Glaser and Strauss, the traditional 'scientific' approach and the use of quantitative methods had become dominant in sociological research. The introduction of grounded theory was intended to counter prevailing views of qualitative research as 'unsystematic' (Charmaz, 2003), and its ontological assumptions reflect its realist foundations. Grounded theory assumes a real, objective social world 'out there' that can be observed and investigated by researchers. The unambiguous aim of a grounded theory study is to 'generate or discover a theory' (Glaser and Strauss, 1967) – an explanation for what is going on. Nonetheless, grounded theory also recognises that people interpret their own social realities, and that their actions towards things will be based on the particular meaning those things hold for them. According to the system of classification we described earlier in this chapter then, grounded theory can be seen as occupying a limited realist position with a realist ontology and a relativist epistemology. However, constructivist approaches to grounded theory such as those espoused by Charmaz take what we have described as a contextualist stance in terms of their philosophical positioning. Constructivist versions of grounded theory do not claim to capture social reality – they recognise that theories developed through social constructionist versions of grounded theory are, by definition, themselves social constructions of reality (Willig, 2013). They are therefore bound to both a relativist epistemology *and* a relativist ontology.

Key features of the method

Although there are, as we have discussed, different versions of grounded theory, there are certain key features common to all versions. We will outline these now.

The focus of a grounded theory study is on uncovering basic social processes. Researchers start with as few predetermined ideas as possible, and seek *theoretical sensitivity* by engaging with and immersing themselves in the data. Once a substantive area of study has been identified, data pertaining to this area is collected and can include a variety of data types (which might be both qualitative (e.g. observations, interviews) and quantitative (e.g. accessed records)). Data collection and data analysis are conducted together, and developing theories are 'grounded' in the data rather than generated in the abstract using pre-existing conceptualisations. Theory construction is the end point, rather than the starting point, of the research process.

Grounded theory proposes systematic procedures for analysing data in order to build theories. Initial coding considers the data in very small units (e.g. line by line) and is primarily descriptive, but becomes increasingly focused. As coding progresses, emerging codes are grouped into meaningful units (conceptual or analytical categories) that interpret rather than just describe phenomena. Throughout the coding process, the researcher questions the data, thinking about ways in which the features making up categories link and integrate, as well as ways in which particular features of a category might be similar or different (*constant comparative analysis*). The process of data collection and analysis is captured and documented through *memo writing*, which provides a written record of theory development, as well as a way for a researcher to test out and record speculative ideas. As data collection is ongoing, the researcher can use *theoretical sampling* – they can select particular cases, settings or respondents to test out their developing explanations and check how their emerging theory works in practice. Throughout the research process, analytical categories are refined and tested until no new categories are identified and those categories identified are felt to satisfactorily capture all available data. At this point *theoretical saturation* is said to have been reached – although this is, of course, always provisional because the process of theory generation is never 'complete', and there is always the possibility of a change in perspective.

An applied example

In Chapter 10 Harriet Gross and Vicky Alfrey describe two of their grounded theory studies that look at the meanings people attach to natural environments. In their work, Gross and Alfrey explore ways in which such meanings may potentially change during people's lives or when making life changes. Gross and Alfrey describe two studies in which they utilise grounded theory to explore the meanings of gardens and gardening across the lifespan. In the United Kingdom and across the developed world, an ageing population means that identifying ways of combating negative effects of social isolation and promoting better physical health amongst older people have clear applied value.

The first project uses grounded theory to explore the meanings of gardens and gardening with interview participants ranging from 18 to 80 years of age (Gross and Lane, 2007). Using a realist approach to analysis, three themes emerged (escapism, ownership and identity and relationships). Themes were relevant for all participants, but Gross and Alfrey note how they were expressed in different ways across the age groups. The second study therefore focuses on the meanings of garden and gardening for 'older' participants (aged between 56 and 90 years of age) more specifically. A constructivist version of grounded theory is employed in this second piece of work, and the main themes identified are: (1) gardening with an ageing body; (2) manageability (referring both to the way that gardens are understood as a space to be maintained and to the process of identity management); and (3) creating a sense of purpose. Gross and Alfrey explain how the themes relate to different elements of the ageing identity as well as the gardening identity, and to current wider discourses of active ageing and decline.

Phenomenology and IPA

What is it?
The principal founder of phenomenology in the early twentieth century was the German philosopher Edmund Husserl. He suggested that it is only our direct and subjective experience of the world that is 'knowable', and that we can only really know and understand concepts when they are grounded in concrete experience. Over the course of the twentieth century, phenomenology was further developed by other philosophers including Husserl's student Martin Heidegger and the French philosophers Maurice Merleau-Ponty and Jean-Paul Sartre. Phenomenology has been an important source of reference for many qualitative psychologists, providing a solid philosophical rationale for focusing on the study of human experience (Brooks, 2015).

Key concepts in phenomenology are *intentionality*, the *lifeworld*, the *epoche*, *essences* and *embodiment*. *Intentionality* refers to the idea that as human beings we are *conscious* beings – we are not just affected by things around us, we are conscious of these things in our world. Phenomenology contends, though, that there is no such thing as 'pure' consciousness, and that to understand experience we need to consider both *what* we are perceiving and *how* we are perceiving it. The *lifeworld* refers to the focus of phenomenological research: rather than a world of abstract or theoretical concepts, the lifeworld is the world of concrete experience inhabited by us as conscious human beings. Phenomenologists studying the experience of 'feeling scared', for example, would not ask about the feeling of fear in general or abstract terms – their focus would be on specific, concrete examples of this experience.

The *epoche* is a specific attitude required to allow a clear view of the lifeworld: it refers to the process of recognising and setting aside (or *bracketing*) existing presuppositions and judgements about a research phenomenon. Such preconceptions might include academic knowledge of a subject, but also include taken-for-granted or common-sense assumptions, referred to in phenomenology as the *natural attitude*. *Essences* are the key invariant features that make a particular experience what it is (and not something else). For example, to identify the essence of 'feeling scared', a range of different accounts of this phenomenon could be analysed to identify the distinctive qualities that make up this specific experience. *Embodiment* refers to the argument that we are *embodied* beings and cannot, when considering human experience, meaningfully detach mind from body, or subject from object – we experience the world as physical beings, with mind and body completely interconnected.

There are many different forms of phenomenological research method based on different strands of the philosophy, and phenomenological psychology may be thought of as an umbrella term encompassing a variety of rich and useful approaches. The primary distinction is between descriptive approaches (mainly associated with the ideas of Husserl) and interpretive approaches (mainly associated with Heidegger, Merleau-Ponty and existentialist philosophers). The focus of descriptive approaches tends to be on identifying essences from accounts of specific phenomena – for example, Morrow et al. (2015) describe a study looking at the lived experience of camping, with a particular focus on the impact of camping on relationships. Overall, though, it is usually interpretative approaches, with a primary focus on interpreting the lifeworld rather than isolating essences, which are most commonly used in applied qualitative psychology. The best known of the interpretive approaches to phenomenological psychology is interpretative phenomenological analysis (IPA), developed as a distinctive approach in the 1990s by Jonathan Smith (see Smith et al., 2009) with the aim of providing a method to allow in-depth and nuanced analyses of individuals' accounts of lived experience. As the approach currently most widely used, it is IPA we will focus on here, but we would emphasise that it is by no means the only phenomenological approach available to you as an applied qualitative psychologist. If a phenomenological approach appeals to you, it is worth familiarising yourself with the different approaches available so you can be sure that you are using the one that best suits your own research (see Langdridge, 2007, for more on this).

Philosophical positioning

IPA researchers work from a contextualist stance. The central concern of an IPA study is examining how people make sense of their own lived experience. The focus of an IPA study is on accessing the personal world of a research participant, and so IPA clearly takes a relativist stance with regards to ontology. The findings of an IPA study focus on the particular case in context. The epistemological position taken by IPA researchers is also relativist. IPA sees the interpretive activity of sense making (that is, reflecting on the meaning of personal experience) as an inherent and universal activity. IPA assumes that research participants interpret their experiences into a biographical narrative that is understandable and makes sense to them: it recognises that individual accounts are inevitably subjective reports. At the same time, IPA recognises that, for the researcher to access a participant's personal world, he or she will also need to engage in a process of interpretive activity, and that it is therefore the joint reflections and interpretations of both participant *and* researcher that produce the final analytic account (Brocki and Wearden, 2006).

Key features of the method

The focus of an IPA study is on the meaning of an experience that holds some significance for the research participant. A homogenous sample of people who have had the same experience are recruited and the number of participants is usually limited (ten or fewer participants are not uncommon) to allow in-depth analysis. IPA studies have been conducted using data from diaries and from focus group interviews, but the majority of IPA work has been carried out using semi-structured interviews.

Although detailed step-by-step guidelines have been provided for those under-taking IPA (e.g. Smith et al., 2009), it has been emphasised that the aim is to provide a useful guide rather than a prescriptive methodology (e.g. Smith et al., 1999). Analysis in IPA is a cyclical process: you should expect to work through each stage several times whilst developing your interpretation of your data.

Before starting to analyse their data, an IPA researcher should identify and reflect on their own preconceptions about the phenomena under inves-tigation. In the initial stages of analysis, researchers familiarise themselves with their data – this usually involves reading through the data set several times and then going through each piece of data making initial observations and notes. Such notes might include attempts at summarising, reflections on associations and connections, and preliminary interpretations, and it is usu-ally recommended that the left-hand margin of the interview transcript is used to make these notes. Next, the researcher is advised to engage in close line-by-line analysis of the text: this descriptive coding should identify things that matter to the participant, as well as the meaning of those things to the participant. As analysis is ongoing, the right-hand side of the page can be used to document emerging theme titles – that is, key words capturing the essential quality of that being identified in the text. The next stage is to list emerging themes and to think about connections between them: the aim is to group or 'cluster' themes into meaningful groupings so that eventually it is possible to produce a master list detailing superordinate themes made up of subordinate themes. Once this whole process has been undertaken for each transcript, the researcher can start to think about how thematic clusters might be grouped together to create general categories reflecting shared aspects of experience for all participants. Overarching categories thus identified can be selected for more intensive analysis – the researcher returns to their data set looking for data on the selected theme and producing a new and more focused data set. As analysis proceeds, coding moves from the more descriptive to the more interpretative. The final analysis should not just re-tell participants' accounts (it should be interpretive), but it is important that interpretations are grounded in participants' experience. The researcher's task is to translate the themes identified into a narrative account that captures the meanings inherent in the experiences described, whilst clearly differentiating between the participants' accounts and their own interpretations of them.

An applied example

In Chapter 5 Leah Tomkins discusses how she used IPA in a study of working carers. Over three million people in the United Kingdom (the majority of them women) combine paid employment and unpaid care, often for an older family member. Tomkins interviewed eight women working in the public sector in a variety of roles, all of whom identified themselves as working carers. She discusses the impact of their caring role on participants' identity and comments on the 'oscillations' of identity work as participants 'weave between different versions of who they were, who they had been, and who they wanted to be'. Using a critical sense-making framework to structure her findings, Tomkins reflects on ways in which competing understandings of 'normality' explain her participants' uncertainty in terms of their own identity, and the importance of understanding personal experience in the context of organisations.

Discourse analysis

What is it?

Discourse analysis focuses closely on language and the ways in which language can be used to formulate 'reality'. Discourse analysts contend that we do not neutrally use language to reflect reality: language instead is productive and constructs versions of social reality. In discourse analysis, language is seen as action-oriented – verbal expressions are never neutral, they have a purpose and need to be understood as attempting to achieve particular social objectives.

Other academic fields in the social sciences and humanities had begun from the 1950s onwards to consider language as performative, but it was not until the 1980s that there was a 'turn to language' in psychology. There are different ways in which discourse can be analysed, and in psychology there is often a particular distinction drawn between two versions of the discourse analytic method: discursive psychology and Foucauldian discourse analysis (FDA). We cover both here, but it is worth noting that there is some debate as to how separate these two traditions of discourse analysis really are, with some advocating the use of a more combined approach (e.g. Edley and Wetherell, 2001; and see Budds and colleagues in Chapter 9).

Discursive psychology refers to a particular approach introduced and developed by Jonathan Potter, Margaret Wetherell and their colleagues. In their book *Discourse and Social Psychology* (1987), Potter and Wetherell radically challenged cognitivist assumptions prevalent in psychology, which, they argued, were based on a number of unfounded assumptions. In particular, they challenged the notion that talk provides a straightforward way for research participants to express their particular beliefs and attitudes. For discursive psychologists, language is performative and discourse is a tool. The focus in discursive psychology is on what people are doing with their talk, on how they are using language to achieve particular objectives and with what effects.

FDA is less concerned with interpersonal communication and focuses instead upon culturally available discourses. Drawing on the work of the French philosopher Michel Foucault, FDA is concerned with how available discourses shape our social worlds. FDA seeks to identify and critique dominant cultural discourses and explore the implications of such discourses for ways of being. Different societal discourses can 'facilitate and limit' how people are able to experience and participate in social worlds (Willig, 2001; Parker, 1992; Burr, 2015).

Philosophical positioning

Discourse analytic approaches take a radical constructionist approach in terms of their philosophical positioning. For discourse analysts, 'reality' is both constructed and understood through language – language actively constitutes rather than passively reflects reality (e.g. Potter, 1996). Epistemologically, discourse analysts take a strongly relativist stance. Knowledge is culturally and historically located, and co-produced through social interaction. This is a very different way of conceptualising language: from this perspective, psychological concepts (such as identity) are not something we have; they are something we do with language (Willig, 2001). Similarly, a researcher taking this position would acknowledge their own position and involvement in the construction of academic research findings.

In terms of ontology, discourse analysis radically challenges any notion of a singular reality, suggesting instead that there are multiple realities that are socially and culturally produced through language. As we noted earlier, this does present some problems in attempting to locate discourse analytic approaches with regards to ontology – if we unequivocally accept that language creates reality, then 'reality' does not exist outside of our constructions of it. It has been argued that those adopting this position do not really distinguish between ontology and epistemology (Maxwell, 2012). Alternatively, discourse analysts adopting a radical constructionist position may coherently argue that, as it is impossible for us to know 'reality', the issue is best bracketed.

In this book, our focus is on applied psychology, and although these are absorbing debates, this is not the place to explore them in detail (although interested readers might like to read a classic paper by Edwards et al. (1995) entitled 'Death and furniture', which counters common realist arguments levelled at those taking a relativist standpoint in the social sciences). For our purposes, what we need to address is whether this approach is useful in terms of applied research, our focus in this book. Radical constructionist approaches argue that the applied value of their work lies in its emancipatory agenda, that, by increasing awareness of how language contributes to the domination of some groups by others, these approaches can challenge inequity and work towards change (e.g. Wodak and Fairclough 1997). Additionally, it is worth noting that a strongly ontological relativist position is recognised as problematic by some working with discursive approaches, and that some have developed alternatives (e.g. Sims-Schouten et al., 2007 outline a procedure incorporating a critical realist approach to the study of discourse using the example of motherhood and female employment).

Key features of the method

The procedures followed in discursive psychology will be focused on here: the applied example of a discourse analytic approach presented later in this book (Chapter 9) discusses a Foucauldian approach, and Willig (2001, 2013) and Parker (1992) are other good resources for those interested in undertaking FDA.

Discursive psychologists do not follow a specific set of analysis procedures, but Willig (e.g. 2001, 2013) helpfully identifies a number of useful basic guidelines. Although discourse analysis should ideally be carried out on naturally occurring text or talk, practical and ethical difficulties mean that often research interviews are used to generate data. Given the philosophical positioning of this approach, the discursive context within which the text has been produced is an important consideration in analysis. Willig (e.g. 2001, 2013) notes that the provision of demographic information will differ from that presented in other research. Whilst it is important to provide demographic information where relevant (e.g. if participants' talk on 'immigration' is the topic of analysis it may be helpful to know their own ethnic status), standard demographic information such as gender and age may suggest an imposition of social categories in a way that is counter to the aims of this approach. Transcription is more detailed than that required by other methods (including e.g. hesitations and emphases) so that the way in which an utterance is made is recorded in addition to its content. The researcher should familiarise themselves with their data through repeated reading of the transcript. Initially, this should be without any attempt at analysis but with the purpose of reflecting on what the text is doing. Coding is then undertaken to identify material relating to the research question, and it is recommended that the researcher err on the side of inclusivity in the early stages. Analysis of material can then proceed to identify both *what* the text is doing and *how* it is accomplishing this. The task of the researcher is to attend to the *action orientation* of talk: How are those speaking using discursive resources and with what effects? What is the speaker trying to do and achieve with their words? (Willig, 2001, 2013).

Potter and Wetherell (1987) outline three key components to consider in analysis: *construction*, *function* and *variation*. The researcher attends to how the text *constructs* objects and subjects, looking at ways in which the use of, for example, terminology, stylistic features and figures of speech might achieve particular *functions*. For example, the researcher might identify *interpretative repertoires* being employed by the speaker (interpretative repertoires are a way of talking about a topic, incorporating e.g. particular clusters of terms and expressions that provide a coherent and recognised way of talking about or describing something). Different interpretative repertoires can be employed to construct different 'realities' (or versions of events) depending on the speaker's social objectives. The researcher also reflects on *variation* (How might the speaker's talk vary depending on the context of the discourse? Are there contradictions within this particular discourse?).

Willig (2004) notes that guidelines for discourse analysis are not descriptions of a data analysis method but rather introduce ways of approaching a text. Whilst the approach might be criticised as perhaps elitist for its dependence on 'craft skills and tacit knowledge' (Potter and Wetherell, 1987, p. 175), perhaps the most important point is that discourse analysis generally and discursive psychology more specifically do require understanding in terms of their wider theoretical framework and a very different conceptualisation of language from that of other approaches. Such a conceptualisation does, though, offer the researcher the opportunity to ask (and answer) some rather different and potentially very interesting questions in a way that other fields of psychology may not.

An applied example

In Chapter 9 Kirsty Budds, Abigail Locke and Vivien Burr present a critical discursive analysis of 'older motherhood'. 'Older mothers' are typically defined as women who have their first baby at the age of at least 35 and more commonly 40. There is an increase in the number of women becoming mothers later on in life in the United Kingdom and in other parts of the world. Budds and colleagues describe their work, which is made up of two studies: an analysis of how older mothers are represented in newspaper articles in the British press and an interview study with older mothers. Newspaper articles published over an eight-year period were analysed using social constructionist thematic analysis and drawing on a Foucauldian approach. Interviews were analysed using a critical discursive approach that enabled an exploration of the culturally available ways of talking about 'older mothers' (and the implications these might have for shaping experience) *and* a consideration of how participants might use discourse as a tool to construct and negotiate their identity to achieve particular interactional effects. Budds and her colleagues discuss how articles position women as both wholly responsible for choosing the timing of their pregnancy and accountable for associated risks to their own and their child's health. Their interview analysis reveals how mothers resisted and reframed these discourses into the positive 'older mother'.

Conclusion

In this chapter we have described some of the approaches to research taken by applied qualitative researchers. We have explained how ways of thinking about the world have implications for the kind of research that it is possible for applied psychologists to undertake. We have introduced you to a range of philosophical positions from which applied qualitative psychology research might be undertaken. We have also used three well-known specific methodologies to show you how they are linked to particular philosophical positions, as well as demonstrating the type of research that might be undertaken using these.

Acknowledgements

The authors and publisher would also like to thank SAGE Publishing for permission to reproduce Table 2.1, originally published in King, N. and Brooks, J.M. (2017). *Template Analysis for Business and Management Students*. London: SAGE.

References

Archer, M., Bhaskar, R., Collier, A., Lawson, T. and Norrie, A. (Eds.) (1998). *Critical Realism: Essential Readings*. London: Routledge.
Ashworth, P. (2003). The origins of qualitative psychology. In J. Smith (Ed.), *Qualitative Psychology: A Practical Guide to Research Methods*. London: SAGE, pp. 4–24.
Braun, V. and Clarke, V. (2006). Using thematic analysis in psychology. *Qualitative Research in Psychology*, 3(2), 77–101.
Brocki, J.M. and Wearden, A.J. (2006). A critical evaluation of the use of interpretative phenomenological analysis (IPA) in health psychology. *Psychology and Health*, 21(1), 87–108.
Brooks, J. (2015). Learning from the lifeworld: Introducing alternative approaches to phenomenology in psychology. *The Psychologist*, 28(8), 642–643.
Brooks, J., McCluskey, S., Turley, E.L. and King, N. (2015). The utility of template analysis in qualitative psychology research. *Qualitative Research in Psychology*, 12(2), 202–222.
Burr, V. (2015). *Social Constructionism (Third Edition)*. London: Routledge.
Charmaz, K. (2003). Grounded theory. In J. Smith (Ed.), *Qualitative Psychology: A Practical Guide to Research Methods*. London: SAGE, pp. 81–110.
Charmaz, K. (2014). *Constructing Grounded Theory (Second Edition)*. London: SAGE.
Duberley, J., Johnson, P. and Cassell, C. (2012). Philosophies underpinning qualitative research. In G. Symon and C. Cassell (Eds.), *Qualitative Organizational Research: Core Methods and Current Challenges*. London: SAGE, pp. 15–34.
Edley, N. and Wetherell, M. (2001). Jekyll and Hyde: Men's constructions of feminism and feminists. *Feminism & Psychology*, 11(4), 439–457.
Edwards, D., Ashmore, M. and Potter, J. (1995). Death and furniture: The rhetoric, politics and theology of bottom line arguments against relativism. *History of the Human Sciences*, 8, 25–49.

Glaser, B.G. (1992). *Emergence vs. Forcing: Basics of Grounded Theory Analysis*. Mill Valley, CA: Sociology Press.

Glaser, B.G. and Strauss, A.L. (1967). *The Discovery of Grounded Theory*. Chicago: Aldine.

Gross, H. and Lane, N. (2007). Landscapes of the lifespan: Exploring accounts of own gardens and gardening. *Journal of Environmental Psychology*, 27, 225–241.

Hammersley, M. (1992). *What's Wrong with Ethnography?* Routledge: London: Routledge.

King, N. and Brooks, J.M. (2017). *Template Analysis for Business and Management Students*. London: SAGE.

Langdridge, D. (2007). *Phenomenological Psychology: Theory, Research and Method*. Harlow: Pearson Education.

Madill, A. (2008). Realism. In L.M. Given (Ed.), *The SAGE Encyclopaedia of Qualitative Research Methods*. London: SAGE, pp. 731–735.

Madill, A., Jordan, A. and Shirley, C. (2000). Objectivity and reliability in qualitative analysis: Realist, contextualist and radical constructionist epistemologies. *British Journal of Psychology*, 91, 1–20.

Maxwell, J.A. (2012). *A Realist Approach for Qualitative Research*. London: SAGE.

Morrow, R., Rodriguez, A. and King, N. (2015). Colaizzi's descriptive phenomenological method. *The Psychologist*, 28(8), 643–644.

Parker, I. (1992). *Discourse Dynamics: Critical Analysis: Critical Analysis for Social and Individual Psychology*. London: Routledge.

Potter, J. (1996). *Representing Reality: Discourse, Rhetoric and Social Construction*. London: SAGE.

Potter, J. and Wetherell, M. (1987). *Discourse and Social Psychology: Beyond Attitudes and Behaviour*. London: SAGE.

Reicher, S. (2000). Against methodolatry: Some comments on Elliott, Fischer and Rennie. *British Journal of Clinical Psychology*, 39, 1–6.

Sims-Schouten, W., Riley, S.C.E. and Willig, C. (2007). Critical realism in discourse analysis: A presentation of a systematic method of analysis using women's talk of motherhood, childcare and female employment as an example. *Theory and Psychology*, 17(1), 101–124.

Smith, J., Flowers, P. and Larkin, M. (2009). *Interpretative Phenomenological Analysis: Theory, Method and Research*. London: SAGE.

Smith, J.A., Jarman, M. and Osborn, M (1999). Doing interpretative phenomenological analysis. In M. Murray and K. Chamberlain (Eds.), *Qualitative Health Psychology*. London: SAGE.

Strauss, A. and Corbin, J. (1990). *Basics of Qualitative Research Techniques and Procedures for Developing Grounded Theory*. London: SAGE.

Willig, C. (Ed.) (1999). *Applied Discourse Analysis: Social and Psychological Interventions*. Buckingham: Open University Press.

Willig, C. (2001). *Introducing Qualitative Research in Psychology*. Buckingham: Open University Press.

Willig, C. (2004). Discourse analysis. In J. Smith (Ed.), *Qualitative Psychology: A Practical Guide to Research Methods*. London: SAGE, pp. 159–183.

Willig, C. (2013). *Introducing Qualitative Research in Psychology (Third Edition)*. Maidenhead: Open University Press.

Wodak, R. and Fairclough, N. (1997). Critical discourse analysis. In T.A. van Dijk (Ed.), *Discourse as Social Interaction*. London: SAGE, pp. 258–284.

Carrying Out an Applied Qualitative Research Project

Nigel King and Joanna Brooks

3

Introduction

In this chapter we move on from the philosophical underpinnings of applied qualitative research and their methodological implications to the practicalities of carrying out such work. It hardly needs saying that we cannot in a single chapter present a detailed step-by-step guide to even the main types of data collection and analysis, especially given that (as we saw in Chapter 2) philosophical and methodological positions can have a significant impact on choices regarding method. Our aim is rather to offer a roadmap to guide the decisions that need to be made in designing and executing an applied qualitative research project, directing you to helpful literature along the way. The chapter is in six main sections:

- Defining your research question(s)
- Choosing a methodological approach
- Collecting data
- Analysing data
- Addressing quality
- Reflecting on ethics and integrity.

Throughout these we will highlight those issues that pertain particularly to the kind of research we have defined as 'applied qualitative' in Chapter 1 of this volume.

Defining your research question(s)

In any study, research questions focus the researcher's attention on what they want to know about the phenomenon they intend to investigate. As such, they should help guide all stages of the research process, from overall design, through data collection and analysis, to final reporting of findings. A study may have a single research question or a small number of distinct questions – two or three, perhaps. We would caution against having many more research questions than this, as there could be a danger of a study becoming fragmented and incoherent as a result.

Inexperienced researchers are sometimes confused about the difference between research questions, aims and objectives. There is a surprising lack of guidance on this in many qualitative methods textbooks, but we would argue that aims and objectives are best seen as a way of framing a research question rather than something additional to it. *Aims* spell out what a project is trying to achieve, while *objectives* specify how the researcher is going to address the aims. For example, a study of the impact of an outdoor activity scheme on wellbeing might have the following aims and objectives:

Aims:
  To examine how the outdoor activity scheme impacts upon subjective wellbeing.

Objectives:
1. To explore how and why people engage with the outdoor activity scheme.
2. To explore the perceived consequences for participants of such engagement.
3. To learn lessons for the future development of the outdoor activity scheme.

We would not see it as strictly necessary to specify both a research question and aims/objectives for a particular study. Often it is appropriate just to present aims and objectives for a qualitative study, though, where there is a programme of work consisting of several studies, overall research questions can be helpful. This might be the case, for example, in a set of projects that are the basis of a doctoral thesis. Returning to the previous example, an overarching research question for a PhD which included this and other studies might be: 'How do outdoor activity programmes impact on the wellbeing of people across a range of social and economic contexts?'

What we have said so far is relevant to pretty much any study regardless of methodology, including quantitative as well as qualitative research. However, there are two features of qualitative research that create challenge for how we treat research questions that do not tend to occur in quantitative research. Firstly, the strong emphasis on exploration rather than confirmation means that it is not uncommon for a project to take a direction that steers it away from the original research questions. The researcher may be left with a dilemma; does she seek to draw the focus of the study back to the research questions she started with, or does she rephrase the questions in response to her changed perspective on the phenomenon under investigation? We provide a fictionalised example of how a researcher might address such a dilemma in Box 3.1.

BOX 3.1   Research questions – to revise or not revise?

Tim is undertaking a PhD looking at how people respond to problems of personal debt. He has gained access to a local charity called Debt-X, which provides support and advice to people whose lives are affected by significant personal debts. Debt-X holds face-face support groups, runs a helpline and offers individual advice sessions to signpost clients to appropriate services. For his first empirical study, Tim sets out to understand whether and how clients experience the support groups as useful. He is taking a limited realist approach and using one-to-one interviews to collect data. His research question is:

> In what ways, if any, do clients find the Debt-X support groups helpful in managing their debt problems?

Tim seeks a diverse sample of 10–12 clients across the three regular groups that the charity runs. However, by only his third interview, he feels there is a problem with the focus of his research, as driven by his research question. He finds that participants frequently want to talk about what they get from the groups in broader terms than debt management. For instance, all three of the initial participants discussed the impact of the groups on their social world, as this quote from 'Julie' illustrates:

> Since all this [debts and related problems] started, I feel I've drawn back and back into my shell – like I'm some kind of hermit. Coming here has helped me to start creeping out of that shell, it really has!

Data such as this leads Tim to realise that, even though his central concern is the impact of debt and how to help manage it, a good understanding of the topic requires a broader focus on people's lives and circumstances. Since Debt-X has given him the understanding that his research will be of use to them, he doesn't feel he can simply change his research question without their approval. He therefore takes the time to meet with his main contact in the charity and explains how a shift in focus would help him obtain data that will potentially meet their needs as well as those of his PhD. Together they agree to revise the original research question to the following:

> How does participation in the Debt-X support groups impact on clients' self-perceptions, both in relation to their debt problems and more widely?

Some of the factors a researcher may bear in mind in this kind of situation are as follows:

- What impact will a change in research questions have on work done so far?
- Are there other stakeholders in the research project whose views need to be considered? In particular, if the research has been commissioned by an organisation, or is being carried out on their behalf, are they comfortable that the changed questions will still enable the project to meet their needs?
- Are the revised research questions consistent with the methodology and method that have been used to date?

The second distinctive challenge with regard to research questions for qualitative research projects is the philosophical and methodological diversity within the field. The diversity of qualitative psychology means that researchers have to take great care that their research questions are formulated in a way that is in line with their philosophical and methodological position. For example, in a phenomenological study, research questions should be framed in terms of direct, first-person experience. In contrast, in a discursive study from a social constructionist position, a research question focused on personal experience would be inappropriate; it would need instead to be concerned with how the phenomenon is constructed by participants or in pre-existing texts.

Thinking about our particular focus in this volume on applied qualitative research, we would add to the advice above the need to capture the main 'real-world' concerns of a study in the way research questions are defined. Where there is a clear group or organisation who might be considered the end-user of the research it is generally a good idea to involve them in the formulation of research questions. So if a project was examining a community-based computer literacy scheme, representatives of those running the scheme could be consulted as to appropriate research questions. In cases where there is not a specific end-user, the researcher might discuss proposed research questions with people who have an interest in the topic from outside of an academic perspective. For example, in a proposed study looking at representations of refugees and asylum-seekers in local newspapers, the researcher might discuss her draft research questions with a cross-section of those concerned with the issue – journalists and editors, refugee charities and/or support groups, and refugees and asylum-seekers themselves.

Choosing a methodological approach

While research methods texts commonly present the choice of methodological approach as framing the definition of the research question we contend that – especially in applied qualitative research – the starting point in any particular project is with the real-world problem or issue it seeks to address. This therefore needs to guide the choice of methodology, ahead of philosophical or theoretical concerns. In our experience, there is often an iterative process in determining the methodology, moving between the problem at hand and the particular interests and expertise of the researcher(s), but, in line with our discussion of what counts as 'applied' qualitative psychology, grounded in the issues of those the research seeks to benefit, which is essential.

A crucial point in making a methodological choice is to think about the kind of real-world impact you want your research to have. It is helpful to take into account the four broad philosophical positions we discussed in Chapter 2 when thinking about this. If you wanted to influence political (in the widest sense) positions towards a particular area, by drawing attention to the assumptions underlying popular opinions, a discourse analytic methodology would be well suited. Budds et al.'s study of how newspapers represent older mothers (Chapter 9, this volume) is a good example of this. In contrast, if the aim is to make credible claims about the experiences of a particular group, in order to influence practice and/or policy, a limited realist stance may be most effective. Cowie and Jennifer's use of drawings in research into children's experiences of bullying (Chapter 6, this volume) can be seen as taking a position within the limited realist spectrum.

Another aspect of this choice is the decision whether to adopt a pre-existing methodology such as constructivist grounded theory (Charmaz, 2013), IPA (Smith et al., 2009), or discursive psychology (Edwards, 2005), or to develop a methodological approach for your particular study. The former strategy allows you to draw on clear guidelines and examples in the literature. However, even though many qualitative methodologies do not seek to be prescriptive (including those just mentioned) there is a danger that they can become 'off the shelf' solutions, deflecting the researcher from critical thinking about how they should best design and carry out their project (Chamberlain, 2012). Contrastingly, developing your own methodological position can help you to think creatively about the research process, making your own links between the research question, the way you approach it and the philosophical underpinnings. At the same time, this can be a daunting task which if done poorly results either in philosophical and methodological confusion or in a kind of foundation-less use of method from which it is impossible to draw valid conclusions.

Collecting data

The sheer range of data collection methods available to applied qualitative psychologists may be seen as either exciting or intimidating – or perhaps a bit of both! We will cover a good selection of these here, but inevitably we cannot be all-inclusive. The textbooks recommended at the end of Chapter 2 provide a good starting point to explore the range of options for qualitative data collection. In the following sub-sections we will look at individual interviews, group interviews, observational methods, visual methods and the use of pre-existing documents. We will also highlight a range of other methods that we do not have space to discuss in any detail. For each main method, we will outline its key features and consider the choices to be made in deciding how to use it. One of the most striking developments in qualitative data collection has been the growing using of online methods; rather than treat this as a category in its own right, we will examine the role of online research within each of the main methods identified. Throughout we will make reference to the exemplar chapters in the second section of this book as illustrations of the use of particular methods.

Individual interviews

Historically, individual interviews have been the most widely used method of data collection in qualitative research. While there have been some strong critiques of the method, which we summarise at the end of this section, interviews remain ubiquitous. In essence, an interview is a form of focused conversation between the researcher and the research participant that seeks to explore the latter's opinions, perceptions and/or experiences of the topic under investigation. There is a huge range of types of interview, varying in terms of the style of questioning, the degree of openness and flexibility, the medium of interaction and so on (we cover group interviews in the next sub-section). We cannot give a comprehensive account in a single chapter, so we will describe below the main forms used in applied qualitative psychology. We will then give some generic guidance on the practicalities of conducting individual interviews.

Individual face-to-face interviews

The individual face-to-face interview can be seen as the archetypal form of the qualitative interview; to a considerable degree, all the others discussed below are variations upon it. As a research tool its history can be traced back to the origins of social anthropology as an empirical discipline in the early twentieth century when 'informant interviews' were used to supplement participant observation (discussed further in the next section). Another important root of the method is in the development of the 'talking cure' in psychiatry and psychotherapy, which popularised the idea that accounts of experience could be elicited from a patient/client using a specialised form of conversation with a skilled therapist (Gubrium and Holstein, 2003). This therapeutic tradition has informed the thinking of qualitative researchers in many and varying ways, going back to its origins in the psychodynamic approaches of Freud and Jung.

Individual interviews are often described in terms of their degree of structure, with qualitative interviews classed as 'unstructured' or 'semi-structured', in contrast to 'structured' interviews used in quantitative surveys. It can be argued that the prefixes *un* and *semi* are misleading when applied to interviews; we know from the study of human interaction that any conversation is richly imbued with structure. What they really indicate is the degree of structure imposed on the questioning process in advance by the researcher, which may vary from little more than an initial generative question to the use of an extensive topic guide detailing areas to cover and useful probes. Regardless of this, qualitative interviews must always retain flexibility in use, so the interviewer can respond to the detail of the account an interviewee is providing. A crucial point to remember is that a qualitative interview is not seeking to gather answers to a succession of discrete questions in the way a survey interview does. Rather, the interview as a whole is a tool to elicit an account from the participant relevant to the study's research questions or aim, and as such it needs to respond to the unique characteristics and circumstances of every interviewee.

As well as differing in the degree of researcher-imposed structure, individual face-to-face interviews vary to some extent in the type of account they seek to elicit from participants. This is strongly linked to the methodology of the study that is using the interview as its data collection method. Thus phenomenological interviews will seek to elicit rich descriptions of concrete lived experience (rather than abstract 'views' or 'opinions'), and may include techniques designed to help the participant bring to conscious awareness aspects of experience that are not normally articulated (e.g. Turley et al., 2016). Narrative interviews encourage participants to reflect on and recount experience in the form of stories (e.g. Mishler, 1986; Hollway and Jefferson, 2000). These examples underline how important it is for the applied qualitative researcher to be clear about her methodological stance from the start, to ensure that interviews are sued as effectively as possible.

Telephone interviews
Although telephone interviews are quite widely used in qualitative research, there is surprisingly little in the research methods literature about when and how they should be used. King and Horrocks (2010) speculate that this reflects the tendency for them to be seen as a 'second choice', to be used when face-to-face interviews are not practicable. Certainly this is often why they are used, and in the pragmatic context of applied research it is not a bad thing if the inclusion of telephone interviews enables a project to access participants who would otherwise not be available. Indeed, all forms of remote interview (telephone, video, online textual) potentially open up a global population of potential participants – though time zone differences may require researchers to collect data at rather unsocial hours! Telephone interviews may, however, be a sensible choice for reasons above and beyond participant availability (Novick, 2008). Like online interviews, they can provide a greater sense of anonymity than in a face-to-face setting, which may be important where research addresses sensitive issues, and especially where the participants may feel themselves to be at risk if their participation is discovered by family members, colleagues or their community. They can provide more of a sense of control for participants than do face-to-face interviews, as the researcher has to 'fit in' to the participants' time and space (Holt, 2010).

It is crucial to ensure a good recording of a telephone interview is obtained. If the researcher is in a quiet room, she may find that simply putting the call on speaker-phone and capturing it on a digital recorder is perfectly adequate. Special fittings to attach a telephone receiver to a recorder directly are available and will give a better quality recording, though they will not fit each and every model of telephone. We would strongly urge researchers using telephone interviews to practise with their chosen means of recording in the setting and with the equipment they intend to use.

Remote video interviews

Increasingly, qualitative researchers are employing remote video technology for interviews at a distance where once they might have used the telephone, as video-calling programs like FaceTime and Skype have become ever more widely available, alongside Webinar software which can readily be used in research contexts (e.g. Adobe Connect and Google+ Hangout). Visual contact is commonly felt to offer more opportunity to build rapport than the purely aural medium of the telephone – indeed, Deakin and Wakefield (2014) report that in some cases rapport may be built quicker in Skype interviews than face-to-face. In terms of practicalities, while the technology is now much more reliable than it was a few years ago, as an interviewer you are still at the mercy of internet connections, and it is a good idea to be prepared for what to do if problems occur. Recording is a key issue; software developed for Webinars and similar teaching purposes will almost certainly include functions to enable simultaneous recording – you need of course to make sure your participants are aware that you are video-recording them and have given consent. Where software does not incorporate the ability to record the interaction, the simplest solution is just to audio-record on a digital recorder, using your computer or tablet's inbuilt speakers.

Online textual interviews

The final form of remote interview is the online textual interview, where the researcher and participant exchange questions and answers over the internet, purely via the written word. Of course, this removes all possibility of visual or aural cues to aid in the interpretation of meaning, though we have been pleasantly surprised at how much of a sense of personal connection can be built up in this medium. Online textual interviews offer the strongest sense of anonymity of any form (Opdenakker, 2006); this can create challenges, though, for a researcher's ability to be confident about the identity of the person they are interviewing (King, 2010).

Online textual interviews take two main forms: synchronous and asynchronous (King and Horrocks, 2010, Chapter 6). The former refers to chat or instant messaging programs that allow interviewer and interviewee to interact in 'real time' (or something very close to it). Such a method retains much of the immediacy of a face-to-face interview; it is particularly useful where a spontaneous response is sought from participants. Synchronous online textual interviews need to be scheduled in just the same way as remote video or telephone interviews. Ayling and Mewse's (2014) article based on a study of gay men's use of the internet to seek sexual partners provides a good account of some of the strengths and weaknesses of the method. Asynchronous forms are usually conducted via email. Typically, the researcher agrees to send a series of main questions over a period of time, with an agreed period within which the participant is required to respond. Often the researcher will send follow-up questions to such responses, before the next main question. This type of online interview tends to produce reflective and considered responses that have more in common with written than spoken language, as James (2016) discusses in the context of educational research.

The practicalities of interviewing: Generic guidance

There is a huge literature on how to conduct interviews in qualitative research, including specialist books (e.g. Brinkmann and Kvale, 2014; King and Horrocks, 2010; Rubin and Rubin, 2011) and chapters in just about every general qualitative methods text. A detailed account of the interview process is beyond our scope here; what we seek to do is simply highlight key features of it that the researcher needs to bear in mind.

The foundation of any interview-based study is the interview guide. (We prefer the term 'guide' to 'schedule' as the latter suggests something rather too fixed for qualitative research.) Guides vary considerably in how extensive they are, reflecting the requirements of different methodological approaches as well as the characteristics of individual studies. Thus, some narrative projects may use little more than a few very open 'generative' questions, while some program evaluation studies may require numerous quite focused questions to ensure evaluation criteria are addressed. Guides may identify in advance probes that the researcher sees as potentially useful in following up on main questions, though it will always be necessary to formulate further probes 'live' – in response to what a participant says in their interview. Above all, interview guides in qualitative research must be used flexibly. The interviewer should not force her interviewee to follow the order in which her topic areas happen to be listed, and must be prepared to ask about unanticipated areas that emerge in the course of the discussion.

All kinds of interview require certain skills on the part of the interviewer. She needs to be able to frame questions in a clear way, without leading the participant. She needs to actively attend to the participant and spot opportunities to use follow-up questions ('probes') to elicit more detail about the topic at hand. She also needs to be able to help the interviewee feel at ease and safe to talk in depth about their personal views and experiences. On a very practical level, she must be highly competent in the use of her recording equipment; there is little more frustrating for a qualitative researcher than to discover at the end of an excellent interview that the recorder was on 'pause' throughout, or that participants' words are drowned out by background noise!

Self-presentation is an important consideration for qualitative interviewers. This includes how the researcher describes herself in the recruitment process – for example, does a postgraduate researcher highlight or downplay his student status? In face-to-face and remote video modes, researchers also need to think carefully about their physical presentation. For instance, will the participants be more comfortable if the interviewer is formally or informally dressed? King and Horrocks (2010, Chapter 4) discuss issues of self-presentation in interviews in some depth.

Critiques of the qualitative research interview

There has been a considerable degree of critique directed towards the way individual interviews are typically used in qualitative research, and towards their continued dominance as the method of choice. Some have criticised the conventional one-off interview for its failure to develop the kind of relationship between researcher and participant that allows for a genuinely in-depth examination of experience. Chamberlain (2012) argues against 'drive-by' interviews that treat the participant as merely a source, and one from which data can be adequately extracted in a single encounter. Potter and Hepburn (2005) have highlighted the failure of most qualitative psychologists to take seriously the interview as a form of social interaction, and have argued that inherent problems with the method mean for many research issues 'naturalistic' data is preferable. A relatively small amount of research has empirically examined what actually happens within individual interviews and what this tells us about their suitability for various types of research approach and topic (see e.g. Madill, 2011).

Group interviews

One of the most widely used alternatives to the individual face-to-face interview is the group interview. This can be defined at its most simple as an interview in which the researcher asks questions of several participants at the same time, seeking to facilitate discussion amongst the participants rather than just elicit a succession of individual answers to questions. Like individual interviews, group interviews may be carried out remotely – by telephone, video-conferencing or online.

Terminology can be confusing in relation to group interviews. Terms such as 'group discussion', 'group interview' and 'focus group' are used more or less interchangeably in much of the literature, but some authors distinguish between them. For clarity, we will refer to any interview with multiple interviewees as a 'group interview', and use the term 'focus group' to refer to those where the researcher facilitates real-time interaction amongst the participants as well as between herself and them. So-defined, the focus group is clearly the predominant form of qualitative group interview (Finch et al., 2014) and the one we will concentrate on here. We will comment more briefly on the types of group interview that do not fit the 'focus group' definition, including structured forms of group deliberation (Delphi and nominal group techniques), group 'workshop' activities and the use of asynchronous online group methods.

Focus groups

At the start of a focus group study there are some crucial decisions to be made about the nature of the groups that are to be recruited, which can have a significant impact on the type and quality of data that are collected. Firstly, researchers need to consider the desired size of the group. The aim here is to have enough people to stimulate lively interaction and ensure some diversity of views, but not so many that the whole thing becomes unmanageable. Recommendations for focus group size vary in the literature: Braun and Clarke (2013) argue for three to eight, Finch et al. (2014) for six to eight and Flick (2014) for five to ten. We are reluctant to state an 'ideal' size as other features of group composition are likely to have an effect on this. For instance, if a highly heterogeneous group is sought a group size of three or four would be inadequate, but such a size might be acceptable for a very homogenous group. However, we would be highly cautious about recruiting more than ten participants as it would be very difficult to ensure a free-flowing discussion in which all members could contribute. Equally, we would not consider that an interview with two participants could be classed as a focus group. This creates a very different dynamic from even three or four participants. Morgan et al. (2013) view the 'dyadic' interview as a separate form that can be very useful where research addresses interpersonal issues and meanings – for instance between friends, parent and child or couples.

Other than group size, key questions for researchers designing a focus group study are the degree of homogeneity/heterogeneity (i.e. similarity or difference) to be sought, and whether to use pre-existing or researcher-constructed groups. These decisions are not a matter of right or wrong; rather, researchers need to reflect upon what is appropriate to their research question(s) and methodology. To address the first question, we will use a hypothetical example of a project interested in inter-professional relations in a hospital setting. We could organise focus groups with representatives from a variety of professions; doctors, nurses, physiotherapists and so on. These would be relatively heterogeneous groups and would have the advantage of diverse perspectives that might reflect in quite direct ways the inter-professional phenomena in which we are interested. On the downside, though, there could be issues of power (perhaps compounded by gender differences) that might make it difficult for some members to speak freely and openly. In contrast, homogenous (i.e. uni-professional) groups may enable more open conversation but might result in an 'official' professional line being presented, and would not provide us with direct examples of inter-professional interaction. We would need to weigh these options in the balance, in terms of the aims of our research and our knowledge of the likely relationship dynamics in our setting. To complicate things further, what counts as heterogeneity or homogeneity is not straightforward. In our example, it may be that for some hospital staff, the group with whom they feel a sense of common identity is not their profession but their multi-professional team – trauma, paediatrics, mental health and so on. It may be necessary to carry out some preliminary exploration of the context before making firm decisions about this aspect of focus group composition.

Another question for researchers using focus groups is whether to use pre-existing groups or construct groups themselves. Sometimes other decisions about research design leave no choice about this – for instance, in the hypothetical example above, if the researcher chose to use specialism-based groups they would *de facto* also be pre-existing groups. Often, though, this is a choice the researcher must make. If a project set out to examine the experiences of victims of crime, for instance, the researcher could use existing support groups, or could advertise widely and recruit focus groups made up of people who were strangers to each other. In fact, there is an in-between point too, as Braun and Clarke (2013) point out. As well as constructing groups from those who are already close to each other and those who are strangers, a researcher might use people who know each other but are not especially close – 'acquaintances' rather than 'friends'. On the whole, we would expect that the stronger the pre-existing relationships amongst group members, the more comfortable they will be talking amongst themselves, and the more they will be able to draw on a shared history in their discussions. However, there is a danger of 'taken for granted' knowledge in close pre-existing groups which is never properly articulated because everyone has (or thinks they have) a tacit understanding of it. Also, some sensitive topics may be more easily shared with strangers than friends and acquaintances.

The researcher's role in a focus group is rather more complex than in an individual interview. Not only does she have to attend to the way she asks questions and listen for chances to probe, she also needs to manage the interaction amongst participants and ensure that they are all able to contribute. Because of this, it is common for group interviews to be conducted by two researchers. The 'moderator' leads the questioning and manages the flow of the discussion – for example, encouraging a quiet member of the group to give their view or diplomatically steering the discussion away from someone who has been dominating it. The 'observer' takes notes on the process, especially things that the moderator may miss, such as nuances of non-verbal communication amongst the group. He may intervene occasionally to support the moderator; for instance, when a good opportunity to probe has been missed or when someone is trying to attract attention in order to enter the discussion. He also manages the recording equipment and any other practicalities such as group tasks that are part of the interview process, or, in longer sessions, ensuring there is a suitable refreshment and comfort break.

Ever-increasing access to the internet makes online focus groups an option for many studies. As with online individual interviews, these can take synchronous or asynchronous forms. There are the same kinds of difference between the types as we have already seen; synchronous tending to produce spontaneous responses and asynchronous eliciting more considered, reflective contributions. However, as Stewart and Williams (2005) show, the group setting means that other factors need to be considered in choosing a form. From their own and others' work they argue that synchronous focus groups can be extremely hard to moderate as they often proceed very rapidly and unpredictably. In fact moderation may well be more complex than in face-to-face groups. In contrast, asynchronous groups are easy to moderate, which allows for considerably larger numbers to be handled than in face-to-face or synchronous online. Indeed, there is evidence that asynchronous groups are more successful when group sizes are on the higher side, as they are less likely to atrophy than smaller groups. This is seen in Williams's study (2003, cited in Stewart and Williams, 2005) which directly compared group cohesion in smaller (n=15) and larger (n=45) asynchronous online focus groups.

Other types of group interview
There are several types of structured group that have been developed for tasks such as decision-making, creative idea generation or consensus-building that have been adapted for use in qualitative research. The literature on such usage is rather sparse; within it, probably the most common form to appear is the Delphi technique. The method was developed in the 1950s by the RAND Corporation to develop consensual future predictions on the basis of expert opinion – initially for the military (Dalkey and Helmer, 1963). Since then it has been used in a wide range of settings, including health care, education and consumer behaviour. Numerous variations on the original form have been proposed, but all involve a process of gathering views from experts (almost always anonymously), sharing, rating and refining those views, and reiterating the procedure until consensus is reached (Hasson et al., 2000). In its classic form much of the analysis of ratings and levels of consensus is quantitative, though even here there may be qualitative elements especially in the initial thematising of suggested ideas for feedback.

There are a few examples in the literature of the use of the Delphi technique in applied qualitative research. Sobaih et al. (2012) used it in two studies in the hospitality industry, while Robertson et al. (2000) present findings from a Delphi study of international students' experiences with a strong emphasis on qualitative aspects. The goal of achieving consensus in classic Delphi technique surveys may be off-putting for qualitative researchers – especially those at the more relativist end of the philosophical spectrum. Fletcher and Marchildon (2014), however, describe a genuinely qualitative use of a modified Delphi technique in research into health leadership, and provide useful guidelines for other qualitative researchers.

Participatory approaches to qualitative research involve actively engaging with those traditionally regarded as 'research participants' as co-researchers in the research process. Group activities are frequently used in such approaches, often drawing on innovative methods to facilitate democratic participation. 'World Café' or 'knowledge café' style events (see Brown, 2001) can provide opportunities for informal café-style conversations with both potential research participants, as well as allowing interactions between different groups who might otherwise not relate to each other on an equal footing (e.g. Brooks et al., 2015a). Rather than relying on traditional verbal or text-based activities, group activities utilising a more creative format can also offer alternative strategies to empower and engage participants as well as taking into account the skills and abilities of vulnerable populations (Boydell et al., 2012). In Chapter 8 of this book, Murray and Wright-Bevans reflect on their use of community arts-based methods in a project working with older residents of a disadvantaged urban neighbourhood. In this project, they worked with a community arts worker and local residents in weekly sessions exploring a wide range of different art activities. A final public exhibition of the artwork was followed by a reflection on the work by the participants. Informal conversations with those taking part at the weekly sessions as well as more traditional research interviews with residents were all incorporated into the final project findings. As well as maximising the residents' involvement and participation, using appealing and engaging methods additionally promoted greater social interaction and confidence-building amongst the older people themselves.

Observational methods

Observational methods have a very long history within qualitative research, going back to the ethnographic approach of early social anthropologists. Scholars such as Malinowski, Radcliffe-Brown and Evans-Pritchard immersed themselves in remote cultures (remote, that is, from a Western perspective) observing and taking part in everyday life. The use of such 'participant observation' spread into sociology, but the method was little used in psychology until qualitative approaches began to gain some traction from the 1980s onwards. There are a few earlier exceptions, most famously Festinger and colleagues' study of a UFO cult, published in the book 'When Prophecy Fails' (Festinger et al., 1956). They used the method to test Festinger's theory of cognitive dissonance, interested in what would happen when cult members – some of whom had given up jobs, homes and families – were faced with the reality that the world did not end on the appointed day.

Not all observational studies in qualitative psychology involve the researcher as a participant in the research setting, in the way we see in Festinger et al.'s study or classic ethnographic work in sociology and social anthropology. However, what counts as 'participation' is not a straightforward matter; the mere presence of an observer may very well have an impact on the social setting even if she is doing no more than taking notes. And a covert observer – who does not make his identity known – may find it harder than an overt observer to avoid getting involved in the social world he is observing. (We will return to issues about covert and overt observation shortly.) In reality, when designing a qualitative observational study, it is generally not a two-way choice between participant and non-participant positions, but rather it is about the degree of participation. The aims of the study, its philosophical, theoretical and methodological stance will determine what level of participation is suitable. In the kind of applied qualitative research presented in this volume, there can be practical constraints on the degree of participation possible; for example, if the setting involves a high level of technical professional skill, such as an operating theatre, a high school classroom or a forensic laboratory.

As with level of participation, the issue of how the researcher presents herself to the people with whom she comes into contact is complex. It is not just a matter of being either covert (where no one knows the researcher's identity) or overt (where everyone knows); in most cases the question is how much is revealed to whom. Entirely covert observation is rare these days, as the degree of deception involved is hard to justify in ethical terms. The exceptions are when observation is in a public place where people would expect to be observed, or where it can be argued that the topic is of such social importance that concerns about deception are outweighed (see our discussion below of the ethics of deception and withholding of information). Festinger et al.'s work could not have been carried out without covert observation; cult members would hardly have agreed to let researchers in whose starting assumption was that their leader and prophet was either deluded or a fraud. We doubt, however, that most ethics committees would now consider the topic to be of such importance that concealment of identity was justified. They would probably take the view that, even with anonymisation, such an unusual group could easily be identified in publications (as indeed it was) and members could find themselves open to ridicule or worse. In some situations, a covert observer's cover being blown could constitute a physical risk to them; in almost all situations, it could effectively terminate the project – as almost happened to Festinger's team.

In most cases, the researcher will reveal differing levels of information about herself and her role to different people. This will depend on such things as the degree of regular contact that she has with them, the possible ethical implications of such contact, and the extent to which the spaces where observation takes place are considered 'private' or 'public'. It can be very hard to specify in advance exactly what to reveal to whom, so the researcher will often have to make judgements on the spot, informed by ethical and methodological principles. In Box 3.2 we present an example of how these types of decision are made, from a participant observation study Nigel undertook in his doctoral research.

BOX 3.2   Who to tell what about researcher identity in participant observation – an example

My (Nigel's) PhD was a mixed-methods investigation of processes of innovation and change, mostly focused on older people's care institutions. Having conducted an interview-based study in two care homes (King et al., 1991) I saw the value of spending an extended period of time in an organisational setting, observing changes as they happened and talking to those involved. I therefore carried out a participant observational study in a psycho-geriatric ward (King, 1992), working as a volunteer nursing assistant. Because of my focus on change within the organisation, I carried out the observations in two blocks, each of approximately one month's duration, during which I worked three full shifts and also attended all ward meetings and ward rounds. There was a five-month gap between the blocks of observations.

Thinking about what I told to whom about myself and my research, I used three distinct levels of self-disclosure. For the ward staff, and those staff from outside the ward with whom I was in regular contact (e.g. the two consultant psychiatrists) I gave quite a full account of myself: that I was a PhD student, that I was interested in organisational innovation and change, and what my participation in the life of the ward as a researcher would involve. In contrast, I did not make any attempt to explain my researcher status to the patients on the ward. The patients all had quite advanced dementia and my assumption was that they would struggle to understand my researcher role and may even have been made anxious if I attempted to explain it – for instance, at the thought of 'being observed'. The staff did not encourage me to talk to patients about this either. While I think this was a reasonable decision, I now feel that my failure to even consider how I might explain myself to patients with dementia reflected attitudes at the time (i.e. the late 1980s). These days there is more recognition that researchers should make a serious effort to involve people with dementia as active participants in the research process.

The third group of people for whom I needed to consider how I presented myself were those who had intermittent contact with the ward; principally patients' visitors and hospital staff who were not regularly present. It was difficult to have a standard position regarding self-disclosure with these people, as the kind of contact I had with them varied enormously. At one extreme were occasions such as my attendance at a day hospital run once a week on the ward for outpatients plus a few of the more able inpatients, where I spent several hours with the nurses running it. At the other were one-off encounters with family members who gave me a brief 'hello' as they met with their relative. In dealing with this diverse set of people I took the decision that I would explain my PhD student status to anyone who asked me directly who I was and why I was there (which was rare, as I wore a uniform similar to those of the regular nursing assistants). Otherwise, I would volunteer information where I had extended contact with an individual, such as the day hospital nurses or a few regular visitors.

It is interesting that the only problems I had with regard to self-disclosure were with the 'full disclosure' group. One member of staff, an attached social worker, was quite hostile to me for a long time after I explained myself; for example, miming looking through binoculars at me as an ironic reference to me as an 'observer'. It was only after I'd carried out a long informant interview with him and attended some outreach visits in the community that he became friendlier towards me. I also learned the important lesson that just because people hear your explanation of your role and say they understand it, they may not actually do so. This became clear when a few of the nursing assistants reacted quite suspiciously to discovering I was keeping notes about experiences throughout the day, and not just in meetings. I had said I was doing this in initial meetings, but evidently had not made it clear enough and needed to make more effort to help these core staff understand what I was doing and why.

Researchers need to think carefully about how to record observations during fieldwork. One question is whether to take notes publicly or to wait until there is an opportunity to do so in private. There may be a trade-off here between the immediacy of the field notes and the potential impact on the social setting of open note-taking. Often different strategies will be appropriate for different parts of the research. In the psycho-geriatric ward study described in Box 3.2, Nigel took notes openly in ward meetings as he judged this would seem 'natural' to those present, but otherwise did so privately to avoid disruption to everyday interactions in his nursing assistant role.

A second question about the recording of observations is whether to use a relatively structured or unstructured format for field notes. Structured formats usually involve a prepared observational record sheet with headings and sub-headings that relate to facets of the setting identified as being of particular relevance to a study's research questions. Nigel used a sheet like this in the psycho-geriatric ward study. An unstructured format would simply involve taking notes in a notebook of events, interactions, personal responses and so on that strike the researcher as potentially of interest. This might be done using voice memos on a smart phone or a digital audio recorder instead of making written notes. It is usually a good idea to write up the 'raw' field notes more formally after observational sessions. McNaughton Nicholls et al. (2014) suggest organising these under headings such as 'detailed descriptions', 'analytic notes/observer comments about the setting' and 'subjective reflections'.

The decision about how to take notes is not necessarily an either/or choice; it may be that a combination of structured and unstructured observations works best. It is also the case that sometimes it makes sense for a researcher to start with very open recording of observations and then, as understanding of the social setting increases, move to more structured forms that reflect key emerging issues. Even in unstructured recording, it is crucial to record time, date, some basic details of where the observation took place and who was present. Field notes, of whatever form, may be supplemented by photographs and diagrams, where helpful. Observational data is also commonly accompanied by more formal individual 'informant interviews' to explore issues in depth with key people in the setting.

Visual methods

The term 'visual methods' in qualitative research refers to work which collects data in visual forms then analyses the visual material and/or participants' responses to such material. In the main, in applied psychology visual methods are used within the setting of an interview or focus group; the visual material may be produced in the session or selected by the participant or researcher beforehand, and discussed as part of the interview. Visual methods may in this context be seen as a form of data elicitation, in that they are used to help enhance the quality of the (verbal) textual data produced in an interview.

However, where visual materials are produced by participants themselves (rather than simply supplied to them), these are increasingly recognised as part of the data and subject to analysis in their own right alongside the interview transcript. Visual methods are relatively new to qualitative psychology, though they have grown rapidly in popularity (Reavey, 2011; Rania et al., 2015).

Given the very wide range of visual methods, it is useful to make some broad distinctions amongst them. A fundamental one is between those that involve the creation of some kind of visual product, and those in which pre-existing material is used. An example of the former is photo-elicitation, where participants are asked to take photographs of people, places and/or items relating to the aim of the research and bring them to an interview where they discuss them with the researcher (Smith and Papathomas included this method in their research described in this volume, Chapter 11). In contrast, an example of the latter is the project by Viv Burr and Nigel King in which they provided participants with images of a wide range of styles and types of female footwear and used personal construct psychology methods to explore responses to them (see Burr et al., 2014). In the present volume, Cowie and Jennifer (Chapter 6) presented children with cartoons to elicit responses on the topic of bullying.

Amongst the methods that involve the creation of visual products in the course of the research process we can further distinguish according to the mode of production. Modes include photography (still and video), drawing tasks (with greater or lesser degrees of direction by the researcher), diagram construction tasks and performative approaches such as the use of dance or drama. Methods also vary in whether the visual product is created solely by the participant or jointly with the researcher. For instance, if we consider diagrammatic methods, the Pictor technique (King et al., 2013; see also Chapter 14, this volume) is normally very much participant-led, while Eco-maps (e.g. Rempel et al., 2007) are often produced jointly with the researcher in the course of an interview.

Pre-existing texts

Pre-existing texts, sometimes referred to as 'secondary sources', can be a valuable form of data for qualitative research. A huge variety of different types of text can and have been used, including articles in newspapers and magazines (e.g. Eagleman, 2011), organisational documents (e.g. Lee, 2012), television and radio programmes (e.g. Wilson et al., 2000) and so on. The internet is also a significant source of such material, including the analysis of material on social media such as Facebook, blogs and web forums (e.g. Bazarova et al., 2013).

A key issue for research based on secondary sources is sampling; how does the researcher ensure that she has selected the right material to address her research question(s), and in a way that is congruent with her philosophical position and methodological approach? Often there is a vast range of possible sources from which to draw a sample; there needs to be a very clear and coherent rationale for how this is actually done. Budds and colleagues (this volume) provide an example of this in their study of how older mothers are represented in British newspaper articles. The use of secondary sources can also create ethical challenges when there is ambiguity about whether the material can be considered 'public'; this applies particularly to web-based text, as we discuss further below.

Other methods of data collection

As well as the methods we have described above, there are many other ways to collect qualitative data in applied research projects. *Diary techniques* are quite widely used; they include written, audio and video diaries. The great strengths of diaries are their ability to capture experience over time, though they do need a fair degree of commitment from participants if they are to complete them effectively. Researchers may ask participants to record their experiences in a relatively structured format, focusing on specific facets that relate to the research question – for example, Radcliffe and Cassell's (2014) study of how couples addressed work–family conflicts. Alternatively, diaries may take quite an open and unstructured form, as in Furness and Garrud's (2010) study of responses to facial surgery. Another form of participant-generated written data is the *qualitative questionnaire*. These are well suited to projects where the aim is to collect a broad-brush overview of opinions on or experiences of a particular topic area; inevitably they provide less depth and flexibility than interactive forms of data collection. They may also be useful for sensitive topics as they offer a high degree of anonymity (see Braun and Clarke, 2013, Chapter 6, for a good discussion of the use of qualitative surveys).

Personal construct psychology (PCP) has a strong tradition of methodological creativity, with methods originally designed for use in psychotherapy adapted for research purposes. We have already discussed Pictor, which has its roots in PCP, in the section above on visual methods. The best-known PCP method is the repertory grid, which, though often used to collect and analyse data quantitatively, can be employed in a purely qualitative manner, as Proctor (2014) explains. Burr et al. (2014) review a range of PCP methods that can be used in qualitative research.

Analysing data

The differences between qualitative methodologies tend to be greater in terms of how data is analysed than they are regarding data collection. Giving generic guidance on qualitative data analysis is therefore problematic. In Chapter 2 we provided an introduction to the types of data analysis associated with the specific methodologies of grounded theory, IPA and discursive psychology. The examples of applied qualitative studies in part two of this book offer more detail of a wider range of methodological approaches. For the present chapter we will concentrate on providing some general guidance on the most widely used form of qualitative analysis; thematic analysis.

Themes and codes

Thematic analysis is very widely used in qualitative psychology, both as an element of specific methodologies such as IPA and grounded theory, and as a 'stand-alone' generic method. It is not, though, a single method but rather describes numerous variations on two basic components: defining themes and organising them into some kind of structure that represents relationships between themes. The notion of 'theme' borrows from the arts, where scholars might talk about common themes in, say, the symphonies of Beethoven, the paintings of Francis Bacon, or the poems of Wordsworth. In relation to textual qualitative data we define a theme as follows:

> *Themes in qualitative analysis are characterisations of recurrent aspects of textual data that the researcher judges as relevant to the research question.*

Note that in most versions of thematic analysis, researchers would be happy to define something as a theme if it recurred within a single case. In fact, the identification of a theme in one case but not any others in a data set can provide interesting insights for the researcher's interpretation. We would not, though, expect a theme to be developed that was just based on a one-off comment.

There is sometimes confusion or contradiction in the literature regarding the terms *theme* and *code*. We take the view that a code is simply a label – a word or a short phrase – that marks a section of text as being of potential interest to the analysis. Codes are the building blocks from which themes are constructed, and help to index where in the text support can be found for the definition of a particular theme. But not all codes will evolve or feed into themes – some may simply prove redundant; others may capture features of the data that are not themes in themselves but help to organise and/or interpret themes. Gibbs (2008) talks about 'placeholders' that help structure themes; for instance, in a study of client experiences of psychotherapy, we might identify sets of themes under the placeholders 'helpful' and 'unhelpful'.

It is quite common in thematic analysis for a distinction to be made between *descriptive* and *interpretive* coding. Some approaches encourage the researcher to view these as separate stages in the process of developing themes, as is the case in grounded theory and also in some more generic styles (e.g. Langdridge, 2004; Saldaña, 2009). Others such as IPA (Smith et al., 2009) and template analysis (King and Brooks, 2017) do not suggest such a clear separation, but recognise that it is generally sensible for coding to become more interpretive as analysis progresses and the researcher builds her understanding of the data. Another important distinction is between *a priori* and *emergent* themes. The former are defined (at least loosely) in advance, while the latter are identified in the course of the coding process. Given the emphasis on inductive ('bottom-up') understanding in most qualitative research, we would never expect a qualitative thematic analysis to only use *a priori* themes – such an approach is more typical of quantitative content analysis (Riff et al., 2014). However, some forms of thematic analysis do allow the use of some *a priori* themes, notably template analysis (Brooks et al., 2015b).

Thematic structures

It is essential to thematic analysis that themes are organised into some form of thematic structure that shows how they relate to each other. Without this all we would have is a list (often rather a long list!) of discrete themes, which would be of limited use in helping the researcher to draw together and present her overall interpretation of the data. The main form of organisation seen in the literature is hierarchical; narrower themes nested within broader ones. We see this both in generic approaches such as template analysis (King and Brooks, 2017) and Braun and Clarke's style (2006), and in specific approaches such as IPA (Smith et al., 2009). So, in the hypothetical example above of a study of client experiences of psychotherapy, we might have a broad 'top-level' theme of *quality of client-therapist relationship* and within that sub-themes of *openness, ease of communication and sense of shared world-view.*

As well as hierarchical organisation of themes, structures may also incorporate lateral connections between them. These are used to indicate ways in which discrete themes – or clusters of themes – are linked in some meaningful way. In grounded theory, axial coding is used to relate to each other codes and categories that emerged in the early stages of analysis (Corbin and Strauss, 2015). In template analysis, integrative themes capture aspects of the data that may not be in the foreground but that run through many or all thematic clusters. For instance, in their study of the experience of diabetic renal disease, King et al. (2002) identified integrative themes of 'stoicism' and 'uncertainty'.

There are two important goals in developing a thematic structure: clarity and inclusiveness. On the one hand, the structure should be clear and comprehensible to someone reading an account of the analysis – that is, it should not only help organise your thinking as a researcher, it should also help you communicate this to readers. On the other hand, it should be as inclusive as possible in order to capture the detailed distinctions made in the analysis. There can often be a degree of tension between these goals; if a structure is too neat and tidy it may sacrifice inclusiveness for clarity, but if it tries too hard to capture every nuance of analysis it may be confusingly complicated. In applied research, the communicative function of a thematic structure may be especially important; it can be very helpful in encapsulating key aspects of your analysis to funders, host organisations and/or participants. It may be helpful to use a simplified version of the structure in publications and presentations for a non-academic audience, retaining the fuller version for the academic arena.

Addressing quality issues in applied qualitative research

When we talk about *quality* in relation to research we mean those features of a project that would enable a reader to judge that it has been conducted well, and that the conclusions drawn from it are properly supported by the findings. Decisions about what counts as 'good' research and how this can be demonstrated are essentially connected to the philosophical and methodological underpinnings of a study. The variety of positions that exist in qualitative research, as we saw in the previous chapter, mean that quality issues are rather less straightforward than in quantitative research. Since different qualitative approaches disagree about the nature of reality and what we can know about it, there can be no universal procedures for establishing quality.

The process of assessing research quality has two basic components: the criteria on which to base judgements, and the strategies and techniques employed to test against the criteria. In broad terms, in adopting criteria qualitative researchers choose between three options: to borrow from quantitative research, to use criteria developed specifically for qualitative research, or to reject any kind of transferable criteria and instead argue for each study on its own merits. While these options do not map exactly onto the four philosophical positions we outlined in Chapter 2, the types of criteria tend to be more associated with some positions than others. Equally, the strategies and techniques for applying criteria vary according to the philosophical and methodological position taken. Below we consider the issue of deciding upon quality criteria before presenting an overview of the kinds of assessment strategies and techniques that can be used. We will end this section with a discussion of reflexivity, as this is closely bound up with quality in qualitative research.

Quality criteria for qualitative research

Not surprisingly, given their similar ontological and epistemological positions, qualitative neo-positivist research is the most likely to use criteria most commonly associated with quantitative research. This may include the use of *reliability*, understood in terms of the 'accuracy' of coding, though more commonly this type of qualitative research tends to concern itself with *validity* – the extent to which analysis can be shown to correspond to participants' views and experiences, as captured in the data.

For many qualitative researchers, especially outside of the neo-positivist approach, the strong association of quality criteria used in quantitative research with issues of measurement makes them unhelpful. Instead, alternative criteria designed specifically for qualitative research have been proposed. There is no single agreed set, though, and the researcher is left with quite a wide choice of criteria. Lincoln and Guba (1985) proposed a set that is frequently cited in the literature, consisting of: trustworthiness, credibility, dependability and confirmability. Tracy (2010) suggests eight 'big tent' criteria of excellence in qualitative research: worthy topic, rich rigour, sincerity, credibility, resonance, significant contribution, ethics, meaningful coherence. Yardley (2008) proposes a useful set specifically for qualitative psychology which is broad enough to be modified to particular approaches but still provides a focus for quality evaluation. Her 'core principles' are: sensitivity to context, commitment and rigour, coherence and transparency, impact and importance. These three sets are by no means the only ones available. If you wish to use qualitative-specific criteria, it is up to you as a researcher to consider the choices and select a set that meets your needs. Both Tracy and Yardley include criteria that address issues of real-world relevance and importance, which should be a key consideration for applied qualitative psychology.

The option of rejecting any general criteria is most commonly advocated by researchers at the more relativist end of the spectrum. Especially from a radical constructionist position, if one argues that there is no ultimate foundation for knowledge, then attempts to 'impose' general criteria of quality make no sense. Such criteria are themselves rhetorical devices that seek to construct a version of 'good research' for particular purposes. This does not mean that the whole notion of judging the quality of research is meaningless; rather, it must be seen as a matter of contesting claims and competing constructions, just like any other arena of discourse. The task of assessing research quality can be seen as analogous to the way we make judgements about novels, films, TV programmes and so on. We do not need agreed criteria to be able to tell whether we think a cultural artefact is 'good' or 'successful'; we argue it out on the basis of our tastes and values, in response to its particular features.

Techniques for assessing quality

It is important to note that the quality of a piece of qualitative research resides in the coherence of the research design and the care with which it is carried out and reported. It cannot be proven simply by carrying out one or more 'quality tests'. Nevertheless, there are widely used techniques that can help you as a researcher to ensure your work is well executed and presented in a way that enables a reader to judge its quality. We list below six of the main such methods, though this should not be seen as an exhaustive list.

Keeping a research diary: Many qualitative researchers keep a research diary throughout a project, in which to note anything of potential interest about the process. Entries may reflect on such things as how recruitment is progressing, experiences in a particular interview, thoughts about data analysis and so on. The aim is to ensure you can see how the project evolved and recognise your own place in it – it is thus very much an aid to reflexivity.

Keeping an audit trail: This is usually applied to analysis, where it refers to the value of keeping a clear record of the way in which the analytic process progresses. For instance, in any form of thematic analysis, you can keep a record of the development of themes and how they are structured, noting reasons for changes at each stage. (We describe the use of such a strategy for template analysis in King and Brooks, 2017.) However, an audit trail can also encompass the development of the data collection process; for example, noting when and why new questions or probes are added to an interview guide. An audit trail enables a more focused form of reflexivity than a research diary – in particular in relation to methodological reflexivity.

Independent coding: Involving other people in your data analysis is a widely used quality assurance technique. The precise form it takes and the way in which it is used are very much dependent on your overall philosophical and methodological position. For instance, in a limited realist study you might get experts on your topic to review your emerging analysis in order to determine the best possible interpretation. In a contextualist study, the experts' role would be rather to challenge you to consider alternative ways of construing the data, and step out of your habitual perspective, without any claim to identifying one interpretation as better than another.

Respondent feedback: We use this term to include activities sometimes described as 'member checking' or 'respondent validation'. It involves taking your findings back to your participants to elicit their views on them. Again, what you make of such an exercise will be determined by your philosophical assumptions and methodological position. It is always important to think of ethical issues that might arise with respondent feedback; in some circumstances you may feel that asking participants to re-engage with their experiences would not be justifiable, if likely to be highly distressing.

Thick description: This refers to the provision of detailed contextual description of a study to help a reader assess the persuasiveness of conclusions drawn and their potential transferability to other settings. Clearly the format in which a study is reported will influence how much of such description can be given.

Use of direct quotes from participants: Using direct quotes from participants when presenting the findings of qualitative research is standard practice, and is often seen as contributing to quality assurance. Care needs to be taken, though, as to the quality claims that are made in relation to this practice. Even from the perspective of a realist epistemology, they cannot on their own 'validate' analysis; the reader would require access to the entire data set and your analytical procedures to judge whether your chosen quotes were a fair representation of participants' experiences. Most qualitative researchers would therefore steer clear of such arguments and would see direct quotes as serving two main functions: to illustrate how the researcher has analysed and interpreted the data (for instance, supporting their discussion of specific themes), and to allow some insight into the way participants talked about their views and experiences. To meet these purposes, it is generally a good idea to mainly use longer quotes of at least several lines' length, rather than peppering the findings with multiple short quotes. You should consider what contextual information is needed for the reader to grasp the sense you have made of the quote, which may require the inclusion of the interviewer's question in some cases. Of course, it is absolutely essential that quotes clearly support the analytical point that is being made.

Reflexivity

Reflexivity can be defined as the researcher's critical self-awareness of how their involvement in the research shapes the way it unfolds. For any qualitative research except that which uses a realist epistemology (what we refer to as neo-positivism in Chapter 2), reflexivity is thus an essential part of the process, and is intimately bound up with quality. There are many different types of, and approaches to, reflexivity (Finlay, 2003). A key distinction, though, is between *personal* and *methodological* reflexivity. The former relates to reflection on the ways in which personal features of the researcher may impact on data collection and/or analysis. For example, in a focus group with cancer survivors, it may well make a difference to the course of the interaction if the group is aware that the interviewer is herself a cancer survivor. Equally, her shared experience is likely to shape the way in which she interprets the data through thematic analysis. The point is not to try to correct for this position as a form of 'bias' (except in neo-positivist research); rather, it is to take it into consideration and account for it. One point we would stress is that personal reflexivity should not be a licence for mere self-indulgent reflection and revelation on the part of the researcher. The point is to integrate personal critical reflection into the research process, not simply display it as a virtue in its own right.

Methodological reflexivity involves a consideration of how methodological choices impact upon the way a study unfolds and the conclusions that can be drawn from it. Put simply, what you find depends at least to some extent on how you carry out your research. Different methods of data collection gravitate towards different aspects of the phenomenon under investigation – or, from a radical constructionist position, to construct the phenomenon differently. A good example we described early is the different styles of 'talk' that tend to be evoked in synchronous and asynchronous online interviews. Equally, contrasting forms of analysis vary in which aspects of the data are to the fore. A narrative analysis, for example, would highlight how a participant's account as a whole works as a story, while a discursive psychological analysis would attend to the positions taken and the versions of reality constructed in the detail of the conversation.

Reflecting on ethics and integrity

Good ethical practice in any psychological research is first and foremost about protecting the interests and wellbeing of research participants, but also about considering the potential consequences of research for the academic community, the wider society and the researchers themselves. Integrity should be seen as a component of ethical practice, and refers particularly to fair and honest conduct in research. Psychological research ethics are generally governed by codes of conduct of national professional bodies such as the British Psychological Society (BPS, 2009) and the American Psychological Association (APA, 2010). We will summarise below the key ethical issues that any psychological research needs to address, highlighting for each the specific challenges for applied qualitative psychology.

Avoiding harm

Research should be designed to minimise the likelihood of physical, psychological or reputational harm to participants. Risk of harm should be formally assessed prior to the start of research; if there are more than negligible risks involved, potential participants should be warned in advance. Any identifiable risks in a research design must be outweighed by the potential value of the research.

Challenges for applied qualitative psychology
Qualitative research often requires participants to provide in-depth accounts of their experience, whether in an interview, diary entries, online, or through some other medium. This always carries the risk of distress, even if the topic is not an overtly 'sensitive' one. It is important to consider in advance how to respond if it becomes evident that a participant is distressed, so that you can manage the situation in a way that does not exacerbate it. We would advise that in any synchronous form of data collection, you pause to give the participant time to think about what they want to do. You should make it clear that they are entirely free to withdraw, but you should not force that option on them. In our experience, more often than not participants

want to carry on – they may simply need a break to collect themselves first. Remember that distress is not necessarily synonymous with 'harm' – it is more likely to be the way you, as a researcher, deal with the distress that determines whether the experience has any longer-term negative impact on the participant.

As well as the potential for distress, applied qualitative research can entail a high risk of reputational harm, because, even with the use of pseudonyms, participants may be identifiable to some audiences. In some cases, there may be risks of harm to a participant even from a colleague, peer or family member discovering they are taking part in the research; imagine, for example, a study examining how people who choose not to be 'out' as bisexual manage their sexual identity in the workplace. It is important to think through potential risks to reputation for participants at every stage of the research process, from recruitment through to dissemination of findings.

Informed consent and the use of deception

Participants should be as fully informed as possible about the purposes of the research, what will be required of them and how findings will be disseminated. A clear record of their consent should be obtained, which may be written or verbal. Ethical codes recognise that for some psychological research (mostly using experimental methods) full advance information would invalidate a study, because prior knowledge could affect the psychological processes under investigation. In such cases, withholding of information or very minor deception may be allowed, though this should be of a kind that is unlikely to cause distress or anger when revealed. Full information must be given as soon as possible after data collection.

In studies that involve naturalistic observation of participants, where people would expect to be observed and where such observation would not create any significant risk for them, it is not necessary to obtain informed consent. It is, however, not always self-evident what counts as a 'public' space, especially with regard to online research.

Challenges for applied qualitative psychology

The great majority of qualitative research does not rely on any kind of deception or withholding of information, so does not face particular problems with the informed consent process. The main exception is for covert participant observation where the researcher wishes to entirely conceal their status, as in the example of Festinger et al.'s (1956) UFO cult study, discussed earlier. Ethics committees today would need a great deal of convincing that the social and academic value of a study planning to use covert participant observation outweighed the risks of harm associated with the method.

The consent issues around online research can be very tricky for qualitative research. Media such as blogs, discussion forums and social media posts are popular sources of material for qualitative researchers, but it is easy to find yourself in a grey area between 'public' and 'private' space with them. They may be 'public' in the sense that anyone can access them, but their authors may not realise or expect that they could be used for research purposes. Research committees are likely to weigh up such factors as the sensitivity of the topic under investigation, the degree of anonymisation possible and the feasibility of seeking permission in deciding whether to approve this kind of research.

Where online qualitative research does require consent to be given, a further issue is how the researcher can be confident that the person providing the consent is who they say they are. There is no foolproof strategy for this, though it is worth bearing in mind that in face-to-face interviews we take it on trust that people are who they say they are! There are steps that you can take to increase confidence in the identity of participants. King (2010) suggests the following:

- Try to obtain internet contact details through a trusted source.
- Where possible, ask participants to return consent forms via a different medium – for example, by post or fax.
- Consider using webcams within some part of the research, and/or the informed consent process.

Right to withdraw

Participants must have the right to withdraw from a research study at any point, without having to explain their reasons and without any further consequences for them. They should also be able to withdraw their data after data collection.

Challenges for applied qualitative psychology
Researchers need to be aware that participants may feel a sense of commitment to the research that makes withdrawal from it difficult. This may happen, for example, if they see themselves as participating in a project to support or represent an organisation or cause with which they are strongly affiliated. In our own research looking at community groups as 'assets' for health and wellbeing, it was clear that many participants gave their time because they valued 'their' group and wanted to ensure it was represented positively in the evaluation (Brooks et al., 2015a). In the light of this, you need to be very clear about the right to withdraw, not only in terms of information provided in advance but during data collection as well, if you have any suspicion that a participant is uncomfortable about their involvement.

Confidentiality and anonymity

These are related but distinct terms: confidentiality refers to restriction on access to participants' data, while anonymity refers to the concealment of participants' identities. In principle, researchers should maintain as high a level of confidentiality and anonymity as possible. However, there may be legal and/or practical limits to this in practice. For example, if evidence emerges of significant risk of harm to participants themselves or to others, researchers may be obliged to report this to appropriate authorities. In all research, where limits to confidentiality and/or anonymity could be expected, participants should be warned of this as part of the informed consent process.

Challenges for applied qualitative psychology
In many forms of qualitative research participants are providing detailed accounts of personal experience. They may also produce visual material relevant to their everyday world, such as in photo-elicitation techniques. These kinds of data make anonymisation more challenging than in a survey or experiment. Given that in applied research you will almost always be producing some kind of report for the funding and/or hosting organisation, as well as giving feedback to participants, it will often not be enough simply to rely on pseudonyms. Where the contributions of individual participants could be identifiable to colleagues or others close to them, it may be necessary to negotiate with them before a report, article or other form of dissemination is produced. For example, in one study for a health care organisation, we were aware that there was only one member of a particular professional group in the sample. If we referred to her in reports to the organisation by her professional role, her colleagues would in all likelihood be able to identify her. We therefore contacted her, telling her the quotes from her interview we would like to use. She was happy for us to do so, but asked us not to include her professional role in relation to them.

Debriefing

After data has been collected, some kind of debriefing should normally be provided for participants, to ensure they are clear about the purpose of the research in which they have participated and, if applicable, to reduce risks of harm. Debriefing is especially important where deception or withholding of information has occurred. The type and extent of debriefing required will depend on the nature of the research in which people have participated, ranging from short informal discussion to quite extensive procedures. It is common for debriefs to include the provision of information about sources of help or support relevant to the research topic.

Challenges for applied qualitative psychology
Since the vast majority of qualitative psychological research does not rely on deception or withholding of information, debriefing is generally not problematic. The main issue is to reiterate clearly to participants how their data will be used, and what they can expect in terms of access to research findings. Where there might be concerns about a participant's wellbeing, you may be advised

to direct them towards sources of support – these would normally be included on the information sheet provided in the recruitment process, so it is a good idea for face-to-face research to ensure you have spare copies of these with you.

Honesty and integrity

Researchers are expected to present their work honestly and accurately, and not to make unsupportable claims on the basis of it, especially in interactions with those outside academia who may be influenced by it. They are also required to treat fellow researchers and the wider academic community fairly, for example through appropriate assignment of authorship in publications, and through correct citation of the work of others on which they have drawn.

Challenges for applied qualitative psychology

Overall, honesty and integrity issues are not particularly methodology-specific. Applied qualitative psychologists are under the same strictures as any other researcher not to fake or manipulate data, draw false or unsupportable conclusions on the basis of it, or treat their co-researchers unjustly in terms of recognition through authorship. One challenge we have experienced, though, relates to attempts by those on whose behalf research is carried out to influence how findings are reported. In quantitative research, it is quite clear that asking researchers to claim that a relationship between variables is significant when it is not (or vice versa) would be an invitation to commit fraud. But since as qualitative researchers we may well argue for a relativist epistemology that does not allow for objective 'proof' or one true account, a funder or sponsor of research might feel it is legitimate to ask us to emphasise certain aspects of our findings over others. Nigel recalls an incident where a governmental sponsor of research requested that a report on the impact of certain new policies should include more examples of 'best practice' and fewer references to problems. The research team felt that this would misrepresent their interpretation of the data. This led to negotiation between researchers and sponsors that eventually reached a compromise both parties could live with.

These kinds of tension can never be entirely eliminated in applied qualitative research, but the chance of serious conflict over versions of research findings can be reduced by open discussion from the very start of a project about when and how it is legitimate for funders/sponsors to intervene. Providing interim reports and/or informal updates in the course of a project can also help avoid a situation where they are hit with a final set of findings that contains unpleasant surprises for them.

Conclusion

In this chapter we have considered some of the practicalities of carrying out a qualitative research project, considering the choice of research question and methodological approach, along with the range of data collection and analysis methods available. We have also looked at issues of research ethics and quality. Much of this discussion is not specific to the kind of qualitative research we describe as 'applied' in Chapter 1, though we have highlighted throughout the chapter particular points for consideration when taking such an orientation.

Overall, Section 1 of this book has set out what we mean by 'applied qualitative research' and offered insights and advice on what needs to be considered when setting out on work of this kind. In Section 2 we will move into the heart of the volume; a series of 11 chapters presenting a varied collection of research methodologies, methods and topics that illustrate the richness of contemporary applied qualitative research in psychology.

References

American Psychological Association. (2010). Ethical Principles of Psychologists and Code of Conduct. Retrieved 30 January 2017 from: www.apa.org/ethics/code.

Ayling, R. and Mewse, A.J. (2014). Evaluating internet interviews with gay men. *Qualitative Health Research*, 19(4), 566–576.

Bazarova, N.N., Taft, J.G., Yoon, H.C. and Cosley, D. (2013). Managing impressions and relationships on Facebook: Self-presentational and relational concerns revealed through the analysis of language style. *Journal of Language and Social Psychology*, 32(2), 121–141.

Boydell, K.M., Gladstone, B.M., Volpe, T., Allemang, B. and Stasiulis, E. (2012). The production and dissemination of knowledge: A scoping review of arts-based health research. *Forum: Qualitative Social Research*, 13(1), Art. 32.

Braun, V. and Clarke, V. (2006). Using thematic analysis in psychology. *Qualitative Research in Psychology*, 3, 258–267.

Braun, V. and Clarke, V. (2013) *Successful Qualitative Research: A Practical Guide for Beginners*. London: SAGE.

Brinkmann, S. and Kvale, S. (2014). *InterViews: Learning the Craft of Qualitative Research Interviewing (Third Edition)*. London: SAGE.

British Psychological Society (2009). *Code of Ethics and Conduct*. Leicester: BPS.

Brooks, J., Bravington, A., Rodriguez, A., King, N. and Percy-Smith, B. (2015a). *Public Health Participatory Research Project Using an Assets Approach: Final Report to Funder*. University of Huddersfield.

Brooks, J., McCluskey, S., Turley, E. and King, N. (2015b). The utility of template analysis in qualitative psychology research. *Qualitative Research in Psychology*, 12(2), 202–222.

Brown, J. (2001). The World Café: Living knowledge through conversations that matter. *The Systems Thinker*, 12, 1–5.

Burr, V., King, N. and Butt, T. (2014). Personal construct psychology methods for qualitative research. *International Journal of Social Research Methodology*, 17(4), 341–355.

Chamberlain, K. (2012). Do you really need a methodology? *Qualitative Methods in Psychology Bulletin*, 13, 59–63.

Charmaz, K. (2013). *Constructing Grounded Theory (Second Edition)*. London: SAGE.

Corbin, J. and Strauss, A. (2015). *Basics of Qualitative Research: Techniques and Procedures for Developing Grounded Theory (Fourth Edition)*. London: SAGE.

Dalkey, N. and Helmer, O. (1963). An experimental application of the Delphi method to the use of experts. *Management Science*, 9(3), 458–467.

Deakin, H. and Wakefield, K. (2014). Skype interviewing: Reflections of two PhD researchers. *Qualitative Research*, 14(5), 603–616.

Eagleman, A.M. (2011). Stereotypes of race and nationality: A qualitative analysis of sport magazine coverage of MBL players. *Journal of Sport Management*, 25(2), 156–168.

Edwards, D. (2005). Discursive psychology. In K.L. Fitch and R.E. Saunders (Eds.), *Handbook of Language and Social Interaction*. Mahwah, NJ: Lawrence Erlbaum.

Festinger, L., Riecken, H.W. and Schachter, S. (1956). *When Prophecy Fails*. Minneapolis: University of Minnesota Press.

Finch, H., Lewis, J. and Turley, C. (2013). Focus groups. In J. Ritchie, J. Lewis, C. McNaughton Nicholls and R. Ormston (Eds.), *Qualitative Research Practice: A Guide for Social Science Students and Researchers*. London: SAGE, pp. 211–240.

Finlay, L. (2003). The reflexive journey: Mapping multiple routes. In L. Finlay and B. Gough (Eds.), *Reflexivity: A Practical Guide for Researchers in Health and Social Sciences*. Oxford: Blackwell.

Fletcher, A.J. and Marchildon, G.P. (2014). Using the Delphi technique for qualitative, participatory action research in health leadership. *International Journal of Qualitative Methods*, 13(1), 1–18.

Flick, U. (2014). *An Introduction to Qualitative Research (Fifth Edition)*. London: SAGE.

Furness, P.J. and Garrud, P. (2010). Adaptation after facial surgery: Using the diary as a research tool. *Qualitative Health Research*, 20(2), 262–272.

Gibbs, G.R. (2008). *Analyzing Qualitative Data*. London: SAGE.

Gubrium, J.F. and Holstein, J.A. (2003). From the individual interview to the interview society. In J.F. Gubrium and J.A. Holstein (Eds.), *Postmodern Interviewing*. London: SAGE.

Hasson, F., Keeney, S. and McKenna, H. (2000). Research guidelines for the Delphi survey technique. *Journal of Advanced Nursing*, 32(4), 1008–1015.

Hollway, W. and Jefferson, T. (2000). *Doing Qualitative Research Differently: Free Association, Narrative and the Interview Method*. London: SAGE.

Holt, A. (2010). Using the telephone for narrative interviewing: A research note. *Qualitative Research*, 10(1), 113–121.

James, N. (2016). Using email interviews in qualitative educational research: Creating space to think and talk. *International Journal of Qualitative Studies in Education*, 29(2), 150–163.

King, N. (2010). Research ethics in qualitative research. In M.A. Forrester (Ed.), *Doing Qualitative Research in Psychology: A Practical Guide*. London: SAGE.

King, N. (1992). Modelling the innovation process: An empirical comparison of approaches. *Journal of Occupational and Organizational Psychology*, 65(2), 89–100.

King, N., Anderson, N. and West, M. (1991). Organizational innovation in the UK: A case study of perceptions and processes. *Work and Stress*, 5(4), 331–339.

King, N., Bravington, A., Brooks, J., Hardy, B., Melvin, J. and Wilde, D. (2013). The Pictor technique: A method for exploring the experience of collaborative working. *Qualitative Health Research*, 23(8), 1138–1152.

King, N. and Brooks, J. (2017). *Template Analysis for Business and Management Students*. London: SAGE.

King, N., Carroll, C., Newton, P. and Dornan, T. (2002). You can't cure it so you have to endure it: The experience of adaptation to diabetic renal disease. *Qualitative Health Research*, 12(3), 329–346.

King, N. and Horrocks, C. (2010). *Interviews in Qualitative Research*. London: SAGE.

Langdridge, D. (2004). *Introduction to research methods and data analysis in psychology*. Harlow: Pearson Education.

Lee, B. (2012). Using documents in organizational research. In G. Symon and C. Cassell (Eds.), *Qualitative Organizational Research: Core Methods and Current Challenges*. London: SAGE.

Lincoln, Y.S. and Guba, E.G. (1985). *Naturalistic Inquiry*. Newbury Park, CA: SAGE.

Madill, A. (2011). Interaction in the semi-structured interview: A comparative analysis of the use of and response to indirect complaints. *Qualitative Research in Psychology*, 8(4), 333–353.

McNaughton Nicholls, C., Mills, L. and Kotecha, M. (2014). Observation. In J. Ritchie, J. Lewis, C. McNaughton Nicholls and R. Ormston (Eds.), *Qualitative Research Practice: A Guide for Social Science Students and Researchers (Second Edition)*. London: SAGE, pp. 243–268.

Mishler, E.G. (1986). *Research Interviewing: Context and Narrative*. Cambridge, MA: Harvard University Press.

Morgan, D.L., Ataie, J., Carder, P. and Hoffman, K. (2013). Introducing dyadic interviews as a method for collecting qualitative data. *Qualitative Health Research*, 23(9), 1276–1284.

Novick, G. (2008). Is there bias against telephone interviews in qualitative research? *Research in Nursing and Health*, 31(4), 391–398.

Opdenakker, R. (2006). Advantages and disadvantages of four interview techniques in qualitative research. *Forum: Qualitative Social Research*, 7(11), Art. 11.

Potter, J. and Hepburn, A. (2005). Qualitative interviews in psychology: Problems and possibilities. *Qualitative Research in Psychology*, 2(4), 281–307.

Proctor, H. (2014). Qualitative grids, the relationality corollary and the levels of interpersonal construing. *Journal of Constructivist Psychology*, 27(4), 243–262.

Radcliffe, L.S. and Cassell, C. (2014). Resolving couples' work–family conflicts: The complexity of decision making and the introduction of a new framework. *Human Relations*, 67(7), 793–819.

Rania, N., Migliorini, L., Rebora, S. and Cardinali, P. (2015). Photovoice and interpretation of pictures in a group discussion: A community psychology approach. *Qualitative Research in Psychology*, 12, 4, 382–396.

Reavey, P. (Ed.) (2011). *Visual Methods in Psychology: Using and Interpreting Images in Qualitative Research*. Hove: Psychology Press.

Rempel, G.R., Neufeld, A. and Kushner, K.E. (2007). Interactive use of genograms and ecomaps in family caregiving research. *Journal of Family Nursing*, 13(4), 403–419.

Riff, D., Lacy, S. and Fico, F. (2014). *Analyzing Media Messages: Using Quantitative Content Analysis in Research (Third Edition)*. Abingdon: Routledge.

Robertson, M., Line, M., Jones, S. and Thomas, S. (2000). International students, learning environments and perceptions: A case study using the Delphi technique. *Higher Education Research and Development*, 19(1), 89–102.

Rubin, H.J. and Rubin, I.S. (2011). *Qualitative Interviewing: The Art of Hearing Data (Third Edition)*. London: SAGE.

Saldana, J. (2009). *The Coding Manual for Qualitative Researchers*. Los Angeles, CA: SAGE.

Smith, J.A., Flowers, P. and Larkin, M. (2009). *Interpretative Phenomenological Analysis: Theory, Method and Research*. London: SAGE.

Sobaih, A.E.E., Ritchie, C. and Jones, E. (2012). Consulting the oracle? Applications of modified Delphi technique to qualitative research in the hospitality industry. *International Journal of Contemporary Hospitality Management*, 24(6), 886–906.

Stewart, K. and Williams, M. (2005). Researching online populations: The use of online focus groups for social research. *Qualitative Research*, 5(4), 395–416.

Tracy, S.J. (2010). Qualitative quality: Eight 'big-tent' criteria for excellent qualitative research. *Qualitative Inquiry*, 16(10), 837–851.

Turley, E., Monro, S. and King, N. (2016 in press). Doing it differently: Engaging interview participants with imaginative variation. *Indo-Pacific Journal of Phenomenology*.

Williams, M. (2003). Virtually Criminal: Deviance and Harm within Online Environments. Unpublished PhD thesis, University of Wales, Cardiff.

Wilson, C., Nairn, R., Coverdale, J. and Panapa, A. (2000). How mental illness is portrayed in children's television: A prospective study. *British Journal of Psychiatry*, 176(5), 440–443.

Yardley, L. (2008). Demonstrating validity in qualitative psychology. In J.A. Smith (Ed.) *Qualitative Psychology: A Practical Guide to Methods (Second Edition)*. London: SAGE, pp. 235–251.

SECTION II

Real World Examples of Applied Qualitative Research

Exploring Men's Experiences of Diagnosis and Treatment for Prostate Cancer

Peter Branney, Clare Strickland, Frances Darby, Lisa White and Sunjay Jain

Introduction

Public participation in research is when those people who will potentially be affected by the findings of a study have a role beyond being the people from whom data is collected. To 'participate' is a verb that means to get involved, to take part, or to engage in some activity, and so there are boundless ways in which the public can participate in research. The motivations for public participation in research are broadly ideological (e.g. making research democratic, transparent and accountable) and pragmatic (e.g. making recruitment easier or making the particular topic studied more likely to be taken up by the communities involved). It's called *patient and public involvement* (PPI) in health care although *citizen* and *user* are terms that are used in other domains. In this chapter, we will use the term *public participation*.

There is some debate about whether public participation in research is real or merely tokenistic (done to meet a funding or governance requirement). Whilst we think that a minimum requirement for public participation in research is that the study or studies in question should be different as a consequence, we want to sidestep issues of definition by thinking instead about how we conceptualise the autonomy and rationality of those we hope will participate in our research. These concepts provide a framework through which to understand, design and conduct public participation in research.

Briefly, the freedom to make decisions (*autonomy*) lies with the individual (*individual autonomy*) or with the larger community (*communal autonomy*). In between these two are smaller groups and one person can be in many groups (*plural autonomy*). What constitutes a reasonable or *rational* decision within public participation can emerge as a consequence of communication at the communal level (*communicative rationality*), between different identities (*inter-subjective rationality*) or through action (*action rationality*). Figure 4.1 maps these concepts of autonomy and rationality against methods of public participation. For example, if we conceptualise autonomy in participation at the individual level and the rationality of public decisions as emerging through the action in their response then we will want methods of participation that focus on equality of involvement, aiming to be representative of all possible individual responses. As such, a charity may conduct a survey to identify the priorities for its research funding (which shows how being involved as a research participant can also be public participation).

In applied research, it is our experience that there are a number of 'players' or groups usually involved in a study and that, over the course of a study, there is an implicit negotiation over which 'story' of the research is to be taken up as the 'truth' and in which contexts (plural autonomy and inter-subjective rationality in Figure 4.1). 'Players' or groups involved in a study may include, for example, junior researchers, professors, clinicians and staff from the body funding the research. The professors may design the study and their story is the truth in the bid that is funded; the junior researchers conduct the study and their story becomes true in the conduct of the research; the clinicians are the link to the health service and their story becomes true in the return of the findings into practice; the funding staff process the end-of-study reports and their story becomes true in the account of their finances. The role of public participation is to give end-users greater power in the research process and

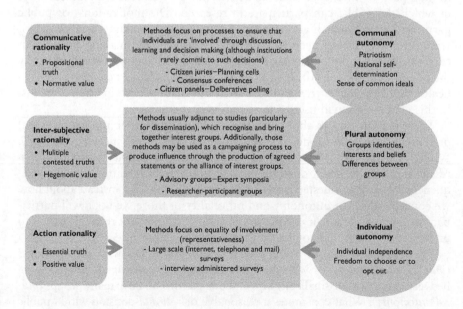

Figure 4.1   Framework for participation

this is often done by giving them a role at the table. A 2011 audit of NHS research governance applications showed that the public are usually involved in research by being a grant holder, or by sitting on what are called 'trial steering groups' or advisory/user groups as 'expert patients' (Tarpey, 2011). However, these roles require a certain degree of confidence as well as a long-term commitment to the research project and we would argue that, because of this, such roles are often taken up by well-educated people of a similar socio-economic background to the research team themselves. One way of broadening the range and type of people involved in public participation is, we suggest, to develop more short-term approaches for participation.

In this chapter we will use an example from our own research to provide an example of a short-term public participation activity which used qualitative methods in an applied setting. First, though, we will briefly outline three principles that we have found useful in the design of short-term participation activities:

1. Framework: you need a framework to understand both (a) how the short-term activities fit into the wider research and (b) what the activity does to enable public participation. Many use the stages of research (design, data collection, analysis and dissemination) as their framework, but we prefer autonomy and rationality.
2. Time is relative: what is 'short term' will depend on your end-users; you need activities that remove the barriers of long-term commitment and confidence to broaden the range of people participating.
3. It takes time: even if the short-term activity is a single day, it takes time to build rapport with your potential participants in the activities and find a time and place that suits as many as possible.

Our case example

Introduction to the study

We will use an example from our own research to illustrate the use of a short-term public participation activity. Our example is taken from a feasibility study which set out to explore the experiences of men diagnosed with prostate cancer in relation to diagnosis and treatment.

Prostate cancer is not necessarily deadly, hence the saying, 'People often die with prostate cancer, rather than of it.' Additionally, clinical guidelines in the United Kingdom (National Institute for Clinical Excellence, 2008) include giving patients the freedom to choose their treatment. If a patient has a low or medium risk diagnosis, he can choose to have his tumour treated but risks incontinence and impotence (Litwin et al., 1999; Litwin et al., 2007; Litwin et al., 2004), which are known to potentially impact on identity (particularly any sense of masculine identity) and overall wellbeing (Chapple and

Ziebland, 2002; Gray et al., 2000; Lucas et al., 1995; Oliffe, 2005, 2006). The alternative is to choose to wait and see what happens (called 'watchful waiting' or 'active surveillance'), treating the tumour if and when it grows. The risk of waiting is that the tumour grows too much, so that treatment is less likely to cure and even more likely to leave the man incontinent and impotent. If cancer spreads, it may become incurable.

Whilst useful for explaining the key issues, this dichotomy of treat-or-wait in choosing treatment for prostate cancer is nevertheless an oversimplification of a diagnostic process with different grades and stages of tumour, the emotional impact of receiving a diagnosis of cancer and then having to navigate health services, relationships with family, friends and professionals and the different types of treatment. We wanted to explore the experiences of choosing treatment for prostate cancer and hoped that what we could learn would help to improve services for patients. We nevertheless felt that we knew too little for us to design good studies. Consequently, our aim was to hold a stand-alone public participation activity from which we could learn about some of the issues for patients choosing treatment while involving our potential end-users in the early stages of a programme of research.

Choice is a complex concept that is both personal and structural. A patient will have personal experiences of making a choice: perhaps hearing their diagnosis from a consultant, talking to a nurse specialist about potential treatments, sharing their diagnosis with family and close friends, searching for information and then a follow-up consultation where they choose a treatment. Personal choice nevertheless occurs within a wider system (not just the system of health services but wider cultural, historical and societal values) that makes such choices possible (and therefore also limits and constrains choice). As Branney et al. (2012) illustrate, even when giving patients choice about where they have elective surgery in the United Kingdom (in an attempt to improve services through competition), the choices made are nevertheless limited by the number of, and demands for, beds available and travel time to the hospital.

Given the distinction between personal and structural choice, it is possible that a patient may make a choice but does not experience it as autonomous; and vice versa, a patient may have an experience of autonomy in choosing their treatment, but there may have been no choice within the system. There is a range of types of choice. For example, Thomas Hobson had a stable of over 40 horses giving the appearance of choice. The proverb is that Hobson offered his customers the horse in the stall closest to the door or none at all. Hobson rotated the horses around the stalls to prevent the best horses from being picked and getting too tired. In a Hobson's choice, we doubt there is much experience of autonomy. Other types of choice include an ultimatum, which is similar to Hobson's choice (this or nothing); a dilemma is a choice between two options when there is little to choose between them; a false dilemma is two choices when there may be other options; catch-22 is a logical problem where the solution is available only if the solution wasn't required (e.g. you could have got the internship if you had more experience); Morton's choice or a double bind is where all options have undesirable outcomes; and blackmail is a choice between doing X or suffering something unpleasant.

Why was the one-day participative workshop the appropriate method?

Consequently, we were interested in methods that would allow us to explore patients' experiences of choosing treatment for prostate cancer, while putting them into the context of their health services and wider cultural, historical and social values. The justification for using a one-day participative workshop comes from our framework for rationality and autonomy (see Figure 4.1).

In terms of individual autonomy and action rationality, we wanted a range of people participating. Every year, over 40,000 men receive a diagnosis of prostate cancer and, while 81 per cent survive for longer than five years, approximately 11,000 die each year.[1] It is a cancer that cuts across socio-economic boundaries, affecting men whatever their educational background or income level. We were under no illusion that we could achieve representativeness for such a large group. Instead, we wanted an approach that would draw in people whose backgrounds were varied. In particular, we hoped that a one-day event would attract people who would be put off by long-term participation.

We also considered men choosing treatment for prostate cancer as a group, not just as individuals. Indeed, they are among a variety of groups that have a stake in treatment choice, including medics, nurses and health managers, for example. Treating autonomy as plural and rationality as inter-subjective, we wanted an approach that would allow us to focus on this group's experiences and give them a chance to take part in the creation of truth that would form later research. The one-day workshop is therefore like a public hearing for a study (South et al., 2012) that focuses on one interest group. As we wanted to explore how we would research this topic, our workshop was similar to the patient and carer co-researcher groups used in the Macmillan Listening Study (Corner et al., 2006; Wright et al., 2005). Using the stages of research, the Macmillan Listening Study had patients and carers involved in the design, data collection and analysis. This included the co-researchers training, and then subsequently conducting, the focus groups, which were the primary method of data collection. The short-term participative workshop includes some design and data collection within one day whereas the Macmillan Listening Study was over a much longer period.

Finally, men choosing treatment for prostate cancer are part of a wider community where truth is created through communication. As such, the process is just as important as the outcome. There is a proviso because the process can also be a way of marginalising people. Having patients involved in research where the researchers and clinicians are experts means

---

[1] www.cancerresearchuk.org/cancer-info/cancerstats/types/prostate/

that their voices risk having no impact. This is particularly so in qualitative methods where the researcher collecting and analysing the data has to draw on their expertise in the way they respond, for example, or how they interpret what was said by participants. Indeed, the questions researchers ask are shaped to some extent by the methods they use for asking them (see Chapter 2 in this volume for more on this). While seeking to explore patients' experiences of choosing treatment for prostate cancer, we therefore wanted to provide an opportunity for those participating to learn about our research methods. The Macmillan Listening Study (ibid.) is an example where the co-researchers learnt about focus group methods over a long period. The one-day participative workshop was a chance for patients to learn about focus groups and semi-structured interviews over a single day.

[Date]

Objectives for the day: To identify questions and prompts that are important for patients (rather than clinicians or researchers).

09:45 –10:15	**Registration** – Sign in and collection of workshop pack. Refreshments will be available throughout the course of the registration.
10:15 –10:45	**Introductions** –The researchers will welcome you to the event and introduce the schedule for the day.

Tea/coffee break

10:45 –12:00	**Discussion Groups** – Workshop participants will be divided into two groups, researchers will help the two groups to make a list of possible interview questions to use when interviewing penile cancer patients.
12:00 –12:45	**Lunch** – A free buffet lunch will be provided for all participants and their companions.
12:45 –14:15	**Interviews** – Pilot, participant-led interviews.

Tea/coffee break

14:15 –15:00	**Feedback** –Participants will be encouraged to give feedback to the researchers.
15:00	**Close**

Figure 4.2 One-day participative workshop schedule

Conducting a one-day participative workshop

Here we will describe how we conducted the one-day participative workshop. The study adopted a participative, mixed-qualitative-methods design combined into a one-day 'workshop' (see Figure 4.2). From our point of view as researchers, we approached the workshop as an event, similar to a one-day conference. As such, we will cover sampling and recruitment, data collection and analysis as planning, running the event and taking stock. To allow us to show the detail of analysis, we focus on a topic (blood) that came up in different ways. Last, we will conclude by highlighting some of the lessons we learned about a participative workshop from this study.

Planning: Sample and recruitment

While the aim of a sampling strategy for qualitative health research is usually to ensure that the analysis can reach saturation, we would argue that participative events require a different approach. Instead, we had to work out how many participants it was possible to recruit given practical limitations, and consider what we could achieve. We aimed to recruit a maximum variation (Marshall, 1996) sample of five to ten men diagnosed and treated for prostate cancer across Yorkshire. The intention of this recruitment strategy was to include the widest possible range of experiences in terms of age, type of treatment and time since treatment. Initially, we aimed to invite potential participations at their six-monthly and annual post-treatment check-ups. Unfortunately, these clinics were so busy that we were unable to find a spare room in which to talk through the study with those interested (even a medium-sized room that was normally used for meetings was required as a waiting room). Subsequently, we recruited from a clinic for men who had robotic prostatectomy; this is probably better known as keyhole surgery, where the robotic devices minimise invasion into the body and therefore improve recovery compared to surgery without a robot. Nevertheless, we were aware that the sampling would be limited by the variety of participants interested in the study and available for the workshop.

A nurse in the clinic approached potential participants, telling them about the study verbally. Those interested were asked to take a recruitment pack away, talk to family and friends and take some time before deciding. The recruitment pack included a reply-slip which asked for demographic and contact details. A researcher followed up all reply-slips to talk through the study, answer questions and (if interested) ask about their availability for three dates. We used the date that was suitable for most of those interested.

The minimum age for inclusion was 16 years due to legal requirements for signing consent forms, but in practice prostate cancer is unlikely under 40 years of age. As many people take a partner, family member or friend with them to health care visits, the workshop incorporated companions in discussions running parallel to the focus groups and participant-conducted interviews. This meant that everyone attending the workshop (except the research team) had been directly or indirectly affected by prostate cancer.

Running the workshop: Data collection

We started with focus groups and then used interviews. In the focus groups, participants designed a one-on-one semi-structured interview schedule. Each focus group had an experienced qualitative researcher who was there to help clarify the aims of the study, and the potential advantages and disadvantages of different aspects of interview technique. The small group format of the focus groups meant that participants could discuss potential interview questions with others who had personal experience of the diagnosis, treatment and rehabilitation of prostate cancer. Group interaction encouraged a range of interview questions and a variety of views about them.

At the end of the discussion each focus group had created an interview schedule, which was subsequently piloted in participant-conducted one-on-one semi-structured interviews. While the interviews would help to identity key issues, their primary aim was to ensure that the pilot workshop was a two-way process in which participants could also learn about the process of conducting interview-based research.

The one-day format was designed to facilitate patients' short but intense involvement in the development of a study about their experiences. The one-day design also meant that a variety of men who had been diagnosed with prostate cancer could be involved in designing the study. Additionally, as a participative workshop running on a single day, the focus groups allowed time for participants to work together, getting to know each other and build rapport, before the one-on-one interviews.

Taking stock: Data analysis

The main aim of the analysis was to illustrate the concerns of the participants by providing examples and highlighting similarities and differences between concerns. Qualitative analysis often aims to inductively identify analytical categories from the data, but the design of this study meant that participants created the key questions (in the form of the interview schedules). Indeed, inductive qualitative approaches engender an analytic scepticism about the talk of the participants (Gondolf, 2000) whereas a deductive approach would mean that we could stick closely to the concerns participants highlighted in interview schedules. Consequently, we applied the five stages of framework analysis (Pope et al., 2000): (1) familiarisation, (2) identifying a thematic framework, (3) coding,[2] (4) charting and (5) mapping and interpretation.

The interview schedule was used as the framework (stage 2) from which to deductively code all data from the focus group according to whether it related to one or more of the 'frames' (topics in the interview schedule). Subsequently, the codes for each frame were combined and rearranged, which allowed for the identification of similarities and differences between the topics (charting, stage 4). The charting stage is where you would change the main, or identify larger, themes but this was unnecessary in our study. The participant-conducted

---

[2] Pope, Ziebland and Mays use the term 'indexing' but we prefer 'coding'.

interviews were analysed to further identify any aspects that elucidated or challenged the themes identified in the focus group. In the final stage of mapping and interpretation, the data was brought together to identify the key issues and their interconnections.

Illustrative findings

Focus groups and interviews are well-used research methods and there is a wide variety of methods for analysing them. As our focus is on the participative workshop, we will not provide an overview of the findings from this study. Instead, we will go through the steps of framework analysis, showing how they were employed in this study.

Identifying a thematic framework

Broadly, analysis of qualitative data can be broken down into data-driven and framework-driven approaches. Data-driven approaches seek to find the framework from within their data. Researchers using bottom-up approaches will often talk and write about their, for example, *themes* emerging from the data as if their findings have agency. In framework-driven approaches, a particular framework, such as culturally shared *discourses* (Parker, 1992) or *interpretative repertoires* (Wetherell, 1998), can be used as a lens through which to code and interpret the data. Even if they look for their findings in the data, analyses looking at discourses or interpretative repertoires draw on a theory of language where knowledge is socially constructed, for example. As the names suggests, framework analysis is driven by the framework used by the researchers, which is often done in the name of pragmatism rather than any explicit theoretical approach. Within framework analysis, the thematic *framework* is usually drawn from the focus group/interview schedules, which in turn are developed from the study aims and literature review (see e.g. South et al., 2010). Framework analysis can be employed to allow the researchers in the last few stops to move beyond the initial framework, so that the final findings are coaxed from the data, blurring the data-driven and framework-driven dichotomy (see e.g. Branney et al., 2012).

In the participative workshop, framework analysis is data-driven then framework-driven (because the framework driving the analysis emerges from the focus group). In the focus groups, participants shared their experiences of diagnosis and treatment for prostate cancer and rehabilitation from robotic prostatectomy. The facilitator (PB) started the focus group off with a few leading but open questions:

Extract 1

Facilitator: *Erm, so really we just, just want a discussion about choosing, you know, your treatment for prostate cancer. You know, what was it like? What happened? What do you think was important? Don't know if anyone wants to kick off?*

Throughout, the facilitator was largely silent but actively listening by giving eye contact, nodding and looking to people who were giving visual cues that suggested they wanted to speak next. The participants were engaged; some speaking at length while others listened. At other times, discussion moved quickly between speakers as each participant spoke for a short amount of time. Participants asked each other general (Participant 6: 'How did everybody get to know they had to go to the doctor?') and specific (Participant 1: 'Which hospital was that then?') questions. There was also agreement (Participant 3 starts with 'Yeah yeah' and continues the topic from Participant 2) and polite disagreement, which we see in this extract:

Extract 2

Participant 6: *Quite interesting, though. We're always searching on the internet.*

Participant 5: *Can I just say I didn't do any.*

This level of discussion meant that, over 96 minutes, the facilitator spoke only four times (including at the start and end). While such a small amount of verbal input from the facilitator does suggest this was an 'easy' discussion (because the facilitator had to say very little), non-verbal input was particularly important for ensuring everyone was involved.

Throughout the discussion, the facilitator kept brief notes about potential items for the interview schedule, which he summarised at the end to participants. This summary is important because it represents an instant analysis from the facilitator's perspective:

Extract 3

Facilitator: *It's been fantastic. You know, really, really grateful. I think what I'll do because I've been kind of making notes and thinking about the main things. I think there's three kind of main areas. They're all quite big. And I probably should start with asking about diagnosis. So that infers, how did they first get to a GP? Erm, it's also about the enormity of diagnosis. You know, the fact that they were facing cancer and dealing with that. And then from that to kind of, erm, the timeline from, you know, having your diagnosis to performing the treatments. And that kind of takes us on to the information gathering. So information gathering is the second thing. So it's quite big and it includes leaflets from the hospital, leaflets you get elsewhere, your own home searches on the internet, erm, looking at web forums or looking for the specific kind of research but also about trust that you place on what you find. And then talking to health professionals, talking to your partner and also the role that your partner had in looking for information and talking to other people. Erm, I've got another thing quite interesting to actually get hold of health professionals to ask them questions afterwards and that's quite, quite a useful thing to add. And so, erm, and I think the, the third one is more about really that it's choosing treatments not so it doesn't stop when you make the decision. That actually there's consequences and you still have lots of choices afterwards where you want more information. So the third area's about practical consequences after treatment. Erm, and I've got a bit about the information you get there, erm, you know seeing both incontinence and erectile dysfunction. A little bit about toilet planning when you're going out and about. Erm, and I think quite a big thing seemed to be the point at which you had the catheter taken out.*

The focus group ended and the participants had a lunch break. Using this summary, the facilitator typed up an interview schedule (see Figure 4.3), which was printed and given to participants for the participant-conducted interviews. From the quote above, you can see how the facilitator's summary was used to create an interview schedule consisting of three main areas (diagnosis, information gathering and practical consequences) and a number of bullet points to act as prompts. These prompts varied between sub-topics (e.g. incontinence and erectile dysfunction as part of practical consequences after treatment) to cross-cutting topics (i.e. blood under both incontinence and erectile dysfunction) and also questions (e.g. what was it like communicating with your health professionals outside of appointments?).

Coding

Using a web-based and open source computer-assisted qualitative data analysis software (CATMA; Computer Aided Textual Markup & Analysis[3]), we read through the focus group and 'tagged'[4] text that we thought illustrated one of the areas and/or prompts on the interview schedule. The topic of blood is a good example, because it came up twice in the interview schedule.

Extract 4

Participant 4: *I know it's a bit of a dodgy subject this, isn't it, but I would say I would imagine I had 90% blood in my semen. And, like, and that went on for about 3 weeks afterwards.*

---

[3] www.catma.de/
[4] The term 'tagging' is specific to the online software and is akin to coding.

Can you tell me about …

1. Your diagnosis

   - How did you get to the GP in the first place (e.g. first symptoms, hearing about the PSA test from friends, etc.)?

   - Dealing with the enormity of getting a cancer diagnosis:

     - Fear

     - Affect on family, children, etc.

   - Timeline from diagnosis to treatment, including appointments and visits for biopsies etc.

2. Information gathering

   - What leaflets did you get/where from/how useful where they?

   - Searching for information online, looking at chat forums, research, etc.

     - How much trust did you place in this information?

   - Was anyone involved in helping you find information (e.g. partner), what did they do?

   - What was it like communicating with your health professionals outside of appointments?

3. Practical consequences after treatment

   - What issues did you have?

     - Incontinence:

       - Blood

       - Dribble

       - Standing up, lifting, working

       - Planning toilet stops during trips

       - Support from health professionals.

     - Erectile dysfunction:

       - Blood

       - What works, how do you deal with it?

       - Support from health professionals.

   - Tell me about the appointment where they took the catheter out (and what happened when you went home).

Figure 4.3   Interview schedule designed by focus group

Extract 5

Participant 5: *Did anybody have, erm, the unfortunate discoloration after, after the operation? Erm …*

Participant 6: *With blood in it?*

Participant 5: *No no. I was thinking more I've always quite fancied being [unrecognisable word] it was the size I was thinking rather than the colour. I mean my, I went home completely black, err, which I didn't read anywhere in any literature and that did worry me for about 10 days before I actually went, I can't remember who I saw now, oh the district nurse I mentioned it to who came up. Err, she said, 'Oh no it does happen in some cases,' but it actually went black. I started thinking, 'Jesus, you know that's ...' because I've had operations before when it hasn't happened so that was quite disconcerting.*

Participant 3: *One of the leaflets did say that that could happen, you know, when it gave you a list of things possible ...*

Participant 2: *Your penis shortens, that's what I got.*

Extract 4 is a single quote that was coded as 'blood-sexual (dys)function' and Extract 5 is a discussion coded as 'blood-sexual (dys)function' and 'blood-incontinence'. In Extract 4, blood is mentioned explicitly as visual (the participant sees blood in his semen) although sexual function is implicit because the process by which semen was produced is left out. Blood is also visual in Extract 5 where discolouration (or bruising) is juxtaposed to penis size. While neither sexual function nor incontinence is mentioned, Extract 5 was given both blood codes – it is linked to Extract 4 by its focus on what happens to the body after surgery (and the bruising could have been a part of incontinence and sexual dysfunction). Additionally, the participant's experience of shocked, or shocking, seems particularly salient to the discussion of blood in both extracts ('I know it's a bit dodgy' and 'Jesus, you know that'). In the case of Extract 4, the coder was using both codes in case a link emerged elsewhere in the data.

Charting

As the coding stage neared completion, we felt that the sub-codes (the prompts under each theme) just didn't quite fit our reading of the dating. Once we had coded all of the focus group, we started to rename sub-codes, combine some and add additional detail. While the 'practical consequences' theme was already separated into erectile function and incontinence, the blood codes showed that time since treatment was also important.

The presence of blood signalled a proximity to treatment and recovery from surgery while its absence suggested that erectile function and incontinence is chronic. As Extract 6 illustrates, what is most salient about the proximity to surgery is just how difficult the experiences were for participants. While the four to five days of bleeding are discounted by the 'a bit worrying', Participant 5 reports that he refused to go back to hospital because the journey had been 'hell'.

Extract 6

Participant 5: *I ruined the mattress when I got home ... These trousers which I had were soaked in blood and my mattress was soaked in blood. Erm, it was four, five days before the bleeding stopped from the drain. Had the district nurse in every day to put me an external bag on to catch it because I was ended up with bandages sort of this big and they were just soaking through and then soaking down into the bed. Err, and I wasn't prepared for that and so that was a bit worrying. He did say at one stage to go back but I said to him 'no' because it was a hell of a journey.*

Mapping and interpretation

The aim of the mapping and interpretation step of analysis is to bring all the data together to identify the key issues and interconnections. In this study, we wanted to stay close to the concerns highlighted by participants in the interview schedule, so, rather than making major changes, this was a step of subtle refinement. The main addition we made as researchers was to emphasise the emotional and experiential aspects of choosing treatment of prostate cancer, which emerged in part from our attempts to code 'bloody'.

Extract 7

Participant 2: *But when you're standing at the urinal we're talking about your penis gets shorter you can't get it out.*

Participant 5: *That leads to problems sometimes if you dribble down your bloody trousers and that now dries and I have to lean right in to go to use the urinal now. You know, you'll arch your back to some extent.*

Extract 8

Participant 5: *And she gives me this bloody massive pad and I think oh hell, you know, what's this going to be like?*

Rather than a description of Participant 5's trousers in Extract 7 or an incontinence pad in Extract 8, 'bloody' is an expletive attributive that adds emotional force. In both cases, the subject of their expletive is an inanimate object (trousers/pad) and they emphasise the 'practical' aspect of the theme; how they stand when urinating, the change in penile length depending on their bodily position, the effect of incontinence on their clothing and what they use to soak up urine. Nevertheless, the 'bloody' in both cases adds emotional force to their descriptions, showing just how frustrating they found these (im)practicalities. Indeed, the 'massive' in Extract 8 is one of the few that ostensibly describes an object; the rest are used as a description of the emotional salience of incontinence and sexual dysfunction.

Extract 9

Participant 1: *Now for me incontinence, right now it's not, right then that was one massive thing.*

Extract 10

Participant 4: *... two things that are massive, aren't they? Incontinence and erectile dysfunction. You know, the surgery you get over.*

While the practical aspects of what happens after treatment are explicit in the name of the theme, our analysis led us to see the emotional side. In terms of choosing treatment for prostate cancer, this theme tells us that it is in the very impracticality of their experiences that the difficult emotions emerge.

Reflections on conducting a one-day participative workshop

To reflect on a one-day participative workshop we must consider both the knowledge produced and the processes of participation. Participants had a chance to learn about designing and conducting interviews (communicative rationality and communal autonomy), to share their experiences of diagnosis, treatment and recovery (inter-subjective rationality and plural autonomy), and to recommend 'your diagnosis', 'information gathering' and 'practical consequences' as topics for use in interviews about decision-making for prostate cancer (action rationality and individual autonomy).

There is a wide range of approaches to public participation and we have noticed that authors are often extremely optimistic when evaluating their specific approach (see e.g. Coote and Lenaghan, 1997). We conducted a one-day participative workshop at the start of a programme of research on penile cancer (Branney et al., 2011); the design of the research had been agreed with the funder and therefore we knew what followed the workshop. In the case given here, what followed the participative workshop on choosing treatment for prostate cancer was unknown. We were going to use the findings to guide future work, which in our case meant grant proposals to funders. In the feedback session at the end of the workshop (see Figure 4.2), this lack of clarity about the next step was frustrating for participants. This highlights the value of a one-day participative workshop as part of a well-defined programme of research rather than work that is still in the development phase.

In conclusion, autonomy and rationality are two concepts that can help us to think about and plan how we enable public participation in research. Long-term involvement in research can put many people off, so the one-day participative workshop is an approach that allows for short-term participation. The workshop gives participants the opportunity to learn about how research is done and researchers gain knowledge about the particular issue under consideration. While we have focused on the health arena, public participation is something researchers are considering across domains, from art to business to physics.

Declaration of interest

Sunjay Jain has received financial support from Ipsen.
The other authors have nothing to disclose.

Acknowledgements

This chapter presents independent research made possible by the generous support of the Leeds Teaching Hospitals Charitable Foundation. The author and publisher would also like to thank Wiley for permission to adapt Figure 4.2 from a figure originally published in Branney, P., Witty, K., Braybrook, D., Bullen, K., White, A., & Eardley, I. (2015). Mortality and sexuality after diagnosis of penile cancer: a participative study. *International Journal of Urological Nursing*, n/a-n/a. doi:10.1111/ijun.12106.

References

Branney, P., Witty, K. and Eardley, I. (2011). Patients' experiences of penile cancer. *European Urology*, 59(6), 959–961. doi:10.1016/j.eururo.2011.02.009.
Branney, P., Witty, K., Bagnall, A.-M., South, J. and White, A. (2012). 'Straight to the GP; that would be where I would go': An analysis of male frequent attenders' constructions of their decisions to use or not use health-care services in the UK. *Psychology and Health*, 27(7), 865–880. doi:10.1080/08870446.2011.63 6443.
Chapple, A. and Ziebland, S. (2002). Prostate cancer: Embodied experience and perceptions of masculinity. *Sociology of Health and Illness*, 24(6), 820–841.
Coote, A. and Lenaghan, J. (1997). *Citizens' Juries: Theory into Practice*. London: Institute for Public Policy Research (IPPR).
Corner, J., Wright, D., Foster, C., Gunaratnam, Y., Hopkinson, J. and Okamoto, I. (2006). *Full Report: The Research Priorities of People Affected by Cancer: Macmillan Listening Study*. London.
Gondolf, E.W. (2000). A 30-month follow-up of court referred batterers in four cities. *International Journal of Offender and Comparative Criminology*, 44(1), 111–128.
Gray, R., Fitch, M., Phillips, C., Labrecque, M. and Fergus, K. (2000). Hegemonic masculinity and the experience of prostate cancer: A narrative approach. *Psycho-oncology*, 9, 273–282.

Litwin, M.S., Gore, J.L., Kwan, L., Brandeis, J.M., Lee, S.P., Withers, H.R. et al. (2007). Quality of life after surgery, external beam irradiation, or brachytherapy for early-stage prostate cancer. *Cancer*, 109(11), 2239–2247.

Litwin, M.S., Sadesky, N., Pasta, D.J. and Lubeck, D.P. (2004). Bowel function and bother after treatment for early stage prostate cancer: A longitudinal quality of life analysis from CaPSURE. *The Journal of Urology*, 172(2), 515–519.

Litwin, M.S., Flanders, S.C., Pasta, D.J., Stoddard, M.L., Lubeck, D.P. and Henning, J.M. (1999). Sexual function and bother after radical prostatectomy or radiation for prostate cancer: Multivariate quality-of-life analysis for CaPSURE. *Urology*, 54(3), 503–508.

Lucas, M., Strijdom, S., Berk, M. and Hart, G. (1995). Quality of life, sexual functioning and sex role identity after surgical orchidectomy in patients with prostatic cancer. *Scandinavian Journal of Urology and Nephrology*, 29(4), 497–500.

Marshall, M.N. (1996). Sampling for qualitative research. *Family Practice*, 13, 522–525.

National Institute for Clinical Excellence (2008). *Prostate Cancer: Diagnosis and Treatment*. London: National Institute for Health and Clinical Excellence.

Oliffe, J. (2006). Embodied masculinity and androgen deprivation therapy. *International Journal of Men's Health*, 3(1), 43–60.

Oliffe, J. (2005). Constructions of masculinity following prostatectomy-induced impotence. *Social Science and Medicine*, 60(10), 2240–2259.

Parker, I. (1992). *Discourse Dynamics: Critical Analysis for Social and Individual Psychology*. London: Routledge.

Pope, C., Ziebland, S. and Mays, N. (2000). Qualitative research in health care: Analysing qualitative data. *British Medical Journal*, 320, 114–116. doi:www.dx.doi.org/10.1136/bmj.320.7227.114.

South, J., Meah, A., Bagnall, A.-M., Kinsella, K., Branney, P., White, J. and Gamsu, M. (2010). *People in Public Health – A Study of Approaches to Develop and Support People in Public Health Roles*. Southhampton, UK: National Co-ordinating Centre for NHS Service Delivery and Organisation R&D.

South, J., Meah, A. and Branney, P. (2012). 'Think differently and be prepared to demonstrate trust': Findings from public hearings, England, on supporting lay people in public health roles. *Health Promotion International*, 27(2), 284–294. doi:10.1093/heapro/dar022.

Tarpey, M. (2011). *Public Involvement in Research Applications to the National Research Ethics Service*. Eastleigh, UK: INVOLVE and the National Research Ethics Service.

Wetherell, M. (1998). Positioning and interpretative repertoires: Conversation analysis and post-structuralism in dialogue. *Discourse Society*, 9(3), 387–412. doi:10.1177/0957926598009003005.

Wright, D., Corner, J., Hopkinson, J. and Foster, C. (2005). Listening to the views of people affected by cancer about cancer research: An example of participatory research in setting the cancer research agenda. *Health Expectations*, 9, 3–12.

Using Interpretative Phenomenological Psychology in Organisational Research with Working Carers

Leah Tomkins

5

Introduction: Interpretative phenomenological analysis (IPA)

IPA is one of the best known and most commonly used qualitative methods in psychology, not only in the United Kingdom but increasingly in other parts of the world, too. Its origins are in health psychology, and most published IPA work is on topics related to the experience of illness, such as chronic pain, cancer and heart disease (Smith, 2011). The second largest domain for IPA work is clinical and counselling psychology, where topics include addiction and eating disorders (Smith, 2011). To date, however, there has been relatively little IPA work in the field of organisational research, and its sub-genres of work/organisational psychology, occupational psychology and organisation studies.

IPA is interested in the systematic exploration of personal experience. Like other experiential methods, it draws on the philosophy of phenomenology for both its central concerns and its approaches, both the 'what' and the 'how'. In particular, it is inspired by the strand of phenomenology concerned with hermeneutics, which is associated most closely with the philosophical work of Heidegger, Gadamer and Ricoeur. Hermeneutic approaches see human beings as inherently interpretative, sense-making creatures; IPA is interested in examining the nature, processes and consequences of this sense-making.

One way of understanding these two core concepts – personal experience and sense-making – is to think about the former as the 'P' in IPA, that is, the phenomenon under investigation, and the latter as the 'I', that is, the ways in which people make sense of, or interpret, that experience. Another way of thinking about this relationship is by drawing on the concept of 'attitudes'. The 'phenomenological attitude' is an idealised state in which things appear in their 'raw', pre-intellectualised being. This is contrasted with the 'natural attitude', which is the state in which we encounter things when we make sense of them, bestow meaning on them, and give them names, labels and definitions. In practical terms, this means that IPA researchers are interested in two key things: firstly, the phenomena of the life-world, or 'What is it like?'; and secondly, the interpretation of these phenomena, or 'What does it mean?'. IPA scholars design their research questions in ways that are intended to tease out both these aspects of experience.

There is an extra complexity to the 'I' of IPA's interpretation. This is because, in an IPA research encounter, there are two people doing the interpreting. The participant is trying to make sense of the phenomena of his/her experience, and the researcher is trying to make sense of the participant's sense-making. In IPA, this twin-faceted interpretation is called the 'double hermeneutic' (Smith et al., 2009). The participant's sense-making is considered first order, whilst the researcher's sense-making is second order.

IPA is normally used with semi-structured interviews with individual participants. This is because we need to collect rich data in order to begin to understand the complexities of human experience, and IPA participants are therefore given the opportunity to tell their own stories, develop their own ideas and express their own concerns. Other data collection methods have been combined with IPA's analytic technique, such as focus groups and participant observations, but these need special care to ensure that they do not result in a loss of experiential richness or focus on the individual human being.

Using IPA

In this section I provide an overview of the key stages in an IPA analysis. I follow the same numbering that appears in the Smith et al. (2009) textbook, so that readers can easily navigate between this chapter and the description there. IPA is not intended to be a prescriptive rule-book for how each and every analysis must be done. Rather, these are general guidelines, which relate both to the processes of research (e.g. moving from the particular to the shared, and from the descriptive to the interpretative) and to the principles of research (e.g. a desire to understand the participant's point of view). Researchers using IPA are encouraged to use these guidelines to engage sensitively and open-mindedly with their topic, their participants and the context of their research.

Step 1: Reading and re-reading

The first step involves immersing oneself in the data. Since most IPA data are in the form of transcribed interviews, this involves a close reading and re-reading of the transcripts. If the audio-tapes are in your possession, you might find it helpful to listen to these tapes whilst you are doing this reading. Hearing the participants can add texture and nuance to the written words on the page. My advice is not to underestimate the importance of step 1 (and not to be afraid to go back to step 1 even after going through the other steps). Each re-reading can throw up new and interesting things, and deepen our engagement in our participants' life-worlds.

Step 2: Initial noting

This step involves exploring the semantics and the use of language in an exploratory and curious way. Researchers pause to reflect on and note points of interest, what they think the participant is saying, and what associations this might trigger. It is useful to think about whether a particular point that the participant is making seems to flow with narrative coherence from what has come before, or whether there is any sense of disruption to that coherence. Whilst this is close to being a free textual analysis, it must stay close to the data. Our aim is to try to understand what the participant is saying, not use what he or she is saying as a springboard for our own personal reflections on a topic.

Step 3: Developing emergent themes

The basic building block of IPA work is the theme. So, step 3 involves converting the initial notes into themes which represent some sort of crystallisation – a kind of psychological gist – of what is happening in each passage of data. Our aim is to derive themes which are particular enough to be grounded: that is, to be clearly traceable back to the raw data, whilst also being abstract enough to be conceptual; that is, to begin to move towards the language of theory. Within a single interview transcript, you may find that the same theme suggests itself for several different passages of data.

Step 4: Searching for connections across themes (within-participant patterning)

Once you have crystallised the data into a list of themes within the transcript, the next step is to move from a chronological ordering (based on the order in which they emerged in the interview) to some other form of patterning which will organise and summarise your data. The aim is to come up with a structure or Gestalt which highlights what you think are the most significant aspects of the participant's experience, and which begins to suggest possible theorisations of it. I will cover several common patterning techniques later in this chapter.

Step 5: Moving to the next case

IPA is sometimes used with just a single case, and this is perhaps the 'purest' way of honouring IPA's commitment to idiography, that is, a focus on the particular. More often, however, IPA is used with small samples. So, step 5 of the process involves moving on to the next participant's transcript and repeating steps 1 to 4 above. The aim is to try to be as open-minded, curious and painstaking with subsequent cases as you were with the first transcript. This means having to sort of forget what you heard during a previous interview and what you did with the data analytically.

Step 6: Looking for patterns across cases

Once we have a thematic Gestalt for each individual participant, the next step is to look for the structures or patterns for the group as a whole. This means looking for two things, both what the accounts seem to have in common and what makes them different. It will depend on the particular research question which of these will take priority for specific projects, but the most persuasive IPA work manages to represent both these qualities, that is, both the shared and the unique. A common theme is one which features in most – not necessarily all – of the participants' accounts (see Smith, 2011, for guidelines on thematic prevalence).

Step 7: Taking it deeper: Influences on interpretation

Interpretation is not a simple task with an obvious end-point. Instead, researchers can go to different levels or depths of interpretation, some more obvious than others, some more speculative than others. These can involve several iterations of steps 1 to 6 above, drawing on different interpretative resources and inspirations each time. This is an important part of how I use IPA for organisational research, so I see it as a core part of the method. It is at this stage that a deeper interpretative engagement can start to really make sense of the participant as a 'person-in-context' (Larkin et al., 2006). I will say more about this later in the chapter, and illustrate this step using data from my own research.

My case example

Introduction to the study

I will now use an example from my own research to illustrate the use of IPA in the real-world setting of organisational life. This example is taken from a project on 'working carers', a label which is often applied to those who combine paid employment with unpaid care-giving, usually for an elderly relative. With our ageing population, an increasing number of employees fall into this category. According to Carers UK,[1] every day another 6,000 people take

---

[1] www.carersuk.org/news-and-campaigns/press-releases/facts-and-figures

on a caring responsibility, with over three million people in the UK already combining work and care (roughly one in eight people in employment). So, if we want to understand people's experiences of organisational life, including the things that nurture or hinder their career development, this is increasingly going to mean exploring how they balance the demands of a career with those of domestic commitments other than childcare.

This project involved talking to working carers in the public sector in the UK. The organisations for which my participants work are considered progressive in that they offer special carers' leave (paid and unpaid) as part of a suite of 'family-friendly' policies. These progressive policies are extremely visible in their office buildings, in both public and private spaces and on intranet and external websites. My participants are involved in a range of caring relationships: most care for an ageing parent; one cares for a disabled (young adult) child; one cares for a disabled sibling; and one cares for a vulnerable friend. Despite these differences in caring relationships, I treated them as a homogenous cohort because of their *self*-definitions. All belong to a working carers' support group, and it was exclusively through this group that I recruited them for my study. This support group offers regular meetings, individual counselling and the opportunity for information-sharing, networking and getting one's voice heard.

Why was IPA the appropriate method to use?

There were several reasons for my choice of IPA for this project. I was specifically interested in the subjective experience of being a working carer, that is, what it is like to be a living, breathing, feeling human being in that situation, and how meaning might be derived from it. Very little research had been conducted into the experience of carers as a topic for *organisational* research (in contrast to the rich heritage of care research in nursing, e.g. Benner, 1994; and education, e.g. Noddings, 2003); so I felt it was important to pick an exploratory method that would support my genuine curiosity about what my participants were experiencing, rather than being constrained by assumptions about what I would find.

Experiential methods are relatively uncommon in organisational research. Researchers of organisational life have tended not to have the subjective human being as their central 'unit of analysis'. Indeed, Nord and Fox (1999) consider the individual employee to be the 'great disappearing act' in organisational research, and suggest that the 'baby' of agency, subjectivity and experience may have been thrown out with the 'bathwater' of essentialism and individualism. As an exploratory experiential method, IPA provided me with an excellent way to try to encourage the individual human being to reappear.

My choice of method was also directly related to my topic of care, which led me towards phenomenological methods in the Heideggerian tradition. For Heidegger (1927/1962), the fundamental human condition is being-in-the-world. This in-the-world-ness refers to engagement and concern rather than location, that is, to our enmeshment in the social, cultural and practical fabric of life. As Cooper (1996, p. 25) puts it, 'I am not in-the-world as a pea in a pod, but more in the sense that someone is in the world of motor-racing or fashion.' In this view, it is impossible to detach ourselves from our cultures and systems of meaning-making to see things 'as they really are'. Instead, the world is meaningful only from *within* those cultures and systems, that is, the meaning of a particular experience is inseparable from the *context* of that experience. At the heart of this vision of the contextualised, grounded, engaged human being lies Heidegger's depiction of care. Care is about *mattering* – being both of-concern and of-matter. It is fundamental to our very existence.

Applying the IPA approach

Here I will describe how I used IPA for data collection and initial analysis (steps 1 to 6) and then began to interpret my findings within a specifically organisational framework (step 7). The interpretative framework I used for step 7 was 'critical sense-making', an approach developed by Helms Mills et al. (2010). I will explain how and why I did this after I have gone through steps 1 to 6.

In saying that I used IPA for data collection and initial analysis and 'critical sense-making' for deeper interpretation, I do not want to imply a rigid divide between these phases of analysis, or to suggest that IPA cannot be used on its own for organisational research. Rather, I want to share my positive experience of IPA's procedural flexibility and hermeneutic orientation to suggest that it can be successfully combined with other theoretical frameworks to make sense of the context as well as the nature of people's experiences of their organisational worlds.

Data collection

For this project, I interviewed eight women between the ages of 48 and 62, representing a range of seniorities, from administrative through to middle management. The interviews were semi-structured, based on a schedule of questions I had developed in advance. There were some questions designed to tease out the 'What is/was it like?' of their experiences (the 'P'), and other questions designed to elicit the 'What does/did this mean?' and 'How do/did you make sense of that?' (the 'I'). An example of the first type is 'what is it like – or how does it feel – when you talk about your mother?' An example of the second type is 'How do you prioritise between doing things for your job and doing things for your mother?'

The interviews were held in a quiet place chosen by the participants themselves. Some preferred to have the interview conducted away from the workplace and invited me to their homes; others chose to be interviewed in a meeting room at work. I was aware of the possibility that participating in these interviews might evoke strong emotions, however sensitively I tried to frame the questions. Consequently, I began each interview by outlining the availability of counselling services upon which we could draw should we need to.

As you will probably be able to gauge from the extracts below, the interviews contained much that was intimate and painful. Two of the participants cried during their interview; two others discussed suicide; two discussed assisted suicide; and all of them seemed to struggle at times to hold it together. In all cases, my instinct was to try to comfort them myself – to the best of my ability – rather than bring any external counsellor into the encounter. All the participants insisted that they wished to continue when I asked them whether they would like to take a break or stop altogether. I was mindful of the need to leave participants 'whole' by the end of the research encounter, and tried to ensure with my final questions and discussion-points that they were not left feeling too drained by the experience. I felt this especially acutely for those women I interviewed during their lunch-break, because I was conscious that they would have to go straight back to work after their interview with me.

Data analysis
Interviews were audio-recorded and transcribed verbatim. For each interview transcript, I followed the standard analytic approach of creating two columns, one each side of the participant's transcribed text. The right-hand column was used to note points of semantic and linguistic interest, to log associations that the text threw up, and to start to unpack what I thought the participant was saying (step 2). I used the left-hand column to develop these initial notes into the basic building block of IPA, namely themes (step 3).

The next step was to look for connections and patterns amongst the themes in order to suggest some sort of shape or Gestalt to the findings, and to synthesise or crystallise them into a summary format (step 4). There are several typical ways of doing this (Figure 5.1), and each project may suggest new ones.

Abstraction	This is the most common technique, involving the development of higher-level or 'superordinate' themes which serve to cluster a number of individual themes under a singleheading –a bit like an umbrella.
Polarisation	This means structuring the themes according to the ways in which they are different from one another in a binary sense of 'on the one hand x; on the other hand y'. Polarisation is especially useful where there are both positive and negative aspects to an experience.
Contextualisation	This technique involves clustering themes around some sort of event or milestone, such as the onset or termination of a particular life experience. Such events might be concrete happenings, or they might be more subjective decision-points or moments that trigger some sort of psychological transition.
Function	This technique involves thinking about the role played by certain themes within the participant's account of an experience, such as how he/she is defending, accounting for, even undermining some aspect of the story.

Based on Smith et al. (2009).

Figure 5.1   Typical patterning techniques

Once I had developed an initial thematic Gestalt for each of the participants individually, I moved towards a cross-case analysis (steps 5 and 6). This involved looking for the patterns across all eight accounts, and developing a provisional thematic summary for the group as a whole.

Illustrative findings

I do not have the space in this chapter to present all the results of this analysis. Instead, I will focus on a particular sub-set of themes that seemed to concern participants' sense-making about identity. Since the concept of identity features strongly in the IPA corpus, it is perhaps not surprising that my analytic efforts were directed this way. Using the technique of abstraction, I initially developed a superordinate theme based on the notion of 'uncertainty about identity'. This was designed to reflect the oscillations of my participants' identity work – how they were weaving between different versions of who they were, who they had been, and who they wanted to be. It was as if the participants were trying out a range of different identities for size; no single identity was right all the time, but all felt right on different occasions.

Being a proper carer

One aspect of participants' 'uncertainty about identity' was their fear that they were not proper carers. I will illustrate this using an extract from Tessa's interview. Tessa is the primary carer for her brother, who was born with hydrocephalus ('water on the brain') and has profound learning and social difficulties. I should preface this extract with a reminder that all these participants had already labelled themselves as 'working carers' insofar as they were all active members of the working carers' support group, through which they had been recruited. So, on one level, Tessa does define herself in terms of care, with all its attendant associations. On another level, however, identification with care is a source of considerable uncertainty. Because she finds her brother difficult to handle, her identification as carer becomes problematic. Her sense-making involves probing the parameters for eligibility for identification, testing the plausibility of fit between the label and her sense of herself:

> Tessa: *I wish I could call myself 'carer' ...' cause that sounds a caring word! But sometimes he has driven me totally crazy! ... So caring is too nice ... That's why I think, am I a carer? Carer for me is ... a bigger ... It's a different word! What do you think? [addressing me] Am I a 'carer'? You have come across all sorts of people doing this. What do you think?*

Such ambivalence about identity has a number of psychological and material implications. If she could find a way to feel comfortable with the label, and allow herself to be classified as such by her organisation, then she would qualify for paid carers' leave, which would make it much easier for her to cope. However, there are a number of things getting in the way of identification with care. One of these – as Tessa's quote suggests – is the potency of our assumptions about what care *ought* to be, that is, what a proper carer is like. The normalised view of care involves very positive associations of kindness, gentleness, patience, etc., such as the view emerging from the care literature in nursing and education. For instance, Benner (1994) sees care as the translation of love from the private to the public domain; and Noddings (2003) considers care as the universal basis of morality. So, it is perhaps not surprising that these participants should have such a strong and positive sense of what care ought to look and feel like; and if they cannot always manage to be loving and kind and gentle, then they are not proper carers.

Within the familial context, there is a sense that being a proper carer is usually a daughterly role. If it cannot be daughterly, then it must be motherly. Either way, it must be asexual, that is, intimate only in the way that a medical nurse might be. For several of my participants, there are suggestions that these acceptable boundaries of intimacy are being breached; and when this happens, anxieties about being the right sort of carer are infused with anxieties about being the right sort of woman.

This is particularly marked with Elisabeth, who cares for a son – now in his early 20s – with myalgic encephalopathy (ME). The fact that she is caring for a child, not a parent, makes her brand of care feel especially challenging, because it is a distortion of the normal generational cycle, but also because it creates a relationship that feels too intimate:

> Elisabeth: *If you're looking after an elderly parent, you can expect to outlive them, can't you? But this is the rest of my life! The rest of my life! ... I don't know how I knew that word [carer], but I did ... because it was just so different from what you'd normally do for a 19-year-old ...*
>
> *And he owns me. It is a symbiotic relationship ... And it's wrong really, because he's my son! Sometimes I have thought about suicide ... Perhaps we might have to go together, a suicide pact type of thing. The Mill on the Floss, it ends with 'in their death, they were not divided', and that was a brother and sister ... So, 'in our deaths we will not be divided' ... It might end up just me and [her son] ... stuck together! Like glue! And it doesn't seem right that it should be that way round. He's my son! Not my husband!*

Elisabeth is deviating from the proper carer role not only because she is not always kind enough (like Tessa), but also because what she is doing feels wrong. In a sense, care is turning her into a *lover* rather than a mother – 'He's my son! Not my husband!' Indeed, her whole narrative is inflected with a strong sense of judgement and punishment, with both Elisabeth and her son serving a life sentence for some unspecified crime that has been committed. It is striking, for instance, how often his health deteriorates just when she is trying to enjoy some independence, such as going on honeymoon with her second husband. In a sense, she feels rebuked or punished for these attempts at independence, and for her confused sense of womanhood.

So, participants want to be able to identify as carers, because this would give them institutional and interpersonal recognition and help them to make sense of the ways in which their lives have been changed by care. However, the public discourses of care are so powerfully associated with goodness, purity and altruism that participants are perhaps bound to fall short of this ideal. When they do, it creates a sense of bewilderment over who they feel they are and what they feel they are doing with their lives.

Being a proper employee

But my participants' identity work is even more complex than this. It is not just the difficult relationship with discourses of care that fuels their uncertain sense of themselves. Their concerns are also linked to another version of what one ought to be, namely, what it means to be a proper employee. Indeed, their anxieties are exacerbated by the sense that the better they get as carers, the worse they will become as employees. Care is associated with the stigma of *absence*, whether literal absence or the absence of not being fully engaged ('presenteeism'). These participants all worry that people at work will think they are not pulling their weight, taking advantage of colleagues' and the organisation's goodwill.

For Tessa, anxieties about identification are linked to her wanting to avoid the charge of unreliability, but also specifically to the fear of the taint of mental illness, particularly if there is any hint that this might be self-inflicted. Her brother may have a physical disability, but it is exacerbated by his alcohol and drug abuse. For her, there is a pecking order for the care conditions that deserve sympathy and recognition from colleagues:

> Tessa: *It depends on what you are caring for ... Say you've got a disabled child ... or maybe a relative with cancer or ... somebody who's been in a car accident ... which wasn't self-imposed ... It just seems more ... on a scale of things that people accept ... As soon as you mention a problem with alcohol or drugs, it's not seen as accepted, maybe, as, say, spina bifida or I don't know ... There's a stigma, isn't there?*

Being a carer marks participants out as different from other people at work, and this difference is especially shameful if there is any hint of mental disorder or self-induced difficulty. So, if participants can distance themselves from identities of care, they can reconnect with identities of professionalism, reliability and sanity.

In this snapshot of my participants' data, I am trying to illustrate how multi-faceted their experiences of identity seem to be. Their uncertainties and anxieties concern both their carer-identity and their employee-identity, and the ways in which these seem bound to collide. Since much of this relates to the specific context of organisation, I wanted to explore how this context might be influencing and infusing their experience and to linger longer with the interpretative process (step 7). I will explain how and why in the next section.

Taking it deeper: using 'critical sense-making' for interpretative framing

Earlier I talked about the IPA research subject as a 'person-in-context'. Context in this sense is not an add-on which provides some kind of background colour. To revisit Cooper's (1996) imagery, context is not the pod from which a pea could be extracted and examined separately. Instead, context is inextricably interwoven with, and constitutive of, the experience itself; just as 'being in the world of fashion' can only be understood by reference to both the being and the fashion. So, researching the 'person-in-context' involves considering how that person is making sense of the practices, possibilities and expectations around them, including institutional and societal norms. This is a kind of context-of-ideas.

Another way of talking about this context-of-ideas is to use the notion of discourse and to connect, in particular, with the way discourse is developed by Foucault – a very influential figure in organisational scholarship. A Foucauldian definition of discourse refers to the way in which certain meanings, ideas and practices come together to produce a particular version of events or body-of-knowledge (see Burr, 2003, for alternative definitions of discourse in psychology). Within IPA research, what we are probably most interested in is the *effects* of such versions of events on participants' sense-making. This means examining experience not as something separate from its institutional setting, but, rather, as something shaped by that setting and absorbed into the person's sense of self.

It may strike readers as surprising that I am talking about discourse in a chapter about IPA, given that some people map the terrain of qualitative psychology in terms of an either/or choice between experiential and discursive methods (Reicher, 2000). In the world of work and organisation, however, our experiences are profoundly infused by popular and official conceptions of how things – and people – are supposed to be. It therefore enriches our interpretative work to be open to discourse as this context-of-ideas. This is not experience *versus* discourse, but, rather, experience *of* discourse; we are studying what it is like to live with several, potentially contradictory, versions of selfhood.

A set of discourses that are very familiar in organisational research relate to the concept of normality. Discourses of normality are interesting to organisational scholars, because they are seen as a form of power. This is not the kind of power that comes through positional, role-based authority such as having the job of CEO. Rather, this is a power that operates more surreptitiously, through the way that some versions of events have more sway than others, some ways of discussing things have greater traction than others, and some ways of being feel more natural and appropriate than others. Perhaps the most potent discourse of organisational normality involves the idea of the 'perfect employee'. Modern Western management theory has been dominated by metaphors of man and organisation as machines, so the 'perfect employee' is characterised by efficiency and reliability. It is no wonder that organisational scholars have remained relatively silent about feelings, bodies and any other kind of 'imperfection'.

Returning to my study, initially I kept my analysis at the level of 'uncertainty about identity', and developed my theoretical arguments using social identity theory (Ashforth and Mael, 1989; Tajfel, 1978). However, this theorisation did not feel as if it was capturing the oscillations, contradictions and ambivalences of my participants' identity work. In particular, I was not doing justice to the way in which participants benchmarked their identity against perceptions of normality. So, to make sense of this identity benchmarking, I looked for a way to frame a deeper interpretation and ground it in an organisational context. The framework I used was 'critical sense-making', an approach developed by Helms Mills et al. (2010), based on the work of Weick (1995). Weick proposes that organisational sense-making is a dynamic process of meaning-making whereby 'people create their environments as those environments create them' (Weick, 1995, p. 34). At the heart of 'critical sense-making' is the concept of identity, which has a number of key properties (Figure 5.2).

'Critical sense-making' directs a spotlight towards the power of discourses of normality to shape people's interpretations of their lives and their identities. These normalisations are not static, but shift across time and place. For instance, 50 years ago, the 'normal' corporate employee would have been male, supported by his 'normal' wife at home. Twenty years ago, the 'normal' corporate employee would have been office-based, whereas now many people work from home. Today's demographically 'normal' employee is increasingly

The experience of identity is...
Driven by plausibility, not accuracy
Context-specific
Interwoven with power relations
Ongoing, not static or definitive
Influenced by discourses of normality

Figure 5.2   Properties of 'critical sense-making'

one who has some form of caring responsibility. But the *discourses* of normality do not seem to be keeping pace with these *demographics* of normality, partly because the notion of the 'perfect employee' as full-time and single-mindedly, super-humanly dedicated to work is so obdurate.

I used this framework to structure my findings, reflecting two inter-related senses in which participants' versions of identity do not always gel (Figure 5.3). The first is a conflict between 'who I am supposed to be' and 'who I feel I am' (the 'versus' on the horizontal axis). The second is a conflict between the various different versions of 'who I am supposed to be' (the 'versus' on the vertical axis in column one).

The patterning approach I used for this was a version of the polarisation technique. Whereas polarisation can be applied to all sorts of oppositions (good versus bad; past versus present; mind versus body, etc.), here it emerges as a useful way of capturing the polarisation between what is and what ought to be. In other words, it can be used to reflect the ways in which the experience of identity is influenced by perceptions of normality. (For a more detailed discussion, see Tomkins and Eatough, 2014.)

Creating connections and conversations: Reflections on the polarisation technique as interpretative framing

This polarisation technique based on discourses of normality is, of course, just one possibility amongst many. It is certainly not the only way to make sense of identity data in an organisational context; indeed, researchers should not be so primed for it that they compromise IPA's inductive sensibility. However, it is an interpretative framing which facilitates both a rich engagement with the data and a connection with the ideas that have currency in organisational

Who I am supposed to be		Who I feel I am
A proper, normal carer is:	versus	*I am:*
Nice, kind, gentle, loving The right kind of woman		Not always nice, kind, gentle or loving The wrong kind of woman
Versus		
A proper, normal employee is:	versus	*I am:*
Reliable and steady Dissociated from mental illness		Stigmatised by absenteeism or 'presenteeism' Stigmatised by association with mental illness

Figure 5.3   Competing discourses of normality

research. As such, it helps me to dialogue with colleagues who are more familiar with Weick's sense-making and Foucault's discourse and power than with the tenets of phenomenology. Working with common ideas and translatable frameworks generates greater potential for cross-fertilisation of ideas, whilst staying true to IPA's concern to make sense of participants' life-worlds.

If we think of experience and discourse as mutually illuminating, rather than mutually exclusive, we have a route towards understanding the 'whole person'. Leading organisational scholars are calling for just such a 'whole person' approach, suggesting something of a rapprochement between the experiential and the discursive in organisational research. In a landmark paper on professional and organisational identities, Alvesson and Willmott (2002) discuss the connection between the efficacy of identity discourses and the intensity of their subjective meaning. For me, this is what researching the 'person-in-context' of organisational experience is all about.

I see the interplay between experience and discourse as fundamental to reflexivity, drawing on Wilkinson's model of personal, functional and disciplinary reflexivities (Wilkinson, 1988; Tomkins and Eatough, 2010). Personal reflexivity refers to the influence of the researcher's biography and interests on research, and is probably the definition with which researchers are most familiar. However, her functional and disciplinary reflexivities are equally significant for experiential research. Functional reflexivity considers the influence of the researcher's professional values, assumptions and biases; and disciplinary reflexivity refers to the effects of institutional, social and cultural ideas on research. In other words, reflexivity involves attending to the ways in which ideas – particularly those that make up the popular and accepted versions of events – influence both our participants' data and our interpretations of those data.

This approach also connects with other methods in the phenomenological family. For instance, Ashworth (2003) considers discourse as one of the phenomenological structures of the life-world. Van Manen (1990) emphasises the power of language to generate meaning, and suggests we pay particular attention to ideas with taken-for-granted status. Langdridge (2007) considers the narratives with which participants construct and inhabit their life-worlds, including 'canonical narratives' of how things are supposed to be. Like IPA, all three of these approaches bear the hallmarks of Heideggerian philosophy, in which discourse is interwoven with understanding, attunement and absorption as ways of approaching the fundamental question of Being (Heidegger, 1927/1962).

Ultimately, though, it is for practical rather than philosophical reasons that I get excited about using IPA to explore the experience of discourse. A huge amount of our lives is lived within the context of institutions, including schools, universities, hospitals and governments, as well as the corporations we tend to think of when we use the term 'organisation'. So it feels important to try to understand the effects of these institutions – and the discourses that animate them – on our sense of who we are, who we might become, and what constrains or liberates such projects of being.

References

Alvesson, M. and Willmott, H. (2002). Identity regulation as organizational control: Producing the appropriate individual. *Journal of Management Studies*, 39(5), 619–644.

Ashforth, B.E. and Mael, F. (1989). Social identity theory and the organization. *Academy of Management Review*, 14(1), 20–39.

Ashworth, P. (2003). An approach to phenomenological psychology: The contingencies of the lifeworld. *Journal of Phenomenological Psychology*, 34(2), 145–156.

Benner, P. (1994). *Interpretive Phenomenology: Embodiment, Caring and Ethics in Health and Illness*. Thousand Oaks, CA: SAGE.

Burr, V. (2003). *Social Constructionism*. Hove: Routledge.

Cooper, D.E. (1996). *Thinkers of Our Time: Heidegger*. London: The Claridge Press.

Heidegger, M. (1927/1962). *Being and Time* (J. Macquarrie and E. Robinson trans.). Oxford: Blackwell.

Helms Mills, J., Thurlow, A. and Mills, A.J. (2010). Making sense of the sensemaking: The critical sensemaking approach. *Qualitative Research in Organizations and Management*, 5(2), 182–195.

Langdridge, D. (2007). *Phenomenological Psychology: Theory, Research and Method*. Harlow: Pearson.

Larkin, M., Watts, S. and Clifton, E. (2006). Giving voice and making sense in interpretative phenomenological analysis. *Qualitative Research in Psychology*, 3(2), 102–120.

Noddings, N. (2003). *Caring: A Feminine Approach to Ethics and Moral Education*. Berkeley: University of California Press.

Nord, W.R. and Fox, S. (1999). The individual in organizational studies: The great disappearing act? In S.R. Clegg and C. Hardy (Eds.), *Studying Organization: Theory and Method*. Thousand Oaks, CA: SAGE, pp. 142–169.

Reicher, S. (2000). Against methodolatry: Some comments on Elliott, Fischer, and Rennie. *British Journal of Clinical Psychology*, 39(1), 1–6.

Smith, J.A. (2011). Evaluating the contribution of interpretative phenomenological analysis. *Health Psychology Review*, 5(1), 9–27.

Smith, J.A., Flowers, P. and Larkin, M. (2009). *Interpretative Phenomenological Analysis: Theory, Method and Research*. London: SAGE.

Tajfel, H. (1978). Social categorization, social identity and social comparison. In H. Tajfel (Ed.), *Differentiation Between Social Groups: Studies in the Social Psychology of Intergroup Relations*. London: Academic Press, pp. 27–60.

Tomkins, L. and Eatough, V. (2010). Towards an integrative reflexivity in organizational research. *Qualitative Research in Organizations and Management*, 5(2), 162–181.

Tomkins, L. and Eatough, V. (2014). Stop 'helping' me! Identity, recognition and agency in the nexus of work and care. *Organization*, 21(1), 3–21.

van Manen, M. (1990). *Researching Lived Experience: Human Science for an Action Sensitive Pedagogy*. Albany, NY: SUNY Press.

Weick, K.E. (1995). *Sensemaking in Organizations*. Thousand Oaks, CA: SAGE.

Wilkinson, S. (1988). The role of reflexivity in feminist psychology. *Women's Studies International Forum*, 11(5), 493–502.

Participatory Methods in Research with Children: The Scripted Cartoons Narrative of Bullying (SCAN) Drawings Method

Helen Cowie and Dawn Jennifer

Introduction: Participatory methods

For over 15 years, there has been a growing concern amongst some research-ers (e.g. Alderson, 2008; Birbeck and Drummond, 2007; Christensen and James, 2008; Cowie et al., 2014; Harcourt and Einarsdottir, 2011; Mayall, 2008; Veale, 2005) to capture the unique voices of children and young people. This approach has a wider brief since it also encompasses efforts on the part of researchers to give voice to people who, in a variety of ways, are disempow-ered. A key concept here is a belief in the competency of children to construct their own meanings. The challenge for the researcher is to design tools to facilitate the expression of that voice. As Jennifer and Cowie (2012) indicate, researchers need to think carefully about designing methods that appeal to children and young people by using materials that are typically used in their everyday lives, for example, through drawings or play (for pre-schoolers), through cartoons (for primary school children) or through cameras and inter-net communication (for adolescents).

The influential multi-method Mosaic Approach (Clark, 2011; Clark and Moss, 2005) creates playful methods to access the child's everyday experience. To this end, the researchers try to listen and learn from the children. For example, they do group conferences, give children cameras to record their everyday lived experience and encourage children to create maps of their environment through photos and drawings. Huser (2010) used drawing, as a typical activity in kindergarten, to explore how pre-schoolers experience their favourite play episode with a friend; here the children were invited to express their meanings through their drawings. Other participatory researchers have designed methods that are appropriate for older children and adolescents. Kernaghan and Elwood (2013) established a young participants' Research Advisory Group (RAG) to monitor their research into cyberbullying. The RAG offered illuminating insights into issues of communication, recruitment and interpretation. Researchers have also developed methods that show sensitivity to the particular emotional needs of participants. Veale (2005) used participatory methods (social mapping, story games, drawings and drama) in rural Rwanda post-genocide to explore the impact of violence on social relations as it impacted on children. These methods were chosen as they would avoid asking children for their personal story, and ownership and control of the material generated rested with the participants. Children's workshops used activities that children engage in spontaneously, such as storytelling and drawing.

There are critical ethical issues associated with this approach. Research must be designed and conducted to give children real choices about participation and to ensure that their views, perceptions and experiences are properly captured (Masson, 2004). Jennifer (2007) involved the junior school children in her research by inviting them to critique the informed consent letters. The researcher found that they had strong views on the layout, colour and typeset of such documents and that they provided useful ideas on how to ensure that children were appropriately informed of their right to participate as well as their right to withdraw at any stage in the research process. In the case of very young children and vulnerable groups, there is even more need for child-friendly forms of gaining consent. Huser (2010) responded to pre-school children's wish to receive their own letter (parents had signed a participation letter before) to be read out to them which they could sign by drawing themselves if they could not write their names. Simultaneously she identified the need to recognise children's non-verbal messages throughout the research process if they wanted to withdraw, for example, if a child turned away, stopped the research activity or changed the subject under discussion.

It is essential to be sensitive to the child's competencies, especially if the participant child or adolescent has limited verbal and literacy skills. Of course, children are usually protected by adult gatekeepers in that parents, carers, teachers, youth workers and any adult in authority are usually able to decide whether or not the young person takes part, so that the researcher can never access children or young people directly. However, this can pose problems because the gatekeeper may prohibit the young person's involvement during the initial recruitment stage. Additionally, adults as gatekeepers can withhold permission for children to participate thus denying them the opportunity to take part if they wish. So overprotection can undermine the concept of children's rights where adults are defensive about what the child might reveal (see, for example, Birbeck and Drummond, 2007; Cowie et al., 2014; Kjørholt et al., 2005).

Doing participatory methods

Using vignettes and cartoons to access the perceptions and experiences of children: the Scripted Cartoons Narrative of Bullying (SCAN) drawings method

A number of researchers have used pictorial vignettes as a child-friendly way of gaining access to the thoughts and feelings of children about sensitive topics. For example, Ttofi and Farrington (2008) asked children aged 10 to 12 years questions about the emotions they felt if they were in the position of the child in a series of pictorial vignettes. The researchers were able to discover the complexity of emotions experienced by bystanders in bullying situations, including anger, shame, remorse or guilt. They also found that the social context in which bullying takes place has a powerful impact on how the bystanders react, whether they intervene to help the victim or actively support the bullies. The use of the cartoon characters in the vignettes appeared to free the children to explore difficult emotions in more detail than they would have done through direct questioning about their own behaviour in such situations.

In this chapter, we focus on the use of pictorial vignettes, adapted from the SCAN method (Almeida et al., 2001; del Barrio et al., 2003), as a way of accessing primary school children's feelings, experiences and perspectives of peer bullying. The method is intended to be flexible and modifications may be necessary to allow for such factors as culture and gender. Here the pictorial vignettes were adapted and modified for a UK sample from the SCAN drawings developed in Portugal and Spain (see Figure 6.2 for an example). The vignettes were redesigned by a young art student to reflect the UK sample in terms of: primary school age, ethnic diversity and primary school culture (i.e. the wearing of school uniform).

The intention of the story illustrated by the drawings is to convey the idea of an imbalance of power and repeated aggressive behaviours such that the interpretation of the story is in terms of intentional and hurtful actions, rather than isolated or irregular events. The set of 14 A4-size drawings includes one neutral vignette, followed by nine vignettes (depicting mean and unpleasant behaviours) performed by one individual or by a group of peers (see Figure 6.3 for an example). A short caption describing the content of the vignette is included with each (e.g. 'She sees the other children playing a game and wants to join in'; see Figure 6.1 for a summary). The remaining four vignettes complete the set of drawings, each representing a different outcome to the story in terms of distinct roles taken by adults and peers (optimistic: the children all play together; pessimistic: the victim remains alone; peer social support: the victim seeks the support of a peer; and adult social support: the victim seeks the support of an adult). A masculine and a feminine version of the same story are used for males and females, respectively. Where necessary, captions are rewritten to address anomalies arising from translation into English, and

Behaviour	Caption
1. Neutral	A new boy or girl arrives at school on his or her first day observed by a group of peers.
2. Social exclusion	The new boy or girl looks on while a group of peers play together.
3. Teasing	A group of peers laugh and point at the new boy or girl's clothes.
4. Physical obstruction	A peer blocks the door to prevent the new boy or girl from leaving the room.
5. Attack on personal possessions	A group of peers takes the new boy or girl's bag and pulls out his or her books.
6. Real damage to personal possessions	The new boy or girl's book is destroyed; a peer with a pair of scissors in his or hand stands nearby.
7. Group physical attack	The new boy or girl has fallen on the floor and is surrounded by his/her books; the group of peers look on.
8. Coercion	The group of peers force the new boy or girl to smoke.
9. Blackmail	The peer group physically threaten the new boy or girl to carry out their orders.
10. Social isolation	The new boy or girl looks at the group of peers from a distance.

Figure 6.1   Content of the Ten Pictorial Vignettes

to incorporate idiomatic vocabulary; for example, in vignette 5, 'recess' was changed to 'playtime'; and in vignette 7, 'ground' was changed to 'floor'.

To assess the modifications to the vignettes, pre-test interviews were carried out with 12 participants from the main sample. The majority of these participants (82 per cent) described the nature of the relationship as bullying. The remainder described the behaviours as aggression, without explicitly mentioning bullying. This was the intended outcome and supported the effectiveness of vignettes to study children's constructions of bullying in school (Ojala and Nesdale, 2004). The data from the pre-test interviews was analysed along with the data from the main study.

Below we provide guidelines for implementing SCAN as a way of accessing primary school children's feelings, experiences and perspectives of peer bullying.

1. This girl is new to the school and it is her first day.

Figure 6.2   An example of one of the original SCAN bullying cartoons
(Almeida et al., 2001)

1. This girl is new to the school and it's her first day

Figure 6.3   An example of one of the pictorial vignettes used in our study
(female version)

1. During presentation of the vignettes, participants are interviewed using a semi-structured interview schedule devised to capture children's knowledge and reasoning about bullying in school (del Barrio et al., 2003).
2. Each participant is asked questions about narrative and causal attributions (e.g. 'After looking carefully at the drawings, what would you say is happening in the story, from the beginning to the end?'; 'What do you think is happening with this girl/boy? [pointing to one character in two or three different drawings, then another character]').
3. Then participants are asked about moral emotional attributions (worry, shame, indifference, pride) to the characters in the story (e.g. 'Can anyone in this story feel ashamed? Why?'), moral emotional attributions to self in the role of the characters (e.g. 'And if you were one of these boys/girls could you also feel ashamed? [pointing to the characters in turn]. Why?') and coping strategies.
4. Interview questions are rewritten to incorporate idiomatic vocabulary where necessary.
5. In addition, in consideration of bullying from a wider social group context, questions relating to the role of characters other than the bully and the victim are included in the interview schedule. (The full interview schedule can be obtained from the second author on request.)

Our case example

Introduction to the study

The broad aim of the research was to engage children meaningfully as active participants in the research process in order to explore their understanding of bullying in primary school in their own voices. Participants, aged 10 to 11, were drawn from the Year 6 classes of two primary schools in a borough of south-west London, one a voluntary-aided faith school, the other a state school. Following parental permission to approach their child, all pupils from Year 6 were invited to participate in the programme of research. The final sample consisted of 30 males (47 per cent) and 34 females.

Why was SCAN the appropriate method to use?

As we discussed in the first section of this chapter, there are particular methodological and ethical challenges associated with exploring the experiences of children. There are ethical issues especially in the context of the power imbalance between the adult researcher and the child participant. Furthermore, it is essential for the researcher to take account of the vulnerability of the young participants and to ensure that they are not emotionally damaged by taking part. This is particularly the case when interviewing children about bullying since, as we know, the experience can be deeply distressing for the child, whether as target, perpetrator or bystander. The researcher needs to have sensitive awareness of the subtle balance between protecting the child on the one hand and enabling that child's voice to be heard on the other. This involves a genuine engagement with the young participant and the demonstration by the researcher that he/she is prepared to work to the strengths of the children by listening and learning from them. Thus the researcher must adopt an authentically enquiring stance. SCAN is appropriate because it capitalises on participants' strengths thereby allowing children with different competencies and preferences to take part in research (Clark, 2004). SCAN can be used to work with children of different ages, abilities and literacy levels, and can be adapted to suit different languages and cultures (O'Kane, 2000), such that any child can make a valid and meaningful contribution to the research.

For those children who have limited experience of direct communication with an unfamiliar adult in a formal interview situation, and who might find the experience intimidating, the use of SCAN helps create a relaxed atmosphere, and rapport, which is likely to increase participants' confidence (Punch, 2002) and, ultimately, the value of the research in terms of validity and reliability (Thomas and O'Kane, 2000). Furthermore, SCAN provides a useful method for discussing school bullying with children since the method shifts the focus away from face-to-face discussions that can involve intrusive eye contact to the task, thereby creating a comfortable distance between the researcher and the participant, which facilitates a non-threatening environment. Indeed, the method provides a safe context within which young participants can produce an account of the events portrayed, which combines previous personal knowledge and experience with the narrative elements of the hypothetical story. It is much less threatening for participants to talk about peer bullying scenarios that they can personally relate to rather than being asked directly about bullying in their school.

In addition, SCAN provides children with space and time to think about what they want to express, and to talk freely about issues that concern them, without creating pressure for them to respond quickly with the 'correct' answer (Punch, 2002). It is also possible that the use of SCAN helps to minimise the power differential between adult researcher and child participant (Kellet and Ding, 2004).

Applying SCAN

Here we will describe how we collected data with SCAN and how we used the narrative material in our analysis, highlighting some of the lessons we learned.

Data collection with SCAN

Semi-structured interviews were conducted during lesson time by the second author, each lasting approximately 20 minutes. Each interview commenced with standardised instructions regarding the general nature of the interview, confidentiality, anonymity and the right to withdraw, and ended with a debriefing, including resources for outside support should the need arise. With the agreement of all participants, audio tape recordings were collected for later transcription.

The first ten drawings, which conveyed temporal and space continuity for the various mean and unpleasant behaviours, were laid out on a table one by one, in ascending order (see Figure 6.1). The researcher did not enter into discussion with participants regarding the script headings. If any doubts were expressed by the participant, the researcher avoided personal interpretation; rather children were probed about what they thought might be happening in the particular drawing. At no point did the interviewer introduce the terms 'bullying', 'aggression', 'victim', 'bully/ies', 'bystander' or 'follower'. Following presentation of the drawings, participants were interviewed using a semi-structured interview schedule. The final stage of the interview required the presentation of the four story outcomes, which were displayed in a randomised order to control for order of presentation effects. Each participant was asked to state how they thought the hypothetical story would probably end.

Analysis of SCAN data

Audio tape recordings were transcribed verbatim and analysis of the interview transcripts was carried out using a qualitative approach to content analysis as described by Millward (2000) and Woods et al. (2002) (see Jennifer and Cowie, 2012, for more information). To capture the richness and complexity of what the children were telling us with regard to their understanding of interpersonal relationships, peer processes and involvement in bullying, detailed cases studies for six of the interviews were carried out using an adapted version of the voice-centred relational method (Brown and Gilligan, 1992). With its emphasis on human relationships, the voice-centred relational method was attractive as it recognised the importance of the social context in which bullying takes place and provided a basis for thinking about peer bullying in school as a relational issue. As Brown et al. (1989) acknowledge, very few individuals experience moral conflict in a vacuum; rather, people function in an ongoing context of relationship.

The analysis revolved around a set of four readings of each interview transcript, in some cases while listening to the audio tape recording simultaneously. For the first reading, transcripts were read for a general understanding of what the participant was saying, to identify the main events, the protagonists and the sub-plots, and for our reflexive response to the narrative. The second reading focused upon the voice of the self, the 'I', represented in the account including self in the role of the victim, bully and assistant. In the third and fourth readings, we listened to how participants spoke about their experiences of bullying in school in terms of their interpersonal relationships with others within the school setting. Specifically, the third reading focused upon concerns of care, responsibilities, interdependence and connection, whereas the fourth reading focused upon concerns of justice, rights, independence and autonomy.

The latter three readings involved a three-step process. First, coloured crayons were used to trace and underline certain statements in the transcripts that represented each reading, that is, the voices of the self (green), care (red) and justice (blue). Second, after reading and underlining for self, care and justice concerns, summary worksheets were completed, which documented participants' voices in one column and our interpretative summaries in the other. Finally, based on the readings, case studies were compiled for each participant. Since time restrictions meant it was impossible to apply this method of analysis to all interviews, our attention was concentrated on six cases (three males; three females), the selection of which was based on a number of criteria. These included interviews that were deemed stimulating or challenging; interviews that seemed to illuminate the research aims; and interviews that provided a contrasting account to a previous participant (Mauthner and Doucet, 1998). To protect participant confidentiality and maintain anonymity each case was assigned a pseudonym: Annie, Mustafa, Karin, Alistair, Freema and Henry.

Illustrative findings

This section focuses on illustrative findings related to the case studies as described above. The analysis revealed that participants used moral language in their explanations and justifications for school bullying, making rich and insightful comments about the complexity of interpersonal relationships and peer processes in relation to involvement in bullying others. Central to the task of exploring these understandings of school bullying was the distinction between two relational perspectives or moral orientations, that is, concerns of care (attachment/detachment, connection/disconnection) and justice (equality, reciprocity, fairness).

In reading for interpersonal relationships in terms of care concerns, core themes were evident in the case studies, such as awareness of the harm caused by bullying behaviours and awareness of issues regarding peer attachments and friendships in relation to bullying behaviour. All accounts drew attention, to varying degrees, to the negative emotional effects of bullying on the victim's health and wellbeing (e.g. anger, fear, worry, shame, sadness, unhappiness). In addition, Annie's, Mustafa's, Karin's and Henry's accounts highlighted the negative psychological effects (e.g. lowered self-esteem, sleeping difficulties, crying, hopelessness, loneliness), and Karin's and Alistair's accounts called attention to negative physical effects (e.g. bodily harm). All accounts drew attention to the hierarchical structure of the bully group, with participants identifying one or two leader bullies aided by assistants and/or followers/reinforcers. Annie's and Karin's accounts drew attention to the bullies' manipulation of interpersonal relationships within the peer group (e.g. deciding who is or is not a member of the 'popular' group; not allowing the follower to befriend the new girl). Freema, Karin and Alistair characterised the follower/ reinforcer as minimally involved, while providing support and encouragement to the bullies.

All but Mustafa's account drew attention to the nature of attachments and interpersonal relationships among individuals in the group in terms of the arousal of positive feelings associated with being part of the popular group (Annie), protection from exclusion from the bully group (Annie, Freema), maintenance of friendships with the bullies (Henry) and protection from becoming the bullies' next target (Freema). With regard to the nature of the follower/reinforcer character's attachment to the group, accounts focused on maintenance of friendships with the bullies (Karin, Henry), 'fitting in' with the bullies (Henry), protection from becoming the bullies' next target (Freema, Henry) and protection from exclusion from the bully group (Freema). In addition, both Annie's and Freema's accounts highlighted the ambivalence of the assistant's involvement in bullying others in terms of their participation as a means of protection from exclusion from the group.

Reading for interpersonal relationships in respect of justice concerns drew attention to the notion of bullying behaviour as a violation of fairness, bullying as a transgression of morally acceptable standards of behaviour and justification for bullying. All but Mustafa's account drew notice to bullying as a violation of fairness, whereby the bullies were perceived as taking advantage of perceived inequalities in terms of individual differences (e.g. appearance) or perceived status differences (e.g. 'geeky' versus 'popular' children, newcomers versus established pupils). Further evidence of an awareness and understanding that bullying involves a power imbalance in favour of the bully was found in Mustafa's, Freema's, Karin's and Henry's accounts, which highlighted the notion that the bullies had transgressed the social norms of morally acceptable standards of behaviour, in terms of using threatening, coercive, oppressive and dominating behaviours. Freema's, Mustafa's and Alistair's accounts highlighted justification and support for bullying from the bullies' perspective under a number of conditions. These included responding to provocation from the victim (Freema, Alistair); when the bully was in a position of power and authority (Alistair); when the bullying behaviour was considered minor (e.g. 'not like the worst you can do', Alistair); when the bully remained uncaught and unpunished (Alistair); and 'because the bullies never had a good life' (Mustafa).

Reading for both justice and care orientations clarified the logic of participants' moral thinking. On several occasions, responses that may have appeared morally doubtful when solely viewed from a justice perspective reflected sophisticated social observations regarding involvement in school bullying when analysed from a care perspective. For example, the notion, evident in Annie's and Freema's accounts, that the assistant bullies were only minimally involved in bullying the new girl compared with the perception that such involvement was as a means of self-protection against victimisation from the leader bully (Freema) or from exclusion from the group (Annie, Freema).

While research has begun to focus on the influence of the social group context on the experience of school bullying, in particular the extent of individuals' participation in the process, the present analysis both complements and extends this work by revealing how children themselves think about how and why children become involved in bullying others. The accounts vividly illustrate that children do not face or resolve school bullying in a vacuum. Rather, the ways in which children understand and construct school bullying and their means of facing and addressing conflict in their interpersonal relationships are fluid and complex with children negotiating their involvement from within an ongoing context of peer relations.

Reflections on participatory methods such as SCAN

Participatory methods offer an innovative way of accessing the inner worlds of children and young people in ways that traditional approaches often fail to do. As shown in our case study, SCAN gives participants the opportunity to discuss both their personal experiences of bullying and other types of bullying that they may not have directly experienced, which may have remained undisclosed using traditional methods of data collection. The task, which requires the participant to take the role of the protagonists, provides some emotional distance from the scenario, which on occasions can facilitate the disclosure of a wider range of perspectives that children have about the phenomenon than traditional methods of data collection. Furthermore, the method offers children the opportunity to speak for themselves and engages children as active participants in the research process. Participants in SCAN expressed enthusiasm regarding the use of the pictorial vignettes and were eager to participate in data collection. They were able to identify with the drawings and relate to the characters portrayed in the pictorial vignettes, which resulted in rich and illuminating data which furthered our understanding of the phenomenon from the child's perspective. The safety of the narrative task enabled some participants to disclose their personal experiences of being bullied and bullying others in primary school, a potentially sensitive topic.

Of course there are limitations to such an approach. Participants' responses are about how they believe they would feel or act in a hypothetical bullying situation and, as such, may not accurately reflect how they would behave in actuality. Additionally, masculine/feminine versions of the pictorial vignettes may not always allow for the notion of mixed gender bullying identified in the literature. Future research may want to take into account scenarios depicting mixed gender bullying. The types of bullying behaviours portrayed in the pictorial vignettes only allowed for face-to-face bullying that occurred within the school premises. Future researchers may want to take into account cyberbullying.

Participatory methods have yet to be fully accepted by mainstream journals. Data can appear to be unsystematic or even chaotic. There is a need to develop sophisticated research methods that are participatory in spirit yet at the same time are rigorous in their application, not least because this approach has such potential for enabling unheard voices to be expressed, including those of children with disabilities, communication difficulties, severe illnesses or those living in poverty and deprivation. We hope that the SCAN method demonstrates that active participation by children and well-designed analyses are not incompatible.

Acknowledgements

The authors would like to thank the children and schools who took part, Lauren Doss for preparing the pictorial vignettes and Ana Almeida for kindly allowing the use of the SCAN. The authors and publisher would also like to thank Springer Science+Business Media New York for permission to reproduce Figure 6.2, originally published in M. Bach (ed.) (2001), *Prevention and Control of Aggression and the Impact on its Victims*.

References

Alderson, P. (2008). Children as researchers: Participation rights and research methods. In P. Christensen and A. James (Eds.), *Research with Children. Perspectives and Practices (Second Edition)*. New York and London: Routledge, Taylor and Francis, pp. 276–290.

Almeida, A., del Barrio, C., Marques, M., Gutierrez, H. and van der Meulen, K. (2001). A script-cartoon narrative of bullying in children and adolescents: A research tool to assess cognitions, emotions and coping strategies in bullying situations. In M. Martinez (Ed.), *Prevention and Control of Aggression and the Impact on Its Victims*. New York: Kluwer Academic/Plenum Publishers, pp. 161–168.

Birbeck, D.J. and Drummond, M.J.N. (2007). Research with young children: Contemplating methods and ethics. *Journal of Educational Enquiry*, 7(2), 21–29.

Brown, L.M. and Gilligan, C. (1992). *Meeting at the Crossroads: Women's Psychology and Girls' Development*. Cambridge, MA: Harvard University Press.

Brown, L.M., Tappan, M.B., Gilligan, C., Miller, B.A. and Argyris, D.E. (1989). Reading for self and moral voice: A method for interpreting narratives of real-life moral conflict and choice. In M.J. Packer and R.B. Addison (Eds.), *Entering the Circle: Hermeneutic Investigation in Psychology*. Albany, NY: State University of New York Press, pp. 141–164.

Christensen, P. and James, A. (Eds.) (2008). *Research with Children: Perspectives and Practices (Second Edition)*. New York: Routledge.

Clark, A. (2004). The Mosaic approach and research with young children. In V. Lewis, M. Kellett, C. Robinson, S. Fraser and S. Ding (Eds.), *The Reality of Research with Children and Young People*. London: SAGE, pp. 142–156.

Clark, A. (2011). Breaking methodological boundaries? Exploring visual, participatory methods with adults and young children. *European Early Childhood Education Research Journal*, 19(3), 321–330.

Clark, A. and Moss, P. (2005). *Spaces to Play: More Listening to Young Children Using the Mosaic Approach*. London: National Children's Bureau.

Cowie, H., Huser, C. and Myers, C.A. (2014). The use of participatory methods in researching the experiences of children and young people, *Croatian Journal of Education*, 16, 51–56.

del Barrio, C., Almeida, A., van der Meulen, K., Barrios, Á. and Gutiérrez, H. (2003). Representaciones acerca del maltrato entre iguales, atribuciones emocionales y percepción de estrategias de cambio a partir de un instrumento narrativo: SCAN-Bullying. *Infancia y Aprendizaje*, 26(1), 63–78.

Harcourt, D. and Einarsdottir, J. (2011). Introducing children's perspectives and participation in research. *European Early Childhood Education Research Journal*, 19(3), 301–307.

Huser, C. (2010). Children's voices on play in a Mosaic approach study: Children as conscious participants in a case study. *Boğaziçi University Journal of Education*, 26(1), 35–48.

Jennifer, D. (2007). Understanding bullying in primary school: Listening to children's voices. Unpublished PhD thesis, University of Surrey. Retrieved from www.epubs.surrey.ac.uk/652/.

Jennifer, D. and Cowie, H. (2012). Listening to children's voices: Moral emotional attributions in relation to primary school bullying. *Emotional and Behavioural Difficulties*, 17(3–4), 229–241.

Kellett, M. and Ding, S. (2004). Middle childhood. In S. Fraser, V. Lewis, S. Ding, M. Kellett and C. Robinson (Eds.). *Doing Research with Children and Young People*. London, SAGE, pp. 161–174.

Kernaghan, D. and Elwood, J. (2013). All the cyber world's a stage: Framing cyberbullying as performance. *Journal of Psychosocial Research on Cyberspace*, 7(1), doi:10.5817/CP2013-1-5.

Kjørholt, A.T., Moss, P. and Clark, A. (2005). Beyond listening: Future prospects. In A. Clark, A.T. Kjørholt and P. Moss (Eds.), *Beyond Listening*. Bristol, UK: The Policy Press, pp. 175–188.

Masson, J. (2004). The legal context. In S. Fraser, V. Lewis, S. Ding, M. Kellett and C. Robinson (Eds.), *Doing Research with Children and Young People*. London: SAGE, pp. 43–58.

Mauthner, N. and Doucet, A. (1998). Reflections on a voice-centred relational method: Analysing maternal and domestic voices. In. J. Ribbens and R. Edwards (Eds.) *Feminist Dilemmas in Qualitative Research: Public Knowledge and Private Lives*. London: SAGE, pp. 117–146.

Mayall, B. (2008). Conversations with children: Working with generational issues. In P. Christensen and A. James (Eds.), *Research with Children. Perspectives and Practices (Second Edition)*. New York and London: Routledge, Taylor and Francis, pp. 109–124.

Millward, L. (2000). Focus groups. In. G.M. Breakwell, S. Hammond and C. Fife-Schaw (Eds.), *Research Methods in Psychology*. London: SAGE, pp. 303–324.

O'Kane, C. (2000). The development of participatory techniques. In P. Christensen and A. James (Eds.), *Research with Children*. London: Routledge, Falmer, pp. 136–159.

Ojala, K. and Nesdale, D. (2004). Bullying and social identity: The effects of group norms and distinctiveness threat on attitudes towards bullying. *British Journal of Developmental Psychology*, 22, 19–35.

Punch, S. (2002). Research with children: The same or different from research with adults? *Childhood*, 9(3), 321–341.

Thomas, N. and O'Kane, C. (2000). Discovering what children think: Connections between research and practice. *British Journal of Social Work*, 30, 819–835.

Ttofi, M.M. and Farrington, D.P. (2008). Reintegrative shaming theory, moral emotions and bullying. *Aggressive Behavior*, 34(4), 352–368.

Veale, A. (2005). Creative methodologies in participatory research with children. In S. Greene and D. Hogan (Eds.), *Researching Children's Experience: Approaches and Methods*. London, Thousand Oaks, CA and New Delhi: SAGE, pp. 253–272.

Woods, L., Priest, H. and Roberts, R. (2002). An overview of three different approaches to the interpretation of qualitative data: Part 2: Practical illustrations. *Nurse Researcher*, 10(2), 43–51.

Using Interpretative Phenomenological Analysis in Conjunction with the Think Aloud Technique to Examine Experience of Living with Disfiguring Conditions with a View to Developing Psychosocial Interventions

Andrew Thompson

Introduction

I will begin this chapter by presenting an overview of the field of clinical psychology and introduce some of the particular issues and the historical contextual factors that have influenced the use of qualitative research methods generally in this field of applied psychology. I will then go on to describe how two individual qualitative approaches that are both useful in their own right can be combined to assist in the development of psychosocial interventions. Specifically I will describe how interpretative phenomenological analysis (IPA) can be paired with thematic analysis drawing on two sequential methods of data collection (semi-structured interviewing and an adapted think aloud protocol and interview method). I will describe and show worked examples of the coding process, and explain how this combined approach can provide both a greater understanding of what it is like to live with specific conditions affecting visible appearance as well as usefully gaining participants' perspectives on new psychosocial interventions.

Clinical psychology and qualitative methods

Clinical psychology is a branch of applied psychology that is concerned with carrying out research that forwards the understanding of psychological functioning in such a way that the resulting psychological theory and knowledge can be ultimately used in practice to promote wellbeing and to reduce psychological distress. The use of the title 'clinical psychologist' is protected by law in the UK and is one of the applied psychological professions that requires registration with the Health and Care Professions Council (HCPC: see www.hcpc-uk.org.uk/). Similar forms of registration are required to practise clinical psychology in most countries, although the route to, and the level of, qualification can differ substantially between countries (Llewelyn and Murphy, 2014).

In the UK, the profession of clinical psychology has grown and developed almost entirely within the National Health Service (NHS), and this makes it unique in many ways from both other branches of applied psychology and clinical psychology in other countries (Llewelyn and Murphy, 2014). Clinical psychology's development within the context of the NHS has meant that the discipline has been greatly influenced by the health care sciences (particularly medicine) and also by the evidence-based practice movement (Harper, 2008). That said the profession has also sought to distinguish its identity and approach to treating distress via focusing on an individual approach to the formulation of psychological wellbeing whilst recognising the role played by wider contextual factors (see British Psychological Society, 2013, 2014).

Despite qualitative methods having a long history in relation to the development of psychotherapy, the profession has been widely acknowledged to be relatively late in engaging with qualitative research. This slowness has been suggested by a number of people to have partly arisen as a result of the professions alignment with the scientist-practitioner model (Harper, 2008; Willott and Larkin, 2012). This model is entwined with the health care evidence-based practice model alluded to above, and both models are rooted in a critical realist epistemological position[1] that has driven research that has primarily been concerned with measuring outcome of interventions (Harper, 2008). Thus a naive realist position that places emphasis on being able to identify generalisable truths has arguably been historically dominant within significant parts of the discipline. This focus has undoubtedly influenced the profession's choice of research methodologies.

A full description of qualitative approaches used within the discipline of clinical psychology is beyond the scope of the current chapter and the interested reader is directed to Harper and Thompson (2012). The majority of the qualitative research undertaken within this field of psychology has focused on understanding the experience of particular conditions, or examining processes involved in the delivery of care or therapy, and has

---

[1] See Chapter 2 in this volume.

typically sat towards the critical realist end of the epistemological spectrum of qualitative approaches. Methodologies based on grounded theory and phenomenology are particularly popular (Harper, 2008). For example, phenomenological approaches such as IPA have been used by clinical psychology researchers to address topics such as the patient's experience of change in cognitive analytic therapy (e.g. Rayner et al., 2011) and the experience of mental health professionals working with people engaging in self-harm (e.g. Thompson et al., 2008). Model building approaches such as grounded theory have been used to develop understanding of such experiences as persecutory delusions (e.g. Boyd and Gumley, 2007) and clinical psychologists' understanding of risk and recovery (e.g. Tickle et al., 2014). Researchers in this field have also used (although much less so) approaches that have as the focus not the phenomena themselves, but the way in which given phenomena are constructed or maintained. For example, approaches such as discourse analysis have been used to look at the implications of discourses associated with specific conditions such as autism (e.g. Avdi, 2005), the potential impact of discourses associated with certain psychotherapeutic practices such as the use of outcome measures (e.g. Kelly et al., 2012) and the influence of conceptualisations of gender upon mental health (e.g. Emslie et al., 2006).

Despite a slow start, the growth of qualitative research in clinical psychology has over the last 20 years been exponential, with qualitative research methods now being taught on all UK clinical training programmes, and accounting for up to around 40 per cent of the doctorial theses produced on some programmes (Harper, 2012; Thompson et al., 2011). Indeed, the British Psychological Society's clinical psychology programme accreditation requirements have required teaching of qualitative methods for some years. In addition, dedicated qualitative textbooks now exist that specifically aim to encourage the use of a wider range of qualitative approaches within the mental health and clinical psychology professions (e.g. Harper and Thompson, 2012; Slade and Priebe, 2006). Should the reader wish to know more about the development of qualitative research in clinical psychology, Harper (2008) provides an excellent summary. One of the issues he raises is that frameworks developed by the Department of Health in the UK have typically placed qualitative research towards the bottom of the evidence hierarchy – despite qualitative research being the most appropriate method for addressing some of the key questions of particular interest to clinicians. For example, qualitative methods are particularly suitable for examining *processes*, including processes involved in change within psychological therapy or intervention (Elliott, 2012). Qualitative methods can also be useful in the development of interventions through elucidating views of acceptability and usability of interventions: indeed this approach is recommended by the Medical Research Council (Craig et al., 2008) in the development of complex interventions. It is this that guided my own thinking in the specific qualitative mixed-method approach I describe below.

Overview of the research methods used

Prior to describing some specific examples of studies that have used IPA in conjunction with a think aloud approach, I will provide an introduction to both approaches and reflect on some of the ethical issues that require consideration.

Interpretative Phenomenological Analysis (IPA)

IPA has been well described elsewhere (e.g. Larkin and Thompson, 2012; Smith et al., 2009; Biggerstaff and Thompson, 2008): it is an approach to qualitative research specifically developed with the aim of drawing out how individuals make sense of their experience within a specific context (Smith, 2004). Studies using IPA purposively seek small samples with similar contextual characteristics relevant to the experience of interest (Thompson et al., 2011). It is quality of the data in terms of its depth that is important in IPA rather than the numbers of individuals taking part. IPA differs from many other qualitative approaches in this regard in so far as it is deliberately idiographic. IPA strives to extract themes obtained with research participants, usually via interviews. The themes and associated thematic description are worked up through a hierarchical, reflexive and ultimately interpretative process to provide a nuanced account of the experience of interest. Larkin and Thompson (2012, p. 101) state: 'The outcome of a successful IPA study is likely to include an element of *"giving voice"* (capturing and reflecting upon the principle claims and concerns of the research participants) and *"making sense"* (offering an interpretation of this material, which is grounded in the accounts, but may use psychological concepts to extend beyond them).' As such the epistemological position of IPA is both hermeneutic (i.e. interpretative) and phenomenological (i.e. attempting to gain a close understanding of subjective experience).

Doing IPA

A full description of doing IPA is beyond the scope of this chapter and the interested reader is directed towards Larkin and Thompson (2012) and Smith et al. (2009). The following summary describes the process of the analysis that moves from an individual case analysis gradually to an analysis of the larger sample. It is important to state that the process of analysis is not linear but iterative, and looking critically between analytic stages occurs as a key part of the analysis process.

- Data collection is key in IPA and the methods of encouraging the participant to reflect upon or try to voice their experience need careful construction. Semi-structured interviews are typically used which either take a biographical approach to eliciting information or follow thematically the objectives of the study. An incident type approach can also be used, whereby the interview is structured around questions centred on specific events or issues of interest (for an example see Thompson and Broom, 2009 – a study of positive examples of people with a visible difference managing the intrusive reactions of others). Interviews should be as open as possible and closed and leading questions are to be avoided. A good interview style is to have a very open schedule and to encourage the participant to speak in depth. Follow-up questions (which can be specific) should be asked to ensure that as full an account as possible is obtained. Interviews can be facilitated further with the use of diaries and photographs to act as memory aides or experiential stimulants.

- The analysis should begin ('informally') during and immediately following data collection. Summarising and paraphrasing during the interview not only facilitates participants to share more but also begins to shape up the meaning emerging within the data. Immediately following an interview it is important to record field notes, to capture personal and theoretical assumptions and notes on nonverbal processes.
- The 'formal' analysis begins with data (typically a transcribed interview) from each individual participant being subjected to detailed coding of each response of interest. This will often require line-by-line coding of the content (see Figure 7.1 below). This stage is deliberately descriptive and should result in a thorough summary of the content.
- The next stage is the rarefication of the summary data into tentative themes or clusters. This is achieved by looking for synonyms within the labelled summary terms used and also by beginning to look at the relationships between themes – looking for how themes might be subsumed by others, or how they might be viewed conceptually to have a subordinate or temporal relationship with one another (see Figure 7.3 below).
- As the analysis progresses towards revealing a manageable number of themes the concepts linked to these emerging themes need to be specified. Essentially the meaning and origin of the theme needs to be coded. This requires acknowledging the theoretical and personal factors that have influenced the choice of labels used.
- A structure is then developed, often using visual aids (such as mind-mapping) that show how the themes or clusters fit together to give a fuller account of the experience/s of interest (see Figure 7.4 below). It is also useful to prepare an individual narrative summary of the experience of interest at this stage.
- The above stages are completed for each individual. Comparisons are then made across individuals and themes modified to take into account their frequency and relevance in relation to the research aims. Relevance is more important than frequency and divergences between individuals are often used to elevate themes to a higher conceptual level via interpretation of the meaning of the divergence.
- All of the preceding stages are organised in such a way as to allow for the development of the analysis to be traceable – for example, by storing each

of the above stages electronically or by capturing images of the techniques used. Spreadsheet software or specific qualitative data management software can be particularly useful to aid the analysis process itself and also to facilitate later audit, to demonstrate transparency and to enable later reworking (Spencer and Richie, 2012).

▪ Procedures for facilitating and capturing reflexivity throughout the analysis process are also helpful (Biggerstaff and Thompson, 2008). The use of techniques like reflexive diaries (see Figure 7.2 below) and interviews can be useful in capturing the contemporaneous influences that the researcher is having on the study.

Think aloud

A 'think aloud' technique has been widely (and often pragmatically) used in a number of disciplines as an approach to capturing information on the 'usability' of new devices, interventions, or equipment. Such techniques typically involve enabling participants to verbalise whilst performing or engaging with a specific task (Ericsson and Simon, 1984). Verbalisation has a long history, stemming all the way back to the introspective methods described by some of the founding figures in psychology such as William James and Wilhelm Wundt. Introspection became largely consigned to history as behaviourism developed. However, interest in observing output of verbalisation returned as a method to gaining insights into cognition with the rise of cognitive psychology. Ericsson and Simon (1984) described a seminal method, usually still cited by researchers undertaking 'think aloud' studies, for gaining access to 'reliable' data pertaining to cognitive processes. Ericsson and Simon's 'think aloud protocol' is concerned with the identification of reliable data, such as the sequence of verbalisations related to transformations of images into words, and does not fit well with studies that aim to collect information on participants' views about a psychosocial intervention. Indeed, Ericsson and Simon's approach is very much derived from the far end of the critical realist position and is explicit in not being interested in the subjective content of verbalisations which it views as unreliable.

Boren and Ramey (2000) point out that much of the usability literature has misaligned itself with the Ericsson and Simon model, as some of the aims of the extant studies have been to obtain information on users' opinions of the technology being developed. In such cases, working with the subjective contextually-specific data derived from participants is essential. As such some usability studies might be positioned as coming from a similar epistemological position as IPA (somewhere close to the middle of a critical realist to relativist continuum) and as such they require a different protocol than that provided by the Ericsson and Simon model (this is a good example of the importance of understanding the epistemological position of the research aims and matching this to the methods used – see Chapter 2 in this volume for more on this).

Doing think aloud with thematic analysis

A summary of our approach towards gaining and analysing usability and acceptability data is described below.

- During data collection the emphasis continues from the IPA section of the study to maintain the participant as holding the experiential expertise, but with a switch to a focus on the intervention materials as the subject of discussion (rather than the experience of the participant per se).
- The think aloud protocol requires participants to read through the intervention (in our case this has been self-help booklets or leaflets) and to speak out loud what they are thinking. Typical instructions include:
  - 'Please read this leaflet on X. Please talk to me about it whilst reading it.'
  - Continuous prompts (e.g. 'yes', 'OK', 'keep going') should be used to encourage the participant and to promote further reflection.
  - If the participant is silent for more than a few seconds, prompts should be used to remind them to continue thinking aloud (such as 'Please continue to think aloud,' or 'What are you thinking now?').
- As the think aloud technique is unusual, it is always sensible to have a brief practice with some unrelated materials.
- Following think aloud, participants are then asked structured questions as to the content, layout, usability and utility of the intervention using an interview script.
- The content of the transcribed data collected via the think aloud protocol and associated semi-structured interview is analysed in our work using thematic analysis (Boyatzis, 1998; Braun and Clarke, 2006). The six stages of data analysis described by Braun and Clarke (2006) can be usefully followed to provide structure to the analysis process. These stages include: familiarisation with the data, generation of initial codes, searching for themes, review of themes, naming themes and writing up. Data from all participants is analysed separately and then compared to extract similar themes. The emphasis is on summarising content and not interpretation of that content.
- In addition it is useful to record specific usability problems and to note whether or not problems are observed by the researcher or are verbalised (see Figure 7.6: Boren and Ramey, 2000; Haak et al., 2003).

Ethical considerations in this context

Few people have written about the ethical dilemmas that can face clinical psychologists when conducting qualitative research. However, Thompson and Russo (2012) have provided some specific recommendations for facilitating the ethical research practice of clinical psychologists involved in qualitative research, and some of these recommendations will be described below.

The interested reader is directed for further information to Thompson and Russo (2012 and Thompson and Chambers (2012).

Clinical psychologists typically hold multiple roles (i.e. clinician, researcher, service manager) and this has particular implications for the types of ethical issue likely to be encountered (Thompson and Russo, 2012 Thompson and Chambers, 2012). One obvious overlap of skill set that can be associated with ethical issues is interviewing. There are of course a number of potential ethical issues associated with conducting research interviews that are particularly relevant to approaches such as IPA including issues relating to informed consent and self-determination; confidentiality and privacy; avoiding harm; dual-role and over-involvement; and power (Allmark et al., 2009). Whilst having the skills to manage distress and to build rapport are usefully transferable from practice to research, clinical psychologists should not normally intervene therapeutically whilst collecting data. Clinicians should also guard against using clinical skills that could inadvertently put participants under pressure to reveal more than they would wish to. This is essentially an issue of privacy, which can be partly managed by ensuring that participants are fully informed about the likely topics of exploration and their rights to privacy and confidentiality ahead of studies taking place. However, as one can never predict all the topics that are going to emerge during an interview, seeking ongoing or 'processual' consent which facilitates participants' option to opt out at any point should be routinely built into interviews (Rosenblatt, 1995; Thompson and Russo, 2012).

Carrying out qualitative research with participants from different backgrounds to the researcher also raises a number of ethical issues (Salway et al., 2009; Thompson and Russo, 2012). Conducting research with purposively selected groups, as is typically the case in IPA and think aloud studies, might lead to allegations of 'othering' (selecting issues simply because of difference as perceived by the researcher, which runs the risk of further maintaining stereotypes). This is of particular relevance to the examples described below as the work was directly focused on difference in terms of investigating issues concerned with disfigurement, and in addition, in one example, also ethnicity. One way that I have sought to address this issue is to actively collaborate with and seek guidance from charities and individuals with personal experience at all stages of the research (Faulkner, 2012) and to be guided by recent recommendations in the literature with regards to conducting research concerned with ethnicity (Salway et al., 2009).

An example using IPA and think aloud

Introduction to the case study

A considerable amount of my research has been concerned with examining the psychological, social and cultural experience of living with conditions that are visible to others (which are sometimes referred to as disfigurement),[2] primarily with a view to using the findings to develop interventions aimed at reducing distress and/or at raising awareness of stigmatisation and discrimination (e.g. Thompson et al., 2010).

In one recent project we worked with participants living with vitiligo (a depigmenting skin condition) in Nigeria (Thompson and Taylor, 2014). My colleagues and I have recently developed a self-help leaflet incorporating techniques aimed at reducing social anxiety for use by people living with the visible skin condition vitiligo (see Shah et al., 2014). This intervention had undergone some informal examination of usability via seeking feedback from the UK Vitiligo Society. An approach was received from an African vitiligo support organisation (the Vitiligo Awareness and Support Foundation: VITSAF) who wanted to ascertain if the self-help might also be useful in Nigeria. This approach also led to an opportunity to examine the experience of people with vitiligo living in Lagos so as to better understand their needs (Thompson and Taylor, 2014). The self-help leaflets used in the project along with other similar resources can be found on the web pages of the British Association of Dermatologists (see www.bad.org.uk/).

Why was IPA and the think aloud approach the appropriate method to use?

One key aim of the project – essentially concerned with getting close to the experience of living with vitiligo – clearly fits well with the capabilities of IPA (Smith et al., 2009). Further, I have used IPA previously in building an understanding of the experience of living with a visible difference that has shown that distress and stigmatisation whilst commonplace are often managed naturalistically with techniques akin to those used in low intensity psychosocial interventions (e.g. Saradjian et al., 2008; Thompson et al., 2002; Thompson and Broom, 2009). Indeed, these prior findings had informed the need for, and the development of, the low intensity self-help interventions being developed as part of the project discussed here.

We wanted to formally examine the usability and acceptability of the self-help materials we had developed, and a review of the literature revealed that think aloud protocols had been used in previous health care intervention research (e.g. Protheroe et al., 2010; Sadasivam, et al., 2011; Yardley et al., 2011; Yardley et al., 2010). However, further reading suggested that the Think Aloud Protocol (Ericsson and Simon, 1984), often cited in the literature, required modification. Our concern was to gain some accounts of how

---

[2] Visible difference is sometimes also referred to as disfigurement and includes conditions affecting appearance as a result of acquired (such as burn), congenital (such as cleft-lip and palate), or disease processes (such as psoriasis). See www.changingfaces.org.uk/Home for further information on terminology.

our self-help materials were viewed: a descriptive version of thematic analysis was identified as appropriate and we modified the think aloud technique so as to value participants' subjective accounts of acceptability and usability (Boyatzis, 1998; Braun and Clarke, 2006).

Brief illustration of applying IPA and think aloud

The focus of this chapter is on the combination of IPA with think aloud as a method rather than the research project itself. As I have also described above how the analysis process in general for both approaches is performed, I will simply focus on summarising some of the processes involved in the analysis of data from the project.

For each IPA participant, formal analysis commenced with each transcript being annotated by the primary researcher to include his initial reflections. The comments function in Word was used to contain and store his notes as shown in Figure 7.1.

As previously stated, reflexivity is essential in IPA and it is particularly important in studies where there are multiple differences between the research team and the participant group. An example from the reflexive diary that was used to help contextualise the experience, nature and origin of the interpretations made during the project is shown in Figure 7.2. Such excerpts were discussed within the research team and with the collaborating charity.

The notes from the transcriptions were then added into a spreadsheet (see Figure 7.3) to support identification of preliminary emerging themes. The use of a spreadsheet containing the early themes enabled the easy movement and organisation of data into themes and initial clusters.

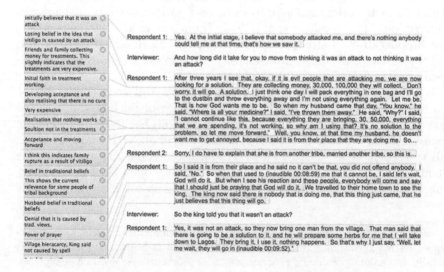

Figure 7.1   Examples of initial coding of IPA transcript

Mrs X is an interesting participant. She was one of the older people taking part, one of the better educated (I think), in one of the better jobs and came from a high socioeconomic group (married to the uncle of the King of a tribe). By some distance she provided the most detail about the traditional belief structures of illness, such as the spirits and incorrect diet leading to vitiligo. However she also spoke confidently in the paradigms of medicine and Christianity. Like other participants she initially suspected that her vitiligo began as a result of some other medical thing, in her case giving birth. She presented as someone who is coping well and who has experienced less impact of from the vitiligo. Throughout the interview she came across as a little evasive on questions of how vitiligo has impacted on her negatively. This could be for a number of reasons, perhaps she did not want to talk about it to a stranger, a man, a Westerner, or in front of X (collaborating charity). I sometimes wonder what impact X's message had on the answers given by participants. X takes the view that people should be confident and outspoken. That the future will be good. I think that this very positive mantra has a lot of advantages but that also it night get in the way of people acknowledging the hurt they feel. This hunch may be completely wrong.

Figure 7.2   Example of a reflexive journal entry

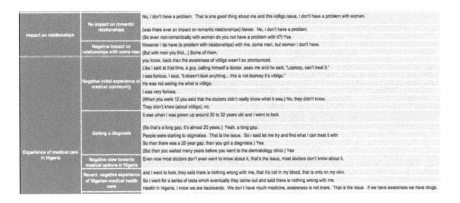

Figure 7.3   Example from spreadsheet of preliminary IPA themes

The spreadsheet was then converted into a mind-map (see Figure 7.4 below) that visually showed how the emerging themes related to one another. The development of the mind-map facilitated further consideration of the conceptual relationship between the experience/s of interest. The spreadsheets and mind-maps for all participants were brought together and the connections between participants were then examined.

Themes were then reorganised taking into account frequency, prominence and relevance. This process was assisted through the use of an overarching mind-map.

For the think aloud part of the study, participants were shown the self-help leaflet after participating in the IPA interview. Transcription was completed in the same manner as for the IPA data. The analysis began with the data being coded and an example is shown in Figure 7.5.

The analysis was conducted in line with the recommendations given by Haak et al. (2003) and focused on four stages. This involved a record being made of the total number of usability problems detected by each participant.

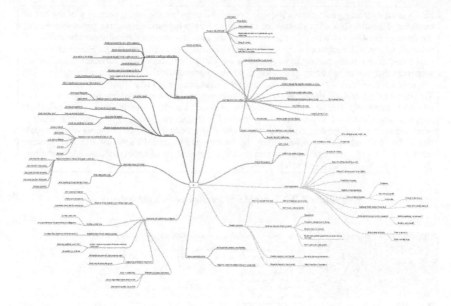

Figure 7.4 Example of mind-map of IPA themes

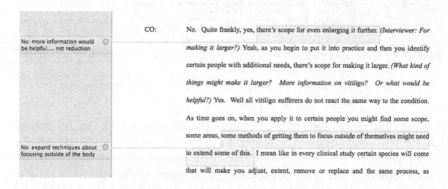

Figure 7.5 Example of a think aloud coding

A distinction was made according to the way that usability problems surfaced in the data: specifically whether they were observed in 'behavioural data' (as recorded by the researcher); were 'verbalised by the participants'; or were a combination of both researcher observation and participant verbalisation. The types of problem identified were also categorised. In addition, a record was made if verbalisations resulted from prompts (Boren and Ramey, 2000). A spreadsheet was used to store this information (see example in Figure 7.6).

Participant	Positive	Prompt	Observation/Verbalization	Usability Problems	Prompted	Observation/Verbalization
JE	Model is appropriate	No	V	Needs to be translated into local languages	Yes	V
	Helpful to hear other people's experiences are similar	Yes	V	The techniques require a lot of self-confidence to begin with	No	V
	Language is appropriate	Yes	V			
	Content is appropriate (including examples)	Yes	V			
	Diagrams are appropriate	Yes	V			
	Okay keeping a diary	Yes	V			
	Techniques are appropriate	Yes	V			
	Relates to the experience of living with vitiligo in Nigeria	Yes	V			
AT	Model of anxiety is appropriate	Yes	V	Paragraph which relates to vitiligo affecting behaviour is not relevant (page 3, 2nd para)	No	V
	Captures the experience very well	Yes	V	impacts on people differently, this needs more highlighting	No	V
	It is informative and educational	Yes	V			
	Relates to the experience of living with vitiligo in Nigeria	Yes	V			
	Good to fill in the diary	Yes	V			
	Exercises are really helpful ("I love the exercise.")	Yes	V			
	Leaflet would help a lot	Yes	V			
FA2	Model is appropriate	Yes	V	More information about how to treat vitiligo	No	V
	Diary is helpful	Yes	V	Diagram is unclear (page 2)	No	V/O
	Techniques are helpful	Yes	V	Wording is not always very clear (i.e. page three) (great quote for this)	Yes	V
				Make leaflet with fewer words	Yes	V
				FA2 was not able to read all of the leaflet	NA	O
				FA2 did not understand the leaflet	NA	V
DO	Appropriate description of vitiligo (particularly the social isolation)	No	V	Some parts not personally appropriate (dysmorphobic)	No	V
	Diagrams are appropriate	Yes	V	Requires a high level of education, would need to be simplified for many people	No	V
	Culturally appropriate	Yes	V	Techniques and ideas could be applied in a group setting	No	V
	Stage two is appropriate	No	V			
	Keeping a diary could be helpful, not definitely	Yes	V			
	Helpful to people in the early stages of vitiligo	No	V			
	Exercises are appropriate	Yes	V			
	Good summary on page seven	Yes	V			
	Would be personally helpful	No	V			
EG	Agree that vitiligo can impact on social life	Yes	V	Diary is not helpful	Yes	V
	Culturally appropriate	Yes	V	Examples are not appropriate to EG	No	V
	Good model/diagram	Yes	V	Needs to be more clearly written	Yes	V
	Good example on page four	Yes	V			
	Well written	Yes	V			
	Technique two is appropriate	NA	Observation			
ZA	Good diagram	Yes	V	Technique two was not immediately understandable	NA	O
	Good example of social anxiety	Yes	V			
	Good description of impact of vitiligo on behaviour	No	V			
	Good technique (one) for reducing self-consciousness	Yes	V			
	First technique is clearer	Yes	V			
Mrs O	Accurate description of experience	No	V	First exercise not clear	No	V
	Both techniques helpful	Yes	V			
	Written appropriately	Yes	V			
OM	Page three (para 1) is very true	No	V	Not appropriate to say people don't notice it, in Nigeria everyone does (skin colour more obvious)	No	V
	Cognitive side of things is very true	No	V	Wording is inappropriate (people sometimes stare out of rudeness/fear not just curiosity)	No	V
	Examples are helpful	No	V	Diagram is not clear enough (model of anxiety)	No	V
	First technique is helpful	No	V	Wording is not clear (2nd para, page 3) (and more generally)		V
	smiled whilst reading technique one	NA	Observation	Anxiety that applying the second technique might be embarrassing	Yes	V
	Techniques are similar to current coping	No	V	important to apply the techniques in the right environment/time	No	V
	Really good that there is no mention of the word meditation (would not be culturally appropriate, clash with religious views)	No	V			

Figure 7.6 Example of spreadsheet used to record analysis of think aloud

Reflections on the exemplar projects and the use of qualitative methods in clinical psychology

In this chapter I have shown how two types of qualitative approach can be used in research population both raising the profile of needs of people living with stigmatising health conditions and conducting preliminary evaluation of the potential acceptability and usability of self-help interventions. Whilst IPA was deliberately chosen so as to enable nuanced investigation of the participants' individual experiences a think aloud protocol and interview was also used to examine issues of usability and acceptability of self-help interventions in a systematic fashion.

Qualitative research has made an important contribution to knowledge, practice and policy in the mental health field and the combination of methods described here has the potential to add to this accomplishment. The large majority of qualitative research conducted more recently in clinical psychology has used either IPA or grounded theory and whilst this might reflect a trend in examining experience, it has been suggested that it might also be reflective of the profession's 'historical commitment to realist epistemologies' (Harper, 2012, p. 11). The project reported here comes from a critical realist perspective but that is not to say that I would not encourage those planning to use qualitative approaches in clinical psychology to not be mindful of other approaches. Clearly, there has to be an epistemological fit between the research question and the approach used, but an over focus on investigating from within a critical realist standpoint runs the risk that some types of question, particularly those that are more critical of systems and criteria, might go unaddressed.

In conclusion, the combination of IPA with a modified form of the think aloud protocol appears to be useful in gaining both nuanced information about specific experiences and feedback on interventions ahead of conducting investigations of effectiveness. Indeed, my experience has been that conducting an IPA interview with a participant in the first instance is useful in building rapport and acknowledging the participant's expertise in such a way as to enable detailed comment on a developing intervention to emerge.

Acknowledgements

Dr Nicholas Taylor carried out the vitiligo study referred to in this chapter as part of his clinical psychology doctorate under the supervision and in collaboration with the author. Figures 7.1 to 7.5 are taken from his dissertation. The vitiligo study was funded by a health partnership grant provided by the Tropical Health Education Trust and the project was also supported by Ogo Maduewesi, founder of the Vitiligo Support and Awareness Foundation.

References

Allmark, P., Boote, J., Chambers, E., Clarke, A., McDonnell, A., Thompson, A.R., et al. (2009). Ethical issues in the use of in-depth interviews: Literature Review and Discussion. *Research Ethics Review*, 5, 48–54.

Avdi, E. (2005). Discursively negotiating a pathological identity in the clinical dialogue: Discourse analysis of a family therapy. *Psychology and Psychotherapy: Theory, Research and Practice*, 78, 493–511.

Biggerstaff, D. and Thompson, A.R. (2008). Interpretative phenomenological analysis (IPA) as a method of choice for research in health care settings. *Qualitative Research in Psychology*, 5, 1–11.

Boren, M.T. and Ramey, J. (2000). Thinking aloud: Reconciling theory and practice. *IEEE Transactions on Professional Communication*, 43, 261–278.

Boyatzis, R. (1998). *Transforming Qualitative Information: Thematic Analysis and Code Development*. Thousand Oaks, CA: SAGE.

Boyd, T. and Gumley, A. (2007). An experiential perspective on persecutory paranoia: A grounded theory construction. *Psychology and Psychotherapy: Theory, Research and Practice*, 80, 1–22. doi: 10.1348/147608306X100536.

Braun, V. and Clarke, V. (2006). Using thematic analysis in psychology. *Qualitative Research in Psychology*, 3, 77–101.

British Psychological Society (2013). *Division of Clinical Psychology Position Statement on the Classification of Behaviour and Experience in Relation to Functional Psychiatric Diagnoses: Time for a Paradigm Shift*. Leicester: British Psychological

Society. www.dcp.bps.org.uk/document-download-area/document-download$.
cfm?restart=trueandfile_uuid=9EF109E9-0FB3-ED4F-DF84-310F745854CB.

British Psychological Society (2014). *Understanding Psychosis and Schizophrenia*. Leicester: British Psychological Society. www.bps.org.uk/networks-and-communities/member-microsite/division-clinical-psychology/understanding-psychosis-and-schizophrenia.

Craig, P., Dieppe, P., Macintyre, S., Michie, S., Nazareth, I. and Petticrew, M. (2008). Developing and evaluating complex interventions: New guidance. Medical Research Council. Retrieved from www.mrc.ac.uk/documents/pdf/complex-interventions-guidance/.

Elliott, R. (2012). Qualitative methods for studying psychotherapy change processes. In D. Harper and A.R. Thompson (Eds.) *Qualitative Research Methods in Mental Health and Psychotherapy: A Guide for Students and Practitioners*. London: Wiley, pp. 243–250.

Emslie, C., Ridge, D., Ziebland, S. and Hunt, K. (2006). Men's accounts of depression: Reconstructing or resisting hegemonic masculinity? *Social Science and Medicine*, 62, 2246–2257. doi: 0.1016/j.socscimed.2005.10.017.

Ericsson, K. and Simon, H. (1984). *Protocol Analysis: Verbal Reports as Data*, Cambridge: MIT Press.

Faulkner, A. (2012). Participation and service user involvement. In D. Harper and A.R. Thompson (Eds.), *Qualitative Research Methods in Mental Health and Psychotherapy: A Guide for Students and Practitioners*. London: Wiley, pp. 39–54.

Haak, M.V.D., de Jong, M. and Schellens, P.J. (2003). Retrospective vs. concurrent think-aloud protocols: Testing the usability of an online library catalogue. *Behaviour and Information Technology*, 22, 339–351. doi:10.1080/0044929031000.

Harper, D. (2008). Clinical psychology. In C. Willig and W. Stainton-Rogers (Eds.), *The SAGE Handbook of Qualitative Research in Psychology*. Thousand Oaks, CA: SAGE Publications, pp. 430–54.

Harper, D. (2012). Surveying qualitative research teaching on British clinical psychology training programmes 1992–2006: A changing relationship? *Qualitative Research in Psychology*, 9, 5–12. doi: 10.1080/14780887.2012.630626.

Harper, D. and Thompson, A.R. (Eds.) (2012). *Qualitative Research Methods in Mental Health and Psychotherapy: A Guide for Students and Practitioners*. London: Wiley.

Kelly, V., Holttum, S., Evans, C. and Shepherd, M. (2012). A discourse analysis of power in relation to PSYCHLOPS (Psychological Outcome Profiles) in the context of CBT for psychosis. *Counselling and Psychotherapy Research*, 12, 247–256.

Larkin, M. and Thompson, A.R. (2012). Interpretative phenomenological analysis in mental health and psychotherapy research. In D. Harper and A.R. Thompson (Eds.), *Qualitative Research Methods in Mental Health and Psychotherapy: A Guide for Students and Practitioners*. London: Wiley, pp. 101–116.

Llewelyn, S. and Murphy, D. (Eds.) (2014). *What Is Clinical Psychology?* Oxford: Oxford University Press.

Protheroe, J., Blakeman, T., Bower, P., Chew-Graham, C. and Kennedy, A. (2010). *An Intervention to Promote Patient Participation and Self-Management in Long Term Conditions: Development and Feasibility Testing*. BMC: Health Services Research, 10.

Rayner, K., Thompson, A.R. and Walsh, S. (2011). Clients' experience of change in cognitive analytic therapy. *Psychology and Psychotherapy: Theory, Research and Practice*, 84, 299–313. doi:10.1348/147608310X531164.

Rosenblatt, P.C. (1995). Ethics of qualitative interviewing with grieving families. *Death Studies*, 19, 139–155.

Sadasivam, R.S., Delaughter, K., Crenshaw, K., Sobko, H.J., Williams, J.H., Coley, H.L., Ray, M.N., Ford, D.E., Allison, J.J. and Houston, T.K. (2011). Development of an interactive, web-delivered system to increase provider-patient engagement in smoking cessation. *Journal of Medical Internet Research*, 13, e87.

Salway, S., Allmark, P., Barley, R., Higgenbottom, G., Gerrish, K. and Ellison, T.H. (2009). Social research for a multiethnic population: Do the research ethics and standards guidelines of UK learned societies address this challenge? *21st Century Society*, 4, 53–81.

Saradjian, A., Thompson, A.R. and Datta, D. (2008). The experience of men using an upper limb prosthesis following amputation: Positive coping and minimizing feeling different. *Disability and Rehabilitation*, 30, 871–883.

Shah, R., Hunt, J., Webb, T. and Thompson. A.R. (2014). Starting to develop self-help for social anxiety associated with vitiligo: Using clinical significance to measure the potential effectiveness of enhanced psychological self-help. *British Journal of Dermatology*, doi:10.1111/bjd.12990.

Slade, M. and Priebe, S. (Eds.) (2006). *Choosing Methods in Mental Health Research: Mental Health Research from Theory to Practice*. London: Routledge.

Smith, J.A. (2004). Reflecting on the development of interpretative phenomenological analysis and its contribution to qualitative psychology. *Qualitative Research in Psychology*, 1, 39–54.

Smith, J.A., Flowers, P. and Larkin, M. (2009). *Interpretative Phenomenological Analysis: Theory, Research, Practice*. London: SAGE.

Spencer, L. and Richie, J. (2012). In pursuit of quality. In D. Harper and A.R. Thompson (Eds.) *Qualitative Research Methods in Mental Health and Psychotherapy: A Guide for Students and Practitioners*. London: Wiley, pp. 227–242.

Thompson, A.R. and Broom, L. (2009). Positively managing intrusive reactions to disfigurement: An interpretative phenomenological analysis of naturalistic coping. *Diversity in Health and Care*, 6, 171–180.

Thompson, A.R. and Chambers, E. (2012). Ethical issues in qualitative mental health research. In D. Harper and A.R. Thompson (Eds.) *Qualitative Research Methods in Mental Health and Psychotherapy: A Guide for Students and Practitioners*. London: Wiley, pp. 23–38.

Thompson, A.R., Clarke, S.A., Newell, R., Gawkrodger, G. and the Appearance Research Collaboration (2010). Vitiligo linked to stigmatisation in British South Asian women: A qualitative study of the experiences of living with vitiligo. *The British Journal of Dermatology*, 163, 481–486.

Thompson, A.R., Kent, G. and Smith, J.A. (2002). Living with vitiligo: Dealing with difference. *British Journal of Health Psychology*, 7, 213–225.

Thompson, A.R., Larkin, M. and Smith, J.A. (2011). Interpretative phenomenological analysis and clinical psychology training: Results from a survey of the group of trainers in clinical psychology. *Clinical Psychology Forum*, 222, 15–19.

Thompson, A.R., Powis, J. and Carradice, A. (2008). Community mental health nurses' experiences of working with people who engage in deliberate self-harm: An interpretative phenomenological analysis. *International Journal of Mental Health Nursing*, 17, 151–159.

Thompson, A.R. and Russo, K. (2012). Ethical dilemmas for clinical psychologists in conducting qualitative research. *Qualitative Research in Psychology*, 9, 32–46. doi: 10.1080/14780887.2012.630636.

Thompson, A.R. and Taylor, N. (2014). Developing a health link partnership with dermatology services in Nigeria: Preliminary feedback from a tropical health education trust start-up project. *Clinical Psychology Forum*, 258, 56–60.

Tickle, A., Brown, D. and Hayward, M. (2014). Can we risk recovery? A grounded theory of clinical psychologists' perceptions of risk and recovery-oriented mental health services. *Psychology and Psychotherapy: Theory, Research, and Practice*, 87, 96–110. doi: 10.1111/j.2044-8341.2012.02079.

Willott, S. and Larkin, M. (2012). Introduction to the special issue on qualitative research and clinical psychology. *Qualitative Research in Psychology*, 9, 1–4. doi: 10.1080/14780887.2012.630622.

Yardley, L., Miller, S., Teasdale, E., Little, P. and Primit, T. (2011). Using mixed methods to design a web-based behavioural intervention to reduce transmission of colds and flu. *Journal of Health Psychology*, 16, 353–364.

Yardley, L., Morrison, L.G., Andreou, P., Joseph, J. and Little, P. (2010). *Understanding reactions to an internet-delivered health-care intervention: Accommodating user preferences for information provision.* BMC: Medical Informatics and Decision Making, 10.

Methods for Community Research, Action and Change

Michael Murray and
Katie Wright-Bevans

8

Introduction: Community research, action and change

Community action research is an approach which combines both research and action designed to enhance the quality of life of the participants. It is an approach that turns away from the predict and control tenets dominant in the positivist approach within psychology. Instead, the concern is with understanding social processes and transforming lives. Whilst traditional social and health psychology approaches are often individualistic in their orientation, community action research works with communities to identify collective opportunities for change (Murray, 2012a). It seeks not only to identify and understand health and social disadvantages but also to mobilise local action to challenge those disadvantages.

Participatory action research is the methodological framework preferred within community action research. The approach is often time-consuming, unpredictable and challenging, but is highly rewarding. What follows is less a step-by-step guide and more a set of guiding principles along with practical recommendations to address the *how* of doing community action research. This is followed by a more specific guide to using community arts for action and change. A case example looking at the CALL-ME project illustrates an example of community action research in practice.

Doing community research in psychology

Participatory action research is a framework utilising a variety of research methods designed to empower communities, mobilising them towards social change. Researchers seek to understand the issues that permeate the everyday lives of communities and to work with them to facilitate localised action. It is a framework that actively seeks not only to understand the everyday lived worlds of communities but also to challenge and take action against the disadvantages faced by those communities (Murray, 2012b).

The sections below consider some of the key principles and steps of community action research as well as some recommendations for how to implement these in practice. Importantly, these are not linear stages or steps to be applied unreflexively. Campbell and Cornish (2014) warn against approaching community action research with a vision of a linear process from inputs through to outputs. Community action research is notoriously 'messy' and open-ended such that the points that follow are intended as some key considerations and not a fixed blueprint.

Collaboration

Collaboration is an essential underpinning facet of community action research. In practical terms, collaboration with gatekeepers is often necessary in order to gain access to disadvantaged community groups. However, more importantly community action research is premised upon the ongoing active involvement of participants (Murray, 2012b). The identification of a community should be an early step in any community action research project to maximise participant involvement in the research design and allow for their concerns and interests to feed the project. Third sector organisations and local authorities offer a traditional avenue to identifying community groups. Other communities may not be as easily approached or identified. Local recruitment flyers, posters and social media posts may serve as a more appropriate means to identify participants that are not a part of an existing network or service. This initial stage can take time and should not be rushed or the researcher may jeopardise any nascent goodwill. During the project the aim is to deepen the collaboration such that the research participants become co-researchers, reflecting on their own experiences and exploring ways to enhance their quality of life.

Empowerment

Central to action research is the notion of empowerment. This is the process by which community participants reflect upon their circumstances and develop strategies of change. The aim is to provide communities with the opportunity to develop their 'voice'. This is the capacity to reflect upon the social roots of their problems and articulate demands for change (Campbell et al., 2010). Practically, empowerment results from the collaborative nature of community action research and the involvement of participants in key decisions throughout the project. Key issues and concerns should be voiced from the community rather than brought to the research setting by the researchers.

Empowerment can also result from the specific methodological tools employed. Many traditional qualitative methods may emphasise pre-existing expert/participant power dynamics particularly within groups that are traditionally disadvantaged or disempowered. Various innovative methods seek to redress power imbalances and encourage democratic participation, many of which steer away from relying solely on participants' talk and text, instead allowing more creative avenues of expression. Two examples of specific action research methods frequently used in community research in psychology are the World Café and Photovoice. World Café provides an opportunity for informal café style conversations with potential research participants (see Brown, 2010). Photovoice involves participants using cameras and taking photographs to explore and express aspects of the community that affect them (see Wang and Burris, 1997; Wang et al., 1998). Such methods were specifically developed to be inclusive, reduce communicative barriers and gain insight into the community as experienced by its members. In practice, empowerment requires reflection on the immediate research setting, the participants' abilities and the broader social context. Such reflection can lead to a better understanding of the participants' abilities and the power structures affecting the community. It enables the researcher to seek to maximise opportunities for the participants to implement action.

Action and reflection
What distinguishes community action research from various other qualitative approaches is its explicit aim not only to develop a greater understanding of the issues faced by the community but also to facilitate collective action towards positive social change. Mobilising for community action and social change requires community members developing a greater awareness of both the socio-cultural conditions that support the challenges they face and their own capacity to change those conditions. This process, termed *conscientization* by the influential Brazilian educator and advocate of critical pedagogy Paulo Freire (1970), is recognised as pivotal to community action and social change. The processes of *conscientization* and community action alike involve continual reflection and more tangible action. Action in this sense can take a variety of forms. Social change is frequently a slow process, characterised by 'ripples' of action. Often community action is characterised by small acts of resistance and challenges to the status quo (Campbell and Cornish, 2014). It is through this process that the community members grow in confidence and begin to explore other change strategies.

In practice, it is important to facilitate transformative spaces both physically and symbolically, within which participants feel comfortable, safe and have the opportunity to collectively reflect and confidently express their beliefs. Reflexivity is recognised as valuable to qualitative researchers in general but particularly to community action researchers. The collaborative nature of community research means that the researcher is immersed in the ongoing processes of reflection and action and can become an advocate for the community in their push for social change. Consequently, reflexivity is integral to action research. Reflexive journals allow the researcher to acknowledge and record their own research priorities, practices and values. As well as the use of more traditional qualitative research methods (e.g. focus groups, interviews, etc.), ethnographic style observations throughout the research can help in attempts to capture as much as possible of the surrounding social context.

Dissemination

If a key principle of community action research is to provide participants with a 'voice', it is equally important to maximise opportunities for that 'voice' to be heard. Community research findings and collaborative actions are frequently showcased in the form of a community event. This enables research findings and community achievements to be disseminated to a wider circle of stakeholders rather than solely academics. Dissemination and celebration of the research project helps to situate local action in a wider social context and should aim at the very least to raise awareness of community issues addressed in the research if not to provoke further action from stakeholders and interest groups.

The involvement of the wider community may attract those with the power and resources to implement further action or to help sustain the project, if that is a community goal. The latter is especially important as in reality the community may have limited power or resources. A showcase of community concerns and needs can attract attention from those with such power and resources. Campbell and Cornish (2010) note that the involvement of those in positions of power is important to increase the 'reach' and sustainability of community projects. At the same time, powerful groups may be resistant to assisting or sharing power. In these cases community action can potentially bring the community into conflict with these more powerful groups. It is for this reason that the community researcher needs to carefully consider the broader social and ethical issues of their work (Brydon-Miller et al., 2006). This does not mean avoiding conflict but ensuring that the community participants are aware of the processes and have access to the necessary support.

In practice, many creative methods such as community arts lend themselves well to wider dissemination. Such methods enable a visual display of the community's collaborative work to be directly showcased. In a time- and resource-bound project, a dissemination event may represent a natural ending point and finale for the community involved. Such events should be negotiated and planned with the community where possible and may also be a source of motivation for the community during periods of struggle or frustration.

Evaluation

Within action research frameworks, evaluation is essential in order to establish if actions have been justified and appropriate. Evaluation involves reflection on all aspects of the research process including the role of the researcher. Aspects of community action research can be traced back to the work of Kurt Lewin (1946). He proposed that action research consists of a series of cycles involving conceptualisation, planning, implementation and evaluation of action after which another cycle may begin. Evaluation is essential in order to understand if actions are appropriate, justified and ethical.

Ideally evaluation and reflection should be built into the research design and should be an ongoing process rather than an isolated stage. Practical recommendations include gaining regular feedback and input from all involved from early in the project. Verbal feedback may be more appropriate and more engaging than multiple monitoring or evaluation forms. Being flexible is equally important as community settings are inevitably more dynamic than other research settings and are subject to change over time.

Community action through arts

While action research offers a methodological framework for community psychology, in practice a variety of methods can be employed. Innovative arts-based methods have great potential to act as a catalyst for action and positive social change and have been used historically to promote solidarity and challenge social exclusion (Murray and Crummett, 2015). Community arts-based methods can involve a variety of creative activities and aim to involve people in developing skills, self-confidence and greater social interaction whilst drawing attention to specific social issues (Murray et al., 2014).

A strength of arts-based methods is how they seek to maximise participant involvement (Brydon-Miller, 2014). Practically, methods may range from activities such as painting, drawing and print-making to theatre, dance and music-making. The art that results often lends itself naturally to wider community engagement through exhibitions, shows or performances. Such wider engagement and dissemination serves to showcase the skills and creative talents of a community, demonstrate resistance to disadvantages faced and allow a wider audience insight into the world as experienced by a community. It is a means of spreading solidarity.

Key to community arts is their capacity to offer a tool with which to create and share stories and express aspects of identity or shared representations. Methodologically, community arts allow for socially shared knowledge and beliefs to be creatively expressed; hence they complement theoretical frameworks that likewise recognise the shared and dynamic nature of social knowledge (Murray, 2012b). Theories such as social representation and narrative theory (Murray, 2002) complement community arts methods because they similarly value the individual in context and knowledge as a dynamic social process. Social representation theory provides a framework for addressing contemporary social disadvantage as it invites 'practical engagement' rather than description of processes (Moscovici and Marková, 1998). Narrative research traditionally focused on individual stories but community narratives can be held by members of a community and depicted or explored through community arts (Murray, 2012b). In any given project, social representations and community narratives can be explored within the creative processes and finished products of the community art. Communities can use the project and space to challenge dominant negative representations of their community or develop new emancipatory narratives (Murray, 2012b). As such, art and arts-based methods can play a key role in facilitating local action and broader social change. Just as community arts are engaging and attractive to participants, they can likewise attract the attention of key figures and local stakeholders.

Practically speaking, implementing community arts for action and change involves recognising and applying the same principles highlighted as key to action research more broadly. Specific practical challenges that researchers may face when facilitating arts-based methods are accessing materials and community spaces as well as engaging artists. Many simple arts materials may be accessed for free or at a low cost. When budgets are limited, often obtaining resources requires some innovation and negotiation. Often projects involve community artists to teach skills and techniques and facilitate sessions. As well as having cost implications, these resources also need to be accessible and inclusive. Coordinating these resources can be time-consuming and require ongoing negotiation.

Our case example

Introduction to the study

Our example is taken from a large study which was concerned with exploring the processes involved in promoting greater social engagement among older people. It is well established that many older people report social isolation and loneliness and express a desire to be more socially involved. This is especially the case for older residents of disadvantaged urban neighbourhoods. The challenge is to clarify the factors which discourage social participation and what steps can be taken to combat these factors. The study was funded as part of the much larger New Dynamics of Ageing initiative which was a cross-council research programme designed to promote a very broad range of research into ageing (Walker, 2015). One particular feature of this research programme was that it deliberately promoted the transfer and integration of the findings into policy and practice. As such, community action research was a particularly suitable approach (see also Murray, 2013).

The research was located in a large city in the north of England. This city was chosen as it had much evidence of social disadvantage as well as a city council which was very keen to explore opportunities for its older residents. Thus from the outset we had the potential opportunity to work closely with the council to explore the sustainability of our project. This is an important consideration in any community action project. Developing these relationships is key to the success of the project.

Why was the community action approach the appropriate method to use?

Community action research emphasises the collaborative nature of its approach. Rather than the distant researcher taking information from the research 'subject', the aim is to work with the study participants such that the research both enhances the life of the participants as well as advancing our understanding of processes. In addition, previous research had shown that many people, and especially older people, have become somewhat suspicious of researchers. They are often perceived as outsiders who are only concerned with their own advancement rather than that of the research participants. Indeed, this is an ongoing tension faced by academic researchers who have to demonstrate to their funding bodies and employers the scholarly contribution of their research. By developing a process which is designed to be collaborative, the aim is to work with participants rather than to work on them. Admittedly there remains the issue of power in the research relationship but we will come back to that later in our reflections on the project.

Doing community action research

In this section we will explore the various stages of the project which we conducted with the older people. We will start with the early planning stages, then proceed through the initial discussions with participants, the development of the community arts projects, the reflections and the challenges around sustaining the projects.

Initial planning

The first contact we had with the community was through the city council. This was very important as the council had substantial information on the various districts in the city, the particular challenges faced by the local residents and the types of service offered. We worked with the council ageing team who were concerned with enhancing the lives of older residents. From the outset we wanted the project to become part of the team's forward planning such that they could learn from how we worked and hopefully adopt some of our lessons in the development and sustaining of initiatives. A member of the ageing team joined the research team such that there was a two-way flow of information between the academic researchers and the council in all our planning from the outset.

The council provided three main types of information: (1) details of the different districts of the city in terms of various measures of disadvantage; (2) details of the potential contacts in the different districts and any local initiatives; and (3) details of potential local resources which could assist with any initiatives. This information was then used by the research team in making decisions as to where to actually investigate the potential locations for the projects.

Although the research took place in different areas of the city, we will focus here on one particular district. This was chosen as it had multiple indicators of social disadvantage and the council was not involved in any local initiatives in the area. We were thus able to build up a profile of the area in terms of its physical characteristics and demographics and begin to explore community initiatives. It was a residential area consisting largely of public sector/social housing with major arterial roads and railway lines marking its boundaries. The older residents had lived in the area largely since it was built about 35 years earlier. There were some small shops in the area but the residents had to travel by public transport to access a larger range of shopping. There were few social facilities in the area.

Through the council we obtained the contact details of certain individuals or social organisations who/which worked in the area. These included churches and social organisations. Two of the researchers visited these individuals/agencies and discussed with them their plans. We also spent time walking about the area familiarising ourselves with its layout and resources. We began to expand our understanding of the area and the key individuals who played important formal and informal roles locally. These included local development workers, clergy and elected officials. After several weeks of informal discussions we made contact with one older local resident who was particularly keen to work with us on the project. This person was key to the subsequent development of the project and it is important to consider the role of this gatekeeper. Through her we began to widen our range of contacts and convened a meeting to discuss forms of community action.

Simultaneously we had been discussing potential forms of community action. One of the researchers had previous experience of community arts and it was decided to explore further the potential of this approach. As explained previously, community arts have a long history in providing a means to combat social exclusion and to enhance the quality of lives of people. We made contact with a community arts worker who agreed to work with us on this project. She was able to access additional resources from a local agency to fund her involvement.

At the initial meeting with the local residents we discussed with them the collaborative nature of the project and enquired if they would be interested in working with us on a community arts project. We discussed the potential project in more detail and the community arts worker explained what her role would be. The collaborative and informal nature of this discussion was very important as it convinced the residents that they would be in control and could manage the pace and character of the project. The key local contact also gave us access to some community rooms which provided space for the project.

As part of the project we also conducted interviews with a range of community workers. Our discussions with community workers helped our understanding of how they operated. Community workers are not formally researchers although their practice is infused with ideas from community action research. Our conversations with them produced additional insight into how they operated, quite often 'under the radar' of official agencies. Their role was to encourage the community residents to articulate their concerns more clearly and to take an active role in shaping their community. The community worker cannot adopt an impartial distanced approach. Rather s/he must demonstrate to the participants their commitment to change.

Developing the project
After the initial meeting it was agreed to meet once a week in the community meeting room. The group included 10 to 12 local residents, the community arts worker and at least one of the researchers. At the initial meeting it had been decided to explore a range of different arts activities including painting, tie dyeing, glass etching, etc.. Each session lasted two hours and was organised very informally, giving the community arts worker the time to work with individuals and sub-groups as well as the researcher opportunity for informal conversations with the participants. Some of these conversations were recorded on audio tape and others in note form. In addition, interviews were subsequently held with some of the participants in their homes. These interviews invited the participants to reflect on their neighbourhood, how it had changed, their neighbours, their social relations, their contact with official agencies and related issues. These interviews were conducted in an informal manner.

The project took place in three-monthly cycles such that at the end of each cycle there was a public exhibition of the artwork in the community rooms followed by a reflection on the work by the participants. The exhibition attracted local residents, elected officials and some media attention. These events were very much welcomed by the participants as it was their opportunity to publicly demonstrate to others their artwork. It was also a marker and provided an opportunity for some participants to withdraw from the project and others to join.

Analysis of data
Multiple forms of data were collected including notes from informal conversations and group discussions through to the more extensive individual interviews. This was supplemented with field notes by the researchers and the actual artworks created as part of the project. An important feature was that these data were collected at different points in time during the project such that it was possible to begin to explore the processes of change. At the beginning many of the participants were apprehensive about the project, but over time they took ownership of it. It was their project, about which they grew in pride. They brought food to the meetings which they shared with each other such that the meetings became very much social occasions. Indeed, it was noted by one of the participants that the meetings became in some ways a refuge from the everyday challenges they faced in the community.

In analysing the data a prime concern was how it could contribute to enhancing the project. This part of the analysis was shared with the participants – exploring what worked well and what did not. Thus it became possible to plan ahead for the next project. In this way the project participants became co-researchers.

At the same time the academic researchers could begin to connect their findings with broader theoretical frameworks. An important point to make here is the underlying social psychological theoretical framework which helps to make sense of the change processes. In our case we found narrative a particularly useful framework. In this project we distinguished between big and small stories and how these could help us understand community processes (Sools and Murray, 2014). Small stories are those accounts of everyday events the exchange of which are central to social interaction. They are sometimes ignored by researchers but they are essential for the reaffirming of identity and the building of social relationships. Conversely, big stories are those that are concerned with larger processes of change. In our case we were concerned with the process of exploring these larger stories of community change. However, to engage participants with these big stories it is essential that the change agent also connected with the participants through the sharing of small stories.

Illustrative findings

The study participants were very enthused by the project. While at the outset they were apprehensive, during the project they grew in confidence. Thus the very process of participating in the arts project contributed to community empowerment. In their discussions they recalled the changes in their neighbourhood since they had first settled there. Initially, they were promised a range of local facilities by the local authority but these had not materialised. Instead they felt that their community was neglected and they had become cynical about the role of the local authority and outside agencies. The community artwork which they produced was in many ways a way of demonstrating their talents which they felt had been ignored. In their conversations and interviews they expressed great enjoyment of all aspects of the project, including the opportunity for social interaction as well as the actual artwork. Particular satisfaction was expressed in the exhibition, which enabled them to challenge the negative social representation of their community.

The role of the community workers was to encourage the community residents to articulate their concerns more clearly and to take an active role in shaping their community. Their everyday work was pervaded by the exchange of small and big stories. To build relationships with local residents they spent much of their time sharing small stories which at the same time provided them with the opportunity to present the big story of community change. Without the relationship-building which was intrinsic to the exchange of small stories it would not have been possible to connect the residents with the big story of community change (Murray and Ziegler, 2015).

Reflections on the community arts project

In many respects the community arts project was very successful. This was reflected in the commentary of the participants but also by the council officials who connected with the project. It demonstrated the power of community arts to promote greater social interaction amongst older people as well as building their confidence. It also increased our understanding of the nature of the lives of older residents of disadvantaged neighbourhoods. The ethnographic nature of the research meant that information was gleaned not just from interviews but also from informal conversations which evolved over time as the participants began to trust the researchers.

However, the project also identified a number of continuing challenges. A key challenge was the reluctance of the participants to take on the project after the academic researchers left. A lifetime of disadvantage and limited opportunity meant that they were anxious about taking on responsibilities. From the outset the issue of sustainability had been a key consideration which was a primary reason for the active consultation with the local council. However, the end of the project coincided with substantial changes in the council such that our plans for continuing support were disrupted. This is an important lesson for similar community projects. The effort put into ensuring that supports are put in place after the project end is of crucial importance.

Reflections on using community action research

This form of research is time-consuming and requires substantial commitment on the part of the academic researcher. It does not follow a linear format and the researcher must accept many delays and challenges. However, that is the very nature of life and working with people rather than imposing our will upon them is surely a more ethical approach to change. The researcher cannot force the process but must take time to listen to the participants.

The ethical challenges are of vital importance. Whilst the aim is to involve the research participants actively in the project, the challenge is not to neglect the participants once the funding for the project has expired. This is very difficult as all research projects have finite funding and this is largely targeted at data collection and analysis and not at project sustainability. An important requirement is for the researchers to be explicit in their aims. They will have to withdraw from the project at some stage and they should prepare the participants for this. They should also explore alternative sources of continuing support.

Another key issue is that of power. Throughout we have emphasised that community action research aims to enhance the power of the community, but this is premised upon an assumption that this will be of value to the participants. At all times the community action researcher must reflect upon his/her assumptions and explore who benefits most from the research. They need also to consider the broader context within which they work which can either facilitate or impede the community action.

References

Brown, J. (2010). The World Café: Shaping our futures through conversations that matter. Available at: www.ReadHowYouWant.com.

Brydon-Miller, M. (2014). Using action research methodologies to address community health issues. In M. Murray (Ed.), *Critical Health Psychology (Second Edition)*. London: Palgrave Macmillan, pp. 217–232.

Brydon-Miller, M., Greenwood, D. and Eikeland, O. (Eds.) (2006). Ethics and action research [Special issue]. *Action Research*, 3(1).

Campbell, C. and Cornish, F. (2010). Towards a 'fourth generation' of approaches to HIV/AIDS management: Creating contexts for effective community mobilisation. *Aids Care*, 22(S2), 1569–1579.

Campbell, C. and Cornish, F. (2014). Reimagining community health psychology: Maps, journeys and new terrains. *Journal of Health Psychology*, 19(1), 3–15.

Campbell, C., Cornish, F., Gibbs, A. and Scott, K. (2010). Heeding the push from below: How do social movements persuade the rich to listen to the poor? *Journal of Health Psychology*, 15, 962–971.

Freire, P. (1970). Cultural action for freedom. *Harvard Educational Review*, 68(4), 476–522.

Lewin, K. (1946). Action research and minority problems. *Journal of Social Issues*, 2, 34–46.

Moscovici, S. and Marková, I. (1998). Presenting social representations: A conversation. *Culture and Psychology*, 4(3), 371–410.

Murray, M. (2002). Connecting narrative and social representation theory in health research. *Social Science Information*, 41, 653–673.

Murray, M. (2012a). Social and political health psychology in action. In M. Forshaw and D. Sheffield (Eds.), *Health Psychology in Action*. London: John Wiley and Sons, pp. 128–137.

Murray, M. (2012b). Art, social action and social change. In C. Walker, K. Johnson and L. Cunningham (Eds.), *Community Psychology and the Economics of Mental Health: Global Perspectives*. London: Palgrave Macmillan, pp. 253–265.

Murray, M. (2013). Implementation: Putting analysis into practice. In U. Flick (Ed.), *The SAGE Handbook of Qualitative Data Analysis*. London: SAGE, pp. 585–599.

Murray, M., Amigoni, D., Bernard, M., Crummet, A., Goulding, A., Munro, L., Newman, A., Rezzano, J., Rickett, M., Tew, P. and Warren, L. (2014). Understanding and transforming ageing through the arts. In A. Walker (Ed.), *The New Science of Ageing*. Bristol: Policy Press, pp. 77–112.

Murray, M. and Crummett, A. (2015). Combating social exclusion through community arts. In A. Walker (Ed.), *New Dynamics of Ageing, Volume 1*. Bristol: Policy Press.

Murray, M. and Ziegler, F. (2015). The narrative psychology of community health workers. *Journal of Health Psychology*, 20, 338–349.

Sools, A. and Murray, M. (2014). Promoting health through narrative practice. In M. Murray (Ed.), *Critical Health Psychology (Second Edition)*. London: Palgrave, pp. 235–253.

Walker, A. (Ed.) (2015). *The New Dynamics of Ageing*. Bristol: Policy Press.

Wang, C. and Burris, M.A. (1997). Photovoice: Concept, methodology, and use for participatory needs assessment. *Health Education and Behavior*, 24(3), 369–387.

Wang, C.C., Yi, W.K., Tao, Z.W. and Carovano, K. (1998). Photovoice as a participatory health promotion strategy. *Health Promotion International*, 13(1), 75–86.

Using Discourse Analysis in Social Psychology

Kirsty Budds, Abigail Locke and
Viv Burr

9

Introduction

Discourse analytic approaches are increasingly used in psychological research. In this chapter, we will briefly introduce the key discourse analytic approaches used within psychological research. Then, using an example from some work carried out by the first author on 'older motherhood', we will guide you through the practical steps associated with an approach to discourse analysis called critical discursive psychology and consider how this approach is successfully applied to qualitative data. Finally, we will consider some of the practical applications of the approach.

Discourse analysis and critical social psychology

The development of discourse analysis in social psychology has been linked to what has commonly been termed 'the crisis in social psychology' during the 1960s and 1970s (Armistead, 1974; Elms, 1975; Parker, 1989). At this time, social psychology was criticised for its individualistic approach, as well as on theoretical and methodological grounds (Hepburn, 2003). There was growing concern over the positivist experimental methods appropriated by social psychology and the artificiality of laboratory settings for studying human behaviour. Key theorists of the time called for a social psychology that would look beyond individual explanations of human behaviour and consider the cultural, historical and social context in which that behaviour takes place (Harré and Secord, 1972; Gergen, 1973). The dissatisfaction many felt with promoting social psychology as a natural science using experimental, individualistic methods led to a review of the methods used by social psychologists. It was within this context and the 'turn to language' that critical approaches to social psychology were established and, as part of this, discourse analysis was first developed within the discipline (Parker, 1990).

One essential similarity and key defining feature of discourse analytic approaches is that they are underpinned by a constructionist ontology (see

Chapter 2 in this book for more on this) and as such demand an alternative stance on the role of language in psychology. That is, for social constructionists, instead of being considered an accurate representation of people's internal thoughts, attitudes and emotions, language ('discourse') is implicated in the construction of social and psychological experience (Burr, 2015). There are a number of approaches to discourse analysis that have largely been developed and appropriated within psychology. The most common are Foucauldian Discourse Analysis (FDA) (e.g. Arribas-Ayllon and Walkerdine, 2008; Willig, 2008), and discursive psychology (DP) (e.g. Edwards, 1997; Edwards and Potter, 1992; Potter and Wetherell, 1987). These two approaches to discourse analysis are distinct and divergent; yet they overlap in some fundamental ways (Burr, 2015). We will now briefly outline these two approaches, before moving on to introduce a more combined approach to the analysis of discourse (critical discursive psychology) which has developed in response to perceived limitations associated with both Foucauldian and discursive approaches.

Foucauldian discourse analysis (FDA)

FDA is concerned with the way in which discourses shape our social worlds and personal experiences, and is influenced by post-structuralism and in particular the work of Michel Foucault. From an FDA approach the term 'discourse' refers to a linguistic system of meaning; a set of discursive resources that constructs a particular version of something in the social world, such as an object, event or category of person. Parker describes a discourse as 'a system of statements which constructs an object' (1989, p. 61). In addition, discourses hold implications for how individuals experience and participate in the social world owing to the subject positions that are made available within them (Willig, 2008).

Subject positions offer individuals different sets of rights, obligations and possibilities for social action, as well as having implications for their subjectivities, as Davies and Harré describe:

> Once having taken up a particular position as one's own, a person inevitably sees the world from the vantage point of that position and in terms of the particular images, metaphors, storylines and concepts which are made relevant within the particular discursive practice in which they are positioned. (Davies and Harré, 1990, p. 35)

Through the subject positions they make available, discourses both enable and constrain certain ways of seeing the world and ways of being in the world for those individuals who take them up (Willig, 2008). Therefore, Foucauldian discourse analysts study the way in which 'discourses facilitate and limit, enable and constrain what can be said (by whom, where and when)' (Parker, 1992, p. xiii) in addition to what people can do or have done to them (Burr, 2015). Typical questions answered through FDA focus on the discourses that are available to people within a given culture or society, and the implications these discourses may have for individuals' subjectivities (Willig, 2008).

FDA is also concerned with the action orientation of discourse, taking into consideration the function of particular discursive constructions and whose interests they serve. In addition, there is a focus on power and the effects of discourse. At any one time there are likely to be multiple discourses that may construct different, possibly competing representations and meanings of the same discursive object that may make different subject positions available to people. However, it is the case that some discourses or versions are more prevalent and appear to be more common-sense than others, such that these discourses are usually the ones that are the most accepted, become entrenched and are considered the most truthful, whilst alternatives are marginalised or invalidated (Willig, 2008). However, that is not to say that alternative discourses will never come into play. Counter-discourses and alternative subject positions emerge and become more 'available' to people over time and can begin with the individual through the resistance of subject positions that do not match an individual's own interests (Weedon, 1997).

FDA enables an exploration of the effects of wider societal discourses on individual subjectivity, the theorisation of subjectivity – a person's sense of self – being a key psychological concern. However, a limitation with FDA is that it positions individuals as largely passive, with their language, practices and subjectivities shaped and therefore effectively limited and constrained by pre-existing societal discourses. As a result, it does not consider the agency with which individuals are able to construct accounts, nor does it allow a consideration of situated language use – how people are able to construct and negotiate meaning to suit particular social situations or how they may construct identities or subjectivities in social interaction to different interactional ends. Although this is a limitation for FDA, the localised action orientation of discourse is a key concern within a discursive psychological approach to discourse analysis.

Discursive psychology (DP)

The focus of DP (Edwards and Potter, 1992; Potter and Wetherell, 1987) lies primarily within the action orientation of discourse. Discursive psychologists concern themselves with the social actions people accomplish in and with their talk and observe precisely how individuals accomplish these actions (Edwards and Potter, 1992). Integral to this approach is the notion that language is performative – it holds a function for individuals in addition to having effects.

From a DP perspective, the task of the discourse analyst is to look at what effects language performs for people within social interaction. It is suggested that people construct versions of the social world through language and use discourse as a tool to formulate versions of events in social interaction that effectively serve their own interests. However, it does not make any claims about the motivation behind such language use – that is, DP does not consider that individuals are necessarily intentionally and consciously constructing versions of events for this purpose. In this way, it contrasts with cognitivist assumptions made in mainstream psychology that talk is a route to cognition and is an accurate representation of a person's memories, thoughts, feelings, beliefs or attitudes. Instead, discursive psychologists would argue that people will draw upon traditional psychological concepts in everyday life in order to make sense of their experience and to construct different versions of events to different interactional ends (Edwards and Potter, 1992). As such, DP reconceptualises how psychologists should research and theorise about traditional areas of psychological enquiry, including cognition, attributions and identity, considering that these are not necessarily things that people *have*, but that they *do* in language to achieve certain social actions, meaning that DP is radically anti-cognitive (e.g. Edwards, 1997; Edwards and Potter, 1992; Potter, 1996; Potter and Wetherell, 1987). More recent versions of DP (e.g. Edwards and Potter, 2005) extend it to use conversation analytic principles in more detail (see also Wiggins and Potter, 2008).

A discursive psychological reading of qualitative data aims to address two fundamental questions: firstly, *what* social actions are individuals accomplishing within their talk? and, secondly, *how* exactly are they doing it? With reference to the first question, discursive psychologists consider what social function is achieved through discourse. For example, discursive psychologists consider how people construct versions of events in order to justify an action, manage stake, blame or accountability, persuade others to believe their version of events and negotiate causal attributions (Edwards and Potter, 1992; Potter and Wetherell, 1987). Secondly, precisely how individuals manage these social functions is considered through an exploration of the discursive and linguistic devices that are used to construct accounts.

As with Foucauldian approaches to discourse analysis, a DP approach has shortcomings. One of the main limitations associated with a discursive approach is that it restricts the analysis of discourse to the interactional episode in question. That is, it is concerned only with the function of discourse within a given interaction; it does not examine anything beyond, such as wider discursive practices (Parker, 1997), and negates the social, cultural and historical context in which the interaction is taking place. Therefore a limitation with this approach is that it focuses on the minutiae of talk-in-interaction and does not attend to how social action is determined, to some extent, by wider social and cultural meaning systems, in that it has little opportunity to critique and challenge meaning systems that are potentially limiting or oppressive for groups of individuals (Parker, 1992).

Critical discursive psychology (CDP)

One suggested way to overcome the limitations associated with both Foucauldian and discursive approaches to discourse analysis is to analyse discourse using a more combined approach. Margaret Wetherell and Nigel Edley have been proponents of this approach to discourse analysis (Edley, 2001; Edley and Wetherell, 2001; Wetherell, 1998; Wetherell and Edley, 1999), which they have termed critical discursive psychology (CDP) and which has gained momentum in recent years. As an approach to discourse analysis, CDP is an attempt at reconciling FDA and DP by stepping outside the analytic boundaries that each single approach defines.

CDP, like DP, advocates an analytic stance whereby attention is paid to the agency with which individuals are able to draw on discursive resources in order to accomplish varying social actions. However, it also recognises that what is available to say is to some extent shaped by social, cultural and historical context and is limited by the discursive terrain that is available to participants at any one time (Edley, 2001). Furthermore, there is a dual focus on the approach to subjectivity within discourse, whereby CDP aims to explore how discourse can to some extent constitute subjectivities, yet on the other hand can be appropriated by participants to construct and negotiate identity in social situations.

At the heart of a CDP approach to discourse analysis, then, is a dual focus on the role of discourse. Discourse is deemed both constitutive in the sense that it, to some extent, shapes, enables and constrains possibilities for identities and social action, yet it is also considered to be constructive. That is, it can be a tool used by participants within social interactions to achieve particular effects.

Wetherell (1998) and Edley (2001) consider that a focus on three particular aspects of discourse is integral to this approach, namely identification of interpretative repertoires (Gilbert and Mulkay, 1984; Potter and Wetherell, 1987), ideological dilemmas (Billig et al., 1988) and subject positions (Davies and Harré, 1990). We will briefly describe each of these analytic concepts before going on to outline the analytic procedure we used. Following that we will introduce our case example and demonstrate how a CDP approach can be applied to social psychological phenomena in a real-world setting.

Interpretative repertoires were first introduced into social psychology by Jonathan Potter and Margaret Wetherell (Potter and Wetherell, 1987). In essence, interpretative repertoires form relatively consistent and coherent ways of representing particular objects or events in the social world. They have been described as:

> recurrently used systems of terms used for characterizing and evaluating actions, events, and other phenomena. A repertoire ... is constituted through a limited range of terms used in particular stylistic and grammatical constructions. Often a repertoire will be organized around specific metaphors and figures of speech (tropes). (Potter and Wetherell, 1987, p. 149)

Edley (2001) considers that the identification of interpretative repertoires in participants' talk is important in CDP because it is through these that we will come to understand the culturally available ways of talking about a particular discursive object. Interpretative repertoires are similar to the Foucauldian notion of discourses in that they constitute 'linguistic repositories of meaning' (Edley, 2001, p. 202) made available to people through culture. Edley (2001) notes that the major difference between the two relates to the methodological and analytic focus of the work being conducted. The term 'discourses' usually signals work from a Foucauldian perspective whereby they are said to construct entire institutions and are implicated with discussions of power, shaping the practices and subjectivities of individuals. Meanwhile, repertoires are said to capture the agency with which people are able to construct the world around them and are considered the 'building blocks' of talk (Wetherell and Potter, 1992) (for a further discussion of this distinction see Edley, 2001). Interpretative repertoires can be seen as something of an available discursive currency which individuals can selectively draw on to suit the interactional task at hand.

If the identification of interpretative repertoires enables an understanding of the ways in which discursive objects are constituted through discourse, locating ideological dilemmas is said to assist with this. The concept of an ideological dilemma represents the dilemmatic nature of our common-sense understandings of the world in which we live (Billig et al., 1988). That is, there is not one singular way in which phenomena are understood, but often contrary or competing ways of making sense of and describing something. Within CDP, identification of ideological dilemmas offers an exploration of the prevalent and perhaps contradictory representations of particular discursive objects and how the tensions within and between, to use Billig's term, our 'lived ideologies' manifest themselves within social interaction.

The final concept central to a CDP analysis, which is also used with the Foucauldian approaches to discourse analysis, is subject positions. Attention to subject positions is useful because, as Edley (2001) notes, 'it is this concept that connects the wider notions of discourses and interpretative repertoires to the social construction of particular selves' (p. 210). Within CDP, subject positions are made available to individuals through interpretative repertoires. These subject positions are said to offer, yet also limit, possibilities for subjectivity and social action in those who take them up. However, van Langenhove and Harré (1999) also describe subject positions as fluid, not fixed – people use them during social interactions to 'cope with the situation they usually find themselves in'. In other words, individuals are not only positioned within discourses or repertoires, which to some extent might constitute their subjectivity, but they also utilise subject positions, taking up particular positions within discourse to use to their own ends – to account for, justify or explain social actions.

Our case example – a CDP analysis of 'older motherhood'

Introduction to the study

Over the past few decades the number of women in the UK becoming mothers later on in life has markedly increased. A similar trend has been observed in the US, Australia and other parts of the Western world (Beets et al., 2011).

'Older mothers' are typically defined as women who have their first baby at an age considered to be advancing of at least 35 and more commonly 40. Health professionals have raised concerns about increasing numbers of 'older mothers', as they have warned of the risks of infertility in women and health risks to mother and baby that increase with advancing maternal age. Moreover, women who come to motherhood later in life are often stereotyped as 'selfish' for 'choosing' to put their careers before mother-hood (Budds et al., 2013). In light of this context, and the relative dearth of qualitative research on older motherhood, particularly within a UK setting, a central aim of this research was to explore what it means to be an older mother. Furthermore, the research set out to examine how societal meanings of older motherhood might impact upon women's experiences of mothering relatively later. In order to meet both these aims, the project consisted of two studies: (1) an analysis of British newspaper articles where the focus was older motherhood; and (2) semi-structured interviews with women defined as 'older mothers' to explore their experiences of pregnancy, maternity care and early motherhood.

Why was a CDP approach appropriate?

A CDP approach to data analysis here is appropriate as it enabled an explo-ration of the culturally available ways of talking about 'older mothers' and the implications these might have for shaping subjectivity and experience. However, it also enabled a consideration of how participants may use discourse as a tool to construct and negotiate their identity from both the interpretative repertoires and subject positions that are available in order to achieve particular interactional effects.

Doing CDP

Data

Similar to Foucauldian approaches to discourse analysis, we would argue that a CDP approach can be applied anywhere there is meaning (Parker, 1992). Most commonly this approach is applied to empirical data collected through interviews or focus groups. However, it can also be applied to secondary data, such as policy documents, newspaper articles or other forms of mass media.

Transcription

If collecting primary data, it is recommended that data is transcribed verba-tim with some basic transcription notation, through which some of the more palpable details of the discourse are marked onto the transcript. As such, we recommend a 'light' version of Jefferson's transcription notation system (Jefferson, 2004) such as that used by Potter and Wetherell (1987). This approach captures some of the key linguistic and discursive features of the discourse, whilst not compromising the readability of the transcript or the ability to attend to the wider discursive meanings in the data.

Analysis

What follows is an explanation of how a CDP approach can be applied to qualitative data. This is a series of six stages that constitute a 'checklist' of concepts that were attended to throughout the analysis. The first four stages of analysis share similarities with steps of FDA outlined by Willig (2008) and focus on the constitutive nature of discourse, the identification of the discursive terrain that is available to discuss 'older motherhood' and how it shapes possibilities for practice and subjectivities. The final two stages draw on a more DP approach and consider how accounts of older motherhood are constructed by participants from the discursive currency available, and to what ends. These stages were applied to both the newspaper and the interview data sets.

One: Discursive constructions

Similar to the first stage of FDA, as outlined by Carla Willig (2008), the first stage of analysis involved the identification of the discursive constructions of the topic under study – in this case, 'older motherhood'. In practice, this preliminary stage involved highlighting all extracts where older motherhood – or mothering later – was referred to. This included both explicit as well as implicit references, and it is this first stage whereby the 'discursive terrain' of older motherhood is identified. Descriptive and interpretative notes or codes were produced at this stage in order to highlight the different ways in which being an older mother was discussed and, as such, the discursive meanings of older motherhood were identified.

Two: Interpretative repertoires

Leading on from this came the identification of interpretative repertoires. At this stage, the discursive constructions of older motherhood are broken down. Interpretative repertoires are usually identified in discourse analytic research through their repetition across a data corpus (Edley and Wetherell, 2001; Potter and Wetherell, 1987). Importantly, variation between constructions of older motherhood is attended to in order to explore and distinguish the different interpretative repertoires or ways of constructing older motherhood.

Three: Subject positions

A further consideration was to identify the subject positions or 'ways of being' that are made available for participants within the discourse, and, by implication, what ways of being are being denied. Further, the implications these subject positions may have for subjectivity and experience were examined.

Four: Practice

This stage involved considering the possibilities for practice opened up by the different interpretative repertoires and subject positions identified. That is, what various constructions of older motherhood, and the positions offered within them tell us about what older mothers can or should do, or have done to them.

Five: Constructions

At this stage, the analysis moved away from the constitutive nature discourse to focus more on the constructive ability of discourse. Here, the focus lay with which discursive resources participants are drawing on, and which they are resisting. There was an additional focus on the action orientation of discourse here. Firstly, there was a consideration of what is achieved, in an ideological sense, by drawing on particular interpretative repertoires and subject positions and resisting others. Moreover, the implications of discourse use were considered more locally, in terms of what participants are able to achieve in the interaction at hand.

Six: Discursive accomplishments

Finally there was a focus on the localised deployment of discourse through examining exactly *how* language used by participants enabled them to achieve particular interactional functions. That is, there was a focus on the discursive and linguistic devices used by participants in order to construct a particular account of something, invoke a particular interpretative repertoire or take up or resist a particular subject position.

Applying CDP to qualitative data

What follows is an example of how we applied the stages of CDP to the interviews with older mothers undertaken in this research project.

Stage one: Discursive constructions

This stage involved identifying the discursive meanings of older motherhood evident in the interviews. In practice, this meant highlighting explicit extracts where women discussed coming to motherhood later on in life and the timing of their pregnancies, as well as their experiences of being an older mother. Additionally, this stage was informed by constructions of older motherhood found in the British press (Budds, 2013; Budds et al., 2013).

Stage two: Interpretative repertoires

Something that was frequently discussed in the interviews with older mothers was the risks associated with advancing maternal age. Generally speaking, through risk categorisation processes, women over 35 mother within a discourse of risk through which they are positioned as 'at risk' (Budds, 2013; Locke and Budds, 2013). Through the analysis, two interpretative repertoires were identified that women drew upon. The first, 'risk as contingent', constructed the level of risk the women faced as dependent on multiple and individualised factors, as opposed to maternal age alone. Secondly, through drawing on a 'normality' repertoire, women's pregnancies were constructed as 'normal', as nothing out of the ordinary, and therefore to be excused of any particular attention or concern about 'risk'.

What follows is a data extract taken from the first repertoire – risk as contingent. We will draw upon this extract to demonstrate how the final four stages of analysis may be carried out on the text by way of identifying subject positions, practices, constructions and discursive accomplishments.

This extract comes from Rebecca, who discusses the risks of fertility problems associated with maternal age. At 36, Rebecca is positioned, and positions herself, as 'at risk' of infertility, and became pregnant unexpectedly.

> R   Just er (2.0) it's, it's just touch and go I mean (.) I don't erm (3.0) I know people talk about the (.) the risks of you (.) being infertile as you get older (1.0) I think that it's more (2.0) I, I think it's more down to sort of (1.0) y' I think more emphasis should be placed on the individual because I think that we're individually quite different (.) and I think it would be helpful if people knew earlier on (.) how, how fertile they were and how long (.) you know what their chances were.
>
> IV   Hmm.
>
> R   Um (1.0) because if (.) somebody had said to me (1.0) you would have no problem getting pregnant right up until the age of 45 (.) I pr' (.) I probably would have waited even longer to be in (.) a (.) relationship and have that support.
>
> IV   Hmm.
>
> R   But it's because you just don't know.
>
> IV   Yeah.
>
> R   That I kind of, you know, I got to 35 and thought (.) y'know I don't want to risk (.) you know, it, it was in my life plan having children (.) don't want to risk not ever having (.) children.

Throughout this extract she invokes a contingent repertoire in which fertility risk is something that is unique, individual and dependent on the individual woman, rather than maternal age necessarily: 'people talk about the risks of you being infertile as you get older ... I think we're individually quite different' (lines 2–6).

Three: Subject positions
The subject position debated within this extract is whether or not Rebecca is positioned as 'at risk'. Within this extract we can see that Rebecca is positioned as 'at risk' of fertility problems owing to her maternal age through wider understandings of age-related fertility categories: 'people talk about the risks of you being infertile as you get older' (line 2). The implications of this in

terms of her subjectivity or 'being' at risk are most felt when she discusses how she did not 'want to risk not ever having children' (line 19). Thus positioned as 'at risk', Rebecca saw the world from the vantage point of that position and considered herself to be 'at risk' of fertility problems.

Four: Practice

The implications of this subject position for practice can be observed as Rebecca alludes to the impact that concerns about age-related fertility problems had on her timing of pregnancy: 'I got to 35 and thought y'know I don't want to risk it...it was in my life plan having children...don't want to risk not ever having children' (lines 17–19). Based on being 'at risk', Rebecca suggests she was prompted to plan motherhood imminently for fear that if she left it any later she would be unable to have children. This was despite the fact that she was in a relationship she described as 'complicated' – a relationship that subsequently ended, leaving Rebecca as a single mother.

Five: Constructions

In drawing upon a contingent repertoire throughout this extract, Rebecca builds up a critique of the taken-for-granted assumption that advancing age is associated with fertility problems in all women. Instead, she constructs fertility as unique and individual, meaning that the subject position of 'at risk' does not necessarily apply to all older mothers – including herself. Further, using her own experience as evidence, she discusses the implications of the absence of this repertoire from women's understandings of fertility and in doing so speaks to the importance of alternative understandings of the relationship between maternal age and fertility problems.

As such, the ideological function of the discourse surrounding risk and maternal age is apparent through this extract. It is this discourse that shapes Rebecca's decision-making about when to have a child. Had she been aware of counter-arguments and different information she talks about waiting longer to be in a relationship and have support, rather than becoming a single mother: 'because if, if somebody had said to me you would have no problem getting pregnant right up until the age of 45 I pr', I probably would have waited even longer to be in a relationship and have that support'. Rebecca's alignment with this discourse and so concern about age-related fertility decline additionally functions to account for her status as a single mother and justify her decision-making regarding the timing of her pregnancy.

Six: Discursive accomplishments

Finally, we can take a look at the discursive accomplishments of Rebecca's talk and examine exactly how the language she uses assists in achieving these different interactional functions. For example, Rebecca's account of her decision-making around the timing of pregnancy is of interest here. In her account she suggests she rushed into pregnancy owing to the pervasiveness of the concerns about infertility in older women and her consequent positioning of being 'at risk' of fertility problems. Her positioning is clearest in lines 17–19 where she discusses not wanting to risk 'not ever having children', which is an extreme case formulation (Pomerantz, 1986). Using this extreme case formulation enables Rebecca to position herself as 'at risk' of the worst case scenario – not ever being able to have children – and functions to justify her decision surrounding the timing of her pregnancy – namely not waiting to be in a relationship. This description also constitutes a three part list (Jefferson, 1990), which is a rhetorical device which bolsters the persuasiveness of her account and shores up her subjective feelings of being 'at risk'. Again, this has the effect of further legitimising her actions.

Reflection of use of this method in this research

Carrying out a CDP approach to data analysis is not exactly straightforward. Although we have outlined a set of six stages in the analytic process, we are not suggesting that these stages should be followed in a linear process, although this may be helpful to a beginner to CDP to provide some analytic structure.

As we have argued in this chapter, the benefit of this approach to discourse analysis is that it avoids the limitations associated with pursuing either FDA or DP in isolation and as such was the best approach to take in order to meet the aims of the research project. As Brown and Locke (2008) in their discussion of contemporary methods in qualitative psychology note, research needs to be 'contextually grounded', 'socially oriented' and offer 'politically informed analysis' (p. 387). Given the different aspects of CDP, we would suggest that it is a key method in being able to fulfil this brief. In this sense, discourse analysis has a clear potential to be applied and there are a variety of research studies that, through their findings, can offer insight in order to work towards social change. Willig (1999) suggests that this view sees discourse as 'social critique'. In this way, the research study here could be viewed in this vein as a social critique of the ways in which 'older mothers' are positioned in the press with the subsequent interview work noting how the mothers resisted and changed these discourses into the positive 'older mother'.

References

Armistead, N. (Ed.). (1974). *Reconstructing Social Psychology*. Harmondsworth: Penguin.

Arribas-Ayllon, M. and Walkerdine, V. (2008). Foucauldian discourse analysis. In W. Stainton-Rogers and C. Willig (Eds.), *Handbook of Qualitative Research in Psychology*. London: SAGE, pp. 91–108.

Beets, G., Schippers, J. and te Velde, E.R. (Eds.). (2011). *The Future of Motherhood in Western Societies: Late Fertility and Its Consequences*. New York: Springer.

Billig, M., Condor, S., Edwards, D., Gane, M., Middleton, D. and Radley, A. (1988). *Ideological Dilemmas*. London: SAGE.

Brown, S.D. and Locke, A. (2008). Social psychology. In C. Willig and W. Stainton-Rogers (Eds.), *The SAGE Handbook of Qualitative Research in Psychology*. London: SAGE, pp. 373–389.

Budds, K. (2013). A critical discursive analysis of 'older' motherhood. Unpublished PhD thesis, University of Huddersfield.

Budds, K., Locke, A. and Burr, V. (2013). 'Risky Business': Constructing the 'Choice' to 'Delay' Motherhood in the British Press. *Feminist Media Studies*, 13(1), 132–147.

Burr, V. (2015). *Social Constructionism (Third Edition)*. London: Routledge.

Edley, N. (2001). Analysing masculinity: Interpretative repertoires, ideological dilemmas and subject positions. In M. Wetherell, S. Taylor and S.J. Yates (Eds.), *Discourse as Data: A Guide for Analysis*. London: Open University Press, pp. 189–288.

Edley, N. and Wetherell, M. (2001). Jekyll and Hyde: Men's constructions of feminism and feminists. *Feminism and Psychology*, 11, 439–457.

Edwards, D. (1997). *Discourse and Cognition*. London: SAGE.

Edwards, D. and Potter, J. (1992). *Discursive Psychology*. London: SAGE.

Edwards, D. and Potter, J. (2005). Discursive psychology, mental states and descriptions. In H. te Molder and J. Potter (Eds.), *Conversation and Cognition*. Cambridge: Cambridge University Press, pp. 241–259.

Elms, A. (1975). The crisis of confidence in social psychology. *American Psychologist*, 30, 967–976.

Davies, B. and Harré, R. (1990). Positioning: The discursive production of selves. *Journal for the Theory of Social Behaviour*, 20, 43–63.

Gergen, K. (1973). Social psychology as history. *Journal of Personality and Social Psychology*, 26, 309–320.

Gilbert, N. and Mulkay, M. (1984). *Opening Pandora's Box: A Sociological Analysis of Scientists' Discourse*. Cambridge: Cambridge University Press.

Harré, R., and Secord, P.S. (1972). *The Explanation of Social Behaviour*. Oxford: Basil Blackwell.

Hepburn, A. (2003). *Critical Social Psychology*. London: SAGE.

Jefferson, G. (1990). List construction as a task and resource. In G. Psathas (Ed.), *Interaction Competence*. Washington: International Institute for Ethnomethodology and Conversation Analysis and University Press America, pp. 63–92.

Jefferson, G. (2004). Glossary of transcript symbols with an introduction. In G.H. Lerner (Ed.), *Conversation Analysis: Studies for the First Generation*. Amsterdam: John Benjamins, pp. 13–31.

Locke, A. and Budds, K. (2013). 'We thought if it's going to take two years then we need to start that now': Age, probabilistic reasoning and the timing of pregnancy in older first-time mothers. *Health, Risk and Society*, 15, 525–542.

Parker, I. (1989). *The Crisis in Modern Social Psychology – And How to End It*. London: Routledge.

Parker, I. (1990). Discourse: Definitions and contradictions. *Philosophical Psychology*, 3(2), 189–204.

Parker, I. (1992). *Discourse Dynamics: Critical Analysis for Social and Individual Psychology*. London: Routledge.

Pomerantz, A. (1986). Extreme case formulations: A way of legitimizing claims. *Human Studies*, 9, 219–229.

Potter, J. (1996). *Representing Reality: Discourse, Rhetoric and Social Construction.* London: SAGE.

Potter, J. and Wetherell, M. (1987). *Discourse and Social Psychology: Beyond Attitudes and Behaviour.* London: SAGE.

Van Langenhove, L. and Harré, R. (1999). Introducing positioning theory. In R. Harré and L. van Langenhove (Eds.), *Positioning Theory: Moral Contexts of Intentional Action.* Blackwell: Oxford, pp. 14-31.

Weedon, C. (1997). *Feminist Practice and Poststructuralist Theory (Second Edition).* Oxford: Blackwell (First Edition 1987).

Wetherell, M. (1998). Positioning and interpretative repertoires: Conversation analysis and post-structuralism in dialogue. *Discourse and Society,* 9, 387–412.

Wetherell, M. and Edley, N. (1999). Negotiating hegemonic masculinity: Imaginary positions and psycho-discursive practices. *Feminism and Psychology,* 9(3), 335–356.

Wetherell, M. and Potter, J. (1992). *Mapping the Language of Racism: Discourse and the Legitimation of Exploitation.* London: Harvester Wheatsheaf.

Wiggins, S. and Potter, J. (2008). Discursive psychology. In C. Willig and W. Stainton-Rogers (Eds.), *Handbook of Qualitative Research in Psychology.* London: SAGE, pp. 73–90.

Willig, C. (Ed.) (1999). *Applied Discourse Analysis: Social and Psychological Interventions.* Buckingham: Open University Press.

Willig, C. (2008). *Introducing Qualitative Research in Psychology: Adventures in Theory and Method (Second Edition).* Maidenhead: McGraw Hill, Open University Press.

Digging Deeper: Using Grounded Theory to Explore Meanings of Gardens and Gardening across the Lifespan

10

Harriet Gross and Vicky Alfrey

Introduction

Environmental psychology overview

Environmental psychology concerns the relationship between human behaviour and the natural and built environment. Research in environmental psychology aims to understand the psychological processes underpinning that relationship; the impact of the environment on behaviour and experience; and how to develop effective strategies for behaviour change.

A core strand of environmental psychology research focuses on the relationship between nature and health and wellbeing. It examines who benefits from activity in natural settings, what interventions are effective (e.g. Beute and de Kort, 2014; Hawkins et al., 2013) and what aspects of the environment are beneficial or restorative. Generally, natural scenes are preferred to urban scenes and White et al. (2013), comparing four different settings, suggest that woodlands or seaside are the most restorative. Key researchers in the area have investigated whether similarly positive effects can be achieved by viewing nature from a window or by engaging directly with it (Kaplan, 2001; Kaplan and Kaplan 1989; Ulrich, 1984). Experimental work exploring physical activity indicates that activity outdoors has a more beneficial impact on psychological wellbeing and health than the same activity undertaken indoors (Pretty et al., 2010). Such benefits have led to 'green exercise' being prescribed as a treatment for depression and being referred to as 'Vitamin G' (Groenewegen et al., 2006). Research in the UK and the USA suggests that the presence of urban green spaces is associated with fewer behavioural and emotional problems in children (Flouri et al., 2014) possibly by acting as a buffer against stress.

A major aspect of research in environmental psychology concerns the ways that individual differences in attitudes and beliefs about nature and the environment are related to engagement with nature, through activities like gardening (Kaplan, 1973) or walking, and to pro-environment sustainable behaviours such as energy conservation and recycling (Gosling and Williams, 2010) as well as to creativity (Leong et al., 2014) and to wellbeing (Nisbet et al., 2010; Howell et al., 2011). The extent to which nature is part of an individual's identity appears to be associated with factors of openness, agreeableness and conscientiousness (Milfont and Sibley, 2012), and includes traits such as connectedness to nature (Schultz, 2002; Mayer and Frantz, 2004), nature relatedness (Nisbet et al., 2009), environmental identity (Clayton, 2012; Clayton and Opotow, 2003) and dispositional empathy with nature (Tam, 2013). The construct of connectedness has an affective dimension and is relevant to people's sense of place and the meanings that they associate with places and settings (Stedman, 2002; Korpela and Hartig, 1996). Place identity (Proshansky et al., 1983) and place attachment (Low and Altman, 1992; Manzo, 2005) also play a part in environmental behaviour, for example resistance to wind farms (Devine-Wright and Howes, 2010). The evolutionary Biophilia Hypothesis (Wilson, 1993) proposes that there are innate human links with the natural world, and an interdependence between humans and nature, expressed as a need to be near plants and animals, particularly for children (Kahn and Kellert, 2002). A powerful explanation for the effect of nearby nature, attention restoration theory proposes that the benefit arises from the characteristics of spaces which allow for recovery from directed attention (Kaplan and Kaplan, 1989). Similarly, the quality of the outdoor activity permits 'flow' (Csikszmentmihalyi, 1990) – the capacity to be completely absorbed and to resist distraction – and thus become detached from the daily routine.

The significance of the natural environment for people's identity, wellbeing and behaviour has far-reaching implications for sustainability in the broadest sense. As well as building knowledge of what works and why, it is important to understand people's own experiences with nature, as this impacts on their willingness to engage or their capacity to benefit, and qualitative research is ideal for this purpose.

Using qualitative methods in environmental psychology

Environmental psychology research is catholic in its approach, using experimental paradigms, surveys, scales and questionnaires and a variety of qualitative methods. A review of the planned contents for volume 40 of the *Journal of Environmental Psychology* accessed during the writing of this chapter (www. sciencedirect.com/science/journal/02724944/40) shows clearly the diversity of research techniques: a comparison of age and gender on a topographical memory test; an experimental study of gaze direction; testing the theory of planned behaviour to predict commuter mode of travel; an online survey of connectedness to nature and creativity; use of GIS and police data to examine rape locations in Sweden; and a paper on spatial discounting and place identity, proposing a new theory of sense of place.

This reflects the diverse nature of applied research; the domain of human interaction with the environment is not exclusive to psychology, crossing many disciplinary boundaries, including sociology, geography, public health, design, planning, horticulture, landscape and architecture. Since identity and meaning are integral to practical and theoretical work in the area, taking a qualitative approach is unexceptional. For instance, methodologies for understanding place identity primarily involve qualitative techniques such as interviewing, participant observation and discourse analysis. Milligan et al. (2004) used diary methods to gather data on the health and activities of older people, including gardening. Relevant research attending to aspects of meaning has long drawn directly on people's accounts of their own experiences of gardens, for example Mark Bhatti used data from the UK Mass Observation Archive (Bhatti, 1999, 2006). Geographers and social policy researchers investigating the benefits of community gardening (Sempik et al., 2005) and allotments (Crouch and Ward, 1997) have also used personal accounts. Therefore, as qualitative researchers working in this field, our decision to use grounded theory sits comfortably with research relevant to environmental psychology.

Overview of research methodology – grounded theory

Grounded theory is an analytical approach comprising a set of guidelines which are applied to develop a theory that can illuminate the processes and relationships under study. The researchers who choose to use grounded theory (GT) typically presume that they may know little or nothing about the meanings that people will have for their actions. The method involves inductive thinking to draw together codes into categories that represent these meanings, in a systematic and flexible way, in order to construct theory from the data. Thus the theory is *grounded* in the data. The theory is then presented through the writing process. There are many excellent texts describing in detail how to undertake GT; see, for example, Charmaz (2014), Chamberlain et al. (2004), Sbaraini et al. (2011) and Willig (2013), all of which address the practicalities of the process.

Key elements of GT are willingness to be open to ideas, interaction with the data from the start of its collection and analysis, and constant comparison across and within data sets, with repeated and developmental progression towards a conclusion (theory). It focuses on actions and social or social psychological processes rather than topics. The starting point is the experiencing individual/ participant, and, through searching out possible themes that may run through the data, analysis can provide an idea of how people's lives work and attend to multiple levels of meaning. GT is particularly helpful when working in new areas with an exploratory focus, as it does not rely on previous theory to identify what should be analysed or to drive the analytical process, and the use of systematic methods permits a deeper understanding of psychological processes.

Our research in environmental psychology is concerned with the meanings that people attach to natural environments, that is, with sense of place, addressing the significance of gardens and gardening, both at home and on the allotment, across the lifespan. The way different people engage with natural settings may be a result of their own personal prior experiences (Parry-Jones, 1990) and the subsequent meanings of nature for any individual are highly personalised, so the life history of gardening for each participant is likely to be unique and varied. This variability lends itself to interviews as the means of data collection. We wanted people to speak freely about their own experiences without directing the discussion to preconceived categories of life stage or ageing. The symbolic interactionist underpinnings of GT as a general approach are in keeping with the constructionist perspective that was taken in some of our research. A number of studies have been successfully carried out using GT with older adult groups (Clare et al., 2008) and on interactions with the environment (Manzo, 2005), which strengthened our view that GT would be a suitable technique.

Ethical considerations

Environmental psychology is embedded in larger ethical issues about people and their place in the world, so there are political as well as ethical aspects to research in this field. This may have ethical implications for the way in which studies involve their participants and data is collected, especially research that involves promotion of environmentally friendly behaviour or that explores behaviour change during any interventions. In fact a meta-analysis by Kornos and Gifford (2014) does express some doubts about the reliability of self-reports of pro-environment behaviours as a basis for designing interventions. The lack of relationship between reported and observed behaviours may reflect demand characteristics of evaluating interventions in such contexts and suggests that information about participation might need to take this into account. Bearing this in mind, however, the range of research methods in use means that ethical considerations will depend on the parameters of any project, such as whether research takes place in the community, in restricted settings, or within universities.

For our own studies, we follow standard ethical protocols for qualitative research projects involving interviews, which require that we must always be aware of personal boundaries and be sensitive to potential distress when working individually with participants and asking them to tell us about their experience. The key ethical issue for us was the recruitment of older participants.

Older people (i.e. those over 65 years) are identified as a 'vulnerable' group under BPS and other guidelines, and require special attention for ethics submissions, particularly with the provision of access, information, timing and consent procedures. To address these we created a simple but comprehensive consent form, presented as a checklist, which we used in the garden research and our subsequent work with allotment holders. Working with opportunity samples in the community, this was sufficient to allow recruitment and data collection. When the research involved residents of sheltered housing, we negotiated with the housing organisation's head office for access to their schemes and then to their residents. They imposed some limitations on access and recruitment and, to comply with their requirements, the recruitment was done indirectly, negotiated via each scheme manager, who distributed leaflets explaining the key features of the study to each resident, who then collected the names of any residents who expressed interest. The names were passed to the researchers and managers advised on the health status of residents, to allow for necessary extra care during the process. Residents were initially contacted by telephone and then called back several days later, to avoid any sense of pressure to take part. Several people who had initially expressed interest retracted their offer on the second call. All those who agreed to participate were given further information and gave their written consent. Some residents remained concerned about the tape recorder and asked for it to be turned off if they were talking about personal matters. This was always done and noted in the transcripts and in any memos made during or after the interview.

Our research

Introduction

For many people, their closest engagement with the natural environment is at home or in their neighbourhoods, and domestic gardens and allotments are probably where people have their most immediate and sustained contact with nature. Importantly, people can engage at any level, not just by having their own garden, but also by having a window with a view of gardens, some outside pots or a window box or indoor plants. When we started researching the topic of people's relationships with their gardens and their gardening activity, we found that, despite evidence that connectedness and behaviour can change, the meaning of gardens was a relatively static concept and did not necessarily take account of potentially changing meanings during people's lives or the relative significance of gardens when making life changes. We have therefore been exploring this in the context of home gardens, gardens in retirement and allotments. In this section, we give a flavour of the work we have been doing and the issues that can be explored using a qualitative approach.

Applying GT in the garden

Our first project used GT to explore the meanings of gardens and gardening across the lifespan (Gross and Lane, 2007) and prefigured some of the work we detail below on gardening and the ageing identity. The study involved qualitative interviews with an opportunity sample of 18 individuals (13 women, five men) representing each decade from 18 to 70+ years (ranging from 18 to 80), and used a realist approach to the analysis. Following standard practice, the process involved preparation (interview guidelines, data collection and storage), pre-analysis (coding), main analysis (the secondary refining stage of linking and defining categories) which was repeated until the categories were saturated, when the key concepts and definitions could be drawn together (outcome and theory). Table 10.1 below shows how the differing and apparently diverse categories that emerged from the iterative analysis of the individual interviews and the comparison of the data for four age periods (childhood, early, middle and later adulthood) led to the emergence of three themes: *escapism, ownership and identity* and *relationships* These three were relevant for all participants expressed in different ways across the age groups, as the categories demonstrate (see Table 10.1). What follows is a summary of the characteristics of these themes.

Table 10.1 A representation of the emergent categories and the convergent themes from the analysis of interviews with people about their gardens, showing which of the categories are most relevant at each life stage. Shading (white, light, dark) indicates which categories define which theme

Age group	Categories	Themes
Childhood 0–18 yrs	sibling relationships	
	play and space	
	socialisation	
	future plans	relationships
Youth 18–30 yrs	outdoor escapism	
	future plans	
	indoor to outdoor	
	coping	escapism
Adulthood 31–70 yrs	transformation	
	addiction	
	coping	
	constraints	ownership and identity
	family interaction	
Late adulthood 70+ yrs	gardening career	
	connection with nature	
	real gardeners	

Escapism reflects how the garden provides a positive distraction from the cares and pressures of everyday life, and links closely with the evidence for the beneficial impact of outdoor activity on mood and the studies of child-hood memories of favourite places (see Korpela, 2002) as well as the relaxing and restorative qualities that recur in personal accounts of spending time in gardens. We did not interview anyone under 18, but when asked about their experience of gardens, many participants mentioned the garden as a space to play as a child and the importance of the plants and trees for that play: '*it was just sort of left to be overgrown which made it more fun – it was like we could explore*' and '*if there wasn't a garden...there would have been nowhere to play*'. Having somewhere to escape to is highly valued, and not just for play, but as a place to take work: '*I can remember sitting out there revising A levels, sitting out in the sun revising*'. The removal of potentially stressful activity into a place associated with escape or fun can be considered a form of coping strategy. This aspect was very prevalent in the adult period, where absorption in an activity allows people to disengage: '*It's good therapy...I switch right off*' and relates to the concept of 'flow'. At this period, the play element of escape was perhaps a more aesthetically driven emotional experience: '*it's a place of absolute curiosity, diversion, colour, pleasure and smell...it's just the feel of it*' and, as this suggests, as people got older, escape was as much about activity as about reflection in the physical space, often through particular plants that could be highly symbolic, commemorating people and past events. The idea of people in the garden links the theme of escape to that of relation-ships. Many participants highlighted the pleasurable and positive social links associated with the garden through friends and family, and the strong recipro-cal relationship forged through working with nature once they started garden-ing: '*It gives you ten times as much back.*' The relationship with nature was ubiquitous in people's talk about their gardens and the attribution of agency also features in the need to work with nature to achieve a shared outcome.

The core themes of ownership and identity were highly salient in adulthood when interest in gardens or gardening was sparked by home ownership: '*it's that little patch of land that's yours, isn't it*', and younger participants also attached importance to owning a garden in the future: '*I definitely want to have a garden when I'm older and plants and stuff*'. Alongside ownership, the garden was clearly presented as a place to develop and to display identity, in terms of choice of plants, structure, components and so on. Very often this was to highlight distinctiveness: '*it's different to everyone else's*'; so the garden represents an individual's interests, preferences and passions (cf. Bhatti and Church, 2001). It was also about identity as a gardener, which incorporated elements of control and working with nature, to create something, often from scratch, which reflected the owner's identity and embodied their effort, and this effort is rewarding: '*I mean, with gardens you can see the efforts you've taken, the results and that can be quite beneficial.*' Being able to make the effort is central to the gardener identity and was mentioned by a number of the older respondents with some concern: '*... when the day comes that we* *can't manage we'll really have to think about moving on*'; the solution of employing other people was seen as an intrusion and a loss of their direct engagement and identity: '*I did lose something else along the way, it's not the same as doing it yourself.*'

In late adulthood, the positive and beneficial elements associated with the garden remain while the concept of retreat or escape may be less relevant. Instead home gardens may visibly reflect individual limitations and changing abilities, and be an indicator of an individual's capacity to manage home main-tenance in later life (Peace et al., 2005). As they age, individuals move from a public work-centred role to a home-based world. Importantly, the activity of gardening continued to provide opportunity for self-expression and creativ-ity while the natural cycle of gardening also represented continuity, ongoing activity and purpose, as well as providing a social context and a focus for shared interests. From this study, we concluded that the concept of the garden as a retreat, as 'escapist and private' (Bhatti and Church, 2001), is psychologi-cally important across the lifespan. The analysis illustrates, too, that, during the course of an individual's lifespan, the garden symbolises all of Francis and Hester's (1990) paradigm of the garden as experience, idea, place and action. However, these concepts could only be experienced simultaneously when a strong connection was established through ownership of a garden.

The study highlighted the importance of place attachment and the garden-ing identity, and led us to consider how the aspects of identity associated with the garden are expressed when gardening takes place away from home, such as allotment gardening, or when people do move on to situations where they may no longer have ownership of a garden. This takes us on to our next example, where we also give more detail about how the GT procedures worked for this study.

Sheltered housing[1]

Research on gardens and gardening meaning had said little about the gardens within specialised retirement housing. In the United Kingdom options for housing in later life include staying 'at home' or moving to sheltered housing, a care home, a nursing home, or a retirement village. We know that older people who take part in more activities like gardening have stronger social connec-tions and better physical health (Milligan et al., 2004) and that horticultural therapy can be a cost-effective and beneficial intervention for a number of client groups, including older adults (Heliker et al., 2000), but these kinds

---

[1] Sheltered housing in the UK usually comprises self-contained accommodation in apartments or bungalows, with some shared facilities such as congregation areas and recreation space and some warden/manager control to provide support if needed. These schemes rarely cater for people with serious health problems requiring nursing care.

of opportunities may not be available within housing schemes. When people leave home for some form of supported or communal housing, they may well be leaving a garden, which may not be replaced in their new location. Many housing schemes have communal gardens, and we wanted to look at how residents engaged with them, and how these were perceived in relation to their own previous experience of gardens or of gardening. In addition, we wanted to relate our findings and emerging theory to wider societal representations of ageing, so we took a social constructionist approach in this study.

Interviews were carried out at seven sheltered housing schemes in the East Midlands, with 29 volunteer participants, 20 women and 9 men, aged between 56 and 90 years old, all of whom were white British or Irish. There was no requirement to be an active gardener, but the sample included more people who engaged in gardening (or had done so) than those who had little engagement with gardens. The gender balance probably reflected the increased likelihood that women will volunteer and the population of women living in sheltered housing.[2]

Interviews using an intensive approach (Charmaz, 2014) were carried out on site. Most took place in residents' own accommodation, but some took place in communal spaces or out of doors. An initial list of open-ended questions was developed and piloted, including questions relating to previous experiences of gardening, moving to sheltered housing and experiences of gardens in sheltered housing. The questions acted as a guide for the interviewer and each interview progressed according to the topics raised by individual residents. Ideas developed during the open coding of the earlier transcripts were used to guide subsequent interviews; in particular, the subject of houseplants was added as a potential subject of discussion. (See also Chapter 3 in this volume, and King and Horrocks, 2010.)

Notes were made at every stage, directly following each interview, concerning the setting and any discussion before or after the interview which could clarify points within the transcript and alert us to our own and others' preconceptions. Detailed descriptions of the schemes were recorded. Memos made during the process of transcription and open coding, and constant comparison and thematic coding, were used throughout the process of analysis, and contributed to the development of theory. As expected, memos generated new questions. For example, a memo made after one interview noted that 'X's name came up again, certainly seems to be some feeling about this person', and after discussion about our category of 'ownership', for subsequent interviews we included a question about who was 'in charge' of gardens or gardening in the schemes.

---

[2] ONS data 2011 indicates that the proportion of women living in non-nursing home communal accommodation is twice that of men in the oldest 85+ age group (ONS, 2011).

From the start of data collection until well after the last interview, transcribing and coding were being carried out simultaneously and the process of open coding was started as soon as possible. In keeping with Charmaz's recommendations, initial codes were kept as active as possible (Charmaz, 2014). Line-by-line coding was carried out with all of the transcripts to ensure that the developing analysis was grounded in the data, and was not diverted down a particular route by categories identified too quickly in the process of analysis. In vivo coding was also utilised. The process of constant comparison was used throughout the project, with comparisons being made at the individual participant and at housing scheme level as well as across all transcripts. The initial code of 'being a gardener', which appeared regularly as the interviews progressed and was subsequently categorised as 'defining self as a gardener', was purposely explored further through the theoretical sampling of a further individual, who was sought out because she was described as exemplifying 'a real gardener'. This confirmed the definitions of this core category and gave confidence that the category was saturated. Once all of the transcripts had been coded, it was judged that sufficient repetition was present within the data set to cease interviewing and focus on the process of analysis.

A limited literature review had taken place during the initial stage of the project development, and widened as the research progressed. Literature relevant to the developing themes was reviewed alongside the development of the analysis. This included existing literature on the meaning of gardens and the meaning of the home, about sheltered housing and constructionist writings on identity in later life. As the theoretical complexity of the analysis developed, the literature review was expanded to accommodate various themes highlighted as significant, such as moral accountability, justifying and 'othering' strategies in conversation, and concepts related to work and retirement.

Three main themes were identified, each with a number of related subthemes: (1) gardening with an ageing body, reflecting the dominance of the topic of the ageing body in residents' talk about the gardens; (2) manageability, referring both to the way that gardens were understood as a space to be maintained that required human input and to the process of identity management; and (3) creating a sense of purpose, referring to the way that gardens and gardening provided a positive and productive focus, whether as a hobby, as work or as a source of direct reward through prizes and external validity.

There is a degree of overlap across these themes because of the complexity of the issues involved, particularly in relation to the category of health, and moral accountability whereby residents tended to contrast their own activity with a generalised idea of being inactive or lazy (see Figure 10.1).

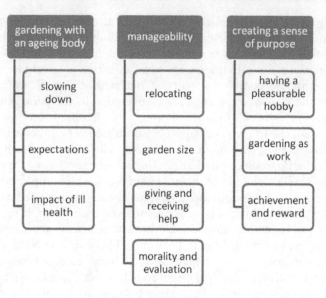

Figure 10.1   The three main themes and their sub-themes from the GT analysis of interviews with 29 residents of sheltered housing schemes

The themes relate to different elements of the ageing identity as well as the gardening identity, and to current discourses of active ageing and decline. What follows is an excerpt from the 'gardening as work' sub-themes of the creating a sense of purpose theme, to illustrate how the analysis draws on wider discourses of ageing and how the residents negotiated these discourses.

Gardening as work
It was clear that the activity of gardening was not only a hobby, but something that required effort and determination; many explicitly referred to gardening as a form of work. Elsie said, '*Well you've got to be one hundred per cent with it. Your heart has really got to be in with what you're doing, you can't just put a plant in today and think that's going to grow, you've got to make sure you water it and look after it, and nurture it all the time, it's constant,*' and not only that, '*When you take on a garden it ... a garden is a place of beauty but a job for life,*' and, asked if it was a commitment, she emphasised that it was indeed a full-time commitment: '*Yeah, yeah and it's not a part, it's a full-time commitment, full-time.*'

This 'job' reflects a theme identified elsewhere in literature on gardens, the need for human input and agency (Cooper, 2006; Francis and Hester, 1990). One interpretation is that by demonstrating that the garden requires their input, older adults may be able to evidence their own agency, through being needed, and thus challenge the idea that moving out of home and work represents a decline and a loss of role (Price, 2000; Barnes and Parry, 2004). By emphasising the work they do in the upkeep of the garden, individuals may be able to successfully manage their identity as active contributors.

Gardening was framed as hard physical work: *'It's heavy work really.'* The gardens at one scheme were entirely communal, and one resident, Sid, described how he and Elsie tended the gardens together: *'There is only two of us do the garden, and we're looking to the future, it's very hard work, I'll tell you that.'* He went on: *'It's all work, and what we've got to try and do is keep the garden looking nice, but we've got to do it to our capability'* and *'We won a lot of awards, and to maintain that standard it meant a tremendous amount of maintenance through the year.'* At one point Sid said: *'But it's always work, you've got to remember that... you're not there just looking at flowers... you're out there for one purpose... you've come out because you've got to do something... if it isn't digging weeds up it's watering, it's doing all sorts of things, but it's always work orientated, you know.'* Interestingly, given the rationale for this research, Sid had little interest in gardening prior to moving to the housing scheme and had only taken it on when another resident left. Elsie did have experience and Sid described her as a leading figure in the managing of the gardens, and himself as 'the labourer', highlighting how the environment can spark involvement.

A possible interpretation of the emphasis on work is that both Sid and Elsie are orienting to gardens in terms of their moral accountability (Antaki, 1994). Firstly, as exemplified by Sid's *'you've got to do something'* and Elsie's *'you've got to make sure'*, which suggest responsibility and duty, they are demonstrating that in their gardening identity, rather than their ageing identity, they are behaving in a manner that befits accepted norms regarding 'tidy' gardens (Taylor, 2008) and responsible gardening. Secondly, by describing their gardening here as work, Sid and Elsie (80 and 74 years, respectively) may be demonstrating their moral accountability as older people to engage with the prevalent discourses of active ageing (Rudman, 2006) and resist a potentially stigmatised identity of retiree (Price, 2000; Barnes and Parry, 2004). While this example is only indicative of the larger analysis, we think it demonstrates the multiple levels of meaning that can be explored through GT and how these can be examined in the development of theory.

In the study the subject of age was identified as a potentially omni-relevant category within the context of sheltered housing, and ageing was generally linked to a perceived reduction in the ability of self and other to carry out the physical tasks associated with garden maintenance. The gardens were frequently the subject of moral evaluations, and unkempt gardens were seen as a sign of laziness or physical inability. Talk about ill-health was conceptualised as a potential justification strategy that residents may have been using to manage their identity within the interview context. Furthermore, residents often used 'othering' strategies in order to distance themselves from the potentially stigmatised category of elderly person, and this technique may have been used to project a more youthful identity.

The garden can be understood as an accountable space which is subject to moral evaluations pertaining to whether a person can be considered to be 'lazy' or 'not bothered', supporting the notion that the garden can serve as a marker of identity. Participants' moral judgements regarding garden upkeep appeared to be linked to perceived levels of independence in later life and therefore whether a person is considered to be elderly or not. This finding indicates that the residents themselves valued notions of independence, which is in keeping with the discourses of successful ageing (Bowling and Dieppe, 2005) and active ageing (Walker, 2006).

As we found in our other work, gardens can provide a space for individuals to engage in physical and meaningful activity as the antithesis to stressful or challenging aspects of their lives, in this case the decline discourse of later life, contesting the notion that domestic gardens are predominantly experienced as problematic in later life (Peace et al., 2005; Bhatti, 2006). Our study of sheltered housing demonstrates that gardens have the potential for residents to resist institutionalisation by engaging with a purposeful activity in an autonomous and agentive manner. This is important because it indicates that the environment of the sheltered housing complex may contribute positively to the experience of living in such a setting. Armed with this knowledge, housing providers might consider adapting their facilities to promote active engagement.

Reflections

The findings from the studies described here suggest that the meanings that people attach to gardens and the role that such spaces play for identity, beyond place, are significant. In the process of doing the research and of writing this chapter, we have been considering the following aspects of the work:

1. Doing this research was an enjoyable process because we were able to ask people about their own experience of a topic that mostly interested them a great deal. With few exceptions, people engaged fully with the interviews and gave details of their gardens and gardening experiences. The benefit of this was that it provided a wealth of rich data. A downside of that is the time taken to code and analyse alongside doing interviews, as required for GT. Using this approach generally worked well. The subtlety and complexity of the categories and the final themes arose from intense reflection and discussion in the team. However, the analytic process meant that we sometimes lost sight of environmental psychology. For example, in examining how people negotiated the discourses of ageing, we had to work to keep in touch with our environmental starting point. Possibly this was due to using a social constructionist approach, which, compared to a more realist approach, seemed to distance the setting from the data, because of a focus on language. Paradoxically this also meant the data was situated

in the context of current discourses, and was helpful in thinking about working in applied settings, which may also reflect these same discourses in their practice. This is something to review for future work.

2. Reflexivity: The project team were all white women, as were most of the participants, and the majority of interviews were done by a researcher who was considerably younger than many of the volunteer participants. This was partly unavoidable since sheltered housing only caters for residents aged 55+. We were aware that this might have increased the salience of age during the interviews and impacted on the way that respondents spoke about their experience in relation to age. For example, some of the analysis suggested that they were trying to both resist and confirm a discourse of decline when discussing their health. Because of this age gap, in memo writing and analysis we were alert to any stereotyping of older people and, conversely, their treatment of us, notably concerning gardening itself. The team varied in its own gardening engagement, and we were careful to be conscious of our own different experience as well as our age during the analysis and coding process.

3. Most of the participants we spoke to were either self-selecting as gardeners or were purposefully sampled as such. This was deliberate. In the interviews with the community sample, we did ask what equivalent activities provoked the feelings described by people about gardens, prompting reference to other outdoor experiences. Many gardeners recognised that they had only become interested once they owned their own homes. Nevertheless, given the undoubted benefits of contact with nature and gardening for identity, future research could explore these issues further with those who currently have little interest.

References

Antaki, C. (1994). *Explaining and Arguing: The Social Organisation of Accounts.* London: SAGE.

Barnes, H. and Parry, J. (2004). Renegotiating identity and relationships: Men's and women's adjustments to retirement. *Ageing and Society*, 24, 213–233.

Beute, F. and de Kort, Y.A.W. (2014). Natural resistance: Exposure to nature and self-regulation, mood and physiology after ego-depletion. *Journal of Environmental Psychology*, 40, 167–178.

Bhatti, M. (1999). The meaning of gardens in an age of risk. In T. Chapman and J. Hockey (Eds.), *Ideal Homes? Social Change and Domestic Life.* London: Routledge, pp. 181–193.

Bhatti, M. (2006). 'When I'm in the garden I can create my own paradise': Homes and gardens in later life. *Sociological Review*, 54, 318–341.

Bhatti, M. and Church, A. (2001). Cultivating natures: Home and gardens in late modernity. *Sociology*, 35, 365–383.

Bowling, A. and Dieppe, P. (2005). What is successful ageing and who should define it? *British Medical Journal*, 331, 1548–1551.

Chamberlain, K., Camic, P. and Yardley, L. (2004). Qualitative analysis of experience: Case studies in grounded theory. In D. Marks and L. Yardley (Eds.), *Research Methods in Clinical and Health Psychology*. London: SAGE, pp. 69–89.

Charmaz, K. (2014). *Constructing Grounded Theory (Second Edition)*. Los Angeles: SAGE.

Clare, L., Rowlands, J., Bruce, E., Surr, C. and Downs, M. (2008). 'I don't do like I used to': A grounded theory approach to conceptualising awareness in people with moderate to severe dementia living in long term care. *Social Science and Medicine*, 66, 2366–2377.

Clayton, S. (Ed.) (2012). *Handbook of Environmental and Conservation Psychology*. New York: Cambridge University Press.

Clayton, S. and Opotow, S. (2003). Identity and the natural environment. In S. Clayton and S. Opotow (Eds.), *Identity and the Natural Environment*. Boston: MIT Press, pp. 1–24.

Cooper, D. (2006). *A Philosophy of Gardens*. Oxford: Clarendon Press.

Crouch, D. and Ward, C. (1997). *The Allotment: Its Landscape and Culture*. Nottingham: Five Leaves Press.

Csikszmentmihalyi, M. (1990). *Flow: The Psychology of Optimal Experience*. New York: Harper and Row.

Devine-Wright, P. and Howes, Y. (2010). Disruption to place attachment and the protection of restorative environments: A wind energy case study. *Journal of Environmental Psychology (Special Issue: Identity, Place and Environmental Behaviour)*, 30, 271–280.

Flouri, E., Midouhas, E. and Joshi, H. (2014). The role of urban neighbourhood green space in children's emotional and behavioural resilience. *Journal of Environmental Psychology*, 40, 179–198.

Francis, M. and Hester, R.T. (1990). *The Meaning of Gardens*. Cambridge, MA: MIT Press.

Gosling, E. and Williams, K.J.H. (2010). Connectedness to nature, place attachment and conservation behaviours: Testing connectedness theory among farmers. *Journal of Environmental Psychology*, 30, 298–304.

Groenewegen, P.P., den Berg, A.E., de Vries, S. and Verheij, R.A. (2006). Vitamin G: Effects of green space on health, wellbeing and social safety. *BMC Public Health*, 6, 149. Retrieved 30 January 2017 from: www.bmcpublichealth.biomedcentral.com/articles/10.1186/1471-2458-6-149.

Gross, H. and Lane, N. (2007). Landscapes of the lifespan: Exploring accounts of own gardens and gardening. *Journal of Environmental Psychology*, 27, 225–241.

Hawkins, J., Mercer, J., Thirlaway, K.J. and Clayton, D.A. (2013), 'Doing' gardening and 'being' at the allotment site: Exploring the benefits of allotment gardening for stress reduction and healthy ageing. *Ecopsychology*, 5, 110–125.

Heliker, D., Chadwick, A. and O'Connell, T. (2000). The meaning of gardening and the effects on perceived well being of a gardening project on diverse populations of elders. *Activities, Adaptation and Aging*, 24(3), 35–56.

Howell, A.J., Dopko, R.L., Passmore, H. and Buro, K. (2011). Nature connectedness: Associations with well-being and mindfulness. *Personality and Individual Differences*, 51, 166–171.

Kahn, P.H. and Kellert, S.R. (Eds.) (2002). *Children and Nature: Psychological, Sociocultural and Evolutionary Investigations*. Cambridge, MA: MIT Press.

Kaplan, R. (1973). Some psychological benefits of gardening. *Environment and Behavior*, 5, 145–162.

Kaplan, R. (2001). The nature of the view from home: Psychological benefits. *Environment and Behaviour*, 33(4), 507–542.

Kaplan, R. and Kaplan, S. (1989). *The Experience of Nature: A Psychological Perspective*. Cambridge: CUP.

King, N. and Horrocks, C. (2010). *Interviews in Qualitative Research*. London: SAGE.

Kornos, C. and Gifford, R. (2014). The validity of self-report measures of pro-environmental behaviour: A meta-analytic review. *Journal of Environmental Psychology*, 40, 359–371.

Korpela, K. (2002). Children's environments. In R.B. Bechtel and A. Churchman (Eds.), *Handbook of Environmental Psychology*. New York: Wiley, pp. 363–371.

Korpela, K. and Hartig, T. (1996). Restorative qualities of favourite places. *Journal of Environmental Psychology*, 9, 241–256.

Leong, L.Y.C., Fischer, R. and McClure, J. (2014). Are nature lovers more innovative? The relationship between connectedness with nature and cognitive styles. *Journal of Environmental Psychology*, 40, 57–63.

Low, S.M. and Altman, I. (1992). *Place Attachment*. New York: Springer.

Manzo, L. (2005). For better or worse: Exploring multiple dimensions of place meaning. *Journal of Environmental Psychology*, 25(1), 67–86.

Mayer, F.S. and Frantz, C.M. (2004). The nature connectedness scale: A measure of individuals' feeling in community with nature. *Journal of Environmental Psychology*, 24, 503–515.

Milfont, T.L. and Sibley, C.G. (2012). The big five personality traits and environmental engagement: Associations at the individual and societal level. *Journal of Environmental Psychology*, 32, 187–195. doi:10.1016/j.jenvp.2011.12.006.

Milligan, C., Gatrell, A. and Bingley, A. (2004). 'Cultivating health': Therapeutic landscapes and older people in northern England. *Social Science and Medicine*, 58, 1781–1793.

Nisbet, E.K., Zelenski, J.A. and Murphy, S.A. (2009). The nature relatedness scale: Linking individuals' connection with nature to environmental concern and behaviour. *Environment and Behaviour*, 41, 715–740.

Nisbet, E.K., Zelenski, J.M. and Murphy, S.A. (2010). Happiness is in our nature: Exploring nature relatedness as a contributor to subjective well-being. *Journal of Happiness Studies*, 12, 303–322. doi:10.1007/s10902-010-9197-7.

Parry-Jones, W. (1990), Natural landscape: Psychological wellbeing and mental health. *Landscape Research*, 15(2), 113–140.

Peace, S., Holland, C. and Kellaher, L. (2005). *Environment and Identity in Later Life*. New York: Open University Press.

Pretty, J., Peacock, J., Hine, R., Sellens, M., South, N. and Griffin, M. (2010). Green exercise in the UK countryside: Effects of health and psychological wellbeing, and implications for policy and planning. *Journal of Environmental Planning and Management*, 50(2), 211–231.

Price, C. (2000). Women and retirement: Relinquishing professional identity. *Journal of Aging Studies*, 14(1), 81–101.

Proshansky, H.M., Fabian, A.K. and Kaminoff, R. (1983). Place-identity: Physical world socialization of the self. *Journal of Environmental Psychology*, 3, 57–83.

Rudman, D.L. (2006). Shaping the active, autonomous and responsible modern retiree: An analysis of discursive technologies and their links with neoliberal political rationality. *Ageing and Society*, 26, 181–201.

Sbaraini, A., Carter, S.M., Evans, R.W. and Blinkhorn, A. (2011). How to do a grounded theory study: A worked example of a study of dental practices. *BMC Medical Research Methodology*, 11, 128–138.

Schultz, P.W. (2002). Inclusion with nature: The psychology of human-nature relationships. In P. Schmuck and W.P. Schultz (Eds.), *Psychology of Sustainable Development*. Norwell, MA: Springer, pp. 61–78.

Sempik, J., Aldridge, J. and Becker, S. (2005). *Social and Therapeutic Horticulture: Evidence and Messages from Research*. Reading: UK Thrive.

Stedman, R.C. (2002). Towards a social psychology of place: Predicting behaviour from place-based cognitions. *Environment and Behaviour*, 34, 561–581.

Tam, K. (2013). Dispositional empathy with nature. *Journal of Environmental Psychology*, 35, 92–104.

Taylor, L. (2008). *A Taste for Gardening: Classed and Gendered Practices*. Aldershot: Ashgate Publishing, pp. 40–51.

Ulrich, R.S. (1984). View through a window may influence recovery from surgery. *Science*, 224, 420–422.

Walker, A. (2006). Active ageing in employment: Its meaning and potential. *Asia-Pacific Review*, 13, 78–93.

White, M.P., Pahl, S., Ashbullby, K., Herbert, S. and Depledge, M.H. (2013). Feelings of restoration from recent nature visits. *Journal of Environmental Psychology*, 35(1), 40–51.

Willig, C. (2013). *Introducing Qualitative Research in Psychology (Third Edition)*. Buckingham: Open University Press.

Wilson, E.O. (1993). Biophilia and the conservation ethic. In S.R. Kellert and E.O. Wilson (Eds.), *The Biophilia Hypothesis*. Washington, DC: Island Press, pp. 31–41.

Understanding Disability, Physical Activity and Sport through Innovative Qualitative Methods: Mobile Interviewing, Autophotography and Creative Non-fiction

11

Brett Smith and Anthony Papathomas

Introduction

Being regularly active can be beneficial not just for physical health, but also for psychological health and wellbeing. For example, engaging in sport or exercise can boost happiness, self-compassion and mood. Despite this, many people remain inactive for long periods of time. For several years we have examined why this is the case in relation to disabled people and how physical activity or sport might be promoted in order to promote health and wellbeing within this population. Qualitative methods have played a vital role in this research. In this chapter, a brief introduction to some of the more innovative methods used in our research is first offered. The remainder of the chapter is then focused on one novel method known as creative non-fiction. We describe what this method is, why it might be used, and how it can be done. We close with some reflections on the use of creative non-fiction in our research on disability, sport and physical activity.

Understanding physical activity and sport through qualitative methods: Mobile interviewing, autophotography and creative non-fiction

For several years our research has focused on physical activity, sport, health and wellbeing among spinal cord injured people. One key reason for this focus is that people with a spinal cord injury are amongst the most inactive people in society (Smith et al., 2013). To understand the complex barriers and facilitators to an active lifestyle, along with how the results of the research could be effectively communicated to different audiences, various qualitative methods were used. Semi-structured interviews with 50 disabled people over a two-year period were first conducted. To reveal more of the complexity of their lives, later our methodological repertoire for collecting data extended to include mobile interviewing and autophotography.

Mobile interviewing

The *mobile interview*, or what is sometimes referred to as the 'go-along' or 'walking' interview, is a means of interviewing participants as they move through space(s) (Buscher et al., 2011). In mobile interviewing, rather than two or more people sitting down in one indoor space as is often the case when conducting an interview, the researcher interviews the participant as they move together through everyday or selected spaces that either the participant or the researcher chooses. For example, in our research spinal cord injured adults wheeled alongside us as we walked, guiding us into environments that restricted and facilitated their ability to be active. The result of all this was a deeply embodied, multi-sensorial, spatial and contextual understanding of disabled people's lives. The corporeal movement across personally meaningful spaces, the different senses (e.g. smell, touch, sight) that were used through-out, and the memories that different contexts recreated, stimulated new barriers and ways to facilitate activity that were not identified in the first 'sit down'/'sedentary' interview. Thus, this method produced additional layers of data that revealed more of the complexity of the participant's psycho-social lives in time and across space. It gave us a deeper appreciation of why physical activity can be so difficult to sustain, even when one is highly intrinsically motivated, as well as the various types of pleasure (Phoenix and Orr, 2014) that can be experienced. Other work with visually impaired adults, who led the lead researcher on a walk that was guided by sounds, touch and smells, rather than sight, offered support for such benefits of mobile interviewing (Phoenix et al., 2015).

Autophotography

Autophotography refers to a type of visual method in which the participants themselves take photographs that represent their sense of self, emotions, or, for example, who they are in relation to a given phenomenon or topic (Cope et al., 2015; Phoenix, 2010a, b; Phoenix and Rich, 2016). For example, we asked each participant who described themselves as inactive in our study to take ten pictures using their own smart mobile phone, or a disposable camera we gave them, that said 'This is why I'm not physically active.' We also asked those who described themselves as highly active to take ten photographs that represented 'This is why I do sport or am very active.' The visual images taken by the participants then formed the basis of a follow-up photo-elicitation interview.

In our photo-elicitation interview, conducted after the initial semi-structured interview, participants were asked about the meaning of the photographs they took. We also used the images to elicit more stories about physical activity and sport in the context of their everyday lives as a spinal cord injured person. When asked in follow-up conversations about how they found the autophotography task the participants said that it was an enjoyable and empowering process that provided an enhanced sense of collaboration compared to traditional interviews. It was possible for participants to 'show' rather than just 'tell' things about their own lives. The inclusion of photographs into the research made it more collaborative, human and emotionally evocative than words alone. The participants also found that the use of photographs had catalytic properties. Similar to the mobile interviews, this method helped stimulate forgotten or taken-for-granted aspects about sport and physical activity. Despite such strengths, participants did raise practical challenges when doing the autophotography task. For instance, some indicated that their photograph-taking was challenged by issues such as weather, time, access to certain places or people, and the absence of a camera during photograph-worthy moments.

Having collected all this qualitative data, as well as other kinds through timelining (see Sparkes and Smith, 2014) and observation (Smith, 2013a), we operated as a story analyst (see Bochner and Riggs, 2013; Smith and Sparkes, 2009a; Smith, 2016) by subjecting all data to a thematic and structural narrative analysis (see Sparkes and Smith, 2014). A qualitative meta-synthesis was also conducted (see Williams et al., 2014). The findings of the results were then 'written up' as realist tales (e.g. Papathomas et al., 2015; Smith, 2013a). A realist tale is a genre of 'writing up' qualitative research. It is the most common way of communicating qualitative research and has three key characteristics (van Maanen, 1988). First, the researcher/author is almost completely absent from most segments of the finished text. This is termed experiential authority. Second, the researcher/author presents extensive and closely edited data to reveal what is known as the participant's point of view. Third, illustrated through empirical data, the researcher/author tells a theoretical account of the data to provide an explanation of it. This is known as interpretive omnipotence.

Although a realist tale is very useful to communicate qualitative research to academics, we found it was limited for serving various purposes. When we shared our published realist tales with disabled people, disability user groups, disability sport organisations and health professionals in spinal cord injury rehabilitation units, most people found our work inaccessible and boring. One key reason for this was the highly specialised academic terminology used. In addition, we hoped to write one paper that could capture the complexity and large amount of empirical and theoretical knowledge that was being generated in our research. A single realist tale could not meet this purpose either. Given such concerns, and without wishing to jettison realist tales, we looked elsewhere for another qualitative method that could communicate our research. Our search led us to the genre of creative non-fiction.

Creative non-fiction

Although often psychologists doing qualitative research write what is known as a realist tale, there are numerous creative analytical methods to legitimately represent research findings. These include ethnodrama, poetic representations and autoethnography (see Sparkes and Smith, 2014). Another legitimate method is creative non-fiction. This is a type of creative analytic practice (Richardson, 2000) that presents a story rather than, as a realist tale does, an account of research. The story is crafted using literary conventions but is grounded in research data and analytical results. Thus, a creative non-fictional representation of qualitative data is not made up or wholly imagined. Rather, it is based on research evidence (Caulley, 2008; Smith, 2013b).

Our case example

Having described what is a creative non-fiction, it is useful at this point to see an example of one in action. For space reasons, the one offered is brief and partial. Grounded in our research findings that emerged from a narrative analysis (Smith and Sparkes, 2009a, b) of semi-structured interviews, mobile interviews, an autophotography task, observation and a qualitative meta-synthesis, the creative non-fiction aimed to show in an accessible way the complexities of engaging in physical activity or sport following spinal cord injury. For example, as the story below hopefully shows, peer support and then physiotherapists were found to be the best type of messengers to share information about physical activity, and the best place to start sharing was in rehabilitation; the barriers to being active included time and added inconvenience on top of much bodily care that goes with a spinal injury, a past dislike of sport, travel restrictions, structural problems, motivation and unsuitable equipment; and, supporting the theory of implementation intentions, planning activities with a friend was a useful means to facilitate physical activity. With all this in mind, here is an edited version of one of the stories produced.

'How are you, Jennifer?' asks Cathy softly.

'Y'know, good days, bad days.' After taking a sip of her warm tea through a straw, Jennifer adds, 'I'm worried, anxious, about leaving here...I feel, I feel this gurgling in me, this deep sense of sickly anxiety about leaving.'

A few moments later Sarah arrives at the round table, and pushes her wheelchair slightly under it.

'Sarah, this is Cathy. Cathy, Sarah.'

'Nice to meet you. You're Jennifer's guardian angel, she tells me,' says Sarah with a gentle smile.

'That's nice. But, in all honesty, I think she's as big a help to me as I might be for her. I'm supposed to be her peer support!' adds Cathy with a laugh.

'And you?' butts in Jennifer, smiling. Turning to Sarah, she adds, 'How are you?'

'So, so. Feeling a little down, a little, a little despondent, if I'm honest. I've just come back from physio. We were talking about what I need to do when I leave here.'

'That's with Krista, right?' interjects Jennifer, before adding for the benefit of Cathy, 'She's the new physio. She's really up on the latest things, really good, forward thinking.'

'Yeah, that's her,' confirms Sarah. 'I like her. But we were talking about doing exercise, being more active now, and planning on being physically active when I leave. I'm struggling to feel motivated about it all. It's not so much worried me. But, I was never an exerciser before my accident. And I've hated sports since I was in public school. Hated it. Being active wasn't me. I really wasn't interested. Now, on top of everything else, I'm being advised to take up exercise, and be active. It's another thing to do. It seems never-ending what we should and shouldn't do. And progress is just so small, sometimes I feel as if I've gone backward in physio. How is exercise going to make any big difference?'

'I wonder that too,' says Jennifer. 'I was fairly active before my accident. I loved my horse riding of course. But I'm not sure exercising, sports, all that is for me either. My physiotherapist hasn't said anything to me, though. No one really has. What do you make of it all, Cathy? Load of nonsense?' With the corners of her mouth curving into a smile, Jennifer quickly adds, 'Cathy's a bit of a cynic sometimes.'

'I can be,' Cathy says with a wry smile. 'What do I make of it? Well, Krista, your physio, has a point. The experts have shown there are so many benefits to being active physically, and equally it's not good for you if you don't move around. I'd agree. My experiences of being active now, as well as what I've heard and seen from other spinal women, support all this. When I went through rehab, no one told me to be active. They told me lots of things I should and should not do. But physical activity or sport was not talked about. I think that's a shame as I look back. Don't get me wrong. Like you, I wasn't particularly interested in exercise. I was very uninterested in sport. Now, though, things are different, and what a difference.'

'Such as?' asks Sarah.

'Well, I've been exercising for about eight months now. At first, it was tough. I gave up a few times. I had seen from other disabled women there are benefits to being active, and I thought things would happen overnight. They didn't, and I stopped a few times. There were other things too that made a difference. Where I first lived, it was a long way to travel to a gym, and there were no bus stops close by my house either. The gym I did end up joining was okay, but most of the equipment wasn't suitable for people in wheelchairs. So the facilities weren't perfect. And during the winter, I found it tough too. It wasn't just the snow, or moving around in the cold that made going to the gym difficult. Truth be told, I was a little concerned about my safety too.'

'That's understandable,' says Jennifer in a soft voice.

'I'd agree,' adds Sarah before gently saying, 'I'm not surprised you gave up. It sounds as though there is barrier after barrier.'

'I won't deny there are a few barriers. But what I realised, thanks to a friend, was that I really hadn't thought exercising through. Most things in my life now are planned to a "T", as you'll appreciate when you leave. But I didn't really plan about where best to exercise, when, how, or even think about different types of activity.'

'And so what happened?' asks Sarah, leaning forward.

'A friend visited. And I opened up about how awful I was feeling, physically, mentally. I was sick of being offered just pills by the doctors, and I didn't feel like a woman anymore. I felt as though life was passing me by. I didn't like my body, and who I was anymore. My friend listened and after a while we made a plan about changing my life. Part of the plan was to stick at exercising, and be active.'

'And how did you do that? Where did you start? I just couldn't even contemplate thinking about it now,' Jennifer proclaims ...

> Originally published in Smith et al. Understanding physical activity in spinal cord injury rehabilitation: translating and communicating research through stories. *Disability and Rehabilitation*, 2013. 35(24), 2048–2049.

Clearly, creative non-fictions are very different from how research is traditionally represented. These differences, however, are neither good nor bad in themselves. Rather, they invite us to think reflexively and critically about the ways we choose to represent, that is write about, the results of our research. This is important because not only do students and academics have to write up their research as a thesis, a journal article, or book chapter; writing is also a method of analysis in itself. As Richardson (2000, p. 923) argued:

I consider writing as a method of inquiry, a way of finding out about yourself and your topic. Although we usually think about writing as a mode of 'telling' about the social world, writing is not just a mopping-up activity at the end of the research project. Writing is also a way of 'knowing' – a method of discovery and analysis. By writing in different ways, we discover new aspects of our topic and our relationship to it.

In support of this conjunction of analysis and writing, Latour (2005) notes: 'Textual accounts are the social scientist's laboratory' and analysis happens in 'continuous and obsessive attention' (p. 127) to writing a well-written report. Given this, along with the fact that there are now numerous ways to legitimately write about research, researchers need to make informed, principled and disciplined choices about just which kind of genre they might use to represent their research (Sparkes and Smith, 2014). Vital in this process of choosing is the 'why' question – why is this method of writing appropriate for this piece of research?

In our work on disability, sport, physical activity and psychological wellbeing, a creative non-fiction was chosen as a method of inquiry for several reasons. First, it had the potential benefit of being highly accessible to many people beyond academia. In addition, highly accessible research could enhance the translation of knowledge and generate wider practical impact. These claims are supported by narrative theory, which argues that stories are a crucial means of knowing, as well as being performative in that they do things on and for people (Frank, 2010; Smith, 2013a).

Second, because a story can uniquely contain a lot of complex information, a creative non-fiction can potentially allow a researcher to show not just one, two, or three key findings or theories, but in one paper an array of research findings and theoretical points that interlace together. It has the benefit of providing insights into the complex, ambiguous contingency of human life without, following Bakhtin (1984), finalising (i.e. offering the final word) participants. Third, a creative non-fiction could capture, rather than cool or wash out, the deeply embodied, sensorial and relational nature of sport or physical activity that was captured in the mobile interviews and autophotography task. Fourth, given that analysis takes place in writing, this method of inquiry could provide additional analytic insights. Through the process of writing, analytical thoughts could deepen and a richer account be developed.

Having said what an ethnographic creative non-fiction is and offered some reasons as to why it might be chosen, how might a researcher go about writing this kind of creative analytical practice? The following are some tips, not recipes to strictly adhere to, which might help to do this. Some of the tips are drawn from other scholars (e.g. Barone and Eisner, 2012; Caulley, 2008; Cheney, 2001; Ellis, 2004), whilst others are based on our experiences of doing an ethnographic creative non-fiction.

■ *Synthesise the results of the analyses and identify various theories*: To create our ethnographic creative non-fiction, we first identified what should be included in the story and why. To do this, findings from our analyses of the qualitative data, along with theoretical interpretations of these, were synthesised using what can be described as the systematic search and review method (Grant and Booth, 2009). This is a technique that aims for exhaustive, comprehensive searching of research to produce a 'best evidence synthesis' of findings. All analytic results and theories collated were then presented in a table. This was useful as it condensed points to be made, was easily accessible when writing started and helped jog the memory about ideas to be included when crafting and editing the story. In short, the table that summarised results helped ensure our imaginations did not wander off and the story stayed grounded in research evidence.

- *Select and develop characters*: When thinking about writing, consider how many characters are needed to tell the story that captures the research findings and theoretical points to be made, who the characters will be and become, how they will drive the story along, what stories they will each tell, and how they will interact. For us, we chose to write two stories, one with three male characters and the other with three female characters. Three characters per story was deemed sufficient to capture in dialogue the different processes and trajectories that spinal cord injured people reported when it came to their experiences of physical (in)activity and sport. Also our analyses of the data revealed differences between men and women in how a physically active lifestyle was initiated and maintained, and what was involved in hindering and promoting this physical, social and psychological process. To reflect these differences, but recognising that gender is relational in origin and reproduction (Smith, 2013b), the decision was made to write one story with male characters and another with female characters.

- *Show rather than tell*: When crafting the story we aimed to predominately show experiences, results and theory, which means delivering a rich, vivid description that aims to create images and conjure up emotions within a reader. Telling concisely catalogues actions and emotional life. Here is an example of telling: 'Helen felt scared when she wheeled into the gym. "Get moving," her trainer said impatiently.' In contrast, here is show-ing: 'Helen's face went ashen when she wheeled herself, bit by bit, into the gym. Her breathing came in ragged gasps. "Get moving!" her trainer snapped.'

- *Use dialogue*: When writing, where appropriate through conversations between characters and/or in a character's head (soliloquy) show what has happened, the point of the story, emotions, and so on.

- *Write evocatively and engagingly*: As well as showing through dialogue, use different senses (e.g. smell, sound, taste) to evocate emotions, create suspension and engage the readers viscerally as well as cognitively. We also found it can be useful to use flashback, metaphor and dramatic evocation.

- *Embodiment and social relations*: When writing, evoke a sense of the characters' bodies in motion and being still. We tried to also show bodies being emotionally expressive (or not) and enacting on, within and against stories other people told. Our characters acted out the story in relation to other people and, we hoped, revealed things about themselves (e.g. why they are not motivated to be active) to others through these actions.

- *Develop a plot*: A plot can't always contain tension, as everyday life is not like that. But a story needs to have some dramatic tension. It needs to connect points (e.g. about results and theories that emerged from the data) across time, be cohesive and have a consequence(s). A story needs a beginning, middle and end (not the final word), but not always told in that order. To help drive the plot along, we found it useful also to consider the characters, what obstacles along the story they will face, what they care about and how they might change, even if only very subtly.
- *Scene setting*: Think about where (e.g. places) and when (e.g. morning breakfast) to locate people and their conversations (including internal dialogues with phantom others). Ask yourself about the back stages and front stages people behave in as well as how many scenes readers are willing to move in and out of. The data generated from the mobile interviews and autophotography were particularly useful in terms of scene setting, proving a deeper contextual understanding of lives.
- *Selectivity*: Recognise early on then that no one can tell the 'whole' story of a research topic. Select what needs to be told in this paper, to meet a certain purpose and to communicate important points for a particular audience.
- *Edit*: Revise your story numerous times – editing, revising, editing more and revising again – over a period of time (often this is over many months). Make every word count.
- *Share the story with critical friends*: When you are satisfied with the story, share it with colleagues and/or participants. Do not look at this as a form of traditional member checking in which other people verify the story and the researcher can, with truth-as-correspondence and (post)positivist overtones, then claim they have got at the truth independent of them and ensured the validity of the research (for a critique of member checking see Sparkes and Smith, 2014). Instead, the people with whom you shared the story are 'critical friends' who may offer advice about the quality of the story and different interpretations of it. We found that any advice and differences in perspectives offered by our critical friends were useful resources for challenging and developing the interpretations made by us as we sought to construct a coherent and theoretically sound argument to defend and/or further develop the case being made in relation to our study.

Reflections

As we reflected on the process of doing an ethnographic creative non-fiction, part of us would have liked to describe it as a neat and tidy procedure that could be packaged into a prescriptive, linear set of steps for others to simply follow. The process did involve first collecting data via numerous techniques, analysing these data, synthesising results and documenting them in a comprehensive table, and then writing the story. But doing all this as we look back was an iterative and often messy process. This recognised, we hope the chapter acts a heuristic guide or exemplar for others, who wish for certain purposes to produce a creative non-fiction, to learn from, use, add to, critically engage with and develop.

It should also be noted that our content and tone in the chapter about creative non-fictions have largely been positive. There are, however, weaknesses and risks that go with doing this kind of creative analytical practice. For example, as we reflected on the process of doing a creative non-fiction and the product, we were surprised by the amount of work we put into it when compared to writing realist tales. We took courses in creative writing and read books on the subject. We also spent many hours crafting sentences that were, when re-read the next day, insipid and theoretically vacuous. In terms of criteria that researchers might use to judge the quality of a creative non-fiction, many of our previous drafts lacked *aesthetic merit, expression of a reality, evocation and illumination, engagement* and an *incitement to action*.

Another risk that goes with doing a creative non-fiction is that *some* influential people, such as journal editors, university project supervisors and PhD committees, may greet creative non-fictional work with suspicion, even hostility, and questions are raised as to whether it constitutes 'proper' research. There are, however, many journal editors and people within universities that do accept good creative analytical practices. Key here is an appreciation that different criteria from those often used to judge a qualitative realist tale are needed to judge a creative non-fiction (see Sparkes and Smith, 2014).

Finally, here, we have become aware that our rationales for using creative non-fictions as a method of inquiry, along with many of the claims in the literature for and about this type of creative analytical practice, are based on 'potential'. For example, two reasons often highlighted for using a creative non-fiction are that it is highly accessible to audiences beyond academia and that stories can have some real impact on people, thereby impacting on society. Whilst recognising that the term 'evidence' is not straightforward, there is very little research within psychology that has examined if there is some substance to such potentials. This point is particularly pertinent given that stories are always out of control. That is, when one offers a story in the form of a creative non-fiction there is no guarantee that the purpose behind the story, analytical insights, theoretical points, attempts to translate knowledge, or desire to generate impact will be realised. Such uncertainty needs to be lived with. But, we were curious about the effectiveness of our creative non-fictions. This has led recently to a number of studies that examine their potential. Thus far the results have supported the claims.

For instance, in a qualitative study (Smith et al., 2015) 30 spinal cord injured people and 15 health care professionals working in rehabilitation were offered the stories. Later we conducted interviews with each person to ascertain their thoughts about the creative non-fictions. The results of an inductive thematic analysis of the interview data revealed that the stories were accessible to these audiences. They likewise considered them an effective form of communicating evidence-based knowledge. This was because each story was seen to be authentic (e.g. credible characters, messengers, dialogues and contexts/scenes) and evocative. The results also revealed that story was a useful resource for those interviewed. As performative – a form of action – the stories were useful for opening up dialogues about an active lifestyle, teaching people new knowledge about physical activity, and reminding, reinvigorating and reassuring the people interviewed about the need to promote different activities.

Conclusion

With a view to giving relatively novel qualitative methods of inquiry within psychology deeper exposure, in this chapter autophotography and mobile methods were first briefly described. We then sketched out creative non-fiction through three questions: What is it, why might it be useful, and how might we go about doing one? We do not encourage the use of this creative analytical practice if one wishes to experiment with this method simply for the sake of experimenting. Nor do we advocate choosing it because it is quite novel or because the more traditional way of representing qualitative work (i.e. realist tales) is not to one's taste. Choices about how to represent research need to be made in informed, principled and disciplined ways. It is hoped that this chapter has helped in the process. We hope it acts as an invitation to expand one's representational literacy and appreciate that there are various ways in which psychological research can be done and communicated.

References

Bakhtin, M. (1984). *Problems of Dostoevsky's Poetics* (Caryl Emerson trans. and ed.). Minneapolis, MN: University of Minnesota Press.
Barone, T. and Eisner, E.W. (2012). *Arts Based Research*. London: SAGE.
Bochner, A. and Riggs, N. (2013). Practicing narrative inquiry. In P. Levy (Ed.), *Oxford Handbook of Qualitative Research*. Oxford: Oxford University Press, pp. 195–222.
Buscher, M., Urry, J. and Witchger, K. (2011). *Mobile Methods*. London: Routledge.
Caulley, D. (2008). Making qualitative research reports less boring: The techniques of writing creative nonfiction. *Qualitative Inquiry*, 14, 424–449. doi:10.1177/1077800407311961.
Cheney, T.A.R. (2001). *Writing Creative Nonfiction: Fiction Techniques for Crafting Great Nonfiction*. Berkeley, CA: Ten Speed Press.
Cope, E., Harvery, S. and Kirk, D. (2015). Reflections on using visual research methods in sports coaching. *Qualitative Research in Sport, Exercise and Health*, 7, 88–108.

Ellis, C. (2004). *The Ethnographic I*. Walnut Creek, CA: Altamira Press.

Frank, A.W. (2010). *Letting Stories Breathe*. Chicago: University of Chicago Press.

Grant, M. and Booth, A. (2009). A typology of reviews: An analysis of 14 review types and associated methodologies. *Health Information and Libraries Journal*, 26, 91–108.

Latour, B. (2005). *Reassembling the Social: An Introduction to Actor-Network Theory*. New York: Oxford.

Papathomas, A., Williams, T.L. and Smith, B. (2015). Understanding physical activity, health and rehabilitation in spinal cord injured population: Shifting the landscape through methodological innovation. *International Journal of Qualitative Studies on Health and Well-Being*, 10, 27295. Retrieved 30 January 2017 from: www.dx.doi. org/10.3402/qhw.v10.27295.

Phoenix, C. (2010a). Auto-photography in aging studies: Exploring issues of identity construction in mature bodybuilders. *Journal of Aging Studies*, 24,167–180.

Phoenix, C. (2010b). Seeing the world of physical culture: The potential of visual methods for qualitative research in sport and exercise. *Qualitative Research in Sport, Exercise and Health*, 2, 93–108.

Phoenix, C. and Orr, N. (2014). Pleasure: A forgotten dimension of ageing and physical activity. *Social Science and Medicine*, 33, 243–266.

Phoenix, C., Griffin, M. and Smith, B. (2015). Physical activity among older people with sight loss: A qualitative research study to inform policy and practice. *Public Health*, 129, 124–130.

Phoenix, C. and Rich, E. (2016). Visual research methods. In B. Smith and A.C. Sparkes (Eds.), *Routledge Handbook of Qualitative Research Methods in Sport and Exercise*. London: Routledge, pp. 139–151.

Richardson, L. (2000). Writing: A method of inquiry. In N. Denzin and Y. Lincoln (Eds.), *Handbook of Qualitative Research (Second Edition)*. London: SAGE, pp. 923–948.

Smith, B. (2013a). Disability, sport, and men's narratives of health: A qualitative study. *Health Psychology*, 32, 110–119. doi:10.1037/a0029187.

Smith, B. (2013b). Sporting spinal cord injuries, social relations, and rehabilitation narratives: An ethnographic creative non-fiction of becoming disabled through sport. *Sociology of Sport Journal*, 30, 132–152.

Smith, B. (2016). Narrative analysis. In E. Lyons and A. Coyle (Eds.), *Analysing Qualitative Data in Psychology (Second Edition)*. London: SAGE, pp. 202–221.

Smith, B., Papathomas, A., Martin Ginis, K.A. and Latimer-Cheung, A.E. (2013). Understanding physical activity in spinal cord injury rehabilitation: Translating and communicating research through stories. *Disability Rehabilitation*, 35, 2046–2055. doi:10.3109/09638288.2013.805821.

Smith, B., Tomasone, J., Latimer-Cheung, A. and Martin Ginis, K. (2015). Narrative as a knowledge translation tool for facilitating impact: Translating physical activity knowledge to disabled people and health professionals. *Health Psychology*, 34(4), 303–313.

Smith, B. and Sparkes, A.C. (2009a). Narrative analysis and sport and exercise psychology: Understanding lives in diverse ways. *Psychology of Sport and Exercise*, 10, 279–288. doi:10.1016/j.psychsport.2008.07.012.

Smith, B. and Sparkes, A.C. (2009b). Narrative inquiry in sport and exercise psychology: What is it, and why might we do it? *Psychology of Sport and Exercise*, 10(1), 1–11.

Sparkes, A.C. and Smith, B. (2014). *Qualitative Research Methods in Sport, Exercise and Health: From Process to Product*. London: Routledge.

Van Maanen, J. (1988). *Tales from the Field: On Writing Ethnography*. Chicago: University of Chicago Press.

Williams, T., Smith, B. and Papathomas, A. (2014). The barriers, benefits and facilitators of leisure time physical activity among people with spinal cord injury: A meta-synthesis of qualitative findings. *Health Psychology Review*, 8, 404–425.

Exploring the Response to Diversity and Equality in English Prisons: An Appreciative Inquiry

Victoria Lavis, Charles Elliott and Malcolm Cowburn

12

Introduction: Appreciative inquiry methods

Qualitative researchers, perhaps most notably those working within a participatory action framework, have long argued that research should actively engage and involve members of the communities about whom knowledge is to be generated and whose lives it will impact (Lewin, 1951, 1952; Whyte, 1991; Kemmis and McTaggart, 2000). Such calls have prompted a significant shift towards the development of methodologies that seek to generate knowledge 'with' communities (Fine et al., 2003; Israel et al., 1998) rather than research 'for' or 'on' communities. Appreciative inquiry (AI) typifies such inclusive, collaborative approaches to the generation of knowledge whilst simultaneously being focused explicitly towards facilitating enhancement; whether personal, collective or organisational. This quality makes AI ideal for use in research sites characterised by an existing collective or organisational framework: public sector (e.g. NHS, prison service, education, local councils), private sector (e.g. telecommunications, petrochemicals, pharmaceuticals) and third sector (e.g. charities and non-profit organisations). Whilst typically employed as a mechanism for facilitating organisational change we have adapted the principles of AI to generate an AI research methodology and illustrate in this chapter an example of its use in prisons research. Before considering this case study in detail we outline some of the foundations and principles which underlie AI.

Doing appreciative inquiry

AI is best represented as a broad 'family' of techniques and processes which share the same positively framed values-based principles. Its uniqueness lies in its departure from traditional problem-based approaches to research and development by acknowledging the importance of positivity through identifying an organisation's 'energy for change' (Elliott, 1999, p. 2). This inclination towards the positive is often referred to as the 'heliotropic principle'; this principle suggests that just as plants in the natural world orient towards the sun which sustains and nurtures their growth, so people also incline towards that which energises and sustains them. AI aims to co-facilitate the generation of this energy by identifying an organisation's self-reflective peak performances or historical 'best', in short its strengths, and then imagining and designing how this could best become more frequent and prevalent (Elliott, 1999, p. 43).

Originating as a methodology of organisational change (Cooperrider and Srivastva, 1987; Cooperrider and Whitney, 1999), AI has since been applied to a number of other challenging problem areas including transforming health care settings (Carter et al., 2007), conflict resolution (Larson and Tian, 2005), sustainable development (Elliott, 1999) and researching equality and diversity and the quality of prison life (Cowburn and Lavis, 2013; Liebling et al., 1999; Liebling et al., 2001). In this chapter we draw the distinction between AI as an organisational change process (facilitated by an AI practitioner in conjunction with a workgroup of stakeholders from the organisation) and our utilisation and adaptation of AI methods to create an *applied* research methodology, generating knowledge which guides actions and produces real and lasting impact within an organisation.

The underlying principles of AI afford the researcher an organising structure to formulate a sound research design. This organising structure is typically focused on four basic elements: *discovery*, *dreaming*, *designing* and *destiny* (Cooperrider and Srivastva, 1987; Elliott, 1999). However, the researcher may need to adapt these phases to suit the nature and purpose of their inquiry or the participant group with which they are working. Thus different exponents of the method sometimes use slightly different terms to represent these elements. Reed (2007), for example, replaces *destiny* with *delivery*, shifting the focus from 'sustainability' to 'planning for action'. Other researchers, for example Stavros and Hinrichs (2009) have adapted AI introducing a fifth 'D' – *defining* – which acts as a precursor to the other elements and focuses on *defining* the target of the inquiry when used in a business context. When AI takes a research rather than an organisational change focus (as in our research), this fifth D is commonly already present in the form of the research questions or aims. Hence, the structure we outline here is for conducting AI research based on the 4D model (Figure 12.1).

- *Discovery* is the start of the inquiry. Here the goal of the researcher is to identify 'best' experiences and 'peak' performance within the organisation rather than commencing the inquiry with a problem to be solved. Understanding the underlying elements or conditions which enable or promote peak performance allows them to be replicated or applied to new or developmental areas of the organisation. It also reveals, at a

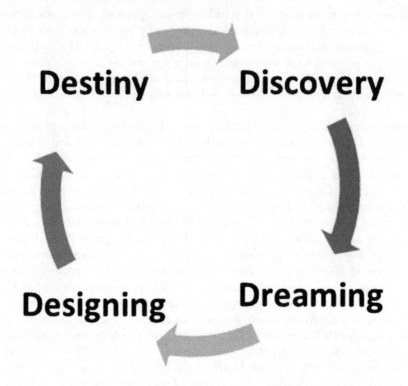

Figure 12.1   Appreciative inquiry four stage structure

human level, what participants value most highly, promoting engagement with the research and revealing the energy within the organisation. It is important to be clear that, although this element aims at identifying best experience, it also inevitably gathers important information about experiences that are not 'best' or that inhibit peak performance.

■ *Dreaming* moves the inquiry on and also changes the focus. In this phase research participants are invited to imagine how the subject under inquiry (in the case of the worked example in this chapter, the response to diversity in prisons) might be improved. *Dreaming* enables participants to link their 'best' experience to how things may be further enhanced thereby highlighting elements and issues which are important and promote their personal engagement with potential future action.

■ *Designing* moves the inquiry from the abstract quality of the 'dream' to a more concrete reality. Research participants actively engage in identifying practices, relationships, resources and processes which might be necessary to support the ideas they have outlined in *dreaming* and articulated as 'best' in *discovery*.

■ *Destiny* is the final phase of AI and concentrates on what is needed to maintain and sustain the changes that have been dreamed about and designed. This phase is an important factor in maximising the potential of the process to have enduring future impact; increasingly a key feature of funded research activity.

We use these four elements to form the underlying framework for data collection and analysis strategies. We outline the process by which this can be achieved below:

1. First, the researcher considers who the stakeholders relevant to the research are. This stage is significant to the ultimate success of the research and its capacity to be impactful. Representatives of all stakeholders relevant to the research topic should be included as participants in the research design. Researchers can use a multitude of sampling strategies to identify these participant groups dependent upon the case being studied. For example, in the case study which follows stakeholders included prisoners (the 'service user'), prison staff (prison officers, non-operational and partnership agency staff), prison managers (including initial level and more senior managers) and the governing governor (the person ultimately in charge of the prison).

2. The researcher then convenes a steering group which draws together representatives from each of these stakeholder groups. The steering group has several important functions:

    ▪ It is a resource to the researcher generating a network of collaborative partners who can disseminate information and facilitate access to different areas of the organisation and to information.

    ▪ The formation of a group helps to disrupt the often unequal power relations between stakeholders and promotes transparency of the research aims, process and findings to all the stakeholder groups.

    ▪ It provides a mechanism through which the researcher comes to understand and take account of those things known to insiders that the researcher, as an outsider, cannot know.

    ▪ Over time steering group members become advocates for the research and it is often within this group that the 'energy' for change begins to emerge first (Cowburn and Lavis, 2013). In some research studies it is necessary to have more than one such group – as we will illustrate later in our case study example where we developed an additional advisory group.

3. The researcher next considers what methods of data collection are most appropriate to the aims of the research and the organisation in which the research takes place. This consideration may be theoretically or pragmatically driven. Traditionally, the AI approach is mobilised around one-to-one interviews, small workshops or focus groups. However, a number of variants have emerged condensing the process into one or two day events or 'summits', often involving large numbers of people (see e.g. Ludmena et al., 2003). AI also lends itself to the use of multiple methods of data collection enabling the researcher to draw upon a range of existing

techniques or develop new activities and tasks relevant to the participant group or organisation. The use of multiple methods with multiple stakeholders has the advantage of enhancing confidence in the robustness, comprehensiveness and quality of the research offering the potential to triangulate method and/or source (Patton, 1999; Mays and Pope, 2000). In our worked example we illustrate the use of multiple methods of data collection in the form of appreciative ethnography, interviews, survey and focus groups.

4. Once the researcher has identified relevant methods of data collection s/he can attend to the development of the protocols they will use to generate data with the participants. The protocol should be oriented by the goals or aims of the research and is constituted by a number of generative appreciatively framed questions. It is important when using AI to draw the distinction between a 'protocol' and the more familiar 'schedule' that is commonly developed to guide interviews or focus groups. A schedule implies a framework of questions to be asked within a more or less structured process (see e.g. King and Horrocks, 2010). In contrast, a protocol consists of a series of appreciatively framed generative questions which are designed to elicit a storied account. The creation of the questions is therefore a key component of successful AI research.

■   Appreciatively framed questions can be characterised as prompting participants to recount memories of their historical best experiences. They aim to uncover not only information but also the emotions associated with this peak performance enabling understanding of what happened and also how this was experienced by the person. The appreciative question should also excite the participant, generating interest and enthusiasm for the future and its possibilities.

■   Enabling these appreciative questions to be generative means moving away from some of the more conventional, often directive starting points for question development. By that we mean avoiding questions which begin with 'what, how, when', etc.. The generative question aims to prompt the participant to provide a story about their experience told in their own words and in their own way. In this sense the approach to question development is similar to that adopted in narrative inquiry (see e.g. King and Horrocks, 2010).

■   These appreciative generative questions are organised to correspond to the 4D elements, for example:
    Discovery: *'Tell me about a point in time when the way in which this prison's procedures for dealing with reports of unfair treatment arising from [ethnicity, sexuality, age, disability] have been at their best? What do you recall as being special about that time?'*
    Dreaming: *'If you had one wish for the ways in which the prison tries to ensure fairness and equal treatment for all prisoners, what would that be?'*

Designing: *'Let's talk in a little more detail about how you think the prison could go about making it possible to achieve the suggestions you have made.'*

Destiny: *'Tell me a story about a member of staff who was regularly able to show respect to ALL prisoners. This could be a real member of staff in any prison, or it could be your "ideal" member of staff. What do you think helps the member of staff to keep being respectful?'*

5. Once the protocol is designed, the researcher then employs their appreciative questions within the framework of methods they have designed for their study. For example, appreciative questions may be informally asked of participants during an observational or ethnographic[1] phase of research and recorded using field notes. Equally they may be employed within the more traditional one-to-one interview setting or within a small focus group where they can be audio recorded.

The vital component in this stage of AI research is the researcher's role in the delivery of the questions. AI is achieved through the development of appreciative conversations; these place the participant at the heart of the inquiry and communicate that they are being taken seriously, and are thus very different from structured interviewing.

- Appreciative conversations are best thought of as a co-constructed and relational activity where the process of eliciting the story is as important as the data the story reveals. The role of the researcher is to open up a physical and interpersonal space within which the conversation can take place. Such activity is challenging and the researcher will need to be fully present in the interaction. By this we mean demonstrating a genuine curiosity and the desire to learn something new through actively listening and engaging with the story being told. Becoming an effective exponent of the appreciative conversation requires the energy and commitment of the researcher to hone their skills. We would therefore recommend that those new to using the approach restrict methods of data collection to a one-to-one mode, such as interviewing, rather than group data collection which requires an experienced facilitator.

- Remaining appreciative is perhaps the most challenging aspect of data collection. The researcher is likely to encounter some participants who are so embedded or well-practised in a critical or problem-solving world view that they find it difficult to attend to the positive. In such cases the researcher should attempt to 're-frame' the conversation towards an appreciative slant. Re-framing does not ignore negative or problem focused responses as these are an important and valuable part of the lived experience of the participant. We

---

[1] The study of a group or culture through close observation, discussion and interpretation of their daily lives, relationships and interactions.

suggest that negative answers often reflect deeply held values that the participant is experiencing as being denied in the story they are telling. Re-framing aims to honour the negativity the participant relates whilst simultaneously seeking to unearth the denied value which is a route to the positive. The example of the process, below, is taken from an interview with a prisoner.

Appreciative question

Interviewer: *'Think back to the induction process you participated in when you first came into prison – what do you most appreciate about that process?'*

Participant: *'Nothing! – It's rubbish. I was made to feel like an idiot – ignored, patronised, mocked.'*

Re-frame of the negative answer

Interviewer: *'So, it's important to you to feel valued, accepted and included?'*

Participant: *'Yes, I suppose it is.'*

Interviewer: *'Can you think of an occasion or place where you did feel accepted and included?'*

Participant: *'Yes, when I went to the workshops. The instructors couldn't have been more welcoming … it made all the difference.'*

6. The researcher may also choose to supplement appreciative conversations with other additional tasks which can elaborate any of the 4D phases. These may focus on activities that participants are required to carry out as part of their role in the organisation; thereby illuminating 'best' or 'peak' performance within a task or activity, for example. Alternatively, they may use more established data collection tools; such as the Pictor technique described in Chapter 14 of this book, or the use of photographs, drawings or visual stimuli which generate discussion about either past peak performance or future orientated ideas.

7. Analysis of the AI data depends upon the specific aims and theoretical position taken by the researcher. For example, the data could be explored using one of the methods of narrative analysis (McAdams, 1993; Riessman, 2005) or Foucauldian Discursive Analysis (Willig, 2008) if this were the underlying theoretical position. However, we have found that thematic analysis, such as that outlined by Braun and Clarke (2006), offers a very effective means of establishing patterns of commonality and difference within the data. In studies where additional tasks are developed

to complement or enhance the appreciative conversations other additional forms of analysis may be required or possible. The researcher should also consider whether analysis is to be a singular (lone researcher) or group activity (researchers with or without research participants (Reed, 2007, provides a useful description of this issue)).

Whilst this AI research method can be used to research any organisation, we have found it is an especially effective method when researching organisations, situations or participant groups where attending to the positive is something that is unfamiliar, counter-intuitive or inherently difficult to achieve. The case study example, below, illustrates this core strength at work in a prison setting.

Our case example

Introduction to the study

The case we illustrate here posed significant challenges to research study. The objective was to design and test a research methodology which could explore how prisons in England and Wales respond to issues of equality and diversity[2] in their prisoner population. The research design needed to generate knowledge about the experience and effectiveness of this response across multiple stakeholders, including prisoners, prison staff and prison managers/governors. A further requirement was that the knowledge generated should illuminate the effectiveness of current policy, procedures and practices and illustrate how these elements could be improved, hence contributing to further development of the prison service's response to diversity nationally and internationally.[3]

---

[2] The requirement to attend to equality and diversity is laid down in the Equalities Act 2010. The response to equalities in prisons is devised nationally and laid out within the Equalities Framework published in 2011 by the National Offender Management Service (NOMS). However, within this broad framework each individual prison is required to develop its own local policies and procedures to promote equality and reduce discrimination in relation to race, faith, gender, sexuality, age and ability/disability, pregnancy and maternity.

[3] These objectives are being met through a series of ESRC (Economic and Social Research Council) funded research projects. The first, conducted in 2009–2010, was a small-scale project to design and pilot a research methodology focusing on one wing of one prison. The second, a large-scale three-year research project (2013–2016) is currently underway to apply the methodology in three very different prisons, each accommodating diverse prisoner populations within a range of security classifications and offence and sentence types.

Why was AI the appropriate method to use?

Prisons are by their very nature challenging environments. Researchers have characterised them as difficult (Bosworth, 2001), ethically complex (Dalen and Jones, 2010), emotionally turbulent and draining (Liebling, 1999), hampered by sexism (Gender and Players, 1985; Cowburn, 2007) and perhaps unsurprisingly bound up with issues of power (Giddens, 1982; Bosworth, 1999; Crewe, 2009). Perhaps most challenging is their overriding remit to security and the requirement to control and constrain their population (Bosworth, 1999; Drake, 2012). Indeed, this requirement to attend to and reduce risks posed by their custodial populations and to anticipate and neutralise problems generates attentiveness in prison staff, managers and prisoners to the negative. We were conscious that prison managers and staff are very suspicious of and demoralised by research which commonly presents them negatively. Thus, adopting a problem-focused methodology held the potential to further highlight what is missing or denied within prison life and to create, in both prisoners and prison staff, unrealistic expectations about what was possible and sustainable in terms of delivering peak performance. Secondly, we had to consider that, in contrast to other research populations, one of the primary stakeholders in the research process – prisoners from diverse minorities – were already disenfranchised and not voluntarily participating in the organisation being studied. Together these issues generated a considerable challenge to the research design.

As we have argued earlier, AI is imbued with characteristics and principles which hold the potential to redress some of the challenges posed by the prison and its population. It aspires to egalitarianism, in an environment where the perspective and worldview of the powerful shape prison life, valuing the stories and experiences of all stakeholders equally. AI promotes empowerment, especially important in an institution where power incrementally decreases hierarchically from the Ministry of Justice through NOMS, to governing governors, senior management teams and staff to prisoners. These last two stakeholder groups are increasingly distanced from the ability to influence and inform the governance of the systems in which they live and work, and adopting AI offers a means through which they can directly contribute to the creation of knowledge which can impact this system. AI ameliorates against exclusion in an environment which is necessarily exclusionary, at the very least in terms of excluding its population from wider society, by incorporating the widest possible range of stakeholders. It is also grounded; basing plans for the future in the real and achievable experiences of the past thus minimising the potential for unrealistic or unachievable goal setting and maximising the potential of research to have impact.

These characteristics arise from AI's social constructionist epistemological position where language is not theorised as a passive tool employed to convey inner 'truths' or 'thoughts' about a common external reality. Rather, language is considered a dynamic process through which the world and our understandings of it are mutually constructed and reconstructed (Gergen, 1999, 2014). Commensurate with this worldview, AI is underpinned by a critical realist ontological position. Within this paradigm there is no singular confirmable view of reality; although we may share the same environmental contexts and practices, our reality and the meanings we ascribe to it are understood, negotiated, agreed and affirmed through everyday interpersonal communication and relationship (Bhaskar, 1989). It was the potentiality afforded by these characteristics, philosophical underpinnings and value bases that made AI such a powerful methodological choice for the prison diversity research.

Applying AI methods

The following section illustrates how we applied AI methods in the research outlined above. We consider the methods of data collection employed, particularly the survey element we designed to complement the data from our appreciative conversations. We describe how we analysed this data and drew from this analysis. This section concludes with a reflection on our use of the method and indicates some of what we are continuing to learn about the application in our current research.

Data collection with AI

The four elements of AI, *discovery, dreaming, designing* and *destiny*, informed four stages of data collection with a range of stakeholders, including prisoners, prison staff and prison managers.

An appreciative ethnography phase

This phase mapped the relationships between official prison documentation, such as policies and procedures, which aim to guide the staff response to diverse minority prisoners and the formal and informal 'learning economy' through which prison staff and managers acquire and exchange knowledge and practice. The research team, working in rotating pairs, spent 37 consecutive days in the prison from morning unlock to evening lock-up. During this time they observed prison life, talked to prisoners and prison staff and where possible participated in activities aimed at equality and diversity, such as religious services and cultural festivals, diversity and wing forums and safer custody and equalities meetings.

Appreciatively framed prisoner interviews

The researchers carried out one-to-one private interviews with prisoners representative of those who directly experience the prison's response to diversity because of their faith, ethnicity, disability, age, sexuality, transgender or foreign national status. The interviews were split into two stages and employed appreciatively framed questions including, but not limited to, those presented earlier in this chapter. The first interview involved appreciative conversations focused on *discovery* of the best experiences of the prison's response to diversity and *dreaming* about how this could best become more frequent and prevalent. To stimulate appreciative conversation the second interview involved the completion of two supplementary tasks. These tasks were designed especially for the research to explore how the ideas identified in the *discovery* and *dreaming* phases could be made achievable and sustainable.

■ Effectiveness of existing equalities practice task

A card was generated to represent each formal practice the prison had instituted to respond to the needs of prisoners who fell within the remit of equality and diversity. In order to discover more about prisoners' experience of these current practices interviewees were asked to place each card on a grid (see Figure 12.2) to show (1) whether they were aware of the practice and (2) how effective they thought the practice was or could be.

■ Prioritisation of dreams task

The second task invited participants to reconsider the dreams they had generated in their own initial interview and the anonymised dreams of other prisoners on their residential wing. The purpose of the task was to understand (1) how important the dreams were to prisoners from diverse minority groups as a whole and in their relevant diversity sub-groups e.g. people of faith and

Task 1: Which equalities practices are effective?

Ability to practise religion/belief	Practice heard of	Practice not heard of	Disability aids
Cultural catering	Very effective		A forum for my PC
Library	Effective		Prisoner reps for my PC
Language line	Neither		PIDS workers
Lifts and ramps	Not effective		Learning mentors
OK club	Very ineffective		DIRF
COMP$_1$			Emotional support from chaplaincy

Figure 12.2   Effectiveness task

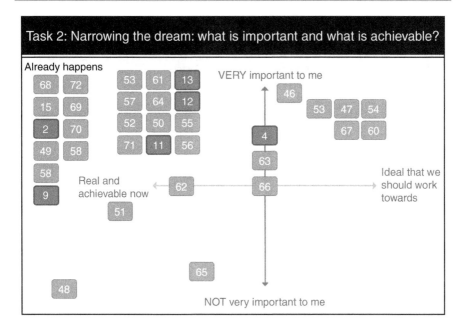

Figure 12.3   Prioritisation task

(2) how real and achievable the dreams were. Numbered cards were generated for each statement and the participants placed each card on a matrix (see Figure 12.3) discussing their views with the interviewer. As each card was placed the interviewer could then invite the participant to express how the idea could be designed into actuality and whether they saw this as something real and achievable now or something that the prison could work towards as part of a future strategy. The task also facilitated appreciative conversation about how the idea could be sustained in the future thereby enabling appreciative conversation about *destiny*.

Survey to all prisoners
The survey stage of the research enabled the views and experiences of the wider prisoner population about the response to diversity and equality to be captured. Consistent with the AI research design, the survey was structured to include four main sections: *discovery, dreaming, designing* and *destiny*. Each section contained a series of statement items which participants rated indicating their level of agreement. Each statement was ideographically derived, elicited from analysis of the one-to-one AI interviews (Pope and Mays, 2006).

However, this presented a challenge as the interview data was so detailed and rich that the number of potential items which could be included in the survey was vast; with some 274 potential items identified across the four AI elements. A conventional approach to addressing these issues would have been to establish the validity of the potential items through a statistical reduction of items; including only those which factored on to one another in statistically meaningful ways (Pett et al., 2003). However, when discussing item validation with our steering group and with prisoner-advisors to the project they expressed concern that a statistical reduction might remove items which had distinct meaning for prisoners belonging to particular minority diversity groups. Ultimately, the validation of items was established by a group of prisoner-advisors drawn from all diversity sub-groups completing a version of the survey which included all the potential items (Cowburn and Lavis, 2013). Content validity was established drawing on the principles outlined by Campanelli et al. (1991). Each prisoner-advisor was asked to rank the individual items and provide qualitative feedback on the ranking. This process enabled us to engage in a structured discussion about the representativeness of the items to the diverse minority groupings from which the prisoners were drawn and to whom they offered support. It also established the face validity of the measure in terms of ease of use, readability and clarity (Fowler, 1995).

Staff focus groups

The research team carried out five appreciatively framed focus groups with small stratified samples of prison staff; officer staff, probation staff, staff working for partnership agencies within the prison such as primary health care and restorative justice staff, middle managers and senior managers. This data was supplemented by a series of informal appreciative conversations with staff as the research team observed them carrying out their daily duties. The focus groups and appreciative conversations were structured to correspond to the 4D process and included questions such as: '*Take a few minutes to reflect on your career as a whole (and that might include your experiences working at other prisons). Can someone tell us about where or when they think the response to issues of diversity have worked best?*' and the follow-on question: '*What was it that made them so effective there/at that point in time?*'

Together, these four stages of data collection enabled the capture of actual practice and the detailed revelation of the experience and impact of the response for prisoners and staff. The data illustrated the strengths and weaknesses of the response and how the response was experienced by staff and prisoners, demonstrating what they were proud of or experienced positively, what more was needed to enable diverse minorities to feel as respected and as well treated as others and what energised both staff and prisoners in terms of achieving this desirable future. This data was then brought together through the analysis process we outline below.

Analysis of data produced through AI

In this section we provide a brief overview of how each type of data was recorded and analysed. Our aim is to provide context for the reader which allows them to make sense of how the data was treated prior to its intellectual interrogation which we review in the next section.

The data produced by the process discussed above took several forms.

1. The appreciative ethnography produced field notes detailing appreciative conversations and activities observed. Field notes were recorded on the day of observation and typed up as soon as possible.
2. The prisoners' interviews and staff focus groups were audio recorded and transcribed verbatim.
3. The survey produced quantitative ratings reflecting participants' views about statements relating to the 4Ds and open-ended qualitative comments. A data set was created using SPSS data for the ratings and the qualitative comments were typed up verbatim.
4. The two appreciative tasks (the effectiveness and the prioritisation tasks) undertaken by prisoners during their second interview produced grids or matrices (see Figures 12.2 and 12.3) which can be both quantitatively and qualitatively analysed.

We brought the field notes, the appreciative conversational data from the interviews and focus groups and the qualitative comments together using N-Vivo[4] as an organising tool.

As we noted earlier in the chapter, many methods of qualitative analysis would lend themselves to the analysis of AI data. In the present study we used thematic analysis (Braun and Clarke, 2006) to generate codes and then themes in N-Vivo. We do not describe this method or make detailed reference to the structure, organisation or analytic methods employed with N-Vivo here as there are sources which focus on this aspect of analysis (see Braun and Clarke, 2006; Bazeley and Jackson, 2013).

We used SPSS as a means of producing descriptive data on how survey respondents rated the statements that had been generated from the qualitative prisoner interviews. We produced descriptive statistics for the prisoner population as a whole and explored how diversity sub-groups rated statements about actual practices or ideas for the future that related specifically to them.

Illustrating the power of AI to guide future action

Since the focus of this chapter is on the application of AI techniques to develop a research methodology, we do not provide a comprehensive discussion of the findings of the equalities and diversity research we have used as

---

[4] N-Vivo is one of several brands of computer-assisted qualitative data analysis software package (CAQDAS). This software facilitates the organisation of qualitative data sets and is particularly useful where data sets are large, produced across multiple research sites or contain multiple participant types. The package does not analyse the data for the researcher, it merely acts as an organising system for holding and enabling retrieval of the data.

our case study. Rather we focus here on the process of interrogating data arising from the AI approach, the kinds of finding it is able to produce and their utility to an organisation in terms of guiding actions that produce real and lasting impact.

Intellectually interrogating the coded data and descriptive statistics

As with other qualitative approaches, analysis of the data does not end with the coding or breaking down of the raw data into useful units of meaning. A powerful analysis must also involve further interpretative activity; the drawing together and synthesis of meaning. This is especially true of AI with its epistemological roots in social constructionism where sense-making is a social, dialogical and interpersonal activity (Gergen, 1999). However, this can be daunting when faced with large amounts of data from diverse sources produced by multiple methods.

Our approach to the interpretive level of analysis was to devise a process where our sense-making related closely to addressing the issues the research was aiming to explore. We began by mapping our coded data sources (field notes, focus groups, interview transcripts, the effectiveness and the prioritisation task data, etc.) on to the research aims to see the 'layers' of data which related to (a) the aims and (b) the 4D structure which we used as a route to identify data which related to the present (*discovery* and *dreaming*) and the future (*dreaming, designing* and *destiny*).

We then explored this data collaboratively to generate 'propositions'. Working individually initially we identified key points in the data and began to construct challenging statements or propositions which might assist us to interrogate the data further. The aim of these propositions was to move us beyond a descriptive interpretation of the data and allow us to attend to the dynamics of particular participant groups, whilst not being constrained into, necessarily, seeing those groups as different. In this way we could attend to the specificity of data relating, for example, to only disabled prisoners whilst at the same time not missing the way in which the needs of disabled prisoners mirrored those of prisoners of faith. Equally, we explored data which specifically indicated the views of different types of prison staff whilst also attending to how this mirrored or diverged from the views of prisoners. Thus our analysis became a process of generating 'propositions', exploring these within the data, critically reflecting upon what was emerging and using this to challenge our interpretations and propose alternatives. Vital to this process was the generation of research memos, noted in our journals and also in N-Vivo through which we recorded our analytic journey, noting our discussions and the decisions arising from them.

Generating foundations for action

A common difficulty experienced by researchers is to translate their analytic and theoretical findings into a format that has utility for the organisations they are working with and for. Too often research is conducted only for the report to 'sit on the shelf' because it is not clear to those working within the organisation how to take action which might address the knowledge that has been generated. Our application of AI principles and techniques helped us to address this difficulty and generate what we refer to as 'foundations for action'. Foundations for action aim to (1) highlight for the organisation what is already working effectively and what has been experienced as effective in the past; (2) indicate what improvements could form the basis of an initial short-term response and which could be part of a longer-term improvement based on the views of the stakeholders who participated in the research; (3) enable the organisation to appreciate what the likely impact of making those improvements is for the various stakeholders; and (4) identify where the energy to support change has been most strongly expressed and by which stakeholders.

Helping the organisation understand what is already working effectively
The generation of descriptive statistics from the effectiveness task grid (Figure 12.2) and the survey enables the prison to see clearly how effective its current practices are being. When synthesised with the qualitative analysis of the appreciative conversation between the interviewer and the prisoner when completing the task the prison can appreciate how these practices are actually experienced and in what ways they might be improved.

Establishing the foundations for future action
Similarly, the prioritisation task matrix (Figure 12.4) can be analysed descriptively in SPSS to contextualise the ideas dreamed of by prisoners from diverse minority groups. Plotting the placement of each statement in a quadrant of the matrix reveals prisoners' views about the relative importance of the ideas dreamed of. It also establishes their views about whether the ideas are achievable in the short term or more likely to be achieved as part of a longer-term strategy. Grids can be plotted to analyse and compare the priorities of diversity sub-groups, as in Figure 12.4 below, which uses fictional data to illustrate the potential prioritisation of the dreams of disabled prisoners. Each of the numbers in the illustration (e.g. S40-3 relates to a specific dream – *people with mobility issues would have access to the same areas of the prison as prisoners who do not have disabilities.* The placement of this dream in the upper left-hand quadrant signifies its prioritisation as an issue of importance which was real and achievable in the short term.

Synthesising these grids with the qualitative analysis of the appreciative conversations between the interviewer and the prisoner when completing the task provides weight and depth about why these issues are important to prisoners and what impact they will have on improving respect and feeling fairly treated. It also reveals prisoners' views about how these ideas could be put into action (*designing*) and sustained (*destiny*).

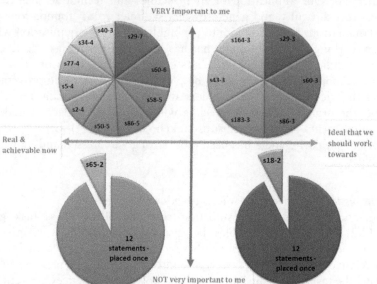

Figure 12.4   Prioritisation of the dreams of disabled prisoners

Cross-referencing this composite data with the analysis arising from the appreciative conversations with staff in the focus groups adds further depth to the emerging picture, allowing consideration of where staff's and prisoners' views converge and diverge.

Identifying the energy for change and generating a plan for future action
Together this layering of the data from each phase of the research and participant group reveals factors which reflect the issues prioritised by prisoners in each diverse minority and across all diverse minorities. These factors enable the researcher to offer an interpretation of where the 'energy for change' is strongest and to form the basis of what we term 'foundations for action'. The foundations for action aid the organisation to prioritise improvements and distinguish between those which could form the basis of an initial short-term response and those which may need to be part of a longer-term improvement strategy. In doing so they address the *destiny* element of AI which seeks to maintain and sustain the ideas dreamed about and designed.

Foundations for action can often be stratified into those which relate to taking global or specific action. Global foundations for action target the priorities of all participant groups (in this example all diverse minority prisoners), but cannot on their own address the specific priorities identified by some minority groups. Specific foundations for action are needed to ensure that the

Factors	Ethnicity	FNPs	Disability	Sexuality	Age	Faith
Affiliation with others						
Being understood						
Challenging discrimination						
Communication						
Mutual respectfulness						
Responsiveness						
Trust						

Figure 12.5   Fictional global foundations for action

issues given highest priority by one or more minority groups are addressed. Figures 12.5 and 12.6 below use fictional data to illustrate factors which could inform foundations for action at a global and at a specific level. A colour has been assigned to each factor so it can clearly be seen which diverse minority has identified this factor as a priority.

In Figure 12.6 below the factor 'maintaining cultural identity' is something identified as a priority by ethnic minorities and foreign national prisoners (FNP).

Factors	Ethnicity	FNPs	Disability	Sexuality	Age	Faith
Access to meaningful activity						
Confidentiality						
Consequences of inattentiveness						
Discipline						
Fairness						
Feeling safe						
Maintaining cultural identity						
Physical comfort						
Support						

Figure 12.6   Fictional specific foundations for action

When combined, these two fictional sets of foundations for action would address the priorities identified by all diverse minority stakeholders.

Reflections on using AI methods

The AI research methodology presented in this chapter is still an emergent and developing approach. It is currently being applied in a three-year project which targets three different types of prison, each with very different prisoner populations. A key aspect of this new research project is to explore how the methodology can be adapted for use in the different contexts posed by these research sites and to develop its analytic strategies. For example, where a prisoner population is relatively static a research team could deliver all the stage 1 interviews, elicit discovery and dreaming statements for the effectiveness and prioritisation tasks and then return to complete the stage 2 interviews at a later date. However, in prisons whose population is typified by remand or short sentences the stage 1 and stage 2 interviews must occur within a few days of one another to avoid participant attrition. The adaptations to process required by this and other emergent issues during the project will further refine and develop the application of AI in this context.

In addition to advancing the AI methodology, our work is also challenging assumptions with regards to the appreciative focus of AI; identifying peak performance as the starting point of any inquiry might prevent discovery of the negative aspects of prison life. Our work is adding to the growing body of research which is illustrating that AI identifies strengths and weaknesses, whilst actively engaging the interest and involvement of prisoners, prison staff and senior prison management (Cowburn and Lavis, 2013; Lavis and Cowburn, 2010; Liebling et al., 2001; Liebling et al., 1999). Two members of the current research team, both of whom have recently completed their PhD research and are using AI for the first time, have remarked that their research would have positively benefitted from the application of the method had they known about it at the time. Moreover, our recent work on the current three-year project is already indicating that adopting an appreciative starting point alters the dynamics of the way in which the participants and stakeholders engage with the research process; breaking down taken-for-granted ways of viewing prison life.

A further benefit of adopting an AI methodology for research is the level of *energy for change* the process generates in comparison with methodologies which take the problematic as their starting point. Research from the field of positive psychology suggests that being placed in a positive affective state creates an opening of the mind towards participation, facilitating thinking and working collaboratively (Freidrickson, 2001). This has particular resonance for contexts like prisons, where staff and prisoners defend against negativity from the press and wider society which often fails to take account of the complex circumstances and environment in which services are being delivered.

Whilst we acknowledge the work of researchers such as Bright and Cameron (2009) who note that negative associations can have a stronger and more enduring resonance for people than positive experiences, it appears that in prisons, at least, AI, with its emphasis not only on positive experience but also on the positive emotions which accompany such experience, offers a distinct and refreshing departure point from which to consider events, situations and interactions.

AI research also generates and maintains vitality in the research team – it seems there is a personal payback to employing this method in research. Whilst acknowledgement and intellectual consideration of the emotional dimensions of researching prison life have been slow to emerge, these papers document some of the personal cost to the researcher of working in this field (Drake and Harvey, 2014; Jewkes, 2012: Neilsen, 2010). Whilst it is certainly not our suggestion that the use of AI offers a panacea against such costs, some of its techniques, for example re-framing to elicit underlying values, offer the researcher a means of actively working with and negotiating, rather than passively absorbing, the negativity often encountered.

References

Bazeley, P. and Jackson, K. (2009). *Qualitative Data Analysis with N-Vivo*. London: SAGE.

Bhaskar, R. (1989). *Reclaiming Reality*. London: Verso.

Bosworth, M. (1999) *Engendering Resistance: Agency and Power in Women's Prisons*. Aldershot: Ashgate.

Bosworth, M. (2001). The past as a foreign country? Some methodological implications of doing historical criminology. *British Journal of Criminology*, 41(3), 431–442.

Braun, V. and Clarke, V. (2006). Using thematic analysis in psychology. *Qualitative Research in Psychology*, 3, 77–101.

Bright, D.S. and Cameron, K. (2009). Positive organizational change: What the field of POS offers to OD practitioners. In W.J. Rothwell, J.M. Stavros, R.L. Sullivan and A. Sullivan (Eds.), *AI Theory and Critique Organization Development: A Guide for Managing and Leading Change (Third Edition)*. San Francisco: Pfeiffer Wiley, pp. 397–410.

Campanelli, P., Martin, E. and Rothgeb, J. (1991). The use of respondent and interviewer debriefing studies as a way to study response error in survey data. *The Statistician*, 40, 253–264.

Carter, C.A., Ruhe, M.C., Weyer, S., Litaker, D., Fry, R.E. and Stange, K.C. (2007). An appreciative inquiry approach to practice improvement and transformative change in health care settings. *Qualitative Management of Health Care*, 16(3), 194–204.

Cooperrider, D.L. and Srivastva, S. (1987). Appreciative inquiry in organizational life. *Research in Organizational Change and Development*, 1, 129–169.

Cooperrider, D.L. and Whitney, D.K. (1999). *Appreciative Inquiry: A Positive Revolution in Change*. San Francisco, CA: Berrett-Koehler Publishers.

Cowburn, M. (2007). Men researching men in prison: The challenges for profeminist research. *Howard Journal*, 46(3), 276–288.

Cowburn, M. and Lavis, V. (2013). Using a prisoner advisory group to develop diversity research in a maximum-security prison: A means of enhancing prisoner participation. *Groupwork*, 23(3), 67–79.

Cowburn, M., Lavis, V. and Bird, H. (2010). Appreciative inquiry into the diversity strategy of HMP Wakefield. Unpublished report to ESRC. Available at: www.esrc.ac.uk/my-esrc/Grants/RES-000-22-3441/read.

Crewe, B. (2009). *The Prisoner Society: Power, Adaptation and Social Life in an English Prison*. Oxford: OUP, Clarenden.

Dalen, K. and Jones, L.Ø. (2010). Ethical monitoring: Conducting research in a prison setting. *Research Ethics Review*, 6(1), 10–16.

Drake, D. (2012). *Prisons, Punishment and the Pursuit of Security*. Basingstoke: Palgrave Macmillan.

Drake, D. and Harvey, J. (2014). Performing the role of ethnographer: Processing and managing the emotional dimensions of prison research. *International Journal of Social Research Methodology*, 17(5), 489–501.

Elliott, C. (1999). *Locating the Energy for Change: An Introduction to Appreciative Inquiry*. Winnipeg, Canada: International Institute for Sustainable Development.

Fine, M. and Torre, M.E. (2006). Intimate details: Participatory action research in prison. *Action Research*, 4(3), 253–269.

Fine, M., Torre, M.E., Boudin, K., Bowen, I., Clark, J., Hylton, D., Martinez, M., 'Missy' Rivera, M., Roberts, R.A., Smart, P. and Upegui, D. (2003). Participatory action research: Within and beyond bars. In P. Camic, J.E. Rhodes and L. Yardley (Eds.), *Qualitative Research in Psychology: Expanding Perspectives in Methodology and Design*. Washington, DC: American Psychological Association, pp. 173–198.

Fowler, F. (1995). *Improving Survey Questions: Design and Evaluation*. Thousand Oaks, CA: SAGE.

Freidrickson, B. (2001). The role of positive emotions in positive psychology. *American Psychologist*, 56(3), 218–226.

Gergen, K. (1999). *An Invitation to Social Construction*. London: SAGE.

Gergen, K. (2014). From mirroring to world-making: research as future forming. Retrieved 30 January 2017 from: www.taosinstitute.net/Websites/taos/images/ResourcesManuscripts/Mirroring-to-World-Making-Ken-Gergen.pdf.

Giddens, A. (1982). *Profiles and Critiques in Social Theory*. London: Macmillan.

Israel, B., Schultz, A., Parker, E. and Becker, A. (1998). Review of community-based research: Assessing partnership approaches to improve public health. *Annual Review of Public Health*, 19, 173–202.

Jewkes, Y. (2012). Autoethnography and emotion as intellectual resources: Doing prison research differently. *Qualitative Inquiry*, 18(1), 63–75.

Kemmis, S. and McTaggart, R. (2000). Participatory action research. In N.K. Denzin and Y.S. Lincoln (Eds.), *Handbook of Qualitative Research (Second Edition)*. Thousand Oaks, CA: SAGE, pp. 567–605.

King, N. and Horrocks, C. (2010). *Interviews in Qualitative Research*. London: SAGE.

Larson, M.J. and Tian, X. (2005). Strengthening women's contributions to sustainable peace: The benefits of flexibility. *Conflict Resolution Quarterly*, 23(1), 53–70.

Lavis, V. and Cowburn, M. (2010). Race relations in prison: Managing performance and developing engagement. *British Journal of Community Justice*, 7(3), 77–89.

Lewin, K. (1951). *Field Theory in Social Science: Selected Theoretical Papers*. New York: Harper.

Lewin, K. (1952). Group decision and social change. In G.E. Swanson, T.M. Newcomb and E.L. Hartley (Eds.), *Readings in Social Psychology*. New York: Henry Holt, pp. 459–473.

Lewis, S. (2011). *Positive Psychology at Work: How Positive Leadership and Appreciative Inquiry Create Inspiring Organisations*. Chichester, UK: Wiley-Blackwell.

Lewis, S., Passmore, J. and Cantore, S. (2008). *Appreciative Inquiry for Change Management: Using AI to Facilitate Organizational Development*. London: Kogan Page.

Liebling, A. (1999). Doing prison research: Breaking the silence. *Theoretical Criminology*, 3(2), 147–173.

Liebling, A. (2005). *Prisons and Their Moral Performance*. Oxford: Oxford University Press.

Liebling, A., Elliott, C. and Arnold, A. (2001). Transforming the prison: Romantic optimism or appreciative realism? *Criminal Justice*, 1(2), 161–180.

Liebling, A., Price, D. and Elliott, C. (1999). Appreciative inquiry and relationships in prison. *Punishment and Society*, 1(2), 71–98.

Ludmena, J.D., Whitney, D., Mohr, B.J. and Griffin, T.J. (2003). *The Appreciative Inquiry Summit*. San Fransisco, CA: Berrett-Koehler.

Mays, N. and Pope, C. (2000). Qualitative research in health care: Assessing quality in qualitative research. *British Medical Journal*, 320(7226), 50–52.

McAdams, D. (1993). *The Stories We Live By: Personal Myths and the Making of the Self*. London: Guildford Press.

Neilson, M. (2010). Pains and possibilities in prison: On the use of emotions and positioning in ethnographic research. *Acta Sociologica*, 53(4), 307–321.

Park, P., Brydon-Miller, M., Hall, B. and Jackson, T. (1993). *Voices of Change: Participatory Research in the United States and Canada*. Wesport, CT: Bergin and Garvey.

Patton, M.Q. (1999). Enhancing the quality and credibility of qualitative analysis. *Health Services Research*, 34(5) Part II, 1189–1208.

Pett, M., Lackey, N. and Sullivan, J. (2003). *Making Sense of Factor Analysis*. Thousand Oaks, CA: SAGE.

Reed, J. (2007). *Appreciative Inquiry: Research for Change*. London: SAGE.

Riessman, C. (2005). Narrative analysis. In N. Kelly, C. Horrocks, K. Milnes, B. Roberts and D. Robinson (Eds.), *Narrative, Memory and Everyday Life*. Huddersfield: University of Huddersfield Press.

Robinson, G., Priede, C., Farrell, S. and Shapland, J. (2012). Doing strengths based research: Appreciative inquiry in a probation setting. *Criminology and Criminal Justice*, 13(1), 3–20.

Stavros, J.M. and Hinrichs, G. (2009). *Thin Book of SOAR: Building Strengths-Based Strategy*. Bend, OR: Thin Book Publishers.

Wengraph, T. (2001). *Qualitative Research Interviewing: Biographic Narrative and Semi-Structured Method*. London: SAGE.

Whyte, W.F. (1991). *Participatory Action Research*. Newbury Park: SAGE.

Willig, C. (2008). *Introducing Qualitative Research in Psychology: Adventures in Theory and Method (Second Edition)*. Buckingham: Open University Press.

Using Construct Elicitation and Laddering in the Education of Social Work Students: Exercises in Reflexive Practice

Viv Burr and Nigel King

Introduction to construct elicitation and laddering

Construct elicitation and laddering are just two examples from a range of fruitful methods drawn from personal construct theory (PCT) (Kelly, 1955) that may be used by qualitative researchers (see Burr et al., 2014). In order to grasp these methods and the kinds of question they can help us to answer, it is useful to first understand their PCT origins. King et al. (Chapter 14) say a little about PCT in their chapter on the Pictor technique. PCT's founder, George Kelly, was a clinical psychologist. He argued that we each 'construe', or perceive, the world in our own personal way, and sometimes the way that we have come to see ourselves and the other people in our lives can cause us problems. As King et al. point out, we are often not consciously aware of our construing; it is our taken-for-granted way of seeing things. Kelly's aim in therapy was to enable the client to externalise and inspect their own construing in order to allow them to understand their own problems and how these might be overcome, and he developed a number of methods for helping him and his clients to understand their psychological difficulties.

According to PCT, each person develops for themselves a 'construct system' which we use to interpret our experience. Our construct system is like a lens through which we perceive the world, giving it a particular appearance and meaning. One's construct system consists of a set of bi-polar dimensions or 'constructs', such as friendly–hostile or interesting–dull, which the person uses to interpret their experience. Although we may not be consciously aware of it, PCT holds that we are constantly interpreting the world through our constructs and anticipating the immediate future with them. For example, when we meet a new acquaintance or colleague for the first time, you may be (non-consciously) asking yourself 'is s/he going to be friendly or distant?' Another person may be asking 'is s/he going to be an ally or an enemy?' Their behaviour, and ours, then takes shape and is interpreted in terms of these constructs, so they can have a powerful influence on our future interactions and relationships.

In PCT terms, if we want to understand a person this means we must understand how they perceive themselves and their world. In other words, we need to understand their construing, to find out about some of the constructs that make up their construct system. People use somewhat different constructs for different areas of their experience. For example, when we are shopping we may typically use constructs such as 'expensive–affordable', whereas when we are listening to a lecture we might use constructs such as 'interesting–dull' or 'clear–confusing'. As social scientists, we usually want to find out about a person's construing in a particular aspect of their lives, such as their close relationships with others, how they have experienced recovery from a major illness, or what they feel about becoming a parent or grandparent.

In order to do this, PCT focuses on concrete examples from that aspect of life. 'Eliciting', or revealing, a person's constructs typically entails the comparison of two or three concrete examples from their experience (termed 'elements'). Kelly defined a construct as any way in which two things are similar and different from a third. This can be any three things. On my desk I can see a book, a glass and a telephone. If I ask myself to think of a way in which two of these are similar and different from the third, I could say that two are 'fragile' and the other is 'sturdy'. Fragile–sturdy is a construct; it doesn't actually matter which of the 'elements' (book, phone and glass) I think is sturdy or fragile – the important point is that the comparison of these 'elements' has elicited a construct. If we wanted to find out about the constructs that a person uses in the realm of relationships we would use people as the 'elements' for our comparison. You could try this now, by comparing, say, your mother, your best friend and your partner and thinking of a way in which two are similar and different from the third.

This focus on concrete things, people and events has further advantages. Qualitative researchers recognise that it can sometimes be difficult for research participants to access and articulate complex aspects of their experience. By focusing on concrete examples, PCT methods can help participants to overcome any difficulties they may have in expressing abstract ideas. With some participant groups it can also be difficult to avoid socially desirable responses, for example where practitioners are keenly aware of what is regarded as 'best practice' in their field. Using concrete examples can give the researcher a means of accessing accounts which reach beyond socially desirable or common-sense responses since they avoid asking participants direct questions about what is important to them.

According to PCT, our construct system is arranged hierarchically, with relatively concrete and mundane constructs, used in relation to quite narrow aspects of life, at the bottom, and more abstract constructs, relating to our overarching values and beliefs, at the top. For example, lower level constructs might include 'tasty–bland' (in relation to food) or 'chatty–quiet' (in relation to acquaintances). A construct higher up the system, to which the lower ones will be related, might be 'exciting–dull' (this could apply to both food and acquaintances), and this might in turn be subsumed under a higher-order (or 'superordinate') construct such as 'life-enhancing–stultifying'.

In this chapter we will demonstrate two PCT methods. The first is construct elicitation, which is a simple method for gaining access to a person's construct system, and the second is 'laddering'. Laddering takes one or more constructs that have emerged from the construct elicitation and uses them to explore the person's superordinate constructs, those that tell us something about their overarching, core values. Although the constructs that we can elicit through these methods are interesting in themselves, in qualitative research constructs are more likely to be used to focus a subsequent interview with the participants so it is important not to think of constructs as ends in themselves (although constructs are often used in this way in quantitative research).

Using construct elicitation and laddering

In this section, we will describe the general procedure for these two methods. Since our case example will focus on people and our perceptions of them (rather than, say, food or shops) we will use people as the elements in our account here.

Construct elicitation

The participant is asked to think of about ten or 12 people they know (the actual number doesn't really matter – it can be more than this or fewer). The list can include people they know well and others that they know only slightly but the participant must feel able to give some opinion of the kind of person they seem to be. It should include people with whom they have different kinds of relationship, and people they dislike as well as those they like. The aim is to get a good range.

They are then asked to write a pseudonym or role (such as mum, dad, sister) for each person on a separate piece of card, and include a further card with 'me' on it. The researcher would then select three of these more or less at random and set them in front of the participant, asking them to think of a way in which any two are similar and different from the third. The researcher takes a sheet of paper and writes down the response as two ends of a dimension, with each 'end' of the construct at opposite sides of the page, for example:

warm   reserved

If the person finds it difficult to work with three cards, one may be removed and the participant asked to think of a way in which the remaining two are either similar to or different from each other. If they focus on a difference you can record the construct as usual, for example they might say, 'My mum is outgoing but my dad is shy.' But if the person focuses on a similarity, it is important to follow up with an enquiry about the opposite 'pole'. For example, the participant may say, 'These two people are both warm.' You would then follow up with: 'As opposed to what? What might be the contrast to being warm?' When recording constructs, it is important to use the participant's own wording as far as possible – avoid the temptation to rephrase the construct in terms that seem more logical to *you*, even if their verbal label is quite long-winded, for example 'treats others with respect and listens to them – treats people like a doormat and tells them what to do'.

Continue offering the participant different combinations of cards, being sure to include 'me' in some of them, recording them in the same way as the first one, until they can offer no further new constructs. You will probably end up with a list of between about five and 20 constructs.

Inspecting the constructs

The next step could be to inspect the list of constructs you have elicited and interview the participant about interesting themes. For example, here is a list of the constructs elicited from one participant (Katherine) in a piece of research focusing on what it might mean to 'be oneself' (Butt et al., 1997). In this piece of research, rather than using different people as the elements for comparison, participants were asked to think of themselves in their relationships with a variety of different people. So the elements were, for example, 'me when I'm with my husband', 'me when I'm with my best friend', etc..

Katherine's constructs

feel defensive	don't feel defensive
feel uncomfortable	feel comfortable
I'm guarded	I'm open
feel disinterested	feel concerned
unsure	relaxed
wouldn't share my feelings	would share my feelings
want to protect myself	feel comfortable
feel resentful	don't feel resentful

unstimulated	stimulated
feel vulnerable	don't feel vulnerable
distrust them	trust them

There is a strong theme in Katherine's constructs around feeling defensive and guarded, distrustful and vulnerable. This was a fruitful focus for a subsequent interview with her about her relationships with others and about when she is and is not able to 'be herself'.

Laddering

Once you have elicited a range of constructs from a participant, you might 'ladder' one or more of these to explore the constructs that lie higher up in their construct system, those that are more likely to say something about their core values. Choose a construct that is rather more concrete or specific than abstract or general. For example, constructs such as 'good person–bad person' are less likely to lead 'up' to further important, core issues than more 'lowly' constructs such as 'vegetarian–eats meat'. Write the construct at the bottom of a sheet of paper, with the poles of the construct on opposite sides of the sheet. Ask the participant which pole of the construct they would prefer to see themselves at. Supposing they replied 'vegetarian', you would then inquire about why they prefer this pole, about their reasons for preferring it to the other pole. They may reply, 'It's about recognising the right to life of animals.' You would then follow up by exploring the opposite pole: 'As opposed to what? What are meat-eaters like, then?' The person may answer, 'It's just using animals for your own ends.' This new construct would be written above the first one, aligning the relevant poles. Again, you would explore both ends of this new construct: 'Why is it important to you to recognise animals' rights to life?' The person may respond, 'It's about living in the world in a way that accommodates the needs of others, not just yourself.' Again, you would prompt about the opposite: 'As opposed to what? How does this contrast with using animals for your own ends?' They may reply, 'It's thinking only about yourself and what you want.' Again, this new construct would be recorded above the other two. The arrows denote the process of 'ascending' the construct system:

accommodating the needs of others-----------thinking only about yourself

recognising the right to life of animals-------using animals for your own ends

vegetarian--eats meat

As the constructs become more and more 'superordinate', perhaps more like general moral principles, you need to decide when further enquiry is unlikely to reveal anything of greater importance or relevance. The 'ladder' that you produce with a participant can then be used to focus a subsequent interview.

The case example

Construct elicitation and laddering are good ways of getting people to think about their own behaviour and relationships, allowing the researcher to quickly focus on issues of particular significance for the person. Such focused reflection is something that is now routinely required in a number of professions within health and social care, and becoming a 'reflexive practitioner' is one of the goals in education and training in such fields. We wanted to find out whether these methods would be helpful for students who were currently developing their reflexive skills. We piloted these methods with four social work students, Nadia, Caroline, Jenny and Alice, and it is this pilot study that we will use here as our case example.

Jenny was in her first year of study, and the others were in year three. We wanted them to reflect on what was, for them, good social work practice, and we wanted them to do this without simply reproducing what they had been told on their course; it can be all too easy to 'sign up' to what look like good principles without properly examining what these may look like in practice, and how we personally might enact them. The year three students had some experience of social work practice during their placements, but even though Jenny had not experienced this we felt that she should still have some conception of good practice that could potentially be examined through PCT methods. Nadia, our first participant, was interviewed individually; the other three took part as a group. This enabled us to judge whether such methods were likely to be successful in a classroom setting.

The students were each provided with a number of pieces of card and asked to write on these pseudonyms or roles for a range of people with whose practice they were familiar. In Jenny's case, she drew on a health and social care setting in which she had previously worked. We emphasised that it was important to include people whose practice they felt less positive about as well as those they approved. The students also included a card for 'me'. Working with three cards at a time, as described above, they were asked to focus particularly on the behaviour and practice of the individuals and to identify similarities and differences between them; in this way each of the students produced a list of constructs. Jenny's constructs are provided here as an example:

Jenny's constructs

senior level–entry level

caring–cold

highly strung–calm

harsh–warm

client centred–business centred

detached–mindful of clients

immature–mature

complacent–super keen

We could, at this stage, have interviewed the students about the constructs that had emerged. However, the aim of this exercise was to explore their more 'superordinate' constructs around social work practice and so we chose one or more constructs from each student's list for laddering. It is important to recognise that laddering is not a psychological 'test' which can reveal some previously hidden truth about the person. Usually it reveals something of interest to be explored further during discussion, but sometimes it is not possible to 'ascend' the ladder very far. See, for example, one of Caroline's ladders:

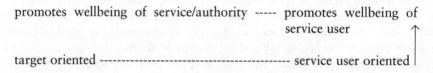

The construct 'target oriented–service user oriented' 'led' only to one more superordinate construct, and it may be that the chosen construct was already fairly superordinate for Caroline. Nevertheless, the exercise revealed something of importance about the contrast Caroline was making, which was about practices that are truly aimed at benefiting clients rather than being for the convenience of the provider.

The ladders sometimes produced counter-intuitive results:

Alice's first ladder

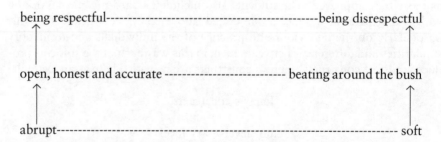

Although this ladder consists of only three 'rungs', it was interesting to find that an 'abrupt' style (rather than being 'soft') was, for her, likely to signal an ultimately more respectful relationship with clients.

Alice's second ladder was longer:

Alice's second ladder

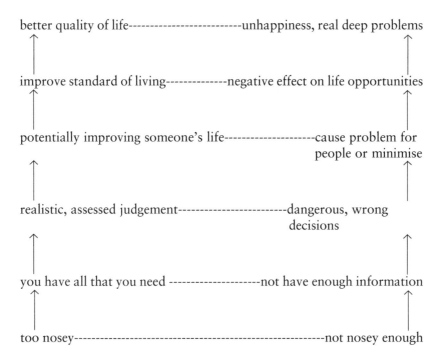

better quality of life------------------------unhappiness, real deep problems

improve standard of living-------------negative effect on life opportunities

potentially improving someone's life--------------------cause problem for
people or minimise

realistic, assessed judgement------------------------dangerous, wrong
decisions

you have all that you need --------------------not have enough information

too nosey---not nosey enough

In the process of completing this ladder, it was clear that Alice was reflecting on her social work values. We chose 'too nosey–not nosey enough' because it seemed a fairly concrete construct. At the outset, it seemed that Alice was unsure of just how 'nosey' a social worker ought to be. However, in the process of laddering she reflected on the implications of these two kinds of behaviour and came to the conclusion that it was important for a social worker to be highly inquisitive about a client's situation as this was the only way to realistically assess the problem and, ultimately, give the client a better quality of life.

Reflections on using construct elicitation and laddering

After completing the exercises, we interviewed our participants about their experience of doing these. One thing they remarked upon was the sometimes unanticipated and counter-intuitive results of their reflection. For example, in a third ladder, Alice began with the construct 'underbearing–overbearing'. She said:

> *I chose that I would rather err on the side of overbearing, so I could get more information [from a client], and that shocked me a little bit actually because I thought actually you think of overbearing as being a very negative thing.*

Nadia was also surprised at the results of one of her ladders. She began with the construct 'doing things their own way–following procedures'. The five 'rungs' of her ladder led from 'following procedures' through 'providing the best for the client without delay' to 'able to achieve potential as a person'. Nadia said:

> *The following procedures thing, that is just sort of drilled into your head when you're at uni … you've got to follow the procedures, but I would never have thought that I would have got to the conclusion that I did to talk about that.*

For Caroline, laddering helped her to gain insight into some of her reactions to others' practice:

> *I didn't realise what my actual main values were in social work until I did that ladder and I didn't realise why sometimes I view things so negatively until I did the ladder. So when I said, erm … 'target oriented–[oriented] to service user' and how that led to my values and that's how I must view it when I'm seeing somebody that's more about targets and money, I must be thinking 'well, you don't think about the service users' and that must be why it annoys me in practice.*

Such insights are arguably evidence of the kind of thorough and effective reflection that social work educators are trying to encourage. The students also suggested that these methods, though challenging for them at times, do potentially result in more effective reflection than the methods they typically use during their course:

> *We have to write a reflective account at the end of the year … and sometimes you feel like you're just reflecting on the same stuff year in, year out. Whereas if you've got this new tool, what they want, the years you go on, is for you to be in more depth … what I took from it was that I was a lot more in-depth in my reflection … and actually it probably takes a hell of a lot less time than an A4 side of reflection that we have to write. (Alice)*

You're drilling down more, aren't you, doing it this way, the whys, you're questioning even further on that action and then you're questioning on that action. So it can take you away from where you've first begun. (Jenny)

The positive feedback we received from our pilot participants encouraged us to trial these methods in a classroom setting. We did this in a two-hour teaching session devoted to reflexive thinking with approximately 60 second year social work students. The students worked in pairs, eliciting and laddering each other's constructs in turn. At the end of the session we asked them for written feedback, and many of these students also found the methods useful for facilitating their own reflectiveness. When asked whether they had been surprised by their reflections or their own values, they responded for example:

It challenged my values and [I] found out things about myself which I never thought about in the past.

I was surprised at how reflective the task made me as I have previously struggled at carrying out a solid thought process.

It was a great learning tool for me. I thought I was aware of most of my prejudices but found I wasn't.

However, for some students the methods did not lead to any fresh insights, and it is hard to say why this was the case. Because the students were inexperienced in using these methods it is possible that some of them were unable to get the most out of them. It is important to point out that construct elicitation and laddering require similar skills to other qualitative methods, such as depth interviewing. The researcher must listen carefully to participants' responses, to help them clarify their own thinking and meanings where necessary and, particularly in the case of laddering, to respond to and follow up interesting and potentially fruitful responses rather than complete the task mechanically.

Our overall experience of using these methods with social work students suggests that they can enable students to reflect on their own values in a fruitful way. They clearly spent a good deal of time thinking through their responses before giving an answer to our questions, and for this reason participants can find such methods quite demanding. Nevertheless, social work students are accustomed to the requirement that they reflect thoroughly upon their own practice and values and so the demands of PCT methods did not seem onerous to them. However, in the case of participants who are not used to thinking about themselves deeply, the researcher may need even more skill and patience if s/he is to produce rich data.

References

Burr, V., King, N. and Butt, T. (2014). Personal construct psychology methods for qualitative research. *International Journal of Social Research Methodology*, 17(4), 341–355.

Butt, T., Burr, V. and Epting, F. (1997). Core construing: Self discovery or self invention? In G.J. Neimeyer. and R.A. Neimeyer (Eds.), *Advances in Personal Construct Psychology*. London: Elsevier, pp. 39–62.

Kelly, G.A. (1955). *The Psychology of Personal Constructs*. New York: Norton.

The Pictor Technique: Exploring Experiences of Collaborative Working from the Perspectives of Generalist and Specialist Nurses

Nigel King, Joanna Brooks, Alison Bravington,
Beth Hardy, Jane Melvin and David Wilde

Introduction: The Pictor technique

Interviews are widely used in qualitative research, and can take many different forms (see King and Horrocks, 2010). In this chapter, we will introduce a particular visual tool developed by the authors and colleagues for use in research interviews: the Pictor technique (e.g. King et al., 2013a). The technique requires research participants to construct a 'Pictor chart' – a visual representation depicting their role and their work – which the researcher and the participant can then use as a basis to explore potentially complex experiences in a research interview setting. We will present here an example from our own applied research to demonstrate how we have used Pictor in research interviews.

Doing Pictor

Before introducing our case example, let us first familiarise ourselves with the main procedural steps undertaken in the technique. Pictor was initially developed from a technique used in family therapy (Hargreaves, 1979) and first used in research with health and social care professionals (Ross, 2005; Ross et al., 2005). It has also been successfully adapted for use with patients and carers, looking at their experiences of being in receipt of multiple care services (Hardy et al., 2012). Research using Pictor has a primary focus on 'collaborative working', which we have previously defined as occurring when two or more people from different professional groups are required to interact to achieve a shared objective (King et al., 2013a, 2013b). In health and social care settings, this shared objective is usually the delivery of appropriate care to a service user.

Below, we provide some generic guidelines for implementing the technique. However, it is important to remember that these are intended to be flexible, and that the primary aim of Pictor is to facilitate reflection and discussion with the research participant. Modifications may be necessary and appropriate when using the approach with different types of participant, as King et al. (2013a) illustrate.

1. First, the researcher asks the research participant to recall a case in which they and others were required to work together to achieve some goal or purpose that fits the criteria of the particular research question.

2. The participant is next asked to think of all the people involved in this case in any way. This must include the participant him or herself but there are otherwise no restrictions placed on who the participant may choose to include. Participants should be encouraged to think as widely as possible. The participant is then provided with a stack of arrow-shaped sticky notes and asked to label these with a pseudonym and/or a role title for each person on a separate note. The notes we use come in three different colours and participants are informed that they are free to use these colours to make distinctions if they so wish, but that there is absolutely no necessity to do so.

3. We have sometimes found that participants want to use notes to refer to groups rather than individuals (e.g. 'social services domestic team' rather than 'Sandra'). Unless the study specifically required only individuals to be represented, there would be no problem with this. Similarly, notes may be used to refer to other factors identified as playing an important role in a case aside from human agents (family pets have made several appearances in our work, as has the weather!).

4. Once the participant has generated their labelled arrows, they are asked to place these on a large sheet of paper in a way which helps them represent the case. This representation is the participant's Pictor chart. Participants are able to use proximity or direction of the arrows to represent aspects of roles and relationships in the particular case if they so wish, but there are no fixed rules about how this should be done; they are encouraged to design their chart in whatever way they can best represent the case in mind. There are no time constraints on chart construction, but participants rarely need longer than around 15 minutes to produce even quite a complex chart.

5. Once the Pictor chart is completed, the participant is asked to talk the interviewer through the story of the case, with the chart serving as the focus for discussion. The interviewer can then use prompts based on the layout of the arrows – for example, it might be appropriate to ask why some

arrows are closer together than others, whether the direction of the arrows represents anything particular about the case, or whether different arrow colours have been used in any systematic way.

6. If, in the course of the discussion, the participant realises that there are additional arrows they would like to add to their chart, they are encouraged to do so. Sometimes, in the course of reflecting on the case, participants want to alter the layout or move the arrows to represent changes over time. This is not problematic, but the interviewer should record where the arrow was originally placed by marking this original position with a dotted line.

7. There are no set rules regarding whether the interviewer should be present whilst the Pictor chart is being created. Our original practice was to give research participants clear instructions with regards to constructing their chart and to audio record this stage. We then left participants alone so as to give them clear autonomy over the creation of their chart, and to prevent them feeling overlooked. Once the participant had completed their chart, the interviewer would then re-enter and recommence audio recording for the discussion. However, some participants may be more unsure about constructing their chart and this may be dependent on the particular participant group being interviewed – for example, in our research, lay people – patients and carers – could be less confident than professionals in this respect. The interviewer can remain with participants if this is appropriate (in this case, audio recording should continue, as participants may wish to discuss their emerging chart as they construct it) but must try to avoid 'leading' the participant in any way, even implicitly.

8. The final stage of data collection, immediately after each interview, is to create a record of the Pictor chart. The interviewer should draw around each arrow, copying the label written by the participant. The colour of the arrow should also be recorded. The interview date and codes to identify the participant and the interviewer are noted on the chart. Finally, the interviewer should take a good-quality digital image of the chart.

9. Analysis of data from Pictor interviews will depend on the overall methodological approach of the study within which the technique was used. Thus, for example, if Pictor was used in a study that took a narrative approach, a suitable form of narrative analysis would be chosen to analyse the participant's discussion of their chart with the researcher, whilst a phenomenological study would look at the account in terms of how it illuminated participants' lived experience of the phenomenon under investigation. Whatever the methodological approach taken, we would encourage researchers to include the Pictor charts as part of the data set for a study. Looking at the chart can help give a sense of where the participant sees him or herself in relation to the others included in the chart. Close scrutiny of the chart may suggest fruitful directions for textual analysis, as we will illustrate in our example below.

Especially in studies where a considerable number of charts are collected, it can be useful to look at patterns of commonality and difference across charts as part of the analytic process. If some groups of participants consistently include or exclude certain people/agencies, place them in particular areas of the chart, or lay out their arrows in particular configurations, this can invite the researcher to examine the data more closely to see what the patterns may mean. In Hardy's 2012 study of patients' and their partners' experiences of receiving services for advanced disease, for example, she found that general practitioners (GPs) were very often placed in a peripheral position on charts, or not included at all. Looking at what participants said about GPs then revealed some important perceptions about their role in care (Hardy, 2012).

As well as being a powerful tool for eliciting and exploring people's accounts of collaborative working, the Pictor technique has a real strength for the dissemination of research findings. We have found in numerous conference papers, workshops and seminars that examples of real charts from our studies provide an effective way of engaging both academic and practitioner audiences with key messages from our work.

Our case example

Introduction to the study

We will now use an example from our own research (King et al., 2013a, b) to illustrate how Pictor can be usefully applied in real-world research settings. Our example is taken from a project undertaken in the UK over three years, funded by Macmillan Cancer Support. The primary focus of the research was to examine how different types of nursing professional worked with each other, with other professionals and with patients and carers to support patients with cancer. Effective collaborative working between different professionals is a crucial part of contemporary health and social care, and essential to the provision of good quality care for patients and their families. In this project, we focused on how different professionals involved in the care of patients understand their own role and the roles of others, and how these understandings impact on inter-professional relationships across different care settings in the provision of patient care. As well as examining what factors might help or hinder collaborative working for nurses, we were also interested in comparing experiences of collaborative working related to cancer patients with experiences relating to patients with long-term conditions such as heart failure and diabetes. We hoped the findings of our study would highlight areas for the further development of services to support patients with a past or current diagnosis of cancer.

The research was set in one mainly urban metropolitan borough in the north of England with high levels of deprivation and health inequalities. This was, in qualitative terms, a large-scale project, and we interviewed a total of 79 participants. Interviews were conducted using Pictor to explore experiences of collaborative working from the different perspectives of our various participants.

Why was Pictor the appropriate method to use?

There are particular methodological challenges associated with exploring experiences of collaborative working with health care professionals. Often, cases are very complex involving many different individuals, and it can be difficult for research participants to recall all those involved when questioned about this in a research setting. This can lead to a tendency to include only 'key' players, omitting those with a more peripheral but nonetheless important role to play. Health care professionals are often very aware of policy rhetoric around the importance of good collaboration, and when asked about their own involvement in and understanding of collaborative working, they can sometimes present an 'official' explanation or ideal version rather than a direct account of their own experiences. Additionally, for experienced professionals, the way they work with others may have become so habitual and ingrained that it can be difficult for them to reflect on it in any depth when questioned by an interviewer. Pictor provided us with an effective technique to help overcome these challenges in our research.

Pictor has its intellectual origins in Personal Construct Theory (PCT) (Kelly, 1955, and also see Chapter 13 in this book), and particularly in phenomenological readings of PCT by more recent scholars (e.g. Butt, 2003). Our thinking about professional roles, relationships and identities in the design of this study was informed by constructivist understandings of the person, and especially by both PCT and by interactionist views on the nature of professions and professional identities (e.g. Macdonald, 1995). In both these traditions, a person's sense of who they are and what they do as a professional are seen as being shaped through their interaction with the social world they inhabit. An understanding of 'self as professional' is something that is achieved through practice, and especially through relationships with fellow professionals, patients and their families. According to PCT, human beings are seen as meaning-makers, formulating personal hypotheses or constructs to explain their worlds. This process of meaning-making, referred to in PCT as 'construing', is not a rationalistic mental operation (Warren, 1990), and happens not 'inside' the person but through his or her actions and interactions in and with the world (e.g. Butt, 1998; Walker and Winter, 2007). From a PCT perspective, we are often not consciously aware of our construing. Much of it becomes taken for granted and accepted as simply the 'natural' way of seeing things, rather than as a perspective that can be altered. In this piece of research, in which we sought to facilitate reflection on collaborative working practices, this approach and our utilisation of Pictor were thus an excellent fit.

Applying the Pictor technique

Here we will describe how we applied Pictor in the study described above. We will cover data collection using Pictor, how we drew on the visual material in our analysis, and conclude by highlighting some of the lessons we learned about the technique from its use in this study.

Data collection with Pictor

Our core participant group in this project was made up of generalist and specialist nurses who worked with cancer and/or long-term condition patients, but we also recruited a substantial number of participants from other professional groups (including managers, general practitioners and social services staff), as well as patients and lay carers. All interviews undertaken with professionals were held in private and quiet settings within participants' workplaces. Interviews with patients and carers were held in their own homes.

We started the interviews with professionals by asking them to describe their own role, and to provide some background information about their professional experience and career history. Then, participants were asked to bring to mind a case of collaborative working they remembered clearly to create their Pictor chart. Where possible, if their role included working with different patient groups, professional participants were asked to construct two Pictor charts: one depicting a case involving a cancer patient and another involving a long-term condition patient. If this were not possible, they were asked for one case in their area of practice. Those who did not have clinical roles (e.g. managers) were asked to provide examples of specific collaborative projects. In interviews with patients and lay carers, the focus was on the patient's own case. In all cases, participants were asked to discuss the roles and relationships amongst those involved, using the Pictor charts to focus their reflection and the interviewer's questioning.

Analysis of Pictor-based data

Interviews were audio-recorded and transcribed verbatim. We could have simply analysed the textual data in the transcripts with no further reference to the Pictor charts. Such a strategy would in effect treat Pictor as just a method of eliciting rich textual data – a worthwhile endeavour in itself. However, we take the view that the Pictor charts should be seen as data in their own right, and that analysis can benefit from a consideration of both the textual and the visual data in relation to each other. In the present study, we used template analysis (King and Brooks, 2017) for the textual data; we will not describe this in detail here (see King et al., 2013a, b, for more information) but rather will concentrate on how we drew on the visual data in the Pictor charts. We did this in two main ways, which might be termed 'within-participant' and 'across-participant' strategies.

'Within-participant' analysis involves moving between examination of the chart and the text to build up an understanding of the participant's experience. In practical terms this meant having the chart(s) produced by a participant in front of us as we went through the steps of coding in template analysis. We would note distinctive features of a chart and turn to the transcript text to see how it shed light on these; for example, we might be surprised to see a particular professional placed in a very peripheral position on the chart, or even to find them absent. This would prompt us to pay attention in the transcript to what the participant said about working relationships with this individual and/or professional group.

'Across-participant' analysis involves consideration of multiple charts, looking for similarities and differences between them that might tell us something of interest about the data as a whole. The kinds of feature that drew our attention in this study included the overall shape of charts, the total number of arrows used, and whether and where particular groups tended to be represented. This is not an exhaustive list, nor is it intended to be prescriptive – the focus of across-participant analysis needs to reflect the aims and objectives of a particular study. Bravington (2011), for example, provides a useful account of how charts were used across participants in a study examining how nursing and midwifery students reflected on collaborative working in their placements.

Illustrative findings

Given that the focus of this chapter is on Pictor as a method rather than the substantive topic of collaborative working, we will not seek to provide a comprehensive overview of the study findings here. Instead, we will present one Pictor case, displaying the chart and summarising the content of the discussion about it between interviewer and interviewee (Figure 14.1). We will then use the chosen case to illustrate the kind of things we do in our 'within-participant' analysis, before presenting some aspects of the 'across-participant' analyses in this study.

This case is taken from an interview with 'Martha' – a staff nurse on a cardiology ward at the district general hospital at the centre of the borough. It relates to a 67-year-old woman ('Angela') who had a long history of heart failure, with a number of other health problems. Angela had been admitted to the ward many times.

On the occasion in question, Angela was admitted feeling 'quite unwell' and required input from a range of services, including the pain team, specialist heart failure nurses, gastrology and haematology consultants and district nurses. The major intervention, though, was the replacement of a heart valve, which required referral to a cardio-thoracic surgeon at a larger hospital outside the district. The ward staff had got to know Angela and her family well over the years; Martha describes the family as very

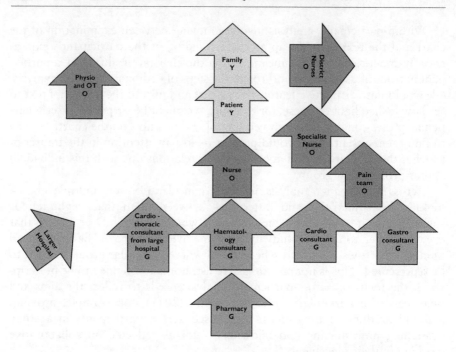

Figure 14.1   Example of a Pictor chart from 'Martha' – staff nurse on a cardiology ward

supportive, but also notes that they themselves required a good deal of support from the nursing staff:

> ... *obviously the family was quite a big input as well because they were quite a close-knit family, there was her and her husband who lived and managed together, outside family like daughters and grandchildren and that, but he was one of these little doting men, wanting to know everything, really anxious, he needed a lot of support, they needed a lot of support as well from that side of it.*

Angela had her surgery at the outside hospital, and returned to Martha's ward for further care and recuperation. The entire episode from admission to her discharge home took about six weeks, which – given the complicated nature of her condition – Martha felt to be 'very quick'. Overall, she described collaborative working between professionals (including across organisations) and with patient and family as highly effective:

> *I think everything went smoothly for her coming back, everything was dealt with really, really well, from all types of levels. Family were involved and kept up to date with everything so they knew what was*

going on, there wasn't an instance where they ever felt, oh they didn't know where they were up to.

On her chart Martha placed the arrow for 'Patient' in the middle and towards the top of the chart. Her own arrow ('Nurse') and that for 'Family' are touching the patient arrow, with those for 'District Nurses' and 'Specialist Nurse' close on one side. A little further out are 'Pain Team' on one side and 'Physio + O.T.' (physiotherapist and occupational therapist) together on one arrow fairly close on the other side. The four different consultants are placed farther down in a line, with 'Pharmacy' in the middle behind them.

Within-participant analysis
When starting to analyse an individual Pictor chart and the accompanying interview, the first step is for researchers simply to familiarise themselves with the 'story' by reading the relevant section of the interview carefully and looking at the overall layout of the chart. Are the arrows laid out in any particular pattern – such as a circle, a series of ranks, a single long line (or combination of such shapes) – and does this seem to coincide with points made in the discussion? Looking more closely, the following features may be worth attending to (although this is not by any means an exhaustive list):

- **Proximity** – how close are arrows to each other? Which are especially close or placed a long way from the rest?
- **Colour** – if different colour arrows were available, does the participant appear to have used them in a systematic way?
- **Direction**– might arrow direction indicate something of significance in the participant's story? For instance, is there one that stands out as being in the opposite direction to others around it?
- **Grouping** – do there appear to be different groupings of arrows in the chart?

In Martha's example, the chart appears to have two main groupings that differ in shape and proximity to the patient – a circle of arrows around the patient, and a straight line underneath this circle. As noted above, the 'agents' represented in these two parts are of different types – mostly nursing groups in the close circle, and consultants in the line. The separation in shape is reinforced by Martha's use of colour. The sticky arrows we used came in three different colours, which we have noted on the figure. Martha has used yellow arrows to represent patient and family, orange for all the nurse groups (and the physiotherapist/occupational therapist) and green for the consultants and pharmacy. The interviewer checked with Martha whether she had a particular purpose in mind in her use of arrow colour:

Interviewer: *Right then, I've noticed you've used three colours, have you used them to represent anything in particular?*

Martha: *Just like the nursing side and like there's physio, so they're like the main team, the darker green is more like the consultants, more of the medical side, and the patient's side is the yellow colour.*

The division into three 'sides' is thus quite explicit, and it is worth noting that Martha describes the nurses as 'the main team'. The way Martha has used grouping, proximity to the patient and colour thus helps convey the way she sees Angela's story of care – that her main support is through the nurses who look after her on the ward (and beyond), while the various medical interventions are temporary intrusions into her experience of care. This is not to suggest that Martha does not value what the consultants do; indeed, she is consistently positive about them. Nevertheless, the image is one that reverses the stereotypical view of nurses supporting doctors; here the doctors are literally depicted as a 'back line' supporting the main team of nurses.

One further point to note in Martha's case is how she represents herself. On the chart, she does this in the form of the arrow immediately underneath that for the patient, labelled 'Nurse'. However, in the discussion of the chart, she almost always refers to herself as part of the ward nursing team, rather than as an individual:

*[Angela] had surgery and came back to **us** post-operatively, was quite, really unwell when she came back, **we** thought maybe there was a possibility she wouldn't improve ...*

*... so **we** were like using infusions to get rid of her oedema and **we** were also keeping her quite anticoagulated because **we** weren't using the Warfarin. Pain control was good, specialist nurse input was only like heart failure at that time, **we** didn't need anything else.*

We have found across several studies that nurses who work in a strongly team-oriented way often present themselves collectively rather than individually, which frequently includes the use of a team rather than individual arrow on the chart. Martha's example highlights the importance of looking closely at the transcribed discussion when considering the chart, and not jumping to conclusions just from the visual material; her use of the singular 'Nurse' on the arrow does not indicate any lack of a team perspective in how she saw her role in the case.

Across-participant analysis
Looking at the Pictor charts from different groups of nurses in this study, one very striking difference was apparent. In the data set as a whole, the most common configuration is what we refer to as a 'network' chart, where the main organising principle used by the participant is to use the arrows to depict the nature and/or quality of relationships between themselves,

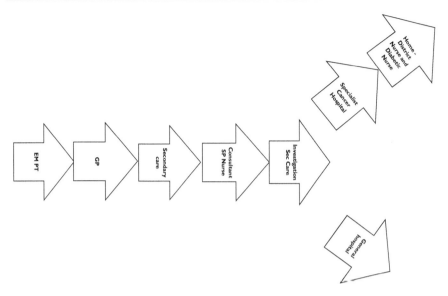

Figure 14.2   Example of a 'timeline' format Pictor chart

the patient and family, and other professionals. (Often these also highlight aspects of relationships amongst other agents on the chart too.) Across a range of studies we have conducted using Pictor, the network form is by far the most common, and in this study this was the case for most of the nursing groups. However, for acute-based (i.e. hospital) specialist nurses the most common configuration was the 'timeline'. In this, arrows are laid out to represent a temporal sequence of events and actions, perhaps with branches to the side to show where several other professionals and/or lay people had an involvement in the case. (An example of a timeline format chart is shown in Figure 14.2.)

Typically, the patient, the professional constructing the chart and other key players are depicted several times along the timeline. Looked at in percentage terms, 72 per cent of community nurse charts were networks and 21 per cent timelines (the remainder used a mixture of the two types). In contrast, 33 per cent of acute specialist nurses' charts were networks and 61 per cent timelines.

Why might acute specialist nurses be much more likely than community nurses to use timeline format charts? To answer this, we needed to go back to look at the individual interviews and charts, especially those of the acute specialist nurses, in detail. One potential influence could be their experience of reflective methods as part of their specialist training. We had not systematically asked participants about this, nor did we have extensive data with regards to post-registration training. However, indirect evidence tends to make us sceptical that past training in reflection was likely to have been a major factor. None of the participants made any reference to other reflective techniques with which they were familiar, neither to highlight similarities to – nor differences from – Pictor. It is unlikely, given their evident variation in age and tenure, that all the acute specialist nurses who used timeline charts went through the same training regime at the same time. Furthermore, if specialist nurse training in general facilitated the timeline style, we would also expect to see it prominently amongst the charts produced by community specialist nurses, but we do not.

A further possible explanation for the prominence of timeline-format charts could lie in the nature of the acute nurse specialist's role. Their involvement with patients is generally episodic; they see patients for check-ups or assessments related to interventions, and when there is a crisis relating to their condition. This may encourage the nurses to conceptualise cases as a series of distinct steps or phases in the trajectory of an illness. Regarding their engagement with other professionals, the charts and interviews show that this is often with other specialist nurses, and consultants and their teams. Commonly, these contacts are for the purpose of referring the patient on for a particular intervention, or seeking advice and information in relation to the urgent situation for which they have consulted. This contrasts with community-based nurses, who tend to describe a wider range of types of interaction with a wider range of other professionals/services. Such a pattern may tend to favour timeline formats for acute specialist nurses but networks for community-based nurses.

The kind of analysis we have described here may appear to be equivalent to the quantitative approach to examining social networks commonly used in some forms of social network analysis (e.g. Patterson et al., 2013). It differs, however, in that when we analyse patterns across participants in Pictor we do not seek to determine objective features of networks that may be summarised statistically. Rather, we use the emerging patterns to raise questions as to what may be going on in participants' experiences. To answer these questions we need to return to the textual data analysis and to consideration of individual Pictor charts in the context of their interview as a whole.

Reflections on using Pictor

This is our largest study to date incorporating Pictor, and it has offered us an important opportunity to learn how best to use the technique. It has confirmed that the great majority of participants are able to follow the technique without trouble, and many commented that they found it interesting and enjoyable to do. The only groups from which participants refused to use the technique were patients and carers, which accords with our previous experience that lay people may find it a little more challenging and/or unfamiliar than professionals – but even here the clear majority were happy to do it.

The fact that we collected a large number of charts gave us our best chance yet to consider the value of cross-participant analyses based primarily on the charts. This proved very worthwhile, enabling some important insights into differences between nursing groups' experiences of collaborative working. We were also able to compare experiences of collaborative working by disease type, since we collected two charts from many participants – one based on a cancer case and one on an LTC. We do not have the space to discuss this in detail here, but the overall picture was that professionals' experiences of the process of collaboration did not appear to vary greatly according to the type of condition, but there were differences in the extent to which there was collaboration across the acute/community sectors.

The project, which collected a large volume of Pictor chart and interview data, highlights the importance of being systematic and well organised in managing data. It would be all too easy to waste a great deal of time matching anonymised charts to audio files, identifying which participant group a chart came from, and so on. We devised a coding system enabling us to identify each chart and audio file by participant type, illness condition and the identity of the interviewer. Even in a much smaller study we would strongly recommend that this kind of system is designed in advance of data collection.

Looking critically at the way we used Pictor in this study, one change we would make in further studies would be to ask participants more questions about the chart itself than we did in some of these interviews. We tended to do so mainly where some aspect of chart construction seemed important to the story the participant was telling, and sometimes did not ask about details that appeared more peripheral. For example, in Martha's case, we did not ask about how the O.T. and physiotherapist were involved, and why they were included in the 'main team' (as represented by both proximity and arrow colour) who otherwise were all nurses. Of course, there is a balance to be struck here; to go through every aspect of a chart with each participant could interfere with the goal of enabling them to tell the story of their case in their own way. Nevertheless, we feel that it would be fruitful to focus a little more consistently and systematically on the chart itself in future.

In conclusion, the Pictor technique has much to offer to qualitative psychologists whose research addresses issues related to collaboration between different professional groups. While our work has concentrated on health and social care settings, there is nothing intrinsic to the technique which means it can only be applied there. Any area of activity where people with different outlooks, backgrounds and/or identities have to work together could be the focus of research using the Pictor technique; for example education, the criminal justice system and many private sector businesses.

References

Bravington, A. (2011). Using the Pictor technique to reflect on collaborative working in undergraduate nursing and midwifery placements. Master's thesis, University of Huddersfield, UK. Available at www.eprints.hud.ac.uk/id/eprint/13720.

Butt, T.W. (1998). Sociality, role and embodiment. *Journal of Constructivist Psychology*, 11(2), 105–116.

Butt, T.W. (2003). The phenomenological context of PCP. In F. Fransella (Ed.), *International Handbook of Personal Construct Psychology*. Chichester, UK: Wiley, pp. 379–386.

Hardy, B. (2012). 'Everyone was like flies around a jam pot': A phenomenological study exploring the experiences of people affected by advanced disease in relation to the involvement of multiple health care services. Unpublished PhD thesis, University of Huddersfield, UK. Available at: www.eprints.hud.ac.uk/17133/.

Hardy, B., King, N. and Firth, J. (2012). Applying the Pictor technique to research interviews with people affected by advanced disease. *Nurse Researcher*, 20(1), 6–10.

Hargreaves, C.P. (1979). Social networks and interpersonal constructs. In P. Stringer and D. Bannister (Eds.), *Constructs of Sociality and Individuality*. London: Academic Press, pp. 153–175.

Kelly, G.A. (1955). *The Psychology of Personal Constructs*. New York: Norton.

King, N. and Horrocks, C. (2010). *Interviews in Qualitative Research*. London: SAGE.

King, N. and Brooks, J.M. (2017). *Template Analysis for Business and Management Students*. London: SAGE.

King, N., Bravington, A., Brooks, J., Hardy, B., Melvin, J. and Wilde, D. (2013a). The Pictor technique: A method for exploring the experience of collaborative working. *Qualitative Health Research*, 23(8), 1138–1152.

King, N., Melvin, J.; Brooks, J., Wilde, D. and Bravington, A. (2013b). Unpicking the threads: How specialist and generalist nurses work with patients, careers, other professionals and each other to support cancer patients in the community. *End of Project Report, Macmillan Cancer Support*. Available at: www.eprints.hud.ac.uk/18481/.

Macdonald, K.M. (1995). *The Sociology of the Professions*. London: SAGE.

Patterson, D., Pfeiffer, A.J., Weaver, M.D., Krackhardt, D., Arnold, R.M., Yealy, D.M. and Lave, J.R. (2013). Network analysis of team communication in a busy emergency department. *BMC Health Services Research*, 13, 109. www.biomedcentral.com/1472-6963/13/109.

Ross, A. (2005). Collaborative working between district nurses and social workers. Unpublished PhD thesis, University of Huddersfield, UK.

Ross, A., King, N. and Firth, J. (2005). Interprofessional relationships and collaborative working: Encouraging reflective practice. *Online Journal of Issues in Nursing*, 10(1), Art. 3. doi:10.3912/ojin.vol10no01man03.

Walker, B.M. and Winter, D.A. (2007). The elaboration of personal construct psychology. *Annual Review of Psychology*, 58, 453–477. doi:10.1146/annurev.psych.58.110405.085535.

Warren, W. (1990). Is personal construct psychology a cognitive psychology? *International Journal of Personal Construct Psychology*, 3(4), 393–414. doi:10.1080/10720539008412828.

SECTION III

Issues in Applying Qualitative Psychology in Real World Settings

Using Multiple Methods in Applied Qualitative Research

Rachel Shaw and David Hiles

15

Introduction

Applied research begins with a problem in practice which is then worked through in research to identify a solution. Research of this kind often involves multidisciplinary teams made up of practitioners and academic researchers, who each bring their different expertise to the project in order to solve the problem. The application of the research findings is the guiding force throughout which means pragmatism dominates decisions made along the research journey. Sometimes there will be multiple elements to the problem which require multiple methods. This chapter will explore the use of multiple methods in applied qualitative research. First, the issue of defining multiple and mixed-methods research will be considered.

The language of multiple and mixed-methods research

Mixed-methods research is typically defined as research which uses both qualitative and quantitative methods. In the second edition of their book, Designing and Conducting Mixed Methods Research, Creswell et al. (2011) spend several pages of the introductory chapter going through various iterations of the definition of mixed-methods research. Each of them requires the collection and analysis of qualitative and quantitative data and the integration of those data. Some authors have argued that mixed-methods research has become an approach in its own right with its own assumptions, a 'third paradigm'[1] (Johnson et al., 2007). This may be because the so-called 'paradigm wars' (Oakley, 1999) made qualitative and quantitative methods incompatible epistemologically; the assumed positivism of those using quantitative methods and the post-positivism or interpretivism among qualitative researchers constructed seemingly contradictory views of the world, the nature of reality and of the human subject, which meant that agreeing on principles in research was challenging. Perhaps creating a third paradigm was the only conceivable way of combining qualitative and quantitative methods without getting into battles that could not be won. It is probably true to say that some qualitative researchers fundamentally disagree with the use of statistical analysis methods to make sense of human experience; similarly, some psychologists who use experimental methods do not believe that qualitative methods can produce valid scientific knowledge. Both sides of the 'quantitative–qualitative divide' have their own paradigmatic assumptions about the nature of the human subject and about what constitutes science which preclude the use of the other method. Hence, using them together would go against their belief system. The idea of mixed-methods research seems to have developed out of a more open approach to research which focuses on finding the best tool for the job rather than beginning from a fixed position in relation to research design and methods. Taking this view enables us to focus on the advantages of using multiple methods to better answer complex research questions. Greene (2007, p. 20) was of this mindset, stating that mixed-methods research 'actively invites us to participate in dialogue about multiple ways of seeing and hearing, multiple ways of making sense of the social world, and multiple standpoints on what is important and to be valued and cherished'.

The openness expressed by Greene is more accommodating than previous definitions which demand the use of both qualitative and quantitative data. Instead Greene's definition advocates a *multi-methods* approach to better understand the social world. In theory this definition permits combinations which may involve more than one quantitative method or more than one qualitative method, making it a potential forerunner for what we now call *pluralism* (Frost, 2011; Frost et al., 2010). Pluralism has developed within psychology and focuses on the use of multiple qualitative methods (Frost, 2011). The definition of pluralism resonates with Greene's open multi-methods approach (Frost and Shaw, 2015, p. 641):

Pluralism suggests the mixing of paradigms, data, and/or analysis techniques to promote engagement with diversity, to actively seek understanding across

---

[1] There are different uses of the term 'paradigm' which make things complicated. Johnson et al. (2007, p. 130) use paradigm here to refer to a 'methodological paradigm', a way of conducting research or specific research design. In this chapter we use Guba and Lincoln's (1994) definition of a paradigm as a set of basic beliefs that 'represents a *worldview* that defines, for its holders, the nature of the "world," the individual's place in it, and the range of possible relationships to that world and its parts' (p. 107). For us, the paradigm is more than the method; it is a way of being and behaving as a researcher.

*lines of difference, and to enter into personal and methodological dialogue
to promote and foster understanding of research inquiry and outcomes.*

Again the focus is on being open and flexible regarding the nature of data
required and in terms of how one makes sense of it. The idea of mixing data
and techniques is familiar, but it is perhaps less familiar to think about mixing
paradigms.[2] In brief, pluralism opens the door to any number of combinations
assuming they will better serve the task of answering the research question(s).
From a pluralist perspective, it is the research question itself which provides
the theoretical underpinnings for the study (Frost and Nolas, 2011). By considering how each method works with the other(s), it also offers a way of
thinking about how different worldviews may be brought to bear on the same
research question to generate alternative understandings to move forward in
unanticipated ways. Such cross-fertilisation of critical thinking may offer new
insights and facilitate a creativity which would otherwise remain untapped.

Another term identified is *qualitatively driven mixed-methods research* which
is defined by Hesse-Biber (2010) as research using qualitative and quantitative
methods that holds the core belief (or assumption) of qualitative methodology,
that is, that social reality is subjective and that there are multiple versions of
it. She follows Denzin and Lincoln (2007) in noting that there are a number
of approaches that hold this belief which identify as qualitative methodologies
which can be split into three categories: constructivist-interpretivist; critical
(Marxist, emancipatory); and feminist. According to Hesse-Biber, the guiding
force behind qualitatively driven mixed-methods research is reminiscent of
Greene's 'multiple ways of seeing and hearing'; it offers a multi-layered view of
social reality, breaks down power imbalances, is transformative and engaged in
social change, and promotes a 'deeper listening' in that it is often more exploratory and theory generating rather than confirmatory and hypothesis-testing
(Hesse-Biber, 2010, p. 456). This approach arose out of dissatisfaction with
the dominance and prioritisation of quantitative methods in mixed-methods
research. Hesse-Biber (2010) outlined a number of mixed-methods designs
that are guided by qualitative methodology; all of her case studies include both
qualitative and quantitative methods. The reasons for deciding to mix methods in Hesse-Biber's examples were: using quantitative methods to increase
the generalisability of findings, to develop research questions or a purposive

---

[2] Returning to the issue of paradigm, Frost and Nolas (2011, p. 116) have argued that
pluralism can entail a mixing of paradigms, not just methods, by which they mean
using 'epistemological and ontological incoherence [to] help to highlight gaps and
contradictions in the data'. This reference to paradigm resonates with Johnson et al.'s
(2007) methodological paradigm and Willig's notion of 'epistemological reflexivity'
(Willig, 2001, p. 10) because its focus is on examining the perspectives of different
researchers using different strategies and techniques to make sense of the same data.
Furthermore, because Frost's pluralism focuses on qualitative methodologies and
methods, researchers are likely to hold the same worldview.

sample for qualitative research; linking qualitative and quantitative methods to enhance validity and reliability; using qualitative methods to explore contradictory findings, for triangulation, and to promote social change. Qualitatively driven mixed-methods research is rooted within qualitative methodology but it remains true to Creswell et al.'s (2011) requirement that mixed-methods research must involve both quantitative and qualitative data.

In short, the language used when combining different methods is highly significant. *Mixed-methods research* has generally come to be understood as research that uses both qualitative and quantitative methods, and for some it is an approach or paradigm in its own right; however, *multi-methods* or *combined methods* are terms that have been used in more open-ended ways to describe research that uses multiple quantitative methods or multiple qualitative methods or indeed qualitative and quantitative methods. Brewer and Hunter (2006) defined **multi-method research** as a 'broader view' which involves the use of multiple methods to overcome the flaws of individual methods:

> A diversity of imperfection allows us to combine methods, not only to gain their individual strengths but also to compensate for their particular faults and limitations. The multimethod approach is largely built upon this insight. Its fundamental strategy is to *attack a research problem with an arsenal of methods that have nonoverlapping weaknesses in addition to their complementary strengths.* (Brewer and Hunter, 2006, p. 4; emphasis in original)

Pluralism describes an approach (usually within qualitative research) involving multiple perspectives and techniques to create a dialogue which will provide a better understanding of the phenomenon under study; and *qualitatively driven mixed-methods research* adopts a paradigm consonant with qualitative methodology and uses both quantitative and qualitative methods.

The rest of this chapter focuses on using multiple methods in applied qualitative research which takes on board the openness of pluralism and multi-methods research. It is driven by qualitative methodology but does not limit the kinds of method used depending on whether they are quantitative or qualitative. The approach described here is best described as multi-methods research. Another way to describe it is as disciplined inquiry.

Disciplined inquiry

Hiles's (2014) model of *disciplined inquiry* (see Figure 15.1) outlines an approach to research which combines the openness of Greene's (2007) definition of mixed-methods research with the need for transparency and coherence (Yardley, 2000; Lincoln and Guba, 1985). The model helps to delineate the different aspects of research and organises them in terms of decisions made along the journey. Disciplined inquiry begins with the research objective and uses that as the driver for subsequent assumptions

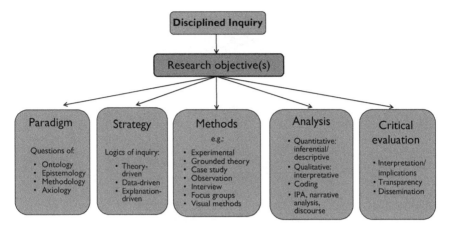

Figure 15.1   Disciplined inquiry
Adapted from Hiles, 2014.

and methodological decisions made. Thus, the approach taken and methods used are built around how research questions for the study come to be formulated, rather than being based on a predetermined belief that one type of design or method is better than others. In formulating the research question(s), the researcher is asked to identify the paradigm which best fits the nature of the research and its subject matter. *Paradigm* is defined by Guba and Lincoln (1994, p. 105) as 'the basic belief system or worldview that guides the investigator, not only in choices of method but in ontologically and epistemologically fundamental ways'. The paradigm creates the framework within which a project will operate; it has its own assumptions about the phenomenon being investigated, the nature of the human subject and about what constitutes valid knowledge, and the values associated with it. For example, positivism was the paradigm of behaviourist psychology which privileged objective observations of measurable behaviour and thus prioritised the experimental method and statistical analysis. In contrast, feminism is a paradigm which challenges taken for granted knowledge and which actively works towards the emancipation of research participants. Feminist researchers are more likely to adopt the strategy of action research and use qualitative methods of data collection and analysis.

The *strategy* is the type of study, for example action research, ethnography, phenomenology, which is related to the logic of the inquiry. Here, logic refers to the strategy taken by the choice of research design to the data and to theory. Hiles (2014) identified three logics of inquiry (see Figure 15.2): theory-driven, which takes a deductive approach; data-driven, which is inductive; and explanation-driven, which uses abductive inference (Pierce, 1903). For example, positivism takes a *theory-driven approach*; it adopts the hypothetico-deductive method which takes a hypothesis from existing theory and then tests it experimentally; feminism is more likely to take a

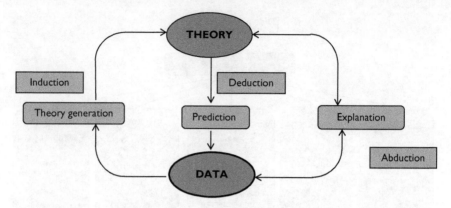

Figure 15.2   The relation between theory and data and the three logics of inquiry
Adapted from Hiles, 2014.

data-driven approach which uses inductive methods and therefore prioritises the participants' accounts in attempting to generate theory from the data. The *explanation-driven approach* employs abductive inference or inference to the best explanation (Lipton, 1991; Harman, 1965), to find the best explanation for the findings from the empirical data generated in the study and/ or from existing theory and/or other evidence including other literature and clinical expertise. This third logic of inquiry is less familiar but it is likely to be the approach which best fits applied research (Hiles, 2014); this is particularly true with case study research, where the emphasis is not on testing an existing theory, or generating a new theory, but on drawing upon a range of theoretical constructs to explain a new body of empirical data. In applied research, findings need to be considered in context, taking into account the acceptability and feasibility of applying them to practice (Shaw et al., 2014). Furthermore, this might mean that clinician expertise, service evaluations, health behaviour change theories and data generated from the study might each be used to guide data collection and analysis methods.

The *method* refers to data collection. Selection will be influenced by the research design strategy or logic of inquiry adopted and it may involve more than one method, for example an experiment, a case study, a series of interviews, a survey, observation techniques, and so on. The approach to data *analysis* will be dictated by the type of data generated. Experimental data will be coded and analysed statistically, survey data may be analysed statistically, or if open-ended questions are used thematic or content analysis may be used. Methods of data collection which generate textual data will usually be analysed using a qualitative approach, such as Interpretative Phenomenological Analysis (IPA), Template Analysis, discourse analysis, narrative analysis, or others.

The final part of disciplined inquiry is the *critical evaluation* which is particularly important in applied research. Existing literature and/or theory may be used to interpret findings and to extrapolate implications for practice.

Therefore, findings need to be evaluated in relation to the transparency of the paradigmatic assumptions, methods of data collection and interpretative analysis. How likely it is that findings are trustworthy should be used to inform or develop new practice. Finally, disciplined inquiry involves appropriate dissemination of findings to all appropriate audiences. The current focus on the impact of research in applied settings demands that findings are not disseminated simply to academic audiences but also to members of the public and to practitioners.

In summary, the model of disciplined inquiry proposes that psychological research is inherently pluralistic, that is, pluralistic in the sense that multiple methods are available in making the methodological decisions that need to be addressed in engaging fully with the research objective(s). Indeed, it is essential that these can be approached transparently to ensure that applied psychological research is of a high quality and therefore can be used to inform policy and practice.

Using disciplined inquiry in applied settings

This book focuses on applied qualitative psychology, that is, psychology research in applied settings which uses qualitative methods. This means it is research which has been influenced by or is conducted (at least in part) by qualitative researchers and which falls within what might be described as 'new paradigm' research (Reason and Rowan, 1981) or qualitative psychology (Smith, 2008). This means that the paradigmatic assumptions made in the research are consonant with a qualitative approach or strategy. In this respect, it resonates with qualitatively driven mixed-methods research (Hesse-Biber, 2010), but it is not restricted to research which uses both quantitative and qualitative methods. Therefore, it takes from pluralism the possibility of using multiple qualitative methods (Frost, 2011). The remainder of the chapter will outline an example of applied research which used multiple methods. The example will be framed within the model of disciplined inquiry (Hiles, 2014) to illustrate its utility as a generic tool for establishing research designs which fit the research questions posed.

An example: Preparing nurses for acute life-threatening events in paediatric hospital settings (Hudson et al., 2015)

The problem

This research grew out of a need identified in practice. Acute life-threatening events (ALTEs) include respiratory or cardiac arrests, apnoea, choking, or a marked change in colour or muscle tone (NIH, 1986). They can be frightening and constitute an additional source of stress for nursing staff. This project focused on ALTEs that were unexpected, that is, those that happened to patients who were not in intensive care. As levels of safety improve, nurses encounter ALTEs less frequently and, although life support training is mandatory, there is no discussion within it about how nurses may feel during or following an event (Resuscitation Council UK, 2013). Research has shown that ALTEs can contribute to the phenomenon of 'second victims' (Scott et al., 2009), that is, staff who lack appropriate skills or who are ill-equipped to deal emotionally with the impact of an ALTE may themselves suffer, which can lead to staff burnout, increased absenteeism, anxiety and stress (McInnes and Bannister, 2002; Bailes, 2001; Cotterill-Walker, 2000). There was little research with nurses about their experiences of ALTEs and a lack of evidence on which to develop an intervention to prepare nurses for ALTEs. Hence, this programme of work was designed to assess the evidence base and gather new empirical evidence to develop an evidence-based and theoretically-informed intervention to equip nurses for ALTEs.

The research question

The central research question was:

■ What are nurses' experiences of ALTEs?

A series of supplementary questions guided the development of the programme of work:

■ What does the evidence tell us about how to prepare nurses for ALTEs?
■ In what ways do nurses need to be prepared for ALTEs?
■ What is an appropriate theoretical basis for an intervention to prepare nurses for ALTEs?

The objective was to:

■ Develop an intervention to prepare nurses for ALTEs in hospital.

The research team

The research was nurse-led and developed by a multidisciplinary team as a programme of work for a PhD. Dr Adrienne Hudson was trained as a midwife and practised as a nurse in a specialist children's hospital. Her clinical supervisor was a consultant intensivist and is manager of the paediatric intensive care unit (PICU). Dr Rachel Shaw was Adrienne's principal academic supervisor, a health psychologist and expert in qualitative methodology. Professor Helen Pattison was associate supervisor, a health psychologist and an expert in trial methodology. Additional stakeholders were also involved in the development of the intervention.

The project

The project involved a series of activities which were developed with the research question and objective in mind using the disciplined inquiry model. The research was conducted under the auspices of evidence-based health care, that is, its aim was to gather evidence from multiple sources using multiple research methods with the goal of changing practice (Figure 15.3).

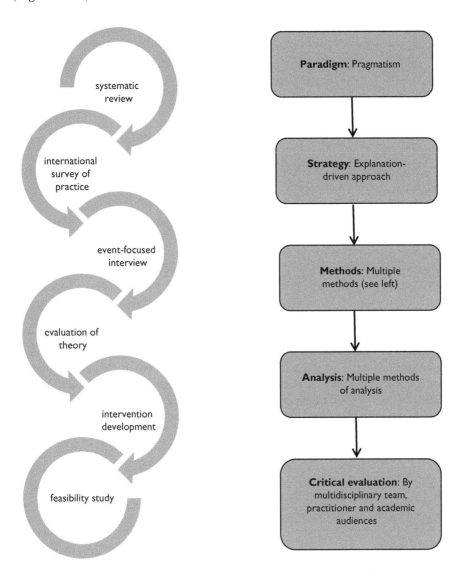

Figure 15.3 Preparing nurses for acute life-threatening events in paediatric hospital settings – multiple methods

Paradigm

Pragmatism was the paradigm within which we were working. Pragmatism takes a functional approach to knowledge and a toolkit approach to method, that is, any research design which fits the research question is permissible.

Strategy

An explanation-driven approach was adopted; we used extant literature, data we gathered and health psychology theory to inform the development of an intervention.

Methods

A number of methods were used. The research began with a systematic review to establish the evidence base. An international survey of practice was then conducted to determine current policy and practice, and to solicit nurses' opinions about the need for an intervention to prepare them for ALTEs. The next phase involved event-focused individual interviews with nurses and doctors attending ALTEs. Staff were invited to participate following an ALTE. A review of health psychology theory and behaviour change techniques was undertaken to develop the content, style and delivery mode of the intervention. Validated measures of stress, anxiety, quality of life, coping, workplace self-efficacy and the impact of events were taken pre- and post-intervention as part of a feasibility study (see Hudson, 2014, for full details).

Analysis

The results of the systematic review were synthesised narratively. The survey data was analysed using descriptive statistics. Interviews were analysed using IPA. Health psychology theories were critically evaluated alongside the findings of the survey and interviews. The validated measures were analysed using descriptive statistics, parametric tests and exploratory inferential analyses.

Critical evaluation

The multidisciplinary supervisory team provided support throughout the project to ensure that interpretations made were consonant with the theoretical background of the work and that implications were considered appropriately within the context of practice. An iterative method was employed to develop the intervention, which involved a multidisciplinary working group. Experts from senior medical and nursing staff were engaged to ensure that the intervention developed was deliverable and feasible within the context of a busy specialist children's hospital.

Throughout the life of the project, findings were presented at international conferences to audiences from PICU, specialist children's hospitals and those working in the areas of safety and rapid response. More importantly, we worked very closely with nursing and medical management teams at the host hospital to facilitate fiscal and structural support while running the feasibility study. Regular feedback sessions were held with staff to keep them informed of how the project was developing.

Reflecting on the use of multiple methods in applied qualitative research

Using mixed methods in applied qualitative research makes sense because there are often a number of research questions to answer or a complex set of interlinking objectives. Psychologists have always felt strongly about method and so it is not surprising to discover a history of terminology and rules about what is and what is not mixed-methods research. Indeed, the dominant definition of mixed-methods research as work that involves the collection, analysis and integration of both quantitative and qualitative data felt quite restrictive. The development of qualitatively driven mixed-methods research felt like a move in the right direction for this chapter, but it still required the use of quantitative and qualitative methods. This definition of methods according to the type of data they generate represents the legacy of the turn to language in the late 1980s and early 1990s in psychology, when scholars rejected the experimental method of behaviourism and the process models of cognitive psychology in favour of methods which focused on language and meaning (see e.g. Smith et al., 1995). Indeed, Hiles (2014) has argued that distinguishing between quantitative and qualitative methods is a red herring. Instead of getting hung up on the type of data generated in a study, we feel that research should be question-driven and inherently pluralistic to enable the answering of diverse and multifactorial research questions. Instead of being driven by tradition or some other arbitrary convention, we argue that research design should be led purely by the question it aims to answer. Hiles (2014) has developed the model of disciplined inquiry over recent years to shift the focus away from the quantitative–qualitative divide and towards a rational approach which prioritises function over form. Disciplined inquiry also promotes explicit and transparent decision-making. We are aware of the risk involved in introducing yet another term in an already jargon-heavy field, but feel that the model of disciplined inquiry could make redundant those other terms and, more importantly, it could provide a helpful mechanism for researchers using multiple methods in their work.

There are great benefits of using multiple methods in applied research. Furthermore, as the ALTE study illustrated, there are benefits of taking an explanation-driven approach in applied research. This meant we were engaged in an iterative process across the series of activities involved in the research and in developing the intervention itself. Extant literature, empirical data from the survey and individual interviews, and theoretical evidence were each used to identify the optimum design and mode of delivery for the intervention. The programme of work involved both inductive and deductive processing of data; the survey and interviews were exploratory and data-driven; and those findings were then used to generate hypotheses about how the intervention might impact on stress, anxiety, workplace self-efficacy and the other outcomes identified above. Finally, predictions were made about the possible impact of the intervention based on theoretical evidence from the theories incorporated into the intervention development (for full details see Hudson et al., 2015).

The current focus on the impact of research and the focus on public involvement in the development and processes of research have demanded that researchers take seriously the context in which their studies will be applied. This will often mean that multiple participant groups will be involved, for example patients, their families and/or carers, health care professionals and other professional groups who may be involved depending on the research question. Collecting data from multiple sources may require different methods of data collection, which may require different methods of analysis. The important thing is that decision-making in research is transparent and that projects adhere to a coherent goal that makes sense. Hence, transparency and coherence are central indicators of quality in research which uses multiple methods. The model of disciplined inquiry provides a framework within which research designs and their logic of inquiry can be developed and made explicit.

References

Bailes, G. (2001). Critical incident management. *Nursing Times*, 9725, 184–190.

Brewer, J. and Hunter, A. (2006). *Foundations of Multimethod Research*. Thousand Oaks, CA: SAGE.

Cotterill-Walker, S. (2000). Debriefing in the intensive care unit: A personal experience of critical incident stress. *Nursing in Critical Care*, 5(2), 82–86.

Creswell, J.W. and Plano Clark, C.L. (2011). *Designing and Conducting Mixed Methods Research (Second Edition)*. Thousand Oaks, CA: SAGE.

Denzin, N.K. and Lincoln, Y.S. (Eds.) (2007). *Collecting and Interpreting Qualitative Materials (Third Edition)*. Thousand Oaks, CA: SAGE.

Frost, N.A. (Ed.) (2011). *Qualitative Research: Combining Core Approaches*. London: Open University Press.

Frost, N. and Nolas, S.-M. (2011). Exploring and expanding on pluralism in qualitative research in psychology. *Qualitative Research in Psychology*, 8, 115–119.

Frost, N. and Shaw, R.L. (2015). Evolving mixed and multi-method approaches for psychology. In S. Hesse-Biber and B. Johnson (Eds.), *The Oxford Handbook of Mixed and Multi-Method Research*. Oxford University Press, pp. 375–392.

Frost, N., Nolas, S.M., Brooks-Gordon, B., Esin, C., Holt, A., Mehdizadeh, L. and Shinebourne, P. (2010). Pluralism in qualitative research: The impact of different researchers and qualitative approaches on the analysis of qualitative data. *Qualitative Research*, 10(4), 441–460.

Greene, J.C. (2007). *Mixed Methods in Social Inquiry*. San Francisco, CA: Jossey-Bass.

Guba, E.G. and Lincoln, Y.S. (1994). Competing paradigms in qualitative research. In N.K. Denzin and Y.S. Lincoln (Eds.), *Handbook of Qualitative Research*. Thousand Oaks, CA: SAGE, pp. 105–117.

Harman, G. (1965). Inference to the best explanation. *Philosophical Review*, 74, 88–95.

Hesse-Biber, S. (2010). Qualitative approaches to mixed methods practice. *Qualitative Inquiry*, 16(6), 455–468.

Hiles, D.R. (2014). Qualitative inquiry, mixed methods and the logic of scientific inquiry. *QMiP Bulletin*, 17 (spring), 49–62. Retrieved 28 November 2014 from: www.shop.bps.org.uk/qmip-bulletin-issue-17-spring-2014.html.

Hudson, A.P. (2014). Exploring the experience of nurses who care for children who have acute life threatening events (ALTE) in hospital. PhD thesis: Aston University. Retrieved 8 December 2014 from: www.ethos.bl.uk/Home.do;jsessionid=3B31390 9FBACB97E2CE74242B3D24774.

Hudson, A.P., Duncan, H., Pattison, H.M. and Shaw, R.L. (2015). Developing an intervention to equip nurses for acute life threatening events (ALTEs) in hospital: A phenomenological approach to healthcare research. *Health Psychology*, 34(4), 361–70.

Johnson, R.B., Onwuegbuzie, A.J. and Turner, I.A. (2007). Toward a definition of mixed methods research. *Journal of Mixed Methods Research*, 1(2), 112–133.

Lincoln, Y.S. and Guba, E.G. (1985). *Naturalistic Inquiry*. Thousand Oaks, CA: SAGE.

Lipton, P. (1991). *Inference to the Best Explanation*. London: Routledge.

McInnes, B. and Bannister, C. (2002). *Working Well Initiative: Guidance on Traumatic Stress Management in the Health Care Sector*. London: Royal College of Nursing.

NIH (National Institute of Health) (1986). Infantile apnoea and home monitoring. Consensus Development Conference Statement, 29 September–1 October 1986. Retrieved 8 December 2014 from: www.consensus.nih.gov/1986/1986InfantApnea Monitoring058html.htm.

Oakley, A. (1999). People's way of knowing: Gender and methodology. In S. Hood, B. Mayall and S. Oliver (Eds.), *Critical Issues in Social Research*. Maidenhead: Open University Press, pp. 154–170.

Pierce, C.S. (1903). Pragmatism as the Logic of Abduction (7th Harvard Lecture). *The Essential Pierce*, Vol. 2. Indiana: Indiana University Press.

Reason, J. and Rowan, J. (Eds.) (1981). *Human Inquiry: A Sourcebook of New Paradigm Research*. New York: Wiley.

Resuscitation Council UK (2013). Quality standards for cardiopulmonary resuscitation practice and training. Retrieved 17 October 2014 from: www.resus.org.uk/ pages/QSCPR_Acute.htm#research.

Scott, S.D., Hirschinger, L.E., Cox, K.R., McCoig, M., Brandt, J. and Hall, L.W. (2009). The natural history of recovery for the healthcare provider 'second victim' after adverse patient events. *Quality and Safety in Health Care*, 18(5), 325–330.

Shaw, R.L., Larkin, M. and Flowers, P. (2014). Expanding the evidence within evidence-based healthcare: Thinking about the context, acceptability and feasibility of interventions. *Evidence Based Medicine*, 19, 201–203.

Smith, J.A. (Ed.) (2008). *Qualitative Psychology: A Practical Guide to Research Methods (Second Edition)*. London: SAGE.

Smith, J.A., Harré, R. and van Langenhove, L. (1995). *Rethinking Psychology*. London: SAGE.

Willig, C. (2001). *Introducing Qualitative Research in Psychology: Adventures and Theory in Method*. Buckingham: Open University Press.

Yardley, L. (2000). Dilemmas in qualitative health research. *Psychology and Health*, 15(2), 215–228.

Public Involvement in Qualitative Research

Delia Muir

16

Introduction

In recent years there has been a change in the way that the public interact with and contribute to health and social care research. Members of the public are moving from passive subjects of research to active members of the research team. This shift has been mirrored by increased public empowerment in other health arenas, such as service design and delivery (Bovaird, 2007), self-management programmes (de Silva, 2011) and health professional education (Towle et al., 2010). At the core of public involvement is the recognition that people gain valuable experience and knowledge through their lived experiences. Researchers from many different methodological backgrounds and disciplines now view public involvement as an important part of their work. Applied qualitative psychologists may find the approach particularly helpful, given their focus on understanding human experiences and talking to people. Working in partnership with those outside of academia can help to develop more inclusive, ethical and meaningful qualitative research.

This chapter will introduce some of the approaches used within public involvement, with a focus on qualitative health and social care research. I will outline how people can be involved at different stages of research, provide real-world examples and discuss some of the practical challenges associated with this work.

Background

The language of involvement

A plethora of terms is used to describe the people and activities which fall under the broad heading of public involvement in research. Terms such as 'patient', 'carer', 'user', 'service user', 'client', 'consumer', 'lay-person', 'co-researcher', 'citizen' and 'survivor' are used interchangeably throughout the literature. One of the reasons for this variation in language is that the types of people who are involved may be dependent on the topic; therefore a single term will not be applicable in every setting. Some research requires a general public perspective, whereas other projects may benefit from the perspective of more specific individuals or groups; for example, people with experience of a particular health condition, people who have used a particular service or other health intervention, people of a certain age, or those from specific cultural or ethnic backgrounds. Terms such as 'engagement', 'participation', 'partnership' and 'collaboration' can also be found in place of 'involvement'.

The language connected with health and health research is potentially emotive and certain terms can be contentious (Coulter, 2011). No single term has been universally accepted across the various health fields which engage in public involvement activities. For example, the term 'patient' is sometimes considered controversial due to the association with patriarchal models of care, where patients play a more passive role. Ward et al. (2009) discuss the pros and cons of considering the people who use health services as 'consumers'. On one hand, the growth of consumerism could be viewed as a positive step towards inclusion, as it recognises the rights of those accessing health services. An alternative view is that this fails to account for the two-way nature of modern health care, where rights come with responsibilities for both care givers and care receivers (Ward et al., 2009).

The lack of standardised terminology or a standard approach to reporting means that the public involvement literature can be challenging to navigate (Shippee et al., 2015). Throughout this chapter we will use the umbrella term 'public involvement' to encompass the myriad of activities and people described in the literature.

Defining public involvement

INVOLVE is a UK-based national advisory group for public involvement in research, funded by the National Institute for Health Research (NIHR). INVOLVE defines public involvement in research as 'research being carried out "with" or "by" members of the public rather than "to", "about" or "for" them' (www.invo.org.uk/find-out-more/what-is-public-involvement-in-research-2/). In this definition, a clear distinction is made between participants in a study, that is, those from whom data is collected to answer a research question, and members of the public who take on a co-researcher role. INVOLVE has described different levels of involvement ranging from consultation through to collaboration and user-led research. Consultation refers to stand-alone activities where researchers consult members of the public about specific elements of a project; a common example of this is reviewing participant information. Collaboration refers to an ongoing partnership where members of the public have an active role in decisions related to the project. User-led or user-controlled research is a growing field where the responsibility for driving a project lies with members of the public; this approach has strong links with emancipatory research (Turner and Beresford, 2005). These levels of involvement have parallels with Arnstein's ladder of citizen participation, a commonly cited model which represents participation as a scale ranging from manipulation to citizen control (Arnstein, 1969).

There are many models which conceptualise involvement in terms of levels or scales (ICPHR, 2013). These can be helpful as they highlight the importance of power dynamics and control within involvement activities. However, these models can sometimes be interpreted as a hierarchy, where absolute public control is seen as the desired approach. Bogart and Uyeda (2009) argue that different approaches are needed in different contexts. Drawing on experience of community-based participatory research, they suggest that researchers should engage in a dialogue with members of the public about the approach needed, taking into account the goals of the study, the time frames and the available resources (Bogart and Uyeda, 2009). This is echoed by the International Collaboration for Participatory Health Research (ICPHR), which suggests in its first position paper that no single model or approach is applicable in every context (ICPHR, 2013).

Participatory research is an important field which embraces partnership working as a fundamental element of research. Here the boundaries between researcher and subject are much more blurred, with participants also being viewed as co-researchers. An explicit aim of participatory research is the empowerment of those involved, both at a personal and at a political level. Participatory research begins and ends with the concerns of a group or community:

Put simply, this method of research is about a group of people who are affected by some problem or issue and decide to get together to work out how they want to tackle the problem. (Wimpenny, 2010, pp. 89–90)

The ICPHR argues that participatory research is a paradigm, not a research method. As such any methodological approach can be used if it is a legitimate way of addressing the needs of the community you are working within. In practice, however, qualitative methods are much more common than quantitative methods.

Co-production is another helpful concept which is often applied to the development and delivery of public services. The principles of co-production can also be applied in a research context, where collaborative processes can be seen to co-produce knowledge. The New Economics Foundation has outlined several key elements of co-production. It highlights the importance of building reciprocal relationships, that is, considering what members of the public get out of being involved, rather than focusing purely on how it will impact on the research or the researchers. It also advocates an asset-based approach which recognises the capacity of communities rather than concentrating on problems which need to be solved via research or professional intervention (Stephens et al., 2008). In other words, research needs the public as much as the public needs research.

Drivers for public involvement in health and social care research

The public involvement literature describes several drivers for the recent and continuing growth in the field. The most commonly cited are policy, moral imperative, impact on those involved and impact on research.

In the UK, public involvement is now embedded within research policy, both at a local and at a national level. Influential institutions and research funders within the USA, Canada and Australia are also pushing for increased public involvement (Boote et al., 2015a). This has undoubtedly had a direct impact on the number of researchers seeking to involve members of the public. It has been argued, however, that these top-down initiatives can lead to tokenistic involvement and that there is often a gap between what policies require and what researchers are willing/able to do in practice (Walker, 2007; Ward et al., 2009; and see e.g. Chapters 4 and 8 in this book). Ward et al. (2009) describe the moral rationale for public involvement in terms of a citizen's right, within a democratic society, to be involved in decisions and processes which may ultimately impact upon their life. This is especially relevant when you consider that much of health research in the UK is publicly funded or funded by charities which rely heavily on public donations.

There are examples of involvement having a positive impact on the individuals involved. When involvement activities are carried out in an ethical and meaningful way, members of the public have reported that it can be an empowering and rewarding experience (Brett et al., 2010; Nierse et al., 2012). In addition, although some researchers are resistant to public involvement, many greatly value it. In a study looking at researchers' attitudes towards involvement, Thompson et al. (2009) found that the majority of participants valued the different perspective which members of the public brought to research. It is also reported that involvement can have an impact on research methodologies and outcomes (Barber et al., 2011; Boote et al., 2015a; Brett et al., 2014), for example, research questions which are more relevant to the public, improved recruitment or wider dissemination. This is sometimes referred to as the consequentialist argument.

Examples of involvement throughout the qualitative research process

There are examples of successful public involvement throughout all stages of the qualitative research cycle, ranging from generating research ideas through to dissemination and implementation of results. Here I will explore the rationale for public involvement at different stages of research and provide some examples. Although this chapter categorises examples according to the stage of research at which involvement occurs, the importance of developing ongoing relationships throughout the life of an entire project cannot be underestimated. At the start of any collaborative project there will be a period of negotiation where people get to know each other and establish their roles; public involvement is no different. Members of a team will bring different strengths and it's understandable that their efforts may focus on different aspects of the project. However, this process should be negotiated rather than pre-determined by researchers as a means to retaining control over a study.

Identifying/prioritising topics

It is generally considered good practice to engage with members of the public as early as possible in the development of a research project (Shippee et al., 2015). The rationale behind this is two-fold. Firstly, it's easier to build a meaningful partnership if all parties work together to set the agenda and aims for a project. Secondly, involvement at this stage can lead to research topics, questions and results which are relevant to the population which they are ultimately aiming to help (Brett et al., 2014; Staley, 2009). Prioritisation can take place at a local level, whereby a single institution or team undertakes work to develop its own research strategy.

Large-scale prioritisation projects are also undertaken to elicit what matters to members of the public at a national level. This approach tends to focus on a particular condition or health issue and informs work in that field more broadly, including influencing research funders. One example of this national approach is the work of the James Lind Alliance (JLA) in the UK. The JLA facilitates priority setting partnerships which bring together members of the public and health professionals to develop research priorities around a particular topic. The methods used in each partnership vary and are influenced by the needs, skills and resources of the partners involved. However, all projects are guided by a set of underpinning principles which include transparency of process; seeking a balance between clinical and public perspectives; and exclusion of groups who may have a conflict of interest, such as drug companies (Crowe, 2009). Partners work together to develop a set of 'treatment uncertainties' which are then cross-checked against existing literature, ranked in order of importance and published.

Research design

Members of the public bring real-life experience which can help researchers to understand if and how a study may work for the population being targeted. This can lead to more inclusive, ethical research and better recruitment (Staley, 2009). It's common for people to be involved in developing recruitment strategies and materials, for example information leaflets. Members of the public can also help researchers consider the level of burden which a study may place on participants and whether this is justified by the potential benefit to the individual or to the wider population. Burden may include practical issues such as the cost and time involved or emotional burden when, for example, discussing sensitive issues during qualitative data collection. One of the challenges of working collaboratively at this stage is that a lot of design takes place before research funding has been awarded; therefore finding funds for this work can be difficult (Coulter, 2011; Boote et al., 2015b). Another challenge relates to managing different perspectives and expectations. Some report tensions between what the public see as important and what academics see as robust research (Brett et al., 2010). Careful facilitation is needed to ensure that different perspectives are valued and that collaboration can continue throughout the project.

Data collection

Some qualitative researchers have challenged the term 'data collection', suggesting instead that data is 'generated' or 'made' with participants and that the researcher plays a part in the development of that data (Holloway, 1997). Therefore it is reasonable to assume that different researchers will bring different things to that process. Involvement at this stage is particularly common in research with 'seldom heard' or 'hard to reach' groups. The rationale is that, in certain circumstances, participants may be more able to open up to people who have had similar experiences to them. Particular individuals or organisations such as charities and community groups can also bring a level of credibility to a project (Staley, 2013) and provide access to people who researchers may otherwise struggle to engage with (Elliott et al., 2002; Brett et al., 2010).

Members of the public have conducted peer-to-peer interviews and led focus groups; Staley (2009) provides several examples of how these activities can have a positive impact on studies. She suggests this may be particularly relevant within research which explores people's experience of accessing services, as people may be wary of criticising a system or institution which they view the researcher as part of (Staley, 2009).

Involvement at this stage is not without challenges. Elliott et al. (2002) describe a project which used peer-to-peer interviews with parents who use drugs. They raise an ethical concern regarding whether the 'stable' interviewers were putting their 'drug-free status' at risk by being in contact with current drug users. They also describe how the shared language of interviewers and interviewees had both a positive and a negative impact on the project. The use of shared language helped to build a rapport and professional researchers acknowledged that they did not understand some of the colloquial terms used by participants. However, this shared experience also led to some issues not being explored in depth (Elliott et al., 2002). Adequate support and preparation are vital throughout these sorts of activity, and experienced researchers may work alongside less experienced members of the team. For example, Williams and England describe the role of 'research supporters' within a project where people with learning disabilities led focus groups (Williams and England, 2005).

Even when members of the public are not directly involved in collecting data, they can still have an influence on this stage of research, for example, by helping to train researchers; being part of recruitment processes for researchers, such as interview panels; helping to develop and test interview schedules or focus group facilitation techniques; or observing researchers at work and providing feedback.

Data analysis and interpretation

Many teams report that involvement at this stage had a positive impact on their studies. This is perhaps not surprising given that qualitative research is about people's experiences and interpretations of the world, rather than collecting facts and figures. Papers highlight the ability of members of the public to pick up and reflect upon the emotional content of data (Gillard et al., 2010; Tanner, 2012); to highlight the complexities of living with a particular condition (Nierse et al., 2012); to identify gaps in research (Brett et al., 2014); to add cultural and/or linguistic insight (Brett et al., 2014; Cashman et al., 2008); to contextualise findings (Shippee et al., 2015); and to challenge academic conventions (Gillard et al., 2012). Authors also describe involvement as adding to the validity of research (Tuffrey-Wijne and Butler, 2010; Gillard et al., 2010; Shippee et al., 2015; Cashman et al., 2008) as people from different backgrounds are more likely to challenge and balance each other's biases whilst trying to reach a consensus (Whitley, 2005).

The way that people are involved varies between projects. Gillard et al. (2012) used training to familiarise members of the public with qualitative analysis techniques, whereas others adapted processes and/or primary data to make the process more accessible, for example looking at vignettes (Tuffrey-Wijne and Butler, 2010) or using visual/experiential facilitation methods (Cashman et al., 2008). Several papers outline a process of dialogue and collaboration between members of the public and researchers, highlighting the importance of support, mutual learning and co-production of knowledge (Tuffrey-Wijne and Butler, 2010; Nierse et al., 2012; Cashman et al., 2008).

An example: the severe pressure ulcer study

The Severe Pressure Ulcer (SPU) study (Pinkney et al., 2014) formed part of the Pressure Ulcer Programme of Research (PURPOSE) funded by NIHR and led by the University of Leeds and Leeds Teaching Hospitals Trust (Nixon et al., In press). A pressure ulcer (sometimes called a bedsore) is an area of damaged skin caused by pressure. It is most commonly caused by lying/sitting in one position for too long. The SPU study investigated why some people develop particularly severe pressure ulcers, with a focus on how the organisational context and culture influenced pressure ulcer development.

A retrospective case study methodology was used, tracing eight people with severe pressure ulcers. Data was collected via interviews with patients and their families, interviews with health professionals, clinical records and other relevant documents such as clinical guidelines. The data was used to construct timelines of events in the development of each pressure ulcer. Summaries of each account were then reviewed by the research team. One important feature of this method is that the patient's account is central to the process and directs further data collection. Despite this approach, there were concerns that the patient's voice could get lost within the wider data (i.e. multiple interviews with health care professionals) and the professionally led review process. One of the ways this was addressed was by involving people with experience of pressure ulcers in the interpretation of data.

A workshop was developed which aimed to facilitate the involvement of people who may have little or no experience of research, and create a meaningful dialogue with other members of the project team. Members of the Pressure Ulcer Research Service User Network (PURSUN) (Muir, 2011) were invited, along with members of the project team (nurses and academics). Due to the volume of data, one case study was selected as the focus of the workshop.

The workshop used the metaphor of a public enquiry, with participants taking on the role of expert witnesses in the case. The first half of the workshop concentrated on the patient's account of what had happened. This was presented to the group as a live interview between the field researcher and a simulated patient (a specialist role-player). Workshop participants observed the interview, which acted as a catalyst for discussion about the case. The simulated patient stayed 'in role' as the patient during the discussion which followed, which allowed workshop participants to interact with her and ask follow-up questions of their own. The next part of the workshop focused on the accounts of the professionals involved. These were presented as short videos, whereby actors playing the role of health care professionals gave their accounts of what happened. Both the live interview and actors' briefs were very closely based on real accounts with key details changed to retain anonymity. The simulated patient also had personal experience of a pressure ulcer, which she was able to draw on to create an authentic role. A visual representation of the timeline of events was also presented.

Workshop participants particularly enjoyed the live interview exercise. A notable feature of the discussion which followed the live interview was the way in which people engaged with the simulated patient, rather than directing comments to the workshop facilitator. This process has parallels with more traditional thematic analysis techniques. Here a lone researcher may code interview data by labelling concepts or categories within a transcript; these can then be grouped together into themes. This often involves continually referring back to the text to check understanding and accuracy. During the live interview, people observed and noted aspects of the case which they felt were particularly important, sometimes recording direct quotes as evidence. In the discussions which followed, the group worked together to identify themes from their individual observations. They were able to go back to the simulated patient to check assumptions and clarify points, which mirrors the way a researcher may move between analysis and transcript.

This exercise forms part of a strategy to limit hindsight bias in the study, by incorporating review by people from different backgrounds. Members of PURSUN identified very similar themes to the project team; however, they weighted their interpretations slightly differently and highlighted certain areas as being particularly important. This influenced the dissemination and implementation of the project findings. Workshop participants found the metaphor of a public inquiry useful, as it helped to clearly explain the project's methodology and their role on the day. Members of PURSUN felt they had a clearly defined role which suited their skills and expertise.

Although this example focuses on involvement at one stage of the research process, data interpretation, it illustrates how research processes can be adapted in order to make them more inclusive. It also demonstrates the importance of a flexible approach to involvement which is built around the needs of both the project and the people involved. These principles can be applied across the spectrum of qualitative research activities.

Dissemination and implementation

Many believe research participants, and the wider general public, have a right to access research findings. Traditional dissemination methods such as journal articles and conference presentations are not easily accessible for people outside of academia and are not always the best way to ensure that research is implemented into practice. Members of the public are well placed to help develop information aimed at people who have had similar experiences to them. Members of the public may also be able to reach practice-based audiences in a powerful way. For example, since completion of the Pressure Ulcer Programme of Research members of PURSUN have spoken to nurses, students and NHS managers at several different events. One member has also become part of an implementation project in her local NHS trust. This real-life testimony has proved to be a powerful dissemination tool, which helps to put research findings back into a real-life context.

Members of the public who are less used to academic conventions may suggest innovative ways of communicating research. For example, a group of people with experience of schizophrenia developed and performed a piece of theatre based on their results (Schneider et al., 2004). Another team developed an 'accessible article' which contained illustrations. This was developed in partnership with people with a learning disability (Garbutt et al., 2009). In a separate article Garbutt reflects on the challenges of disseminating participatory research in a way which is meaningful for the people involved. The article challenges journal editors to accept submissions written in a more accessible way, including visual formats (Garbutt, 2009).

Challenges in applied research

Training, support and preparation

The support offered to members of the public can take many different forms including mentorship, peer support, personal development opportunities and formal training. It is widely accepted that support for members of the public is a vital part of involvement; however, the use of formal training is more contentious. Ives et al. (2013) claim that members of the public require training in research methods and language in order to become equal members of a research team. They go on to suggest that this creates a paradox within public involvement. This paradox relates to the fact that once people have been trained they may become 'professionalised' and are therefore less able to provide a lay perspective (Ives et al., 2013). In a response to that article, Staley argues strongly that the acquisition of research skills and knowledge does not necessarily have to lead to people losing their lay identity. She suggests that training can and should help people to understand the wider research context and see how their perspective can contribute to that landscape.

One could also argue that training members of the public suggests a deficit, that is, a lack of knowledge which needs to be filled. This conflicts with the principle of asset-based involvement and with the notion that different forms of expertise have value. Another way of looking at this issue is that training is part of building a reciprocal relationship with members of the public. Professional researchers have access to training, so why not their research partners? Some research activities may also require a level of quality assurance to protect research participants, for example peer-to-peer interviews or facilitation of focus groups (Staley, 2013). Training may form part of that quality assurance.

Rather than questioning whether training should be offered, it may be more helpful to consider *how* to train in an effective and appropriate way. Training which encourages people to reflect on their personal experiences and consider how they can contribute in a research context is perhaps more helpful than learning in detail about research methods. Thinking about research *preparation* rather than research *training* may also be helpful. Morris and colleagues developed a preparation process called the patient learning journey (PLJ) (Morris et al., 2010). This process was first used to prepare patients and carers to become involved in teaching medical students and has since been adapted for use in a research environment (Muir, 2012). The PLJ model involves facilitated workshops which encourage people to share their experiences of health, reflect on the learning within those experiences and consider how best to communicate that learning to others in a safe and constructive way. The workshops aim to encourage peer support and keep people grounded in their personal experiences. Ultimately training, support and preparation should be based on the needs of the people you are working with and their role within a project.

Evaluating and reporting public involvement activities

Our understanding of public involvement is growing rapidly; this is demonstrated by the large body of literature now available on the topic. Some argue, however, that more systematic evaluation and better reporting are needed in order to develop a stronger evidence base (Barber et al., 2012; Brett et al., 2014; Fudge et al., 2007; Shippee et al., 2015). This perceived lack of evidence is partly because measuring impact in this context is challenging (Barber et al., 2012; Wyatt et al., 2008). It is difficult to isolate the impact of one person or group of people within a collaborative research project. Some have attempted to do this by separating out and comparing the contributions of researchers and members of the public. This approach has some obvious benefits in terms of exploring the impact of involvement; however, it does not account for the complex interactions which take place between collaborators from different backgrounds. Some have raised concerns about this approach, making the point that one of the aims of involvement is the bringing together of different perspectives (Boote et al., 2014; Gillard et al., 2010).

Entwistle (2010) also suggests that caution is needed when conducting or evaluating involvement in this way. Comparing contributions can fail to recognise the complexities of people's roles and the way that different elements of people's professional and personal experiences impact upon how they interpret the world and therefore how they interpret research (Entwistle, 2010). Others report that the boundaries between people's roles can become less defined throughout the life of a project, describing 'public' and 'professional' as transitory states which do not fully describe the diversity of knowledge which people bring (Cornes et al., 2008).

In addition to these practical challenges, there is disagreement in the field about how ethical it is to measure impact when it is considered morally right for members of the public to have a voice within research. Furthermore, you could ask why we are evaluating the impact of public involvement when we do not subject other members of the research team to the same degree of scrutiny. Perhaps all members of the team should be asked to reflect on their contributions, rather than singling out members of the public as an add-on. Staley et al. (2014) suggest more work is needed to understand how the context and nature of involvement link to the impact it has. This is necessary to understand when and where to use different involvement models. Realist evaluation techniques provide one way of doing this (Staley et al., 2014).

Engaging with marginalised groups

The question of how to make projects inclusive and accessible to a variety of people is central to public involvement and to qualitative research more generally. The literature describes certain groups as 'marginalised', 'seldom heard' or 'hard to reach' and there is concern that traditional research activities favour those who act, think and communicate in a certain way. Groups that are often referred to in these terms include, but are not limited to, black and minority ethnic groups, people who do not speak the native language, people with cognitive impairments, homeless people, people with learning disabilities and people with drug or alcohol dependency. It has been suggested that the term 'hard to reach' is in fact a euphemism for groups who are excluded from research because of a lack of opportunity and/or appropriate support (Beresford, 2005). This is relevant in relation to both research participants and members of the public who are conducting research.

Steel (2005) points out that any of us can feel marginalised or vulnerable at points in our lives. Anyone can feel like an outsider in an unfamiliar setting; reflecting on that feeling may help researchers to adopt a more inclusive approach. He argues that researchers and research organisations must be willing to adapt their processes in order to accommodate outsiders (Steel, 2005). Practical support is vital when engaging with marginalised groups, for example providing translators, communication aids, accessible venues or financial support. In addition to thinking about what prohibits marginalised groups from contributing, it's also helpful to consider what skills, experience and expertise they bring to the table. The concept of asset-based involvement is helpful here, as activities can be designed in ways which play to people's strengths rather than add to the feeling of being an outsider. This same principle can be used when thinking about appropriate data collection techniques.

The report 'Beyond the Usual Suspects' (Beresford, 2013) describes in detail the barriers which people can face when becoming involved in research. A key theme throughout this report is the need to find creative, innovative approaches to involvement. Members of the public describe feeling bored and disengaged at research meetings and stress the importance of enjoyable involvement activities. The Severe Pressure Ulcer study, described earlier in this chapter, provides one example of how arts-based approaches can facilitate this.

Conclusion

The public involvement landscape is complex and at times slightly messy. When collaborative projects work they can be an empowering and even transformative experience for all parties. However, there is potential for disempowerment when confusing, professionally led processes leave people feeling unable to contribute or feeling that their contributions were not valued. Equally, researchers can feel that their professional training and experience are devalued by public involvement activities. These issues require careful thought. Involvement should be planned and conducted with the same degree of care accorded to other aspects of research. Just as methodological choices must be well justified, so should approaches to public involvement be appropriate for the research and the needs of the people you are working with.

Although public involvement cuts across many different fields, methodologies and theoretical underpinnings, some core values have emerged as being important to many working in this field. Put simply, public involvement should:

- recognise the power imbalance which can exist between researchers and the communities they work within;
- strive towards shared responsibility between collaborators;
- build rewarding, reciprocal relationships;
- recognise and value the contribution of everyone involved;
- be asset based; and
- be engaging.

References

Arnstein, S. (1969). A ladder of citizen participation. *Journal of the American Institute of Planners*, 35, 216–224.

Barber, R., Beresford, P., Boote, J., Cooper, C. and Faulkner, A. (2011). Evaluating the impact of service user involvement on research: A prospective case study. *International Journal of Consumer Studies*, 35, 609–615.

Barber, R., Boote, J.D., Parry, G.D., Cooper, C.L., Yeeles, P. and Cook, S. (2012). Can the impact of public involvement on research be evaluated? A mixed methods study. *Health Expectations*, 15, 229–241.

Beresford, P. (2005). Theory and practice of user involvement in research: Making the connection with public policy and practice. In L. Lowes and I. Hulatt (Eds.), *Involving Service Users in Heath and Social Care Research*. Oxfordshire: Routledge.

Beresford, P. (2013). *Beyond the Usual Suspects*. London: Shaping Our Lives.

Bogart, L.M. and Uyeda, K. (2009). Community-based participatory research: Partnering with communities for effective and sustainable behavioral health interventions. *Health Psychology*, 28, 391–393.

Boote, J., Wong, R. and Booth, A. (2015a). 'Talking the talk or walking the walk?' A bibliometric review of the literature on public involvement in health research published between 1995 and 2009. *Health Expectations*, 18(1), 44–57.

Boote, J.D., Dalgleish, M., Freeman, J., Jones, Z., Miles, M. and Rodgers, H. (2014). 'But is it a question worth asking?' A reflective case study describing how public involvement can lead to researchers' ideas being abandoned. *Health Expectations*, 17(3), 440–451.

Boote, J.D., Twiddy, M., Baird, W., Birks, Y., Clarke, C. and Beever, D. (2015b). Supporting public involvement in research design and grant development: A case study of a public involvement award scheme managed by a National Institute for Health Research (NIHR) Research Design Service (RDS). *Health Expectations*, 18(5), 1481–1493.

Bovaird, T. (2007). Beyond engagement and participation: User and community coproduction of public services. *Public Administration Review*, 67, 846–860.

Brett, J., Staniszewska, S., Mockford, C., Herron-Marx, S., Hughes, J., Tysall, C. and Suleman, R. (2014). Mapping the impact of patient and public involvement on health and social care research: A systematic review. *Health Expectations*, 17(5), 637–650.

Brett, J., Staniszewska, S., Mockford, C., Seers, K., Herron-Marx, S. and Bayliss, H. (2010). The PIRICOM study: A systematic review of the conceptualisation, measurement, impact and outcomes of patients and public involvement in health and social care research. University of Warwick.

Cashman, S.B., Adeky, S., Allen, A.J., Corburn, J., Israel, B.A., Montano, J., Rafelito, A., Rhodes, S.D., Swanston, S., Wallerstein, N. and Eng, E. (2008). The power and the promise: Working with communities to analyze data, interpret findings, and get to outcomes. *American Journal of Public Health*, 98, 1407–1417.

Cornes, M., Peardon, J., Manthorpe, J. and the Y.O.P.T. (2008). Wise owls and professors: The role of older researchers in the review of the National Service Framework for Older People. *Health Expectations*, 11, 409–417.

Coulter, A. (2011). *Engaging Patients in Healthcare*. Maidenhead: Open University Press.

Crowe, S. (2009). Setting priorities for treatment uncertainties – A review of methods. Retrieved 20 January 2017 from www.jla.nihr.ac.uk/news-and-publications/downloads/review-of-priority-setting-methods-sally-crowe.pdf.

de Silva, D. (2011). Evidence: Helping people help themselves. Retrieved 20 February 2015 from: www.health.org.uk/public/cms/75/76/313/2434/Helping%20people%20help%20themselves.pdf?realName=8mh12J.pdf.

Elliott, E., Watson, A.J. and Harries, U. (2002). Harnessing expertise: Involving peer interviewers in qualitative research with hard-to-reach populations. *Health Expectations*, 5, 172–178.

Entwistle, V.A. (2010). Involving service users in qualitative analysis: Approaches and assessment. *Health Expectations*, 13, 111–112.

Fudge, N., Wolfe, C.D.A. and Mckevitt, C. (2007). Involving older people in health research. *Age and Ageing*, 36, 492–500.

Garbutt, R. (2009). Is there a place within academic journals for articles presented in an accessible format? *Disability and Society*, 24, 357–371.

Garbutt, R., Tattersall, J., Dunn, J. and Boycott-Garnett, R. (2009). Accessible article: Involving people with learning disabilities in research. *British Journal of Learning Disabilities*, 38, 21–34.

Gillard, S., Borschmann, R., Turner, K., Goodrich-Purnell, N., Lovell, K. and Chambers, M. (2010). 'What difference does it make?' Finding evidence of the impact of mental health service user researchers on research into the experiences of detained psychiatric patients. *Health Expectations*, 13, 185–194.

Gillard, S., Simons, L., Turner, K., Lucock, M. and Edwards, C. (2012). Patient and public involvement in the coproduction of knowledge: Reflection on the analysis of qualitative data in a mental health study. *Qualitative Health Research*, 22(8), 1126–1137.

Holloway, I. (1997). *Basic Concepts for Qualitative Research*. Oxford: Blackwell Science.

ICPHR. (2013). Position paper 1: What is participatory health research? International Collaboration for Participatory Health Research.

Ives, J., Damery, S. and Redwod, S. (2013). PPI, paradoxes and Plato: Who's sailing the ship? *Journal of Medical Ethics*, 39, 181–185.

Morris, P., Dalton, E., Mcgoverin, A. and Symons, J. (2010). Preparing for patient-centred practice: Developing the patient voice in health professional learning. In H.

Bradbury, N. Frost, S. Kilminster and M. Zukas (Eds.), *Beyond Reflective Practice.* Oxford: Routledge.

Muir, D. (2011). Patient and public involvement in pressure ulcer research. *Journal of Tissue Viability*, 20, 132–133.

Muir, D. (2012). Training case study 13: Preparing people for involvement in research using the patient learning journey model. University of Leeds.

Nierse, C.J., Schipper, K., Van Zadelhoff, E., Van de Griendt, J. and Abma, T.A. (2012). Collaboration and co-ownership in research: Dynamics and dialogues between patient research partners and professional researchers in a research team. *Health Expectations*, 15, 242–254.

Nixon, J., Nelson, E.A., Rutherford, C., Coleman, S., Muir, D., Keen, J., McCabe, C., Dealey, C., Briggs, M., Brown, S., Collinson, M., Hulme, C., Meads, D., Mcginnis E, Patterson, M., Czoski-Murray, C., Pinkney, L., Smith, I., Stevenson, R., Stubbs, N., Wilson, L. and Brown, J. (2015). Pressure UlceR Programme Of reSEarch (PURPOSE): Using mixed methods (systematic reviews, prospective cohort, case study, consensus and psychometrics) to identify patient and organisational risk, develop a risk assessment tool and patient-reported outcome Quality of Life and Health Utility measures. Southampton: NIHR Journals Library.

Pinkney, L., Nixon, J., Wilson, L., Coleman, S., McGinnis, E., Stubbs, N., Dealey, C., Nelson, A., Patterson, M. and Keen, J. (2014). Why do patients develop severe pressure ulcers? A retrospective case study. *British Medical Journal Open*, 4, e004303.

Schneider, B., Scissons, H., Arney, L., Benson, G., Derry, J., Lucas, K., Misurelli, M., Nickerson, D. and Sunderland, M. (2004). Communication between people with schizophrenia and their medical professionals: A participatory research project. *Qualitative Health Research*, 14, 562–577.

Shippee, N.D., Domecq Garces, J.P., Prutsky Lopez, G.J., Wang, Z., Elraiyah, T.A., Nabhan, M., Brito, J.P., Boehmer, K., Hasan, R., Firwana, B., Erwin, P.J., Montori, V.M. and Murad, M.H. (2015). Patient and service user engagement in research: A systematic review and synthesized framework. *Health Expectations*, 18(5), 1151–1166.

Staley, K. (2009). *Exploring Impact: Public Involvement in NHS, Public Health and Social Care Research*. Eastleigh: INVOLVE.

Staley, K. (2013). *A Series of Case Studies Illustrating the Impact of Service User and Carer Involvement on Research*. The NIHR Mental Health Research Network.

Staley, K., Buckland, S.A., Hayes, H. and Tarpey, M. (2014). 'The missing links': Understanding how context and mechanism influence the impact of public involvement in research. *Health Expectations*, 17(6), 755–764.

Steel, R. (2005). Actively involving marginalised and vulnerable people in research. In L. Lowes and I. Hulatt (Eds.), *Involving Service Users in Health and Social Care Research*. Oxfordshire: Routledge.

Stephens, L., Ryan-Collins, J. and Boyle, D. (2008). *Co-production: A Manifesto for Growing the Core Economy*. London: New Economics Foundation.

Tanner, D. (2012). Co-research with older people with dementia: Experience and reflections. *Journal of Mental Health*, 21, 296–306.

Thompson, J., Barber, R., Ward, P.R., Boote, J.D., Cooper, C.L., Armitage, C.J. and Jones, G. (2009). Health researchers' attitudes towards public involvement in health research. *Health Expectations*, 12, 209–220.

Towle, A., Bainbridge, L., Godolphin, W., Katz, A., Kline, C., Lown, B., Madularu, I., Solomon, P. and Thistlethwaite, J. (2010). Active patient involvement in the education of health professionals. *Medical Education*, 44, 64–74.

Tuffrey-Wijne, I. and Butler, G. (2010). Co-researching with people with learning disabilities: An experience of involvement in qualitative data analysis. *Health Expectations*, 13, 174–184.

Turner, T. and Beresford, P. (2005). *User Controlled Research: Its Meanings and Potential*. Eastleigh: INVOLVE.

Walker, A. (2007). Why involve older people in research? *Age and Ageing*, 36, 481–483.

Ward, P.R., Thompson, J., Barber, R., Armitage, C.J., Boote, J.D., Cooper, C.L. and Jones, G.L. (2009). Critical perspectives on 'consumer involvement' in health research: Epistemological dissonance and the know-do gap. *Journal of Sociology*, 46, 63–82.

Whitley, R. (2005). Letter: Client involvement in services research. *Psychiatric Services*, 56, 1315.

Williams, V. and England, M. (2005). Supporting people with learning dissabilities to do their own research. In L. Lowes and I. Hulatt (Eds.), *Involving Service Users in Health and Social Care Research*. Oxfordshire: Routledge.

Wimpenny, K. (2010). Participatory action research: An integrated approach towards practice development. In M. Savin-Baden and C. Howell Major (Eds.), *New Approaches to Qualitative Research*. Oxfordshire: Routledge.

Wyatt, K., Carter, M.V.M., Barnard, A., Hawton, A. and Britten, N. (2008). The impact of consumer involvement in research: An evaluation of consumer involvement in the London primary care studies programme. *Family Practice*, 5, 154–161.

Disseminating Qualitative Research: From Clarity of Writing to Collaborative Action

17

Flora Cornish and Sarah Honeywell

Introduction

The present chapter seeks to introduce the reader to a range of strategies for getting qualitative research into policy and practice. We begin by outlining the policy context, in which there is a significant demand for research evidence and an increasing appreciation of the value of qualitative evidence. The following sections review what is known, generally, about the barriers to the uptake of research and factors influencing the uptake of research. We then move to discuss specific approaches to (1) communicating qualitative research and (2) undertaking collaborative research and action. The focus throughout is on practical steps and strategies. A key argument is that the depth of engagement between the world of the researcher and the world of social actors (policy-makers, practitioners and citizen communities) matters hugely for the prospects of qualitative research being in a position to make a worthwhile difference in society.

Policy context

Current policy thinking regarding the relationship between research and society is dominated by the evidence-based practice movement (Lambert, 2006; Cartwright and Hardie, 2012). This movement has both pros and cons for applied qualitative researchers. The main advantage is simply the incentivisation of the application of research. Practitioners are incentivised to listen to research evidence. Researchers are increasingly incentivised to demonstrate that their research has 'impact' in society. From origins in evidence-based medicine, the evidence-based practice movement has expanded to be used in a wide range of disciplines (European Social Network, 2014). For instance, the UK coalition government, in 2013, launched a network of independent 'What Works?' centres in certain social policy areas, including economic development, crime reduction and educational attainment. Based on the model of the National Institute for Health and Clinical Excellence (NICE), these centres were tasked with collating evidence on the effectiveness of policy programmes and practices and sharing findings in an accessible way in order to encourage informed decision-making (Cabinet Office, 2013 and see Goldacre, 2013).

Alongside demands for policy to reflect evidence, individual practitioners are also increasingly expected to engage with research, to be research-aware, research-users, or, at the most intensive, research-active. This is reflected in initial training and continuous professional development requirements in different sectors. For example, one of the eight domains in the UK Professional Capabilities Framework (PCF) for social workers, introduced in 2012, is 'knowledge'. According to this framework, a newly qualified social worker is required to demonstrate a critical understanding of research methods and to be beginning to use research to inform practice, while a fully registered social worker is required to demonstrate a comprehensive understanding and use of knowledge related to their area of practice, including critical awareness of current issues and evidence-based practice research. Teaching schools, based on the teaching hospital model, receive funding to develop alliances with a number of other schools to provide six strands of work – one of which is research and development. A large part of this strand is training and supporting teachers to conduct action-research as part of their practice. Overall, this institutional context of the valuing of 'evidence' creates an environment that is, in some respects, conducive to the uptake of research.

However, qualitative research has historically been given less attention and legitimacy in the evidence-based practice paradigm. The paradigm is heavily dependent on an 'evidence hierarchy' in which systematic reviews of randomised controlled trials (RCTs) are the most valuable forms of evidence, followed by individual RCTs, uncontrolled studies, cohort studies, descriptive and case studies. In this hierarchy, qualitative studies do not even appear. The evidence-based movement has often assumed that knowledge derived from patterns in larger populations is inherently better than that derived from smaller studies (Thorne, 2009). Constructivist qualitative researchers have at times been wary of answering 'what works?' questions in the simplified cause and effect terms which policy-makers often demand (Cornish, 2015; Donmoyer, 2012). Qualitative researchers' skills in uncovering complexities, elucidating local meanings, or problematising grand theories or simplistic administrative categories can frustrate those who wish to derive a 'bottom line', 'straight answer' or clear recommendation.

Nonetheless, qualitative research has been increasingly recognised by policy-making and practitioner communities as being good at shedding light on 'how' and 'why' questions. Questions about contextual factors which influence how successfully or unsuccessfully programmes or policies are carried out and questions about the social determinants of complex issues have been mentioned as ones particularly suited to qualitative inquiry (Jack, 2006). Practitioners themselves often appreciate the contribution of qualitative research. Thorne (2009) states that practitioners find it difficult to reconcile their commitment to evidence-based practice, based on quantitative evidence, with their own knowledge of the complexity of the context.

This dual context sets the scene for qualitative researchers interested in disseminating or achieving social impact with their work. They may find an appetite among practitioners for collaboration to bring evidence to bear on practice, but some scepticism about the methods. To make the most of their research, researchers may wish to consider what is known about factors influencing the uptake of research, to which we now turn.

What makes qualitative research more or less likely to be used?

With increasing explicit interest in the process of 'dissemination', also conceptualised as knowledge transfer, knowledge translation, implementation, or research utilisation, there is a growing literature on the process of dissemination itself. While there has been little research on the effectiveness of different types of dissemination activity, there is some literature, particularly from the health sector, that highlights factors found to affect the dissemination and utilisation of research (Lavis, 2009; Grimshaw and Eccles, 2008). For qualitative researchers, the evidence on dissemination is scant. However, it has been suggested that the process of communicating qualitative research does not appear essentially different from that of other kinds of research (Estabrooks, 2001, cited in Keen and Todres, 2006).

Barriers to the use of research

The specific barriers to the take-up of research, both quantitative and qualitative, will vary according to the context. However, Grimshaw and Eccles (2008, pp. 8–24) identify five overarching concerns which can affect research take-up:

1. structural barriers (e.g. financial disincentives);
2. organisational barriers (e.g. inappropriate skill mix, lack of facilities or equipment);
3. peer group barriers (e.g. local standards of care not in line with desired practice);
4. professional barriers (e.g. knowledge, attitudes and skills);
5. professional–patient interaction barriers (e.g. communication and information processing issues).

We use the headings identified by Buse et al. (2012) to explore these barriers in greater detail.

Political and ideological factors

Political and ideological factors can influence the creation and usage of research, for example it can shape who is chosen to conduct research or why certain research is funded over other projects (Buse et al., 2012). Insights from any type of research must also compete with other factors in the policy-making process, such as institutional constraints, interest group pressure and policy-makers' past experiences (Lavis, 2009). Researchers hoping to influence policy-makers must also contend with rapid staff turn-over and the constant reshaping of administrative structures (Grimshaw and Eccles, 2008). The literature suggests that interventions will be unlikely to influence policy without a detailed understanding of all these factors (Oliver et al., 2014).

Policy and scientific uncertainty

Differences between what policy-makers want from research and what that research is able to say can be a potential barrier to use. For example, it can be difficult for researchers to provide evaluations of programmes which often have very broad policy goals and to disentangle the effects of interventions in policy areas where multiple factors are at work (Buse et al., 2012).

In addition, researchers have found that many policy-makers and practitioners are not skilled in research methods and so are not well equipped to digest research and understand its limitations (Grimshaw and Eccles, 2008; Walter et al., 2004, cited in Keen and Todres, 2006).

Different conceptions of risk

Buse et al. (2012) note that there can be differences between individual conceptions of risk and what the evidence shows; for example, media attention often focuses on findings that are new and rare and can thus distort the focus or weight of research.

Perceived utility of research

A common theme in the literature around barriers to research usage is the perceived utility of that evidence by the target audience. Buse et al. (2012) suggest that whether research is used is influenced by whether the findings are considered usable within the specific circumstance.

Qualitative research must also battle the public perception that it has less rigour and legitimacy than quantitative research, as a result of having limited generalisability at population level or being weak at addressing causation

(Jack, 2006). As Nutley et al. (2002b) argue, there is a trade-off in utility between the extremes of generic knowledge, usually quantitative, and local knowledge specific to context, usually qualitative.

Timing

Decision-makers often criticise researchers for taking too long to produce findings when they are under pressure to act (Buse et al., 2012). Practitioners and policy-makers also report having little time or opportunity to engage with and use research evidence (Oliver et al., 2014).

Communication and reputation

The literature suggests that many barriers to the utilisation of qualitative research findings stem from how they are presented. Authors argue that qualitative research is often difficult to understand due to the way reports are written, with authors failing to provide clarity or render findings parsimoniously, failing to differentiate between their findings and those of similar studies, and confusing analysis with interpretation (Sandelowski and Leeman, 2012; Oliver et al., 2014). Furthermore, findings are harder to place in qualitative papers as the results can less easily be written up in an objective data-based results section than in a quantitative study (Sandelowski and Leeman, 2012).

The nature of qualitative research has also made the 'summing up' of studies in systematic reviews of a particular population or intervention extraordinarily difficult (Jack, 2006).

Buse et al. (2012) make a general point that is particularly salient to qualitative research, in that the more complex, opaque and indeterminate are the results and presentation of them, the less likely, all other things being equal, that they are to be taken notice of. That said, no matter how well communicated, if research proposes a radical structural change, it is much more likely to be ignored (Buse et al., 2012).

The barriers challenging the usage of qualitative research findings will be specific to the context. Therefore, researchers must use their judgement and understanding of the context to identify potential barriers and consider addressing these through different dissemination activities. As well as being aware of barriers, in a more positive light, being aware of factors influencing the uptake of qualitative research is also useful, and we now turn to this issue.

Factors influencing the uptake of research

While the contribution of qualitative research has been lauded in many fields, particularly around the development, testing and implementation of interventions in areas such as health, there has been relatively little written on how best to present findings in a way that is usable and that will overcome the barriers identified above (Sandelowski and Leeman, 2012).

To summarise the guidance available on disseminating qualitative research, we have sought to provide preliminary answers to five key questions identified by Lavis and colleagues (Lavis et al., 2003):

- What should be transferred?
- To whom should research knowledge be transferred?
- By whom should research knowledge be transferred?
- How should research knowledge be transferred?
- With what effect should research knowledge be transferred?

What should be transferred?

Grimshaw and Eccles (2008) suggest that the unit of dissemination should be strategic reviews, as individual studies do not provide enough evidence to change policy or practice. Providing strategic reviews and ones that grade the strength of the evidence can help address barriers around the volume of evidence and limited time for reading (Grimshaw and Eccles, 2008; Lavis et al., 2003).

To whom should research knowledge be transferred?

Different types of research will have different target audiences, whether that is policy-makers, decision-makers, practitioners, researchers or the public. Content, message and medium should be tailored towards the specific audience (Keen and Todres, 2006). In this interest, researchers must clearly articulate the outcomes of the qualitative research (to both funding agencies and decision-makers); develop context-specific strategies illustrating how the findings can be used by practitioners and policy-makers (Jack, 2006); define the problem in relation to the knowledge base; and consider users' motivations (Nutley et al., 2002b).

Nutley et al. (2002b) explain that this represents a shift in focus from researcher as disseminator to practitioner as learner. Researchers, therefore, need to be aware that user knowledge and capacity to use research varies (Jack, 2006). As a result, dissemination might include activities to educate decision-makers about the richness and value of qualitative research and to develop an appetite for qualitative research amongst practitioners (Jack, 2006; Grimshaw and Eccles, 2008).

By whom should research knowledge be transferred?

Susan Jack (2006) argues that the onus is on researchers to present the relevance of their findings to policy-makers. To inform policy-making more effectively, researchers need a better systematic understanding of political culture and the policy-making process (Grimshaw and Eccles, 2008). Researchers might also want to involve others, such as opinion leaders, those regarded by their peers as trusted sources of information, third party intermediaries such as think tanks and non-governmental organisations (NGOs) and people involved in artistic sectors when considering non-traditional forms of dissemination, to encourage take-up of findings (LSE Public Policy Group, 2011; Grimshaw and Eccles, 2008; Keen and Todres, 2006).

How should research knowledge be transferred?

One of the barriers to use is the inaccessibility of qualitative research findings. The literature suggests that presenting findings in a clear format that is easy to read and that explains how the evidence can be used to inform decisions and changes in practice will increase uptake (Oliver et al., 2014; Jack, 2006). Researchers will also need to consider the medium for dissemination, that is, how the knowledge is described, packaged and transmitted, and variations in different approaches' coverage, timeliness and cost.

While there is little research on the most effective dissemination activities, the existing literature suggests that interactions, collaboration and increased communication between researchers and decision-makers increase the prospects for research evidence to be used (Oliver et al., 2014; Lavis, 2009; Nutley et al., 2002a). Interactive exchange and active discussion of research findings has also been found to be more likely to lead to changes in behaviour (Nutley et al., 2002b). In addition, the use of multiple dissemination strategies appears to offer the best hope of promoting behaviour change (Estabrooks, 2001, cited in Keen and Todres, 2006).

With what effect should research knowledge be transferred?

Lavis (2009) suggests researchers should approach dissemination strategically, for example by making strategic use of evidence during 'windows of opportunity' created by political events, such as the election of a new government or an interest group pressure campaign. In order to have real impact, policy-makers and researchers must learn to accommodate differences in the timeframes within which they operate (Grimshaw and Eccles, 2008). There is also a need to evaluate the impact of the findings and the effectiveness of different dissemination activities as part of the research process, although this is very difficult (Keen and Todres, 2006).

Communicating qualitative research: Practical strategies

The steps in Table 17.1 below have been suggested as ways researchers can better communicate research findings, promote professional behaviour change and overcome some of the barriers identified earlier in this chapter.

Writing accessible material

Much of the literature on disseminating qualitative research emphasises the importance of presenting findings in a way that is accessible to your audience. These authors advise writing in a clear, jargon-free style and using the language of your target readers (Buse et al., 2012; Sandelowski and Leeman, 2012). Sandelowski and Leeman (2012) suggest translating the main findings into thematic statements using a table with headings such as: 'with this intervention', 'these outcomes occur', 'with this population', and 'in these settings'. The process of setting findings out like this can also help the researcher clarify the main points from their project. Furthermore, findings should be presented in a clear format that is easy to read (Oliver et al., 2014) and researchers

Table 17.1   Communicating qualitative research findings

- Target dissemination strategies and material to the needs of the audience (Nutley et al., 2002a).
- Provide a range of different types of research report and printed materials including newsletters, executive summaries, short policy papers and recommendations for practice (Grimshaw and Eccles, 2008; Buse et al., 2012).
- Provide conferences, seminars, briefings, practical workshops and training to disseminate research findings and educate policy-makers and practitioners about research (Buse et al., 2012; Grimshaw and Eccles, 2008).
- Design studies to maximise utility and include specific policy implications or practice guidelines in research reports (Buse et al., 2012; Nutley et al., 2002a).
- Identify opinion leaders and innovators, and ensure that they understand the implications of research findings (Buse et al., 2012; Grimshaw and Eccles, 2008).
- Undertake systematic reviews of research findings on policy-relevant questions to enable policy-makers to access information more easily (Lavis, 2009; Buse et al., 2012).
- Consider alternative approaches to dissemination, such as Twitter, podcasts or blogging (Dunleavy and Gilson, 2012); non-traditional arts-based approaches (Keen and Todres, 2006); or working with intermediaries and third party organisations (Lavis, 2009) and the media (Nutley et al., 2002a).
- Employ multifaceted interventions which include two or more components. This can potentially target different barriers in the system (Grimshaw and Eccles, 2008; Nutley et al., 2002a).

should explain succinctly how the evidence can be used to inform decisions and where, how and why practice might be changed to improve outcomes (Jack, 2006; Sandelowski and Leeman, 2012). To support this, qualitative researchers should also identify local applicability and equity considerations. Setting out applicability considerations makes it easier for the end-user to judge whether the findings will be relevant in their context (Lavis, 2009; Jack, 2006).

EXAMPLE 1: Writing for your audience

The Key Support (www.thekeysupport.com/) is an example of an intermediary organisation set up to disseminate information to practitioners. The Key Support's focus is on education, and its team of researchers disseminates information, including research, guidance, best practice examples and advice from experts, through online articles. These articles are intended to help professionals make informed decisions when approaching a wide range of issues in their schools.

Researchers are encouraged to think about the audience when constructing an article. Guidelines include adopting a peer-to-peer tone and explaining answers using clear, concise and unambiguous writing. As the target audience are busy school leaders, articles are designed to be read 'in five minutes before a staff meeting'. The format used reflects this: articles are short, the answer or key information is provided up front, headings lead the reader through the article and bullet points are used to summarise information. Non-essential information is excluded, but all material is clearly attributed and hyperlinks are used to direct the reader to further information should they need.

Due to the needs of the audience these articles are intended to be highly practical; highlighting important take-away points and providing good practice case studies and advice and guidance from a range of sources on how the answer can be translated into practice in a school. In order to maximise the utility of answers to the audience, articles are explicit about context limitations and where, when and in what situation an answer might apply.

Non-traditional methods of dissemination

Some researchers have also explored non-traditional arts-based forms of disseminating qualitative research. These have included short stories, research-based theatre/ethnodrama, three-dimensional multi-media presentations, dance, patchwork quilts, documentary film, websites and DVDs and poetic texts (Sandelowski and Leeman, 2012; Keen and Todres, 2006). The 'performative social science' tradition claims that such performative genres can themselves be ideal vehicles for the production and communication of academic research. However, other applied researchers maintain a distinction between their academic scholarship, which aspires to traditional guarantors of rigour and quality, including peer-reviewed article format, and innovative modes of *communication* of that scholarship (Keen and Todres, 2006).

EXAMPLE 2:   Research-based theatre

The research-based play 'Handle with Care?' explores issues around living with terminal cancer (Gray et al., 2000, cited in Keen and Todres, 2006). The play is based on data from focus groups about the information needs of women with metastatic breast cancer and interviews with medical oncologists treating breast cancer patients; both conducted in Ontario, Canada.

Although the study authors did not intend to create a play, this option emerged when thinking about how to disseminate the findings from the two studies. After initial research into the viability of this approach, a team of researchers, actors and women with breast cancer worked on the script. Most of the words used for the script were taken directly from study transcripts. Further amendments were made after piloting the script with service users and physicians.

The play was then performed for health care professionals and the general public in eight Ontario cities hosting a regional cancer centre and had been shown 200 times by 2000. Audience evaluation questionnaires found that the general public enjoyed seeing the drama and agreed that the play made the subject seem more true to life. Health professional audiences agreed that the use of research transcripts to create drama increased its validity substantially, and considered that issues presented were relevant to and useful for thinking about their clinical practice.

Disseminating qualitative research through collaborative action

Writing as clearly as possible and for one's audience is no doubt a good thing. Nonetheless, even researchers who present their findings clearly and engagingly continue to find that their research does not make it into practice or policy. Linear and rationalist models of knowledge translation, in which research-based knowledge, produced by university-based academics, is turned into dissemination materials for practitioners, who then take up that knowledge and use it to change their practice, have long been criticised (Lindblom and Cohen, 1979; Bastow et al., 2014; Ward et al., 2012). Scholars have observed that the kind of literature which we have reviewed above, on barriers to the implementation of research, and communication tips, continue to conceptualise implementation as a linear and rational process, where failure to implement 'good and true' knowledge must be the result of irrational barriers (Best and Holmes, 2010; Ward et al., 2012).

Applied psychologists are familiar with the concept that accurate information does not simply translate into behaviour change, given decades of study on efforts to change health behaviour (Marks et al., 2011). This applies equally to the dissemination of scientific knowledge and its impact on practitioners' behaviour (Lavis, 2009; Sharples, 2013). Informed by pragmatist philosophy, Cornish and Gillespie (2009) develop the position that knowledge, including scientific knowledge, is always located in a particular context, and becomes good or truthful, with respect to particular purposes. Abstract scientific knowledge may have little meaning to a social worker or teacher if it is simply 'disseminated' as bits of information. Instead, for knowledge to be useful, it needs to be collaboratively constructed close to its context of application. The action research and scholar-activist traditions of research have much to offer in this regard, through established experience of collaborative efforts to produce transformative knowledge and action (Campbell and Murray, 2004).

The relevant implication for this chapter is that, for qualitative research to have an impact in terms of policy or practice, waiting until the completion of a project, and then seeking to write findings clearly, is unlikely to be sufficient. Impactful qualitative research is likely to engage the relevant actors early in the research process, so that research questions, research designs, interpretation of findings and changes to practice are embedded in the perspectives, needs and contexts of the possible research users (Buse et al., 2012).

In this section, we discuss three examples of collaborative action to put qualitative research to use: participatory workshops; collaborative knowledge brokering; action research.

Participatory workshops

Engaging the relevant public in participatory activities is premised on the understanding that, for knowledge to be meaningful and actionable, it needs to be 'owned' by the relevant actors. As a first move to more collaborative action, participatory workshops have been proposed as a means not just of 'disseminating' nuggets of research truth, but also of working with research findings to make them relevant to policy-makers, practitioners and citizen communities (Campbell et al., 2012; Priego-Hernandez, 2014; Rusmer and Steven, 2014).

Such workshops aim to move the knowledge-exchange process from research to action. Whereas the researchers contribute knowledge from an external point of view, local actors contribute contextual knowledge and expertise regarding local needs, constraints, resources and opportunities. Bringing these together, it is hoped, may result in new ideas for feasible action. The limitation of such workshops is that, while they may generate enthusiasm and positive ideas for action within the setting of the face-to-face meeting, their sustainability is not ensured (Rusmer and Steven, 2014). The inertia of institutions, with their manifold constraints, may outweigh even apparently feasible and locally owned ideas for putting research into practice.

EXAMPLE 3:   Dissemination workshops as intervention

Following a qualitative study of the local responses to HIV/AIDS in the rural community of Entabeni, South Africa, Campbell et al. (2012) ran a set of 'dissemination as intervention' workshops with community members. Their study had found that, in general, local community members did not discuss HIV/AIDS and had little vision of what might be done to tackle HIV/AIDS, despite high levels of prevalence and suffering. At the same time, a group of about 60 volunteer community health workers were offering significant support to households affected by AIDS and, with greater community and other stakeholder support, could potentially lead a more ambitious and successful community response. Rather than simply presenting their findings to the community, the research team designed a set of participatory workshops, intended to themselves serve as an intervention, to trigger critical and constructive thinking about how community members could support a stronger HIV response.

The workshops proved to be powerful environments for participants to critically discuss HIV/AIDS, the power relations undermining local responses, and possible responses. Participants greatly appreciated the opportunity to speak openly and freely about a highly charged and deeply stigmatised disease. They identified ways they could better support the community health workers. Yet some participants continued to blame individuals for becoming positive, or to recommend punitive action as a response. The more positive strategies identified were mainly relatively small-scale and at an individual level, such as being kinder to HIV positive persons, or acknowledging rather than denying a family member's HIV positive status – rather than acting on the social dimensions of gender, age and leadership which they had identified in discussions as being problematic.

In this particular instance, building on the workshops, the research team were successful in securing funding for a larger intervention to build support for the community volunteers. In the absence of such further investment, the authors argue that such participatory workshops can serve to develop more critical understandings of problems and solutions, which are a necessary but not sufficient condition for further action.

Collaborative knowledge exchange

Taking a longer time-horizon than participatory workshops, qualitative researchers can seek to work collaboratively with practitioner teams from the outset. The evolution of terms in this field, from dissemination, to knowledge translation, to knowledge exchange, and, most recently, impact, highlight an increasing awareness of the interdependence of research and action, and of scholars and practitioners, in the process of putting knowledge into action.

Ward et al. (2012) embedded a knowledge broker within three teams in a mental health organisation in the UK, in order to initiate a productive knowledge-exchange process, and as an opportunity to study knowledge exchange in action. The knowledge broker worked responsively, in response to problems or issues that the team identified that they wanted to work on. This is an important difference from the 'dissemination' model, where the issues are identified by the researcher. The knowledge broker also worked not only by providing information (though that was a part of the role), but also by creating the conditions for knowledge exchange, by linking the teams with other teams and experts, and by building the capacity of the team in knowledge exchange for the future. This knowledge broker model creates a rich engagement between research knowledge, practical knowledge and locally identified concerns. The researchers observed that the knowledge-exchange process was iterative and cyclical rather than linear. For example, the phase of 'problem-definition' did not simply happen at the start of the process and set the scene for the elaboration of solutions to the problem. Problems were often diffuse and a part of broader processes of change, and coming to an actionable definition of the problem was itself an important outcome of the knowledge-exchange process.

Action research

A long tradition of action research (Reason and Bradbury, 2008) and participatory action research (Fals and Rahman, 1991) provides qualitative researchers with an array of experience in working collaboratively with communities to generate action-oriented knowledge. This tradition explicitly rejects the linear concept of knowledge transfer, in which accurate knowledge originates with a disinterested scholar. Instead, knowledge and action are seen as arising together out of critical engagement between perspectives, in a motivated change process. This tradition has typically had politicised objectives to bring out small-scale social change. It has also been extended, in practitioner contexts, such as education or social work, to bring about changes within institutions, and in more ambitious contexts, such as our example below, to yield changes to public understandings and politicians' actions.

EXAMPLE 4:   Collaborative research as political action

The Family100 project in Auckland, New Zealand, is a collaborative endeavour, using research, theory and action to understand and improve the lives of impoverished people who regularly access a food bank (Hodgetts et al., 2014). University-based researchers, a local charity, the Auckland City Mission and clients of charity worked together, firstly, to build an accurate picture of the experiences of families living in desperate poverty, and, secondly, to publicise that understanding, so that the public, state service providers and politicians might take up a more realistic and sympathetic understanding of these experiences.

Researchers conducted interviews with clients every two weeks, across a year, documenting their everyday lives and their interaction with a range of services. Themes including education, employment, housing, food, health, agency supports, income and debt, and justice were explored, and findings highlighted the enormous challenges clients faced in achieving everyday tasks such as securing sufficient food, clothing, or basic attention to health issues. Building on this work, the team engaged

---

EXAMPLE 4:   *Continued*

in a variety of forms of advocacy, including supporting direct action events, fostering service developments, presenting public lectures for wealthier community groups and conversing with government bodies. Importantly, the project engaged actively in media advocacy, aiming to shift discourses away from language such as 'getting tough on solo mums' or 'reducing government welfare liabilities', and towards a more respectful and action-oriented discourse, with some successes. Key messages were picked up by political parties, who echoed the team's wording, including tropes of 'poverty is New Zealand's growth industry' and 'being poor is hard and frustrating work'. The researchers' expertise as scholars of media and communications was no doubt invaluable in engaging journalists and producing media-friendly messages.

Conclusion

We aimed, with this chapter, to review actionable considerations for applied qualitative researchers in planning how to make their research useable by policy-makers, practitioners and citizen communities. We identified a range of factors undermining and influencing the uptake of research, and reviewed strategies for the more effective communication of research and more collaborative working. Across our review, it has emerged repeatedly that research knowledge does not have an easy or straightforward journey from the pages of academic journals into the preoccupations and actions of people working outside the academy. A host of other factors maintains the status quo in everyday life, institutions and politics. To make qualitative research make a difference, we have argued that research needs to become more embedded in the relationships and activities of everyday life, institutions and politics. Our main recommendation is for early and iterative knowledge exchange collaborations.

References

Bastow, S., Dunleavy, P. and Tinkler, J. (2014) *The Impact of the Social Sciences: How Academics and Their Research Make a Difference*. London: SAGE.

Best, A. and Holmes, B. (2010). Systems thinking, knowledge and action: Towards better models and methods. *Evidence and Policy*, 6(2), 145–159.

Buse, K., Mays, N. and Walts, G. (2012). *Making Health Policy*. Milton Keynes, UK: Open University Press.

Cabinet Office (2013). What Works: Evidence Centres for Social Policy. Retrieved 20 January 2017 from: www.gov.uk/government/uploads/system/uploads/attachment_data/file/136227/What_Works_publication.pdf.

Campbell, C. and Murray, M. (2004). Community health psychology: Promoting analysis and action for social change. *Journal of Health Psychology*, 9(2), 187–195.

Campbell, C., Nair, Y., Maimane, S., Sibiya, Z. and Gibbs, A. (2012), 'Dissemination as intervention': Building local HIV competence through the report back of research findings to a South African rural community. *Antipode*, 44, 702–724.

Cartwright, N. and Hardie, J. (2012). *Evidence Based Policy: A Practical Guide to Doing It Better*. Oxford: Oxford University Press.

Cornish, F. (2015). Evidence synthesis in international development: A critique of systematic reviews and a pragmatist alternative. *Anthropology and Medicine*, 22(3), 263–277.

Cornish, F. and Gillespie, A. (2009). A pragmatist approach to the problem of knowledge in health psychology. *Journal of Health Psychology*, 14, 1–10.

Donmoyer, R. (2012). Can qualitative researchers answer policymakers' what-works question? *Qualitative Inquiry*, 18(8), 662–673.

Dunleavy, P. and Gilson, C. (2012). Five minutes with Patrick Dunleavy and Chris Gilson: 'Blogging is quite simply one of the most important things that an academic should be doing right now'. *The Impact Blog*. Retrieved 20 January 2017 from: www.blogs.lse.ac.uk/impactofsocialsciences/2012/02/24/five-minutes-patrick-dunleavy-chris-gilson/.

European Social Network (2014). *Contemporary Issues in the Public Management of Social Services in Europe*. Brighton: European Social Network. Retrieved 20 January 2017 from: www.lx.iriss.org.uk/content/contemporary-issues-public-management-social-services-europe.

Fals Borda, O. and Rahman, M.A. (1991). *Action and Knowledge: Breaking the Monopoly with Participatory Action-Research*. Lanham, MA: Rowman and Littlefield.

Goldacre, B. (2013). *Building Evidence into Education*. London: Department for Education. Retrieved from 20 January 2017 from: www.media.education.gov.uk/assets/files/pdf/b/ben%20goldacre%20paper.pdf.

Grimshaw, J. and Eccles, M. (2008). Knowledge translation of research findings. In *Effective Dissemination of Findings from Research: A Compilation of Essays*. Alberta, Canada: Institute of Health Economics, pp. 8–24. Retrieved 20 January 2017 from: www.ihe.ca/documents/Dissemination_0.pdf.

Hodgetts, D., Chamberlain, K., Tankel, Y. and Groot, S. (2014). Looking within and beyond the community: Lessons learned by researching, theorising and acting to address urban poverty and health. *Journal of Health Psychology*, 19(1), 97–102.

Jack, S. (2006). Utility of qualitative research findings in evidence-based public health practice. *Public Health Nursing*, 23(3), 277–283.

Keen, S. and Todres, L. (2006). *Communicating Qualitative Research Findings: An Annotated Bibliographic Review of Non-traditional Dissemination Strategies*. Bournemouth, UK: Bournemouth University.

Lambert, H. (2006). Accounting for EBM: Contested notions of evidence in medicine. *Social Science and Medicine*, 62(11), 2633–2645.

Lavis, J. (2009). How can we support the use of systematic reviews in policymaking? *Public Library of Science Medicine*, 6(11). doi:10.1371/journal.pmed.1000141.

Lavis, J.N., Robertson, D., Woodside, J.M., McLeod, C.B. and Abelson, J. (2003). How can research organizations more effectively transfer research knowledge to decision makers? *The Milbank Quarterly*, 81(2), 221–248.

Lindblom, C.E. and Cohen, D.K. (1979). *Usable Knowledge: Social Science and Social Problem Solving*. New Haven, CT: Yale University Press.

LSE Public Policy Group (2011). *Maximising the Impacts of Your Research: A Handbook for Social Scientists*. London: LSE. Retrieved 20 January 2017 from: www.blogs.lse.ac.uk/impactofsocialsciences/the-handbook/.

Marks, D.F., Murray, M., Evans, B. and Estacio, E.V. (2011). *Health Psychology: Theory, Research and Practice (Third Edition)*. London: SAGE.

Nutley, S., Davies, H. and Walter, I. (2002a). Evidence Based Policy and Practice: Cross Sector Lessons from the UK. Working Paper 9, Research Unit for Research Utilisation, University of St Andrews, UK. Retrieved 20 January 2017 from: www.kcl.ac.uk/sspp/departments/politicaleconomy/research/cep/pubs/papers/assets/wp9b.pdf.

Nutley, S., Davis, H. and Walter, I. (2002b). From Knowing to Doing: A Framework for Understanding the Evidence into Practice Agenda. National College for School Leadership. Retrieved 20 January 2017 from: www.wmcallan.plus.com/%3C..%3E/Components/Literature%20Review/Knowing%20to%20doing%20Nutley%20et%20al%202002.pdf.

Oliver, K., Innvar, S., Lorenc, T., Woodman, J. and Thomas, J. (2014). A systematic review of barriers to and facilitators of the use of evidence by policymakers. *BMC Health Services Research*, 14(2). doi:10.1186/1472-6963-14-2.

Priego-Hernandez, J. (2014). Participatory workshops with non-academics foster positive social impact and work as a research validation mechanism. *The Impact Blog*. Retrieved 20 January 2017 from: www.blogs.lse.ac.uk/impactofsocialsciences/2014/07/02/participatory-workshops-social-impact-research-quality/.

Reason, P. and Bradbury, H. (2008). *Handbook of Action Research: Participative Inquiry and Practice (Second Edition)*. London: SAGE.

Sandelowski, M. and Leeman, J. (2012). Writing useable qualitative health research findings. *Qualitative Health Research*, 22(10), 1404–1413.

Sharples, J. (2013). Evidence for the Frontline: A Report for the Alliance for Useful Evidence. London: Alliance for Useful Evidence. Retrieved 20 January 2017 from: www.alliance4usefulevidence.org/assets/EVIDENCE-FOR-THE-FRONTLINE-FINAL-5-June-2013.pdf.

Thorne, S. (2009). The role of qualitative research within an evidence-based context: Can metasynthesis be the answer? *International Journal of Nursing Studies*, 46, 569–575.

Ward, V., Smith, S., House, A. and Hamer, S. (2012). Exploring knowledge exchange: A useful framework for practice and policy. *Social Science and Medicine*, 74(3), 297–304.

Index

normality
  demographics of, 968
  discourses of, 96, 97–8
noting
  AI study, 201
  GT interviews and, 166
noting, initial, IPA, 88
Nutley, S., 271, 272
N-Vivo, organisational tool, 201, 202

observation
  ethnographic style, 135
  as selective, 18
observational research methods, 46–9
observer, of focus groups, 44
one-day participative workshop
  charting, 81–2
  coding, 79–81
  facilitator perspective, 78–9
  framework analysis for, 77–83. *See also*
    framework analysis, one-day participa-
    tive workshop
  interview schedule, 80
  mapping/interpretation, 82–3
  planning, sample/recruitment, 75
  reflections on, 83–4
  as short-term participatory format, 73–4
one-to-one interviews, AI study, 191, 193
online focus groups, 44
online textual interviews, 40–41
ontology, 15
  contextualism and, 19
  discourse analysis, 28
  grounded theory, 22
  qualitative neo-positivism and, 18
  radical constructionalism, 20
  realist, 19
open coding, 22
organisational barriers to qualitative
    research use, 269
organisational change, AI and, 189
organisational normality, 96–7
organisational research, IPA use and, 90–1
othering, allegations of, 122
outcome measures, psychotherapeutic prac-
    tices and, 117
overt observer, 46
ownership, GT and, 164, 166

pain, qualitative research and, 7
paradigm
  defined, 241
  participatory research as, 253
paradigmatic assumptions, 243

paradigm wars, 238
Parker, I., 29
participatory methods, children
  analysis of SCAN data, 108–9
  bullying in social group context, 111
  bystander emotions, 103
  data collection with, 107–8
  guidelines to implement, 106
  illustrative findings, 109–11
  introduction to, 101–2
  overprotection of children, 102
  perceptions/experience of children, 102
  pictorial vignette content, 104
  reflections on, 111–12
  use of SCAN method, 106–7
  See community research, action/change
participatory observation, researcher identity
    and, 47–8
participatory research methods, 8
  public involvement and, 252–3
  See also public involvement, in
    qualitative research
partnership, participatory research and, 253
patient and public involvement (PPI), 69
patterning techniques
  polarisation, 98
  thematic Gestalt, 92
patterns across cases, IPA and, 89
Pattison, Helen, 244
PCT. *See* personal construct theory (PCT)
peer group barriers, to qualitative research
    use, 269
peer-to-peer interviews, 256, 260
performative social sciences, 275–6
Persinger, Michael, 5–6
personal choice, 72
personal construct psychology (PCP), 51
personal construct theory (PCT)
  construct elicitation laddering and,
    210–12
  Pictor technique, collaborative experiences
    and, 225
personal experiences, IPA and, 86–7
personal reflexivity, 57, 99
phenomenological attitude, 87
phenomenological methods, IPA and, 90–1
phenomenology
  applied example, 27
  defining, 24–5
  IPA and, 25
  method, key features of, 26–7
  philosophical positioning, 25–6
philosophical approaches, 14–16
philosophical assumptions, 14